Develop on Yammer

Social Integration for Modern Business Applications

Pathik Rawal
Pryank Rohilla

Apress®

Develop on Yammer: Social Integration for Modern Business Applications

Pathik Rawal Pryank Rohilla

ISBN-13 (pbk): 978-1-4842-0944-8 ISBN-13 (electronic): 978-1-4842-0943-1
DOI 10.1007/978-1-4842-0943-1

Library of Congress Control Number: 2015950941

Distributed to the book trade worldwide by Springer Science+Business Media New York, 233 Spring Street, 6th Floor, New York, NY 10013. Phone 1-800-SPRINGER, fax (201) 348-4505, e-mail orders-ny@springer-sbm.com, or visit www.springeronline.com. Apress Media, LLC is a California LLC and the sole member (owner) is Springer Science + Business Media Finance Inc (SSBM Finance Inc). SSBM Finance Inc is a Delaware corporation.

For information on translations, please e-mail rights@apress.com, or visit www.apress.com.

Apress and friends of ED books may be purchased in bulk for academic, corporate, or promotional use. eBook versions and licenses are also available for most titles. For more information, reference our Special Bulk Sales–eBook Licensing web page at www.apress.com/bulk-sales.

Any source code or other supplementary materials referenced by the author in this text is available to readers at www.apress.com. For detailed information about how to locate your book's source code, go to www.apress.com/source-code/. Readers can also access source code at SpringerLink in the Supplementary Material section for each chapter.

Printed on acid-free paper

I dedicate this book to my late father, Shree. H.B Rawal

—Pathik Rawal

Contents at a Glance

Contents

About the Authors

Pryank Rohilla works as a collaboration solutions architect for a Microsoft Gold partner in London. Pryank has 15 years of software development experience in Microsoft technologies. He is Microsoft certified and has worked as a developer, consultant, architect, tech lead, and delivery lead in various engagements. He lives in Reading, UK and his Twitter handle is @Pryankrohilla. In his free time, Pryank enjoy watching sports and spending time with family and friends.

Pathik Rawal is a succesful technical architect and is working as a Microsoft Technology Architect. He has 15 years of software development experience and has worked on many consulting and technical assignments. Pathik is Microsoft certified and he is enthusiastic about cloud and mobile platforms. He lives in London and can be reached on Twitter by @Pathikrawal. Pathik enjoys socializing with friends and family in his free time.

About the Technical Reviewer

Fabio Claudio Ferracchiati is a senior consultant and a senior analyst/developer using Microsoft technologies. He works at BluArancio SpA (`www.bluarancio.com`) as a senior analyst/developer and is a Microsoft Dynamics CRM specialist. He is a Microsoft-certified solution developer for .NET, a Microsoft-certified application developer for .NET, a Microsoft-certified professional, and a prolific author and technical reviewer. Over the past 10 years, he's written articles for Italian and international magazines and coauthored more than 10 books on a variety of computer topics.

Acknowledgments

Writing a book was not an easy task for me. It took a lot of time and a lot of support. Thanks to my wife for her endless support. I also need to thank the co-author and my friend Pathik Rawal, and the talented team of editors and reviewers at Apress. It would have not been competed without your collaboration.

—Pryank Rohilla

I wish to personally thank the following people for their contributions to my inspiration and knowledge and for their help in creating this book.

Pryank Rohilla (my co-author)

Gwenan Spearing (my editor)

Melissa Maldonado (the coordinating editor)

Douglas Pundick (the development editor)

My family (wife Mittu and my two Kids Aayu and Jigi)

—Pathik Rawal

Preface

Yammer is more than just a social network for an organization. Through a range of development options, you can build deep integration across your company's application ecosystem. You can embed relevant conversation feeds where they matter, such as on a company web site or CRM application. You can encourage easy interactions with the Yammer Like and Share buttons in the places where your users will see them. Or, you can even build a standalone app for one or more platforms, and share or collect relevant information with Yammer using Open Graph and Yammer's REST API. In short, Yammer integration with business applications makes collaboration and interaction easier than ever, and it lowers the barrier for user engagement with line-of-business applications and data. It helps make users better connected and more productive.

The examples in this book cover Yammer integration with SharePoint, ASP.NET, and Windows Phone 8. Once you've mastered the Yammer development examples in this book, you will have a head start on integrating Yammer with other enterprise applications, such as Dynamics CRM, and even third-party applications like Salesforce. The possibilities are endless! Start here today. We hope you enjoy it.

Who This Book Is For

This book is targeted at developers with a background in .NET/C# development. Readers should also be familiar with HTML and JavaScript.

Software architects will also find this book valuable for planning social integration across their company's business ecosystems.

What You Will Learn

Chapter 1: You are introduced to Yammer, including its features and benefits, and you find out about Yammer's architecture and the development options available. You also learn how to set up an account with Yammer and meet SPDSUniversity, the case study used throughout the book.

Chapter 2: You find out how to add a Yammer feed to a web page or SharePoint site using Yammer Embed. This is the simplest and quickest way to integrate Yammer content into your business applications. Possible feeds include user feeds, group feeds, topic feeds, and Open Graph/object feeds. You also learn how to add the Yammer action buttons (Like, Follow, and Share) to a web page.

Chapter 3: Covers important information regarding Yammer App development, including registering your app, its configuration options, and how to submit an app to the Yammer Global Apps Directory. This chapter also covers initial configuration of Open Graph.

Chapter 4: This chapter outlines the Yammer authentication process using OAuth, including both client-side and server-side OAuth flows.

Chapter 5: Following on from the initial configuration in Chapter 3, this chapter provides a deep dive into Open Graph. You learn how to create custom Open Graph objects, and find out how to write data into Yammer from your enterprise applications, using the SPDS ASP.NET web application as an example.

Chapter 6: You discover a truly flexible way to integrate with Yammer, using its REST APIs. These APIs allow you to access and write Yammer data between Yammer and many other line-of-business applications, including both inbound and outbound messages. Get a breakdown of Yammer endpoints and learn how to work with each of them.

Chapter 7: You use Yammer's JavaScript SDK to integrate Yammer with an HTML-based enterprise business application, using the SharePoint hosted app from Chapter 4 as an example.

Chapter 8: The final chapter teaches you how to build a new Windows Phone 8 app and use Yammer's Windows Phone 8 SDK to add Yammer functionality.

Source Code

The source code for this book can be found at `www.apress.com/9781484209448`. Scroll down and click the Source Code/Downloads tab to view the download link.

CHAPTER 1

Introduction to Yammer Development

Pryank Rohilla

Today, communication channels are constantly evolving and organizations are discovering that they need a new way to work together to succeed. Organizations have embraced various platforms and tools over time to deliver better employee experiences tuned to how they work and what they need to be successful, thus creating a highly productive workplace that delivers better performance and reduced costs. Figure 1-1 shows how enterprise communications have evolved.

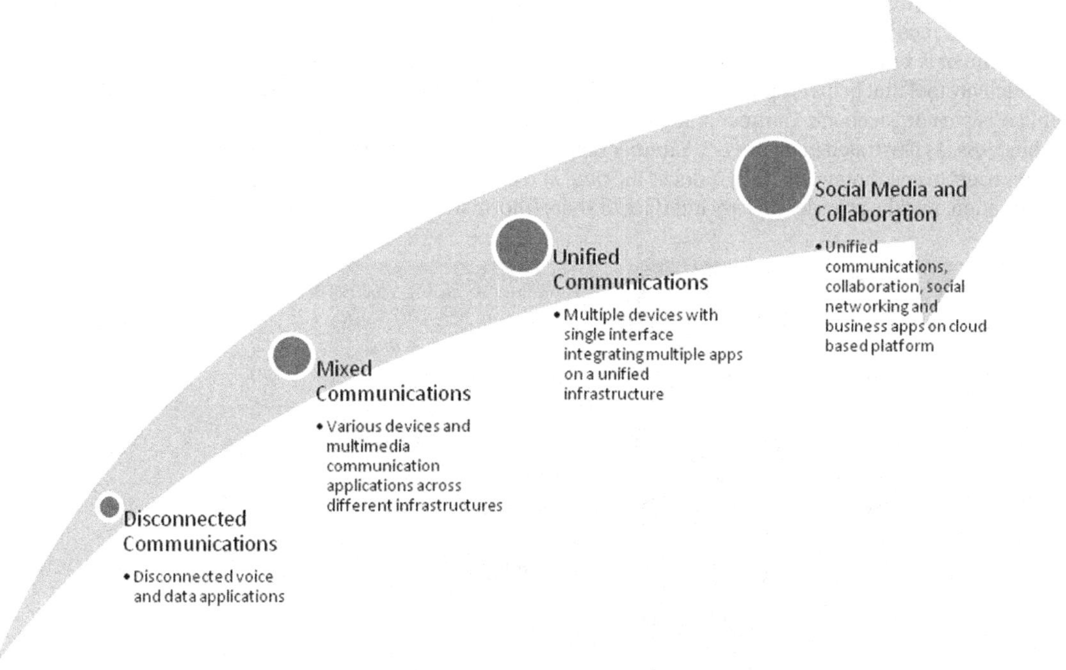

Figure 1-1. *Evolution of enterprise communication channels*

Electronic supplementary material The online version of this chapter (doi:10.1007/978-1-4842-0943-1_1) contains supplementary material, which is available to authorized users.

P. Rawal and P. Rohilla, *Developing on Yammer*, DOI 10.1007/978-1-4842-0943-1_1

Enterprise Social allows you to share information, connect with people, make quick decisions, and share updates. Rather than being a standalone tool, Enterprise Social tools work with existing line-of-business applications and provides value in a digital workplace.

Enterprise Social can be part of the digital workplace in an enterprise and can integrate with adjacent technologies such as Collaboration, company portals, and Customer Relationship Management applications to solve business challenges inside and outside the company.

Yammer is an Enterprise Social networking tool launched in 2008 and acquired by Microsoft in 2012. Yammer provides a simple, scalable solution that lets employees collaborate and connect with coworkers in a private, secure manner. This chapter introduces Microsoft Yammer and explains basics of Yammer development. The chapter provides an introduction to the Yammer platform and the technical offerings that can be used to implement Yammer integration.

In this chapter, we cover the following:

- The Microsoft Yammer platform
- Yammer integration architecture
- How to start on integration with Yammer
- Setting up a Yammer profile
- Introduction to the case study used in the book—the fictitious SPDSUniversity app

What Is Yammer?

Yammer is a leading Enterprise Social network designed for businesses to get work done smarter and faster (`www.Yammer.com`).

Yammer is a micro-blogging and collaboration tool for members of a network. Yammer is also a productivity tool that helps employees collaborate quickly and take effective actions to deliver better results. Unlike Twitter or Facebook, Yammer is aligned to discussions and decisions happening inside your organization or business. As illustrated in Figure 1-2, Yammer helps you get connected to other users in your organization, allows users to collaborate together, reduces the time and effort required to reach people, helps you find information quickly, provides an easy interface to share information and grow ideas to deliver better results.

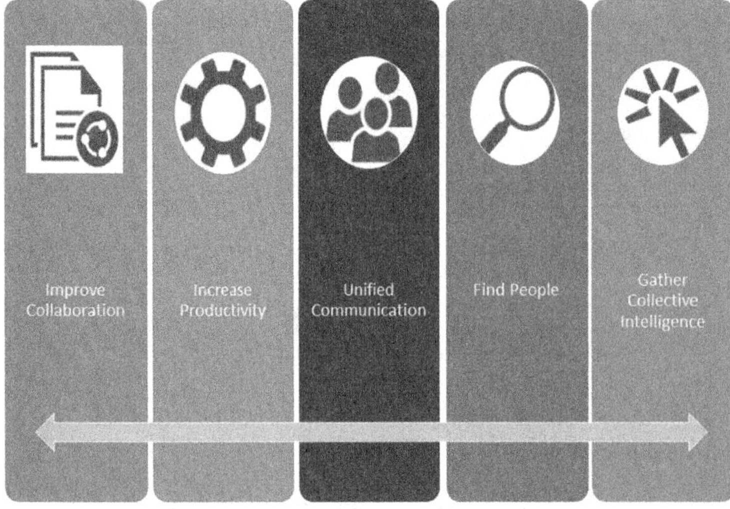

Figure 1-2. *Advantages of Yammer as an Enterprise Social collaboration platform*

Yammer provides a user-friendly web and mobile interface allowing users to stay connected easily. You create groups to collaborate and share information with internal and external people.

Yammer groups can be private or public, providing group owners with an easy way to manage who can see information shared in a group (Figure 1-3).

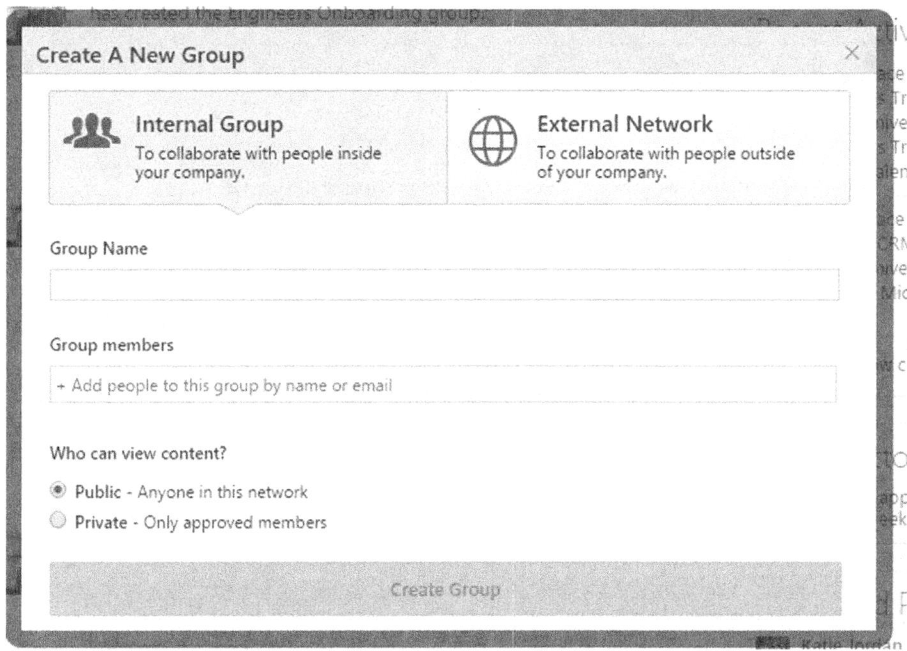

Figure 1-3. *Creating a new Yammer group*

Let's explore further how public groups are different from private groups.

Public Groups

Yammer's public groups are an easy way to collaborate on common topic/agenda/departments/functions. Employees can create a new group or join public groups, as shown in Figure 1-4.

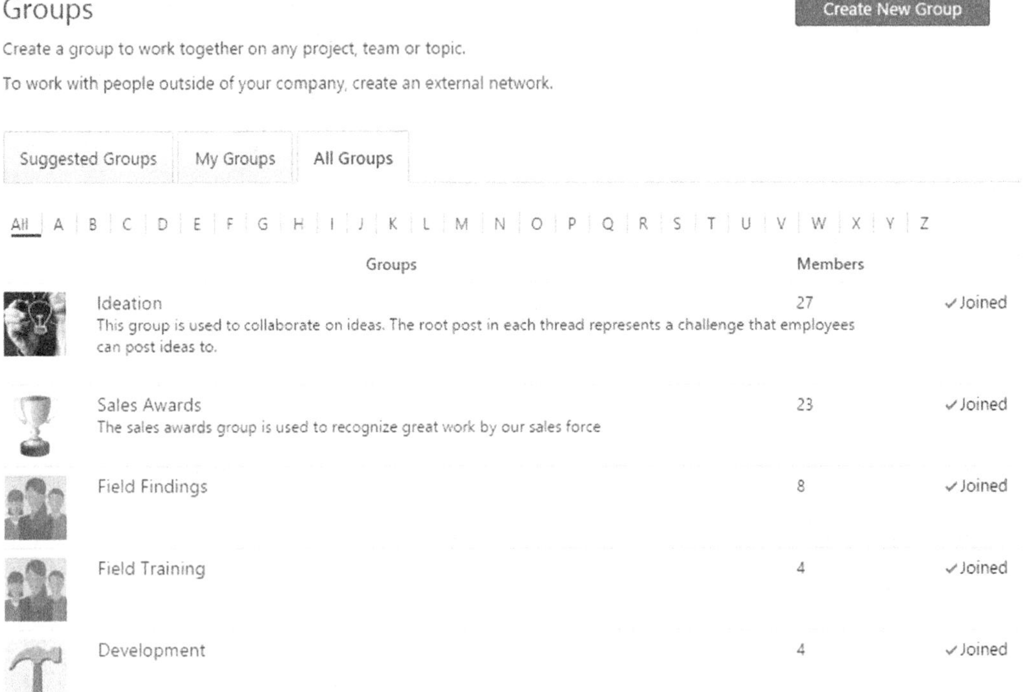

***Figure 1-4.** Creating a Yammer group or joining an existing group*

Messages that are posted in Yammer public groups are displayed in the Home view of every member of the group. Additionally, users who aren't members of a public group can view messages on the group's page. Anyone in a Yammer network can join a public group.

Private Groups

Yammer's private groups are also a great way to improve team communications. Messages posted in private groups in Yammer are displayed in the Home view of every member in the group. However, people who aren't members of the particular private group can't view messages on the group's page. As shown in Figure 1-5, Unlike with public groups, an administrator of a private group must invite members or approve membership.

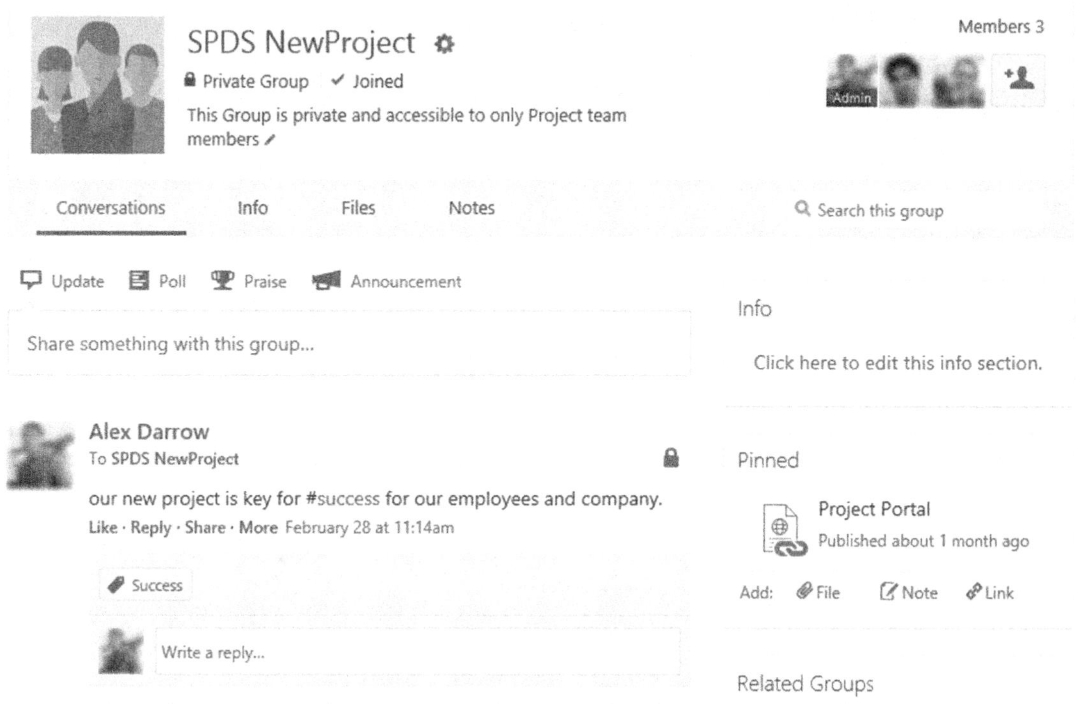

***Figure 1-5.** The Yammer private group is for approved users only*

Private group owners can select whether the group is visible to other members through the network's Groups Directory when a group is created. Or you can do this through its Settings page, as shown in Figure 1-6.

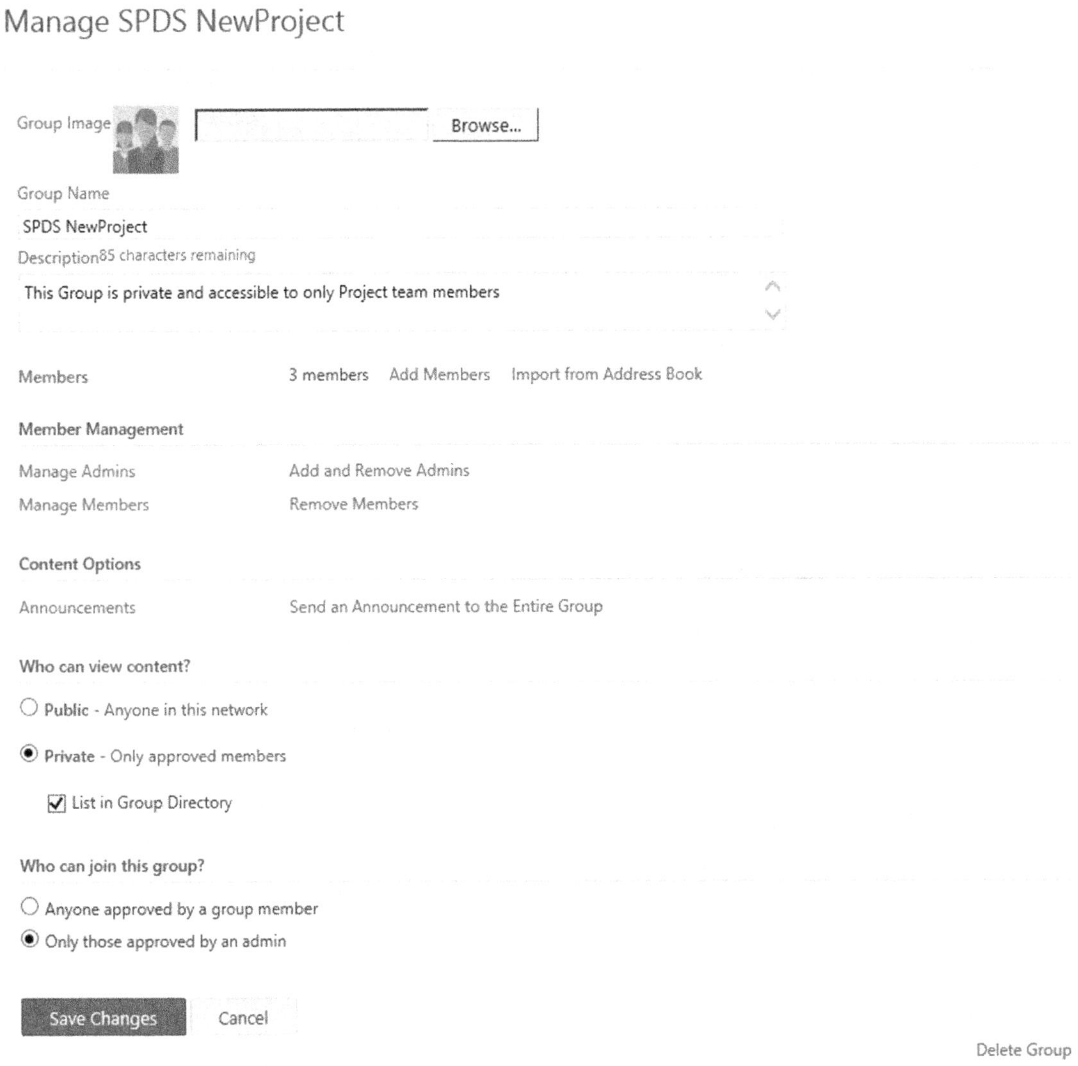

Manage SPDS NewProject

Group Image Browse...

Group Name

SPDS NewProject

Description85 characters remaining

This Group is private and accessible to only Project team members

Members 3 members Add Members Import from Address Book

Member Management

Manage Admins Add and Remove Admins

Manage Members Remove Members

Content Options

Announcements Send an Announcement to the Entire Group

Who can view content?

Public - Anyone in this network

Private - Only approved members

List in Group Directory

Who can join this group?

Anyone approved by a group member

Only those approved by an admin

Save Changes Cancel

Delete Group

Figure 1-6. *Private group Settings page*

Also note that files or documents that are uploaded to private groups are invisible to members who are outside the group. However, their file names are displayed in the network's Files directory.

■ **Note** In Basic Yammer groups, the Network Privacy setting can't be changed after a group is created. However, in Enterprise Yammer networks, the Network Privacy setting can be changed by the Yammer administrator at any time.

Yammer Profiles

Yammer Profile provide an easy and efficient way to let others know about you. Each user on Yammer gets their own Yammer profile. Users can update profiles to share their contact details, skills, knowledge, expertise, and interests with coworkers and company employees, as illustrated in Figure 1-7.

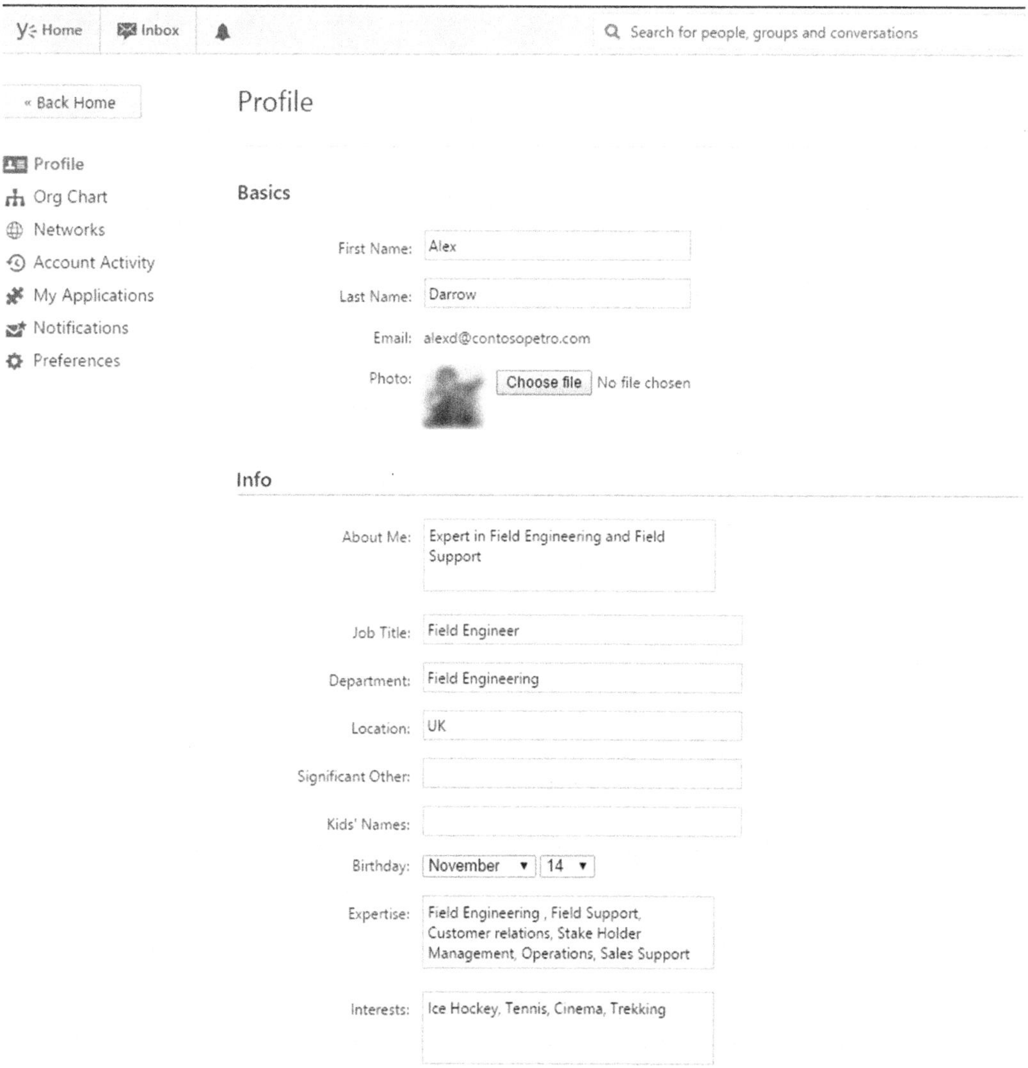

Figure 1-7. *Yammer provides interfaces to view, search, and manage user profiles*

When other users visit a Yammer profile page, they can download the user's electronic business card (vcard) and save it in Outlook (Figure 1-8).

About Alex

Expert in Field Engineering and Field Support

Info download vcard

Department:	Field Engineering
Location:	UK
Birthday:	November 14
Expertise:	Field Engineering , Field Support, Customer relations, Stake Holder Management, Operations, Sales Support
Interests:	Ice Hockey, Tennis, Cinema, Trekking
Email:	
Work:	0124655755 x123
Mobile:	07384884848
Twitter:	testme
Skype:	alexme
Websites:	

Figure 1-8. *Yammer user's vcard, which can be downloaded and saved in Outlook*

Yammer also allows other users to search for contacts and see who is online on Yammer from a web or mobile device interface.

Conversations

Yammer is built around open communication, and it allows users to have conversations and share information in the open. Figure 1-9 is an overview of Yammer interface for sharing information and starting conversations with colleagues. Yammer provides an easy way to update latest events and projects, ask questions, share documents, and link with others.

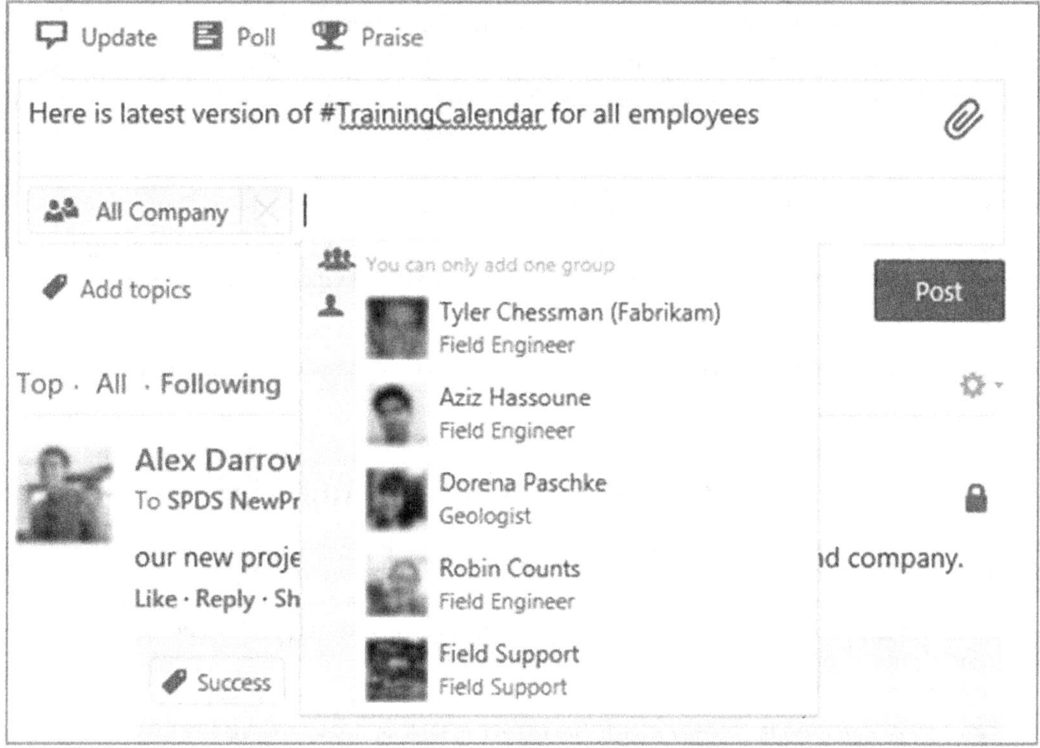

Figure 1-9. *Using Publisher to share the latest information*

Benefits of Integration with Yammer

Some of the main benefits of integration with the Yammer platform and Yammer adoption are:

- *Central repository*: Yammer helps pull activities across business applications into a single place where employees can easily discover relevant information and collaborate.
- *Team collaboration*: Yammer helps improve internal team collaboration and enables quick decision-making.
- *Employee engagement*: Yammer helps employees by providing tools that they need to thrive and unleashes their full productivity:
    - By improving access to information and expertise.
    - By increasing the effectiveness of company-wide communications.
- *Business agility*: With Yammer, you can connect employees, collaborate, and accelerate the feedback loop when entering new markets.
- *Team communication*: Yammer helps break down communication barriers.
- *Increased productivity*: Yammer helps drive productivity by making business applications social and business data easily discoverable, which in turn makes it easier for users to take meaningful actions.

■ **Note** Yammer is a fast-paced platform where new features are developed and released on a regular basis. For full details of new features and future releases, refer to the YCN (Yammer Customer Network) at `https://about.yammer.com/success/engage/grow-your-network/release-schedule/`.

Microsoft Office 365 and Yammer

Microsoft has included Yammer as an Enterprise Social offering in Office 365. Yammer thrives in the Microsoft Office 365 environment by providing deep integration with MS office applications and SharePoint Online.

In Microsoft Ignite 2015, Microsoft showcased the power of Office Graph and showed how Microsoft Delve provides personalized information to users. Users can initiate Yammer conversations directly from Delve.

Core of Yammer Development: The Yammer Platform

The Yammer platform enables users to integrate information across disparate business applications and collaborate through a common interface while working on various business applications.

Yammer platform provides a set of open APIs that enables you to integrate various line-of-business applications within your organization. These can be internal portals, business process automation systems, change and support management applications, or mobile applications.

The main benefits of Yammer integration are:

- *Single sign-on with Yammer credentials*: Users can register to your line-of-business applications using Yammer credentials.
- *Share information and collaborate*: Yammer allows users to get the right information at the right time, making it more valuable, and allows users to make better decisions.
- *Embedded social capabilities*: These are embedded in the business application like surfacing feeds to give context to the users, thus allowing users to share content and extend the reach of organization's information.
- *Ease of use*: Integration with Yammer is a simple and scalable data level integration. Yammer integration enables you to send important updates from business applications and surface social data from Yammer into your applications.
- *Consolidation of data*: In an organization, information is processed and stored in multiple locations and in multiple business applications. By integrating your business applications into Yammer, you can display information in one common interface that makes information easily discoverable, meaningful, and actionable.

The main components of the Yammer platform are:

- *Embed Feed*: Share and display Yammer user feed, group feed, topic feed, or Open Graph objects on other applications.
- *Action Buttons LIKE/FOLLOW/SHARE*: An easy way to enable social interaction and publish an activity story related to that action on Yammer.

- *Open Graph*: An integration protocol that allows you to define an activity that can be posted on Yammer as an object.
- *SDKs*: Available in various programming languages (JavaScript, .Net, Ruby, Python, Windows Phone 8, and iOS). Developers will learn in this book how to use Yammer SDKs to authenticate on Yammer and how to access Yammer APIs to develop integration solutions.

Yammer Integration Architecture

As mentioned, Yammer integration involves simple and scalable data online or on-premises applications:

- Embeddable plug-ins
- REST Application Programming Interface (API)
- Open Graph-enabled social apps

Yammer provides many components for integration with your line-of-business application. These components are REST APIs, JavaScript, Open Graph, embedded widgets, and SDKs for different platforms such a web applications, .NET desktop applications, mobile applications, and backend services. In this section, we will review each of the main elements of Yammer integration in turn.

Yammer Embed

Yammer's embeddable plug-ins allow users to access social content across all of their business applications using their Yammer credentials. There are various embeddable plug-ins available and, in Chapter 2, we will cover the full details of the currently available Yammer Embed.

JavaScript

The JavaScript integration component enables you to integrate line-of-business applications using a client-side script. Yammer provides JavaScript SDK for user authentication and read/write into Yammer. We cover JavaScript in great detail in Chapter 7.

REST APIs

Yammer REST APIs are most commonly used for integration. They provide a secure HTTP interface that allows you to easily add social features to enterprise applications. The REST APIs provide endpoints for authenticated users to read/write data on Yammer. We cover the Yammer REST APIs in great details in Chapter 6.

Open Graph (OG)

Yammer uses the Open Graph (OG) protocol to connect applications to create the Enterprise Graph, which is a single mapping of people and objects they encounter at work. Figure 1-10 shows how Open Graph works.

In Figure 1-10, company employee Alex creates a training schedule on a business application. This business application integrates with Yammer using Yammer apps and Open Graph and allows Alex to share the training schedule with other users on Yammer. It's visible via the Yammer Recent Activity widget.

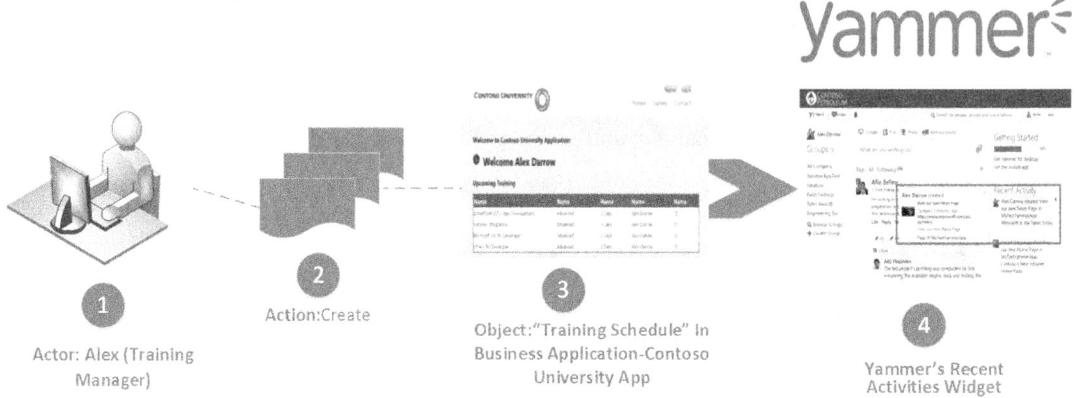

Figure 1-10. *Line-of-business application using Enterprise Social graph to share information in real-time*

SDKs

Yammer SDKs are open source code that enable developers to implement authentication with Yammer and access Yammer APIs from various technology platforms. Yammer has released SDKs for these languages:

- JavaScript SDK
- .NET SDK
- Windows Phone 8 SDK

Chapter 7 describes the details of these SDKs, with examples on how to implement JavaScript SDKs and .NET SDK.

How to Start Yammer Integration

Yammer provides two types of integration:

- Lightweight integration using Yammer Embed feeds, which allow you to get Yammer feeds surfaced on your business applications. Yammer Embed provides the easiest and simplest approach to integrate Yammer into your business applications. This is covered in Chapter 2.
- Yammer Embed does not allow you to write or read Yammer data from your line-of-business application. To overcome this limitation, Yammer provides deep integration using Yammer apps and Yammer SDKs. To get started with deep integration of Yammer with an application, you need to have following components:
    - A valid Yammer account
    - A Yammer app that provides an integration channel (Covered in more detail in Chapter 3)
    - Yammer SDKs of your choice, which provide a platform to quickly integrate Yammer with other applications within your organization

If you want to integrate Yammer with a web application, you can leverage JavaScript SDK. In case you want to integrate Yammer with a mobile application platform such as iOS or Windows Phone, Yammer has released SDKs for mobile platforms. This book explains the JavaScript SDK and Windows Mobile SDK using different examples.

Creating a Yammer Account

As Yammer is an Enterprise private social network and Yammer is also part of Microsoft Office 365 network, there are different ways to create an active Yammer account:

1. Create a Yammer account with a company email address and your personal profile. In this case, there are separate credentials for Yammer and it does not offer single sign-on.
2. Single sign-on using a company email address and configuring your personal profile.
3. Sign in to Yammer using a Microsoft Office 365 account and then manage your personal profile.

Let's look at these three options in detail.

Setting Up Your Profile Without Single Sign-On

You will need your corporate email ID in order to create a Yammer account. Visit `www.yammer.com` and sign up by entering your corporate email address, as shown in Figure 1-11.

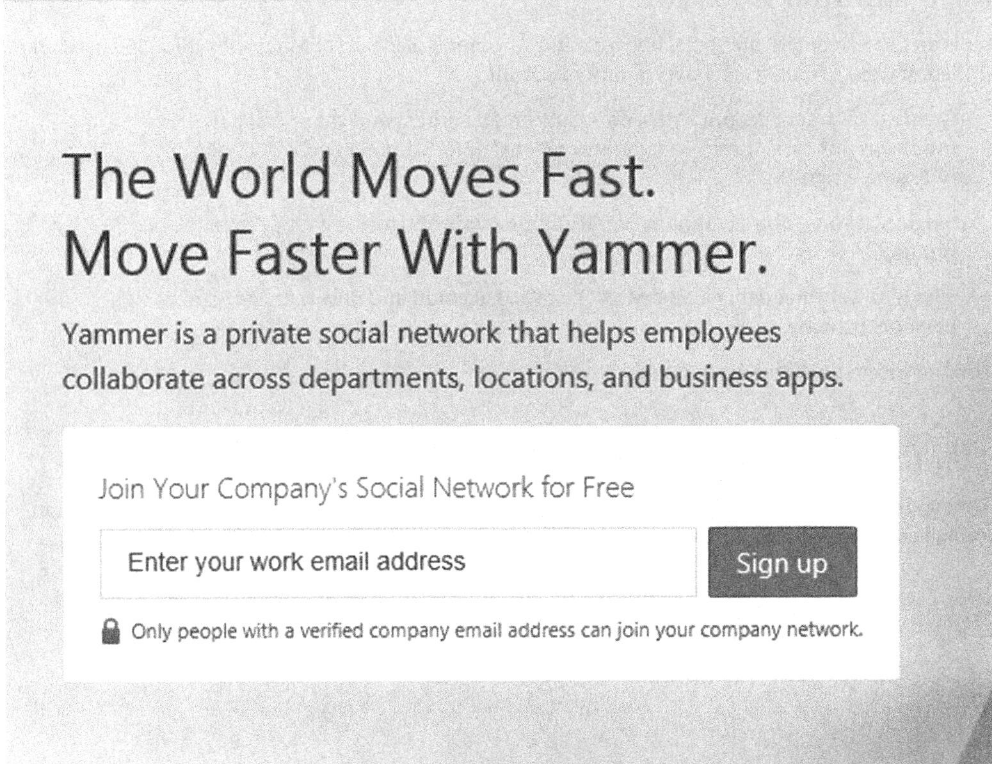

Figure 1-11. *Sign up on Yammer using your company email address*

Yammer will send you an email to confirm your email address. Once your account has been confirmed, you will be taken through the setup process. The setup process requires you do the following:

1. Set up your profile by entering information about yourself such as job title, department name, profile picture, and so on (Figure 1-12).

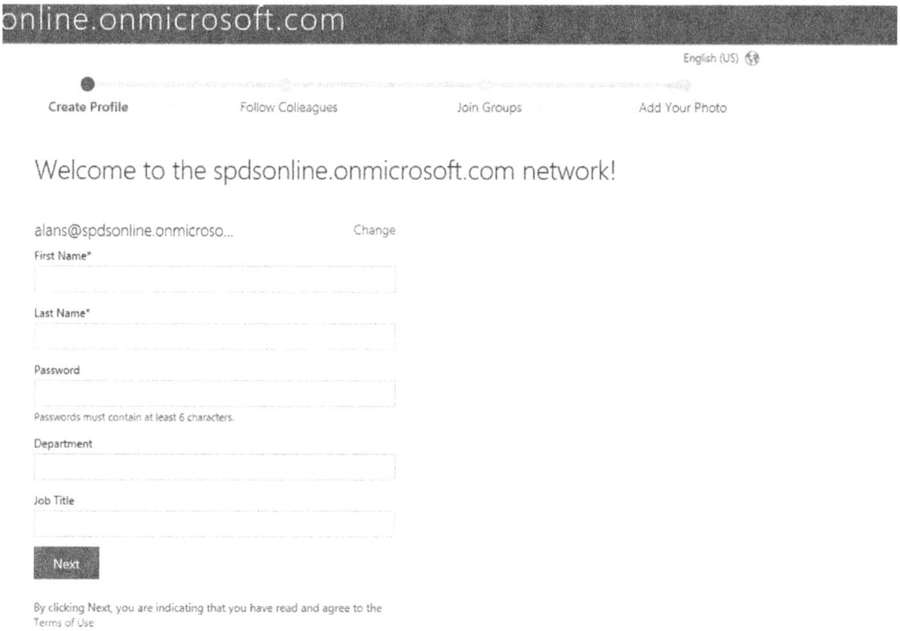

Figure 1-12. *Sign up on Yammer*

2. (Optional) You can invite your colleagues to sign up on Yammer (Figure 1-13).

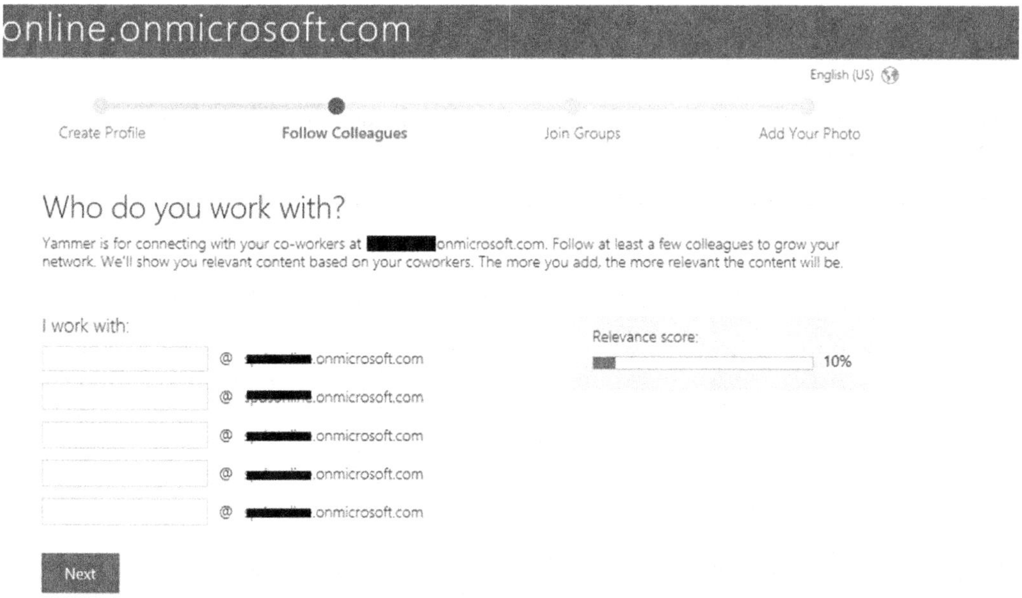

Figure 1-13. *Invite colleagues to join Yammer*

That's it! You can now log in to Yammer with your company email address.

Setting Up Your Yammer Profile with Single Sign-On and a Company Email Address

If your company has already set up single sign-on between Yammer and the company domain, you do not need to sign up on Yammer separately. In order to log into Yammer.com, navigate to `https://www.yammer.com/companyname` or `[Company Name Portal address]`. You will be redirected to the `[COMPANY NAME]` SSO system, as illustrated in Figure 1-14.

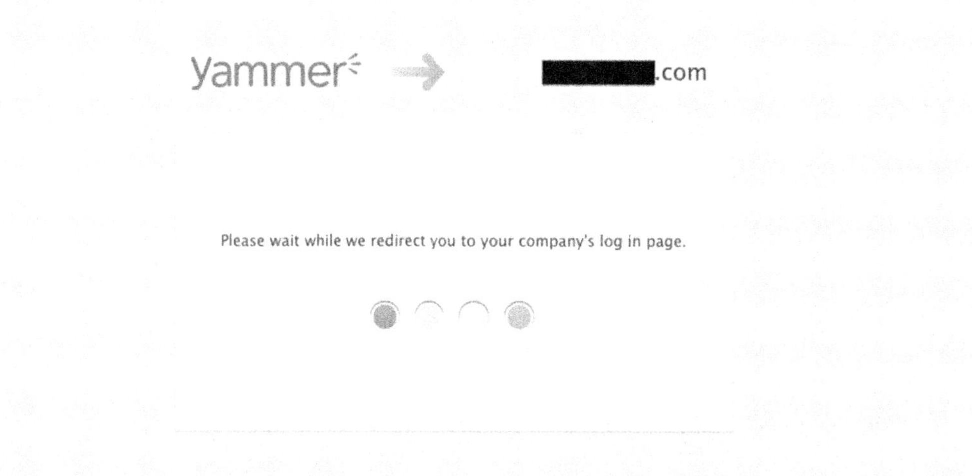

Figure 1-14. *Log on to Yammer*

Occasionally, you will need to log into the `[Company Name Portal address]` to verify your identity. When prompted, simply enter your domain username and password, as shown in Figure 1-15.

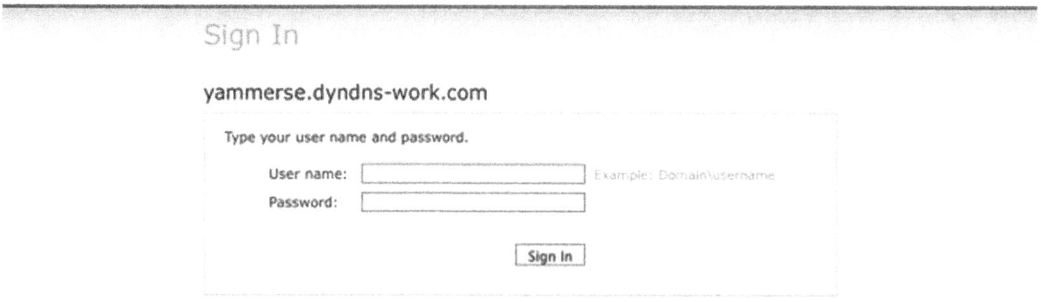

Sign In

yammerse.dyndns-work.com

Type your user name and password.

User name: Example: Domain\username

Password:

Sign In

Figure 1-15. *SSO to Yammer from company federated domain (this page depends on company account federation configuration settings)*

Once you have successfully signed in, you will be redirected back to Yammer to view your company's Yammer feed.

The most important change to understand is that `Yammer.com` will no longer be storing your password information. Instead, this is being handled by your company-implemented single sign-on solution, such as Active Directory Federation Services (ADFS).

Signing in to Yammer with a Microsoft Office 365 Account

With Office 365 sign-in for Yammer, users can access Yammer with their Office 365 credentials. Office 365 users can seamlessly access Yammer from their Office 365 navigation bar, as shown in Figure 1-16, thus providing immediate access to their existing Yammer account linked to Office 365.

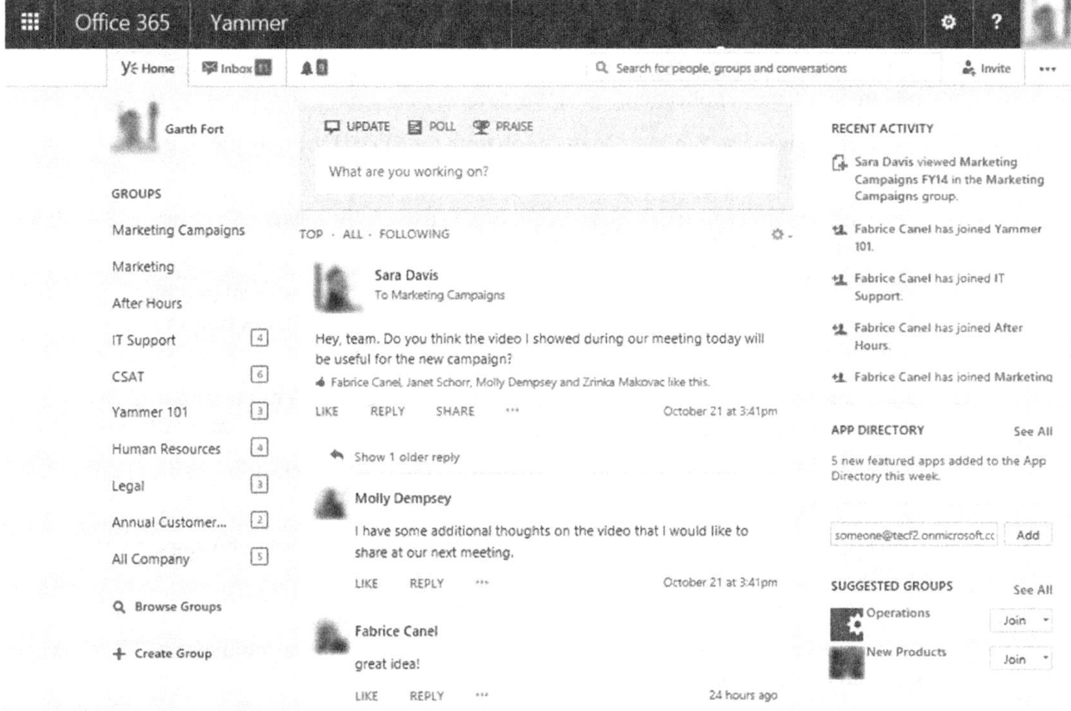

Figure 1-16. *Office 365 suite navigation bar and Yammer integration*

Office 365 sign-in for Yammer is for Office 365 customers with the following criteria: Yammer Enterprise is activated in a network's Office 365 Admin Center and Yammer single sign-on (SSO) is not enabled. Users will notice the Office 365 suite navigation bar (Figure 1-16) at the top of their Yammer network.

Case Study: SPDSUniverisity

In order to guide you to implement Yammer integration with line-of-business applications, we will use a case study of the fictitious global company called SPDS and explain how this company is using Yammer to provide integration with an internal application.

SPDS provides an internal learning and management system (LMS), called "SPDSUniversity," for their employees to learn and develop their skills. The SPDSUniversity application offers different interfaces for web applications, Window mobile apps, and SharePoint apps. Based on the employee's convenience, they use different interfaces. This application provides annual training schedule, recorded trainings, and announcements on future trainings events. But due to lack of user engagement, not all employees are using this application at its full potential.

Also, SPDS has adopted Yammer as their Enterprise Social networking tool to make employees collaborate quickly and take effective actions and deliver better results. SPDS wants to utilize Yammer capabilities and offer Yammer integration with the SPDSUniversity application by implementing Yammer Social features in LMS. There is strong case it will improve the employees' engagement.

In this book, we will show you how to integrate Yammer with the SPDSUniveristy application and provide detailed explanations on the following integration possibilities:

- You will learn how to use Yammer Embed feeds to surface on an internal company portal.
- You will learn to implement "Sign in with Yammer" to provide authentication on a SharePoint app, a web application, and a Windows mobile app.
- You will learn how to use Yammer Open Graph from the SPDSUniversity training portal to:
    - Send updates on Yammer about recent activities that can be used by Yammer users during discussions.
    - Send updates on Yammer about a new training venue from an internal training application. Inform users about training locations and let them know how to reach the destination with a location map.
    - Share important events like a new certification attained by users directly from the SPDSUniveristy application to Yammer using the Yammer Open Graph API.
    - When a new training video is created, share this video link directly from the SPDSUniveristy application to Yammer.
- You will learn how users can share an upcoming training page on Yammer using REST APIs.
- You will also learn how users can bring relevant Yammer posts into the SPDSUniversity application using Yammer REST APIs and how to use Yammer REST APIs to search Yammer posts directly from the LMS web portal.
- You will learn how to develop more social integrations using Yammer JavaScript SDKs and create an app using Windows Phone 8 SDK.

Summary

In this chapter, we explored Yammer as an Enterprise Social platform and discussed its key features. We reviewed the core of Yammer Integration architecture and explained the different components of developing integrations with Yammer. We laid out the plan for integration by creating a Yammer account and provided details about the case study that we will be using throughout this book.

In following chapter we will start with Yammer integration using the Yammer Embed technology, which is simplest way to integrate Yammer with your business application and to view Yammer feeds directly from business applications.

CHAPTER 2

Integrations with Yammer Embed

Pryank Rohilla

Yammer has evolved as one of the top enterprise social networking platforms. Microsoft Office 365 and Yammer integration has helped organizations provide better productivity solutions for users. Along with standard capabilities, there is scope to bring Yammer social features and functionalities directly into line-of-business applications and allow users to collaborate and engage from their main business applications. Yammer Embed provides a way to get Yammer social features into business applications.

In this chapter, we will explain what Yammer Embed is and how to use Yammer Embed in your business applications. We explain with an example how to add Yammer Embed into an online company portal.

Introducing Yammer Embed

Yammer Embed *is made up of* lightweight JavaScript-based widgets *that* can be added to web applications to display snapshot*s* of Yammer feeds based on a defined configuration. Yammer Embed provides an easy and simple approach to integrate Yammer in your business applications. Using Yammer Embed, users can view the latest announcements, comments, posts, add new comments, and share information and files directly from the mainstream business applications without having to visit the Yammer. This allows users to engage quickly with others and achieve better results.

There are different types of Yammer Embed feeds that can be added to external applications based on business needs. You can surface Yammer Embed feeds of a current user (My Feed), a specific Yammer group feed, a topic feed, or a Yammer Open Graph object feed. Figure 2-1 shows you an example of Yammer Embed added to a Project Center site. In this example, users can view and share the latest updates with colleagues directly from the Project Center site, which helps them be updated and share views with team members.

P. Rawal and P. Rohilla, *Developing on Yammer*, DOI 10.1007/978-1-4842-0943-1_2

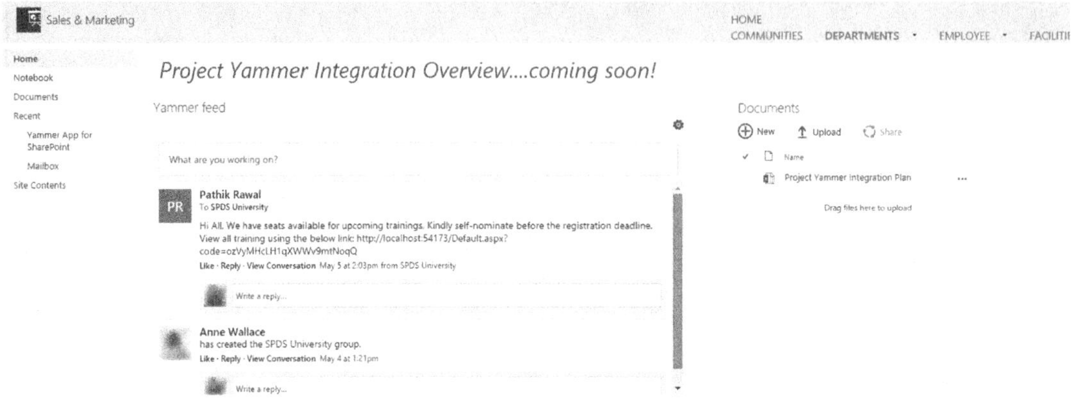

Figure 2-1. *An example of a Yammer group feed embeded in a company's Project Center site*

This is just one example. In this chapter we will explain different types of Yammer Embed and Yammer action buttons, including Like, Share, and Follow.

First let's explore the requirements for adding Yammer Embed to your business applications.

Yammer Embed Prerequisites

In order to use Yammer Embed on a web page, you need to satisfy the following:

- An HTML-based and JavaScript-enabled web interface, preferably in a business system (like your company intranet).
- A Yammer network permalink such as: `https://www.Yammer.com/spdsuniversity.onmicrosoft.com`.
- Editable HTML container that's 400 pixels or larger.

For less than 400 pixel container, Yammer will show Skinny mode, which will be less feature rich.

Note Yammer Embed does not support Microsoft Internet Explorer 8 or lower. Note that Yammer keeps updating its feature set, so some of the prerequisites and usage mechanisms may change in future. For the latest, refer to `https://developer.Yammer.com`.

As you can see, the requirements to have Yammer Embed on your business application are very simple and you do not need to develop any complex code. Let's go through the different types of Yammer Embed feed that you can use in your applications.

Different Types of Yammer Embed Feeds

As Yammer offers various social collaboration features, it is possible with Yammer Embed to surface different types of feeds based on your functional needs. For example, you may want to see the Yammer feeds belonging to your Learning and Training department on your Training and Knowledge management site, or perhaps your Sales and Marketing team wants to get the latest Yammer announcements and updates from the R&D Department's group feeds on the CRM portal.

There are five types of Yammer feeds that can be embedded in HTML-based web applications, as listed in Table 2-1. Most of these feeds are self-explanatory, apart from Object feed, which we will cover more in detail.

Table 2-1. *Different Types of Yammer Embed Feeds*

Feed	Description	Feed Type	Use Case
MyFeed	My feeds are where conversations/posts are delivered for a Yammer user	See MyFeed example	User's personal site/workspace site
User feed	All the posts/conversations posted by a user in the Yammer network	User	Portal Profile page of user
Topic feed	A feed of posts/conversations that are hashtagged in Yammer	Topic	An event or company announcement page in portal Search results page, CRM portal landing page
Group feed	A feed or posts/conversations that are posted in a specific private/public Yammer group	Group	Teamsite page Project page
Open Graph/ object feed	Posts/conversations about a custom object that is created using the Open Graph API	Commenting	Blog page, CRM opportunity page, internal company news page

■ **Note** Users have to log in to Yammer to view the feed on a web application unless that application provides single sign-on to Yammer. For example, Microsoft SharePoint Online.

Yammer Embed Parameters

Before users can use Yammer feeds from a business application, you need to specify the parameters associated with Yammer Embed. These parameters are listed in Table 2-2.

Table 2-2. *Yammer Embed Parameters*

	Embed Parameters	Definition
1	Container	The ID of the HTML <DIV> element in which Yammer Feed is added
2	Network	Network permalink. To retrieve the network permalink, You can navigate to the feed on the Yammer platform and copy it from the URL. More details are in the section to "How to Add Yammer Embed to a Page"
3	feedType	Type of feed to be displayed: group, topic, user, or Open Graph object
4	feedID	ID of the group, topic, or user feed (not applicable for Open Graph or MyFeed)
5	Config	Currently supports headerless, which removes the title bar from the feed
6	objectProperties	Open Graph Feeds/Like/Follow buttons supports all the properties available in the Yammer Activity Stream API If you do not specify any object properties, the object will attempt to get the metadata from the web page, using `<title>` or `<meta>` tags as per the Open Graph specification (`http://ogp.me/`)
7	Private	Open Graph object permissions may be constrained to a list of users, specified by full name and email address
8	Users	The users who may see the private object

Let's now explore how to specify these parameters when adding Yammer Embed to a web page.

Adding Yammer Embed to a Web Page

As mentioned, your application needs to support HTML and JavaScript to add Yammer Embed. Yammer Embed is a JavaScript widget that needs to fit in the HTML `<div>` element. You need a minimum height of 400 pixels for the Yammer Embed `<div>` element.

The code snippet shown in Figure 2-2 is an example of Yammer Embed for a Yammer group.

```
<!DOCTYPE html>

<html lang="en" xmlns="http://www.w3.org/1999/xhtml">
<head>
    <meta charset="utf-8" />
    <title></title>
</head>
<body>
    // JavaScript source code
    <div id="embedded-feed" style="height:800px;width:400px;"></div>
    <script type="text/javascript" src="https://assets.yammer.com/assets/platform_embed.js"></script>
    <script type="text/javascript">
 yam.connect.embedFeed({
    container: "#embedded-feed",
    network: "spdsuniversity.onmicrosoft.com",
    feedType: "group",
    feedId: "5733146"});
    </script>
</body>
</html>
```

Figure 2-2. *An example of a Yammer Embed feed code snippet*

In the example in Figure 2-2, we have specified a Yammer group feed with the following parameters:

- div id: "Embedded feed". Specify the ID of the <div> where you want to add the feed.
- style: Specify the height and width of the container.
- **Source** (src): Yammer Embed code is reference to the platform_Embed.js file. This reference is based on existing Yammer and it may change in the future. Refer to http://developer.yammer.com for the latest references.

Here are the Yammer Embed JavaScript method parameters:

- container: **The name of the <div> ID that's specified in HTML in the previous example is "Embedded-feed" as mentioned.**
- Network: Specify the network name. In Figure 2-2, spdsonline.onmicrosoft.com is highlighted as "Network Permanent Link".
- feedType: Specify the feed type. This is the type of feed you want to render on the page. This can be user, group, or topic. For example, in Figure 2-2, we selected group.
- feedID: Based on feed type, specify the value of object ID. In Figure 2-2, the Yammer group ID 4552935 is set to Feed ID.

You can add this code to any HTML and JS-enabled web page, but Yammer also provides an easy way to get the group feed scriptlet auto-generated from the Yammer site.

To get the Yammer Embed feed for a group, browse to your Yammer network, select the specific group feed page, and then select the Embed This Group in Your Site link, as shown in Figure 2-3.

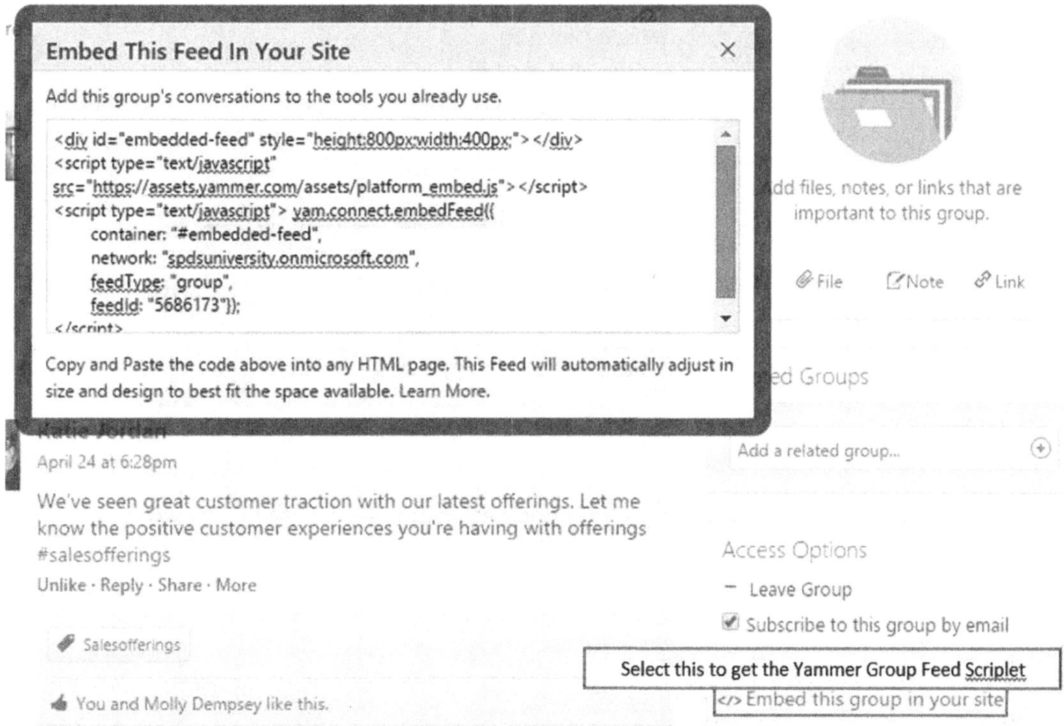

***Figure 2-3.** Yammer group SPDSUniversity feed page to get the Yammer Embed scriptlet*

Copy the script for embedding feeds on your HTML web page to view the Yammer group feed rendered on the web page, as shown in Figure 2-1.

There is another way to get Yammer Embed scriptlets: using the Yammer Embed widget.

Yammer has made life simpler for developers by providing an online tool to generate and preview the Yammer Embed feeds. You can browse to the web site `https://www.Yammer.com/widget/configure` and set the configuration parameters and preview the feed. Figure 2-4 is from the Yammer Embed Widget Configuration web page. As you can see, all the parameters are self-explanatory and described in the section entitled "Yammer Embed Parameters."

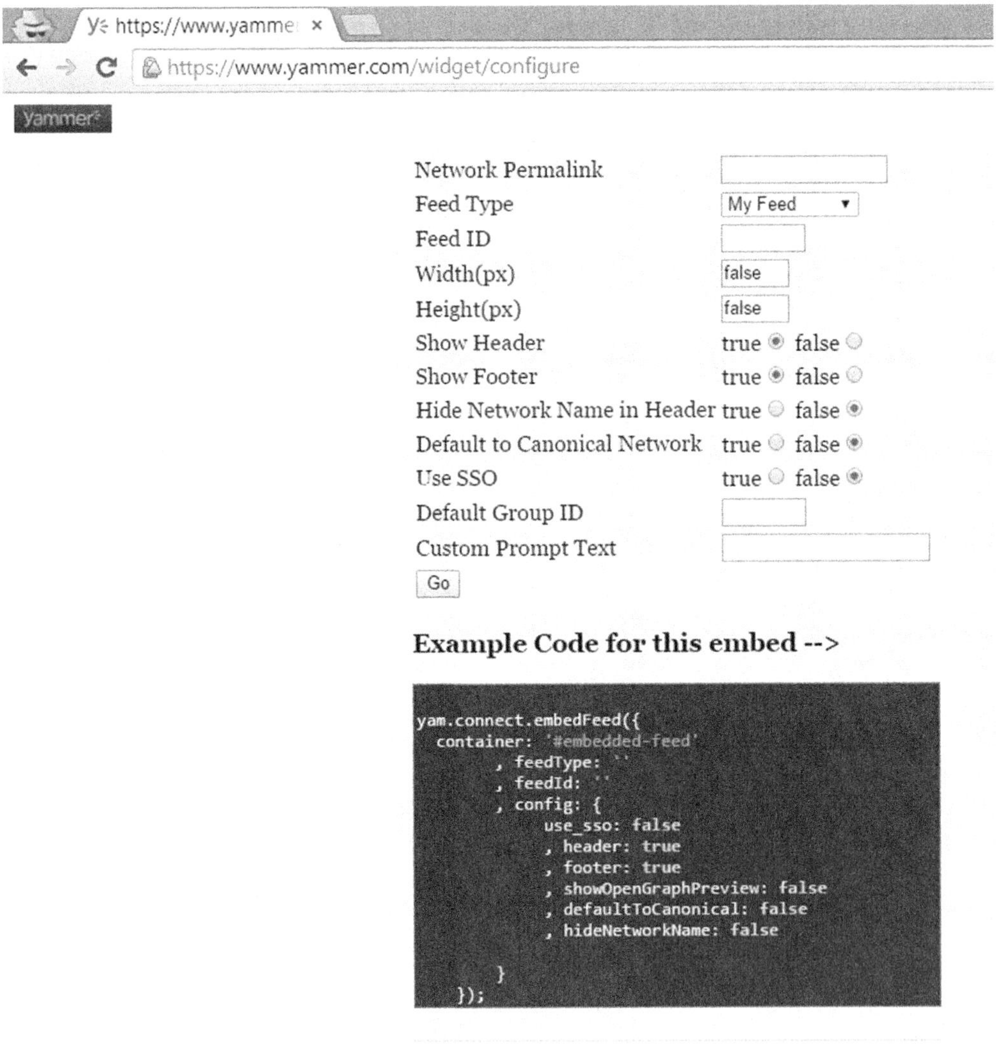

https://www.yammer.com/widget/configure

yammer

Network Permalink	
Feed Type	My Feed
Feed ID	
Width(px)	false
Height(px)	false
Show Header	true ● false ○
Show Footer	true ● false ○
Hide Network Name in Header	true ○ false ●
Default to Canonical Network	true ○ false ●
Use SSO	true ○ false ●
Default Group ID	
Custom Prompt Text	

Go

Example Code for this embed -->

```
yam.connect.embedFeed({
  container: '#embedded-feed'
        , feedType: ''
        , feedId: ''
        , config: {
             use_sso: false
           , header: true
           , footer: true
           , showOpenGraphPreview: false
           , defaultToCanonical: false
           , hideNetworkName: false

        }
    });
```

***Figure 2-4.** Yammer Embed widget configuration page*

Using this configuration web page, you can get a Yammer Embed script for any type of Yammer feeds. This can be for a user feed, a profile feed, a group feed, a topic feed, or Open Graph object feed. Once you get the Yammer Embed script, just add it to your web page using the HTML `<script>` element tag as shown in Figure 2-2.

The next section provides information about the different types of Yammer feeds.

Types of Yammer Feeds

Let's look at various types of Yammer Embed feeds that can be added based on your needs of business process and collaboration.

Yammer User Feed

Figure 2-5 illustrates the Yammer Embed script of the default feed of a currently logged in Yammer user.

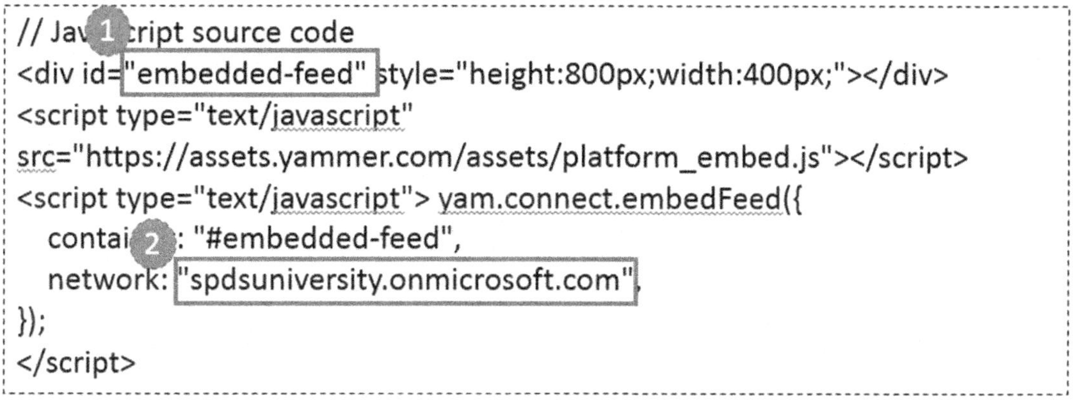

```
// JavaScript source code
<div id="embedded-feed" style="height:800px;width:400px;"></div>
<script type="text/javascript"
src="https://assets.yammer.com/assets/platform_embed.js"></script>
<script type="text/javascript"> yam.connect.embedFeed({
  container: "#embedded-feed",
  network: "spdsuniversity.onmicrosoft.com",
});
</script>
```

Figure 2-5. *Yammer Embed script for a default feed*

In this script, **`<div id="Embedded-feed">`** (label 1) is an important value that needs to specified in the Yammer Embed script method **`yam.connect.EmbedFeed`** container parameter.

The second most important parameter is **`network`** (label 2) and you must specify your Yammer network there.

Yammer Group Feed

In Figure 2-6, you can see that the Yammer feed type is `group` and is set to the default for a `groupid`.

```
// JavaScript source code
<div id="embedded-feed" style="height:800px;width:400px;"></div>
<script type="text/javascript"
src="https://assets.yammer.com/assets/platform_embed.js"></script>
<script type="text/javascript"> yam.connect.embedFeed({
   container: "#embedded-feed",
   network: "spdsuniversity.onmicrosoft.com",
   feedType: 'group',           // can be 'group', 'topic', or 'user'
   feedId: '123'              // feed ID from the instructions above
   ,config: {
        defaultGroupId: 3257958      // specify default group id to post to
});
</script>
```

Figure 2-6. *Yammer Embed script for a group feed in the SPDSUniversity Yammer network*

In this script:

- Label 1 shows the ID of the `<div>` where the feed will be rendered.
- Label 2 is your Yammer network.
- Label 3 shows that the `feedType` is set to `group` to display the feed of a Yammer group.
- Label 4 shows the `feedId`, which is the group ID in this case.
- Label 5 (`config:`) specifies any other specific values, such as the default group to post to.

When this script is added to your HTML page, it will show the feed displayed in Figure 2-7.

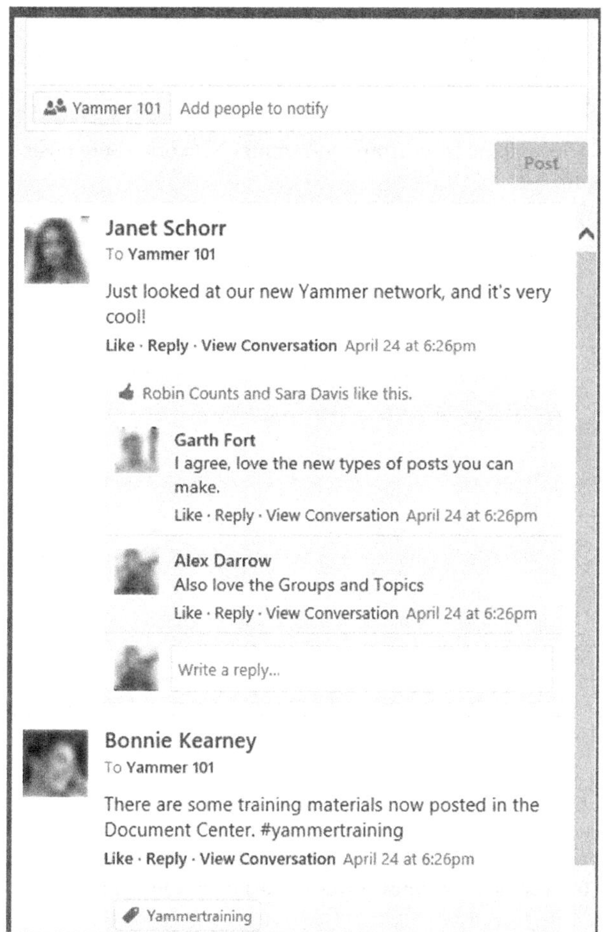

Figure 2-7. *Yammer Embed rendered on a web page for a group feed called "Yammer 101"*

Yammer Topic Feed

In Figure 2-8, `feedType` is set to `"topic"` and `feedId` is `"topic id"`.

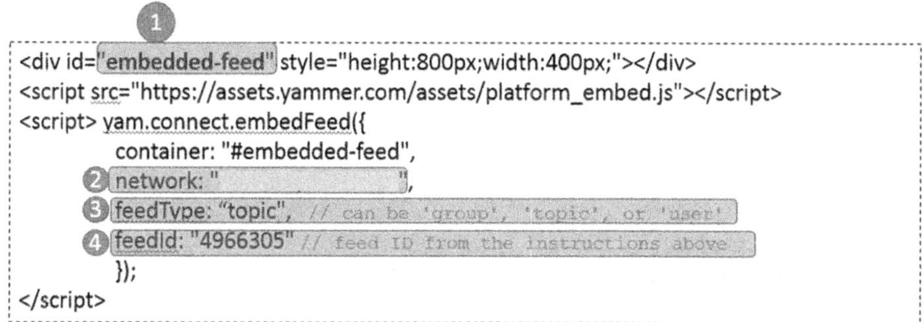

Figure 2-8. *Yammer Embed script for a Yammer topic feed*

In the script shown in Figure 2-8, labels 1 and 2 are same as in the Yammer group feed, except:

- `feedType` (label 3) is changed to `topic` to display the feed of a Yammer topic.
- `feedId` (label 4) is the topic ID in this case.

When this feed is rendered on the page, it will show all the feeds from the Yammer network where posts have the "training" topic specified, as shown in Figure 2-9.

Figure 2-9. *Yammer Embed feed for the "Training" topic*

So far we have explained Yammer Embed for user, group, and topic feeds, which are simple options that allow you to view feeds or a specific object or start a conversation related to a specific configured feed.

Next, let's look at how to use Yammer Embed to provide commenting directly from your business applications.

Yammer Object Feed

Using Yammer Embed, you can comment on your internal communication site, a blog site, or an internal company news portal and then capture the comments or feedback from users directly and surface on Yammer using a Yammer Open Graph object. This is a very effective way to make your company portal more collaborative and get comments from users about specific articles, news, blogs, and so on.

Implementing Commenting Using a Yammer Object Feed

The following script shows Yammer commenting, which can be added to your HTML page.

```
<script src="https://c64.assets-yammer.com/assets/platform_embed.js"
type="text/javascript"></script>
<b>Commenting on Yammer</b>
<div id="embedded-feed" style="width:600px; height:150px;"></div>
<script type="text/javascript">
yam.connect.embedFeed({
 container: '#embedded-feed'
      , network: '[redacted]om'
     , feedType: 'open-graph'
     , config: {
header: false
         , footer: false
         ,promptText: 'Enter Comments'
     }
     , objectProperties: {
       url: 'https://mysiteurl.com/page.aspx'
       , type: 'page'
     }
  });
</script>
```

Figure 2-10. *Yammer Embed script for a Open Graph commenting section*

In this script, you will notice that:

- The **feedType** parameter value is open-graph.
- The **feedId** parameter is blank because we are not rendering any existing feeds in this case.
- The **objectProperties** parameters are important for an open-graph type feed to highlight which type and object allows commenting. In this script, we have used a default page of a portal.

The output of this script will show a free text box that allows users to specify new comments that will appear as posts on Yammer.

The comment box is a Yammer Publisher control and it lets users comment directly from a web site/ portal using their Yammer profiles and shows this activity to their colleagues in the Yammer feed.

Using Embed.ly (`www.Embed.ly`)

As you can see in Figure 2-11, with Open Graph Yammer Embed posts the URL of a page but adds the "Sign in to Office 365" message. Basically, Yammer displays additional properties of the Open Graph object posted on Yammer.

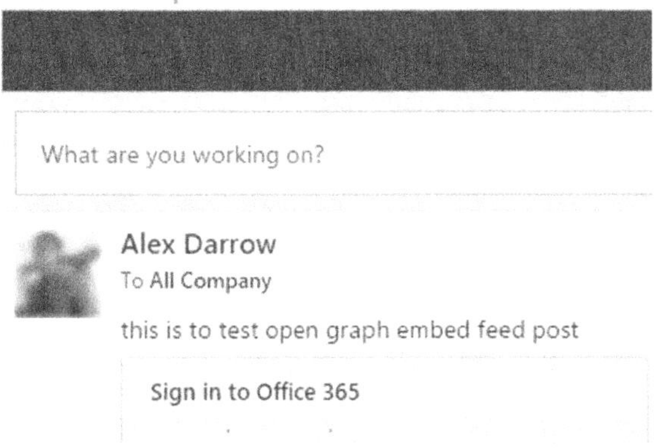

***Figure 2-11.** Yammer Embed using Open Graph feedtype rendered on a web page*

When you use Yammer Embed to post a public URL, Yammer creates an Open Graph object represented as a page object in Yammer, as shown in Figure 2-12. This Open Graph object displays all the open metadata that's pulled from the Embed.ly service. Embed.ly visits the page in the background and retrieves the Open Graph metadata present on the page. This allows Yammer to display more information about the page on the Yammer feed, making it much more user friendly. Later in this chapter, you will learn how to use the Yammer Share button to create an Open Graph object post on Yammer.

■ **Note** `Embed.Ly` is an external service. For more information, refer to the `embed.Ly` web site.

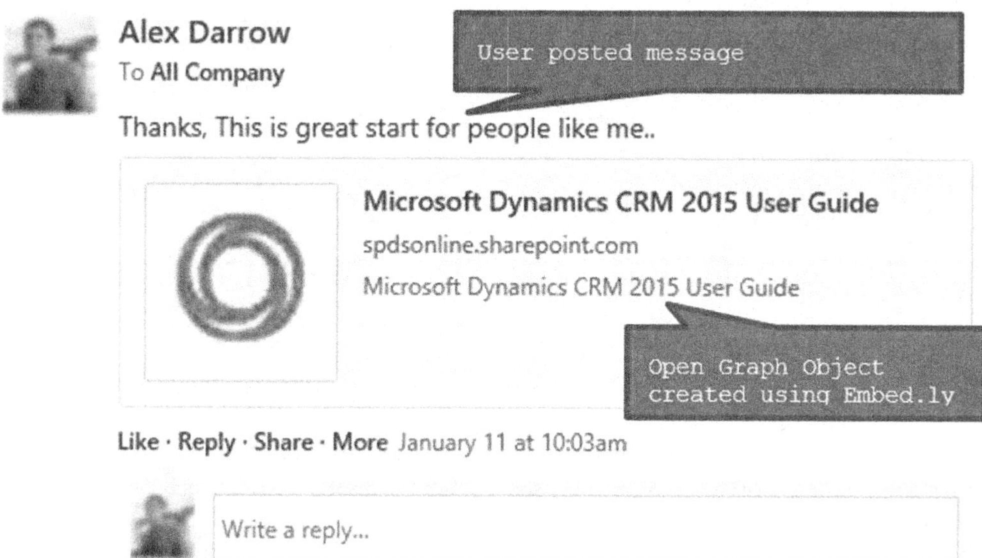

Figure 2-12. *Open Graph object created from posted messages using Embed.ly*

■ **Note** Open Graph and its usage in Yammer is covered in Chapter 5.

Object Feed Configuration Parameters

For the Open Graph feed, you can specify different parameters to manage the different configurable features. The following sections explore the different parameters you can specify.

Headers and Footers in Object Feeds

Figure 2-13 shows the parameters needed to hide the Yammer header or footer in a Yammer Embed Open Graph object.

```
yam.connect.embedFeed({
 container: "#embedded-feed",
 feedType: "open-graph",
 config: {
  header: false,
  footer: false
 }
});
```

Figure 2-13. *Open Graph object script with `config` option to hide headers and footers*

Custom Publisher Messages

You can add custom messages in Publisher by using the `promptText` configuration parameter, as shown in Figure 2-14.

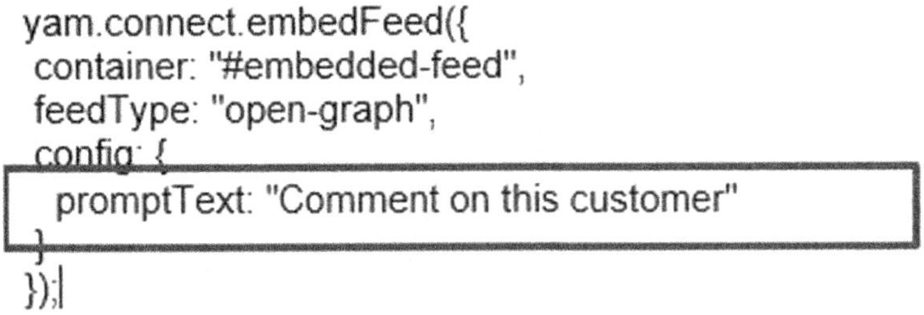

```
yam.connect.embedFeed({
 container: "#embedded-feed",
 feedType: "open-graph",
 config: {
  promptText: "Comment on this customer"
 }
});
```

***Figure 2-14.** Open Graph object script with `promptText` option to specify custom message*

When this script renders on a web page, the Publisher control will display a custom message that reads "Comment on this customer," as shown in Figure 2-15.

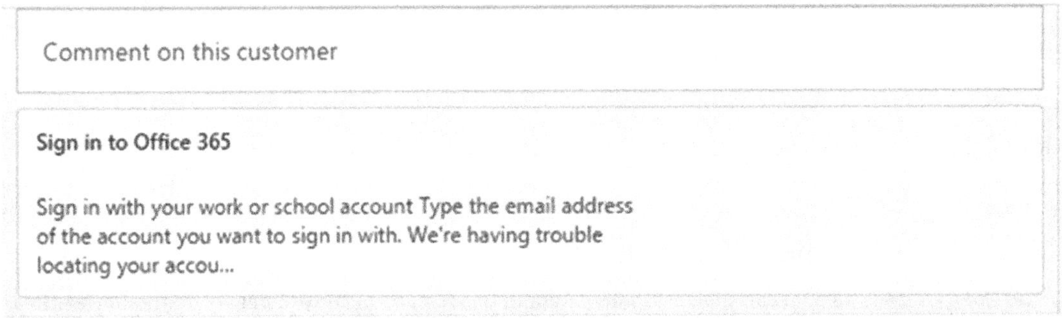

Comment on this customer

Sign in to Office 365

Sign in with your work or school account Type the email address of the account you want to sign in with. We're having trouble locating your accou...

***Figure 2-15.** Open Graph object feed rendered with custom message*

Open Graph Previews

Use the attribute illustrated in Figure 2-16 to display an Open Graph summary preview of the target URL in a new message on Yammer.

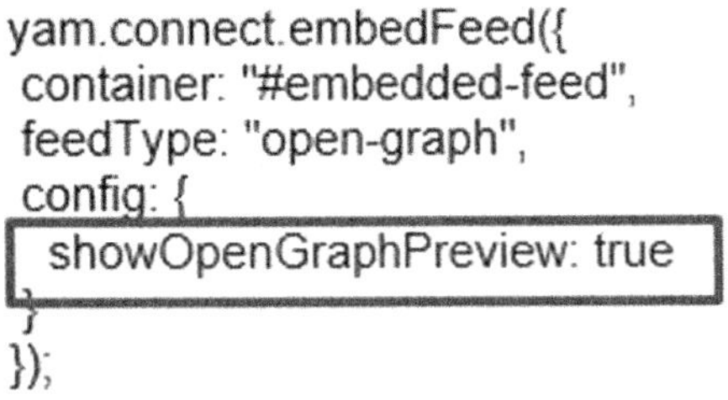

```
yam.connect.embedFeed({
 container: "#embedded-feed",
 feedType: "open-graph",
 config: {
  showOpenGraphPreview: true
 }
});
```

***Figure 2-16.** Open Graph object feed to show the additional values using the Open Graph `Preview` parameter*

When this script is rendered, you will see the preview like you saw in Figure 2-15. If it's set to false, users will not the Open Graph metadata associated with URL specified in the object properties.

Private Specified Object Feed

When Yammer Embed feed is placed on a page within a page, adding the `private` parameter option will allow developers to target audiences to restrict the access to only specified users in the specified Yammer network. Figure 2-17 shows you how to specify specific users using the `private` parameter in a Yammer Embed Feed.

```
yam.connect.embedFeed({
 Container: '#embedded-feed;
     , feedType: 'open-graph'
     , feedId: ''
     , config: {
         showOpenGraphPreview: true
         , promptText: 'Confirm you can make to this event'
     }
     , objectProperties: {
         url:https://lh4.[redacted]tent.com/-v0soe-ievYE/AAAAAAAAAAI/AAAAAAAC4-
w/ZCWLO9dszIM/s120-c/photo.jpg'
         , type: 'image'
     },
 private: true,
 users: [
  {name.: "Aziz Hassoune", "email" : "azizh@[redacted]om"},
  {name.: "Garret Vargas", "email" : "garretv@[redacted]com"}
 ]
  });
```

Figure 2-17. *Open Graph Object feed script allowing only two users to view the feed*

Another important aspect to consider when using Yammer Embed is how authentication works. The next section explains how to configure Yammer Embed for authentication on Yammer.

Yammer Embed with Single Sign-On

Your company can benefit from Yammer single sign-on (SSO), which allows users to log in to Yammer without entering seperate credentials. Using SSO with Yammer reduces the complexity and improves the usalibility of Yammer Embed feeds in business applications.

To use Yammer Embed with SSO, see the `config` section in Figure 2-18.

```
yam.connect.embedFeed({
  container: '#embedded-feed'
        , feedType: ''
        , feedId: ''
        , config: {
            use_sso: true // this line enables SSO
            , header: true
            , footer: true
            , showOpenGraphPreview: false
            , defaultGroupId: 1234879 //specify default group id
        }
    });
```

Figure 2-18. *Yammer Embed script with single sign-on*

If single sign-on is not enabled and you add a Yammer Embed script to your web site, users will be asked to log in to Yammer first before they can see the Yammer feeds, as shown in Figure 2-19.

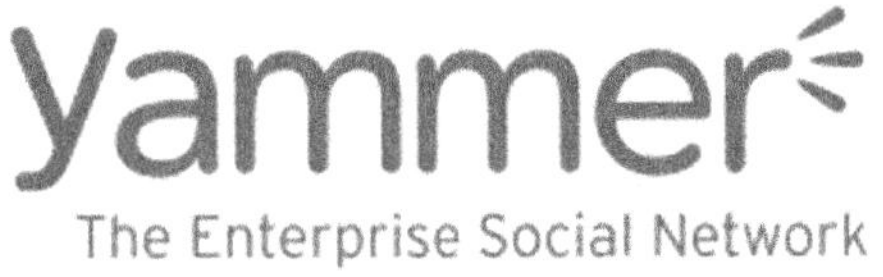

Figure 2-19. *Users will be asked to log in before Yammer Embed displays the Yammer feeds*

So far we have explained Yammer Embed and explored the different types of Yammer Embed feed options that you can add to your business applications. Later in this chapter, we will work on an example to show all the steps required to add Yammer Embed on a SharePoint-based company portal.

Let's now look at the Yammer action buttons, which are part of Yammer Embed functionality.

Using the Yammer Action Buttons

Yammer Embed also provides Open Graph action buttons—Follow, Like, and Share—as shown in Figure 2-20. Using these action buttons, you can make it easier for users to engage and share information with others. These action buttons are similar to other social networking tools that provide these kinds of actionable components. This feature can be useful in company intranets, CRM systems, reporting portals, and so on. They allow users to like a new announcement, follow important documents/reports, share newly published company news with colleagues on Yammer, and more. It's a very quick and easy implementation to see what colleagues have liked, shared, or are following. You can display all three Open Graph buttons next to each other to let people use them as needed.

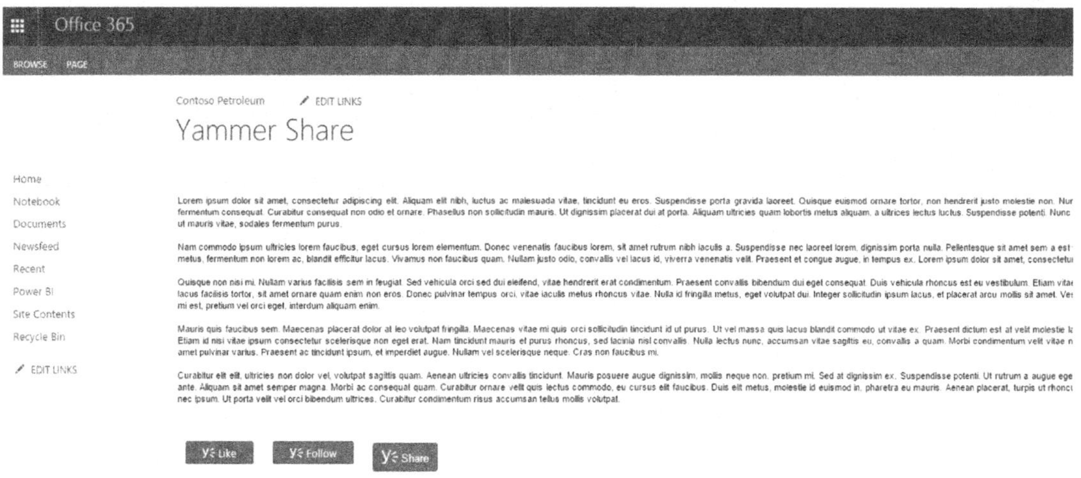

Figure 2-20. *Yammer action buttons on a web page*

These buttons are clickable interfaces. Like and Follow directly create an object on Yammer, and the Share button allows you to specify custom messages and select appropriate audiences for sharing the message.

How to Add a Yammer Action Button

Adding a Yammer action button is similar to adding Yammer Embed using JavaScript. There is a JavaScript snippet that you need to add to your HTML page. Let's look how to add to these buttons to your web applications.

Yammer Like Button

The Yammer Like button is the quickest way for people to share content with colleagues.

A single click on the Yammer Like button will like the content on the web page and share it on Yammer.

When you add the Yammer Like action button to a web page, on initial load users will see the Like button. When this button is clicked, an Open Graph object will be created, which will be visible on Yammer as an activity.

The Yammer Like button code snippet is similar to Yammer Embed and can be added to any HTML page:

```
yam.connect.actionButton({
container: "#Embedded-like",
network: "spdsuniversity.onmicrosoft.com",
action: "like"
});
```

When the Like button is clicked, a new Yammer activity is created against the user on Yammer and is visible in the Recent Activity widget, as shown in Figure 2-21. When users mouse over the widget, they can see the full details of the activity, as shown in Figure 2-21. Yammer also creates a dedicated page for this activity that employees can follow and discuss.

Figure 2-21. *Yammer Recent Activity widget showing the user Alex has liked a page*

■ **Note** The Recent Activity widget displays the most important activities on Yammer. Yammer out-of-the-box features also use the Recent Activity widget to post people's latest activities. You will read more details on Open Graph in Chapter 5.

Once the Like activity is complete, the Like button will change text and color to Liked, as shown in Figure 2-22. This allows users to Unlike the page/object if they want to.

Mauris quis faucibus sem. Maecenas placerat dolor at leo volutpat fringilla. Maecenas vitae mi quis orci sollicitudin tincidunt amet. Etiam id nisi vitae ipsum consectetur scelerisque non eget erat. Nam tincidunt mauris et purus rhoncus, sed lacinia ni quam sit amet pulvinar varius. Praesent ac tincidunt ipsum, et imperdiet augue. Nullam vel scelerisque neque. Cras non fauci

Curabitur elit elit, ultricies non dolor vel, volutpat sagittis quam. Aenean ultricies convallis tincidunt. Mauris posuere augue commodo ante. Aliquam sit amet semper magna. Morbi ac consequat quam. Curabitur ornare velit quis lectus commodo, eu (neque erat nec ipsum. Ut porta velit vel orci bibendum ultrices. Curabitur condimentum risus accumsan tellus mollis volutpat.

Figure 2-22. *The Yammer Like button when a user has clicked it once*

Users can unlike the page/object by clicking the Unlike button and it will change to Like again, as shown in Figure 2-23.

Mauris quis faucibus sem. Maecenas placerat dolor at leo volutpat fringilla. Maecenas vitae mi quis orci sollicitudin tincidunt amet. Etiam id nisi vitae ipsum consectetur scelerisque non eget erat. Nam tincidunt mauris et purus rhoncus, sed lacinia ni quam sit amet pulvinar varius. Praesent ac tincidunt ipsum, et imperdiet augue. Nullam vel scelerisque neque. Cras non fauci
Curabitur elit elit, ultricies non dolor vel, volutpat sagittis quam. Aenean ultricies convallis tincidunt. Mauris posuere augue commodo ante. Aliquam sit amet semper magna. Morbi ac consequat quam. Curabitur ornare velit quis lectus commodo, eu c neque erat nec ipsum. Ut porta velit vel orci bibendum ultrices. Curabitur condimentum risus accumsan tellus mollis volutpat.

Unlike
Follow
Share

Figure 2-23. *The Yammer Like button, now with the text Unlike*

When users click the Unlike button, the action button will change back to Like, thereby allowing users to like it again if they desire. At the same time a new activity is posted on the Yammer Recent Activity widget—"User....Liked <Object title>," as highlighted in Figure 2-24.

Aziz Hassoune
Alex Darrow liked:
Updated 34 minutes ago
Page
Alex Darrow likes .
Alex Darrow liked .
Alex Darrow followed .

Figure 2-24. *A new activity on Yammer is visible when the user clicks the UnLike button*

The Yammer Like button is a very creative way to allow users to update others on information they liked.

Yammer Follow Button

The Yammer Follow button is like the Facebook Follow button. When users click on it, they will automatically be subscribed to an Open Graph object and receive all updates in their activity stream. A new OG object is created on Yammer for the page/object where the Follow button is clicked and an association between the user and the OG object is created.

The following JavaScript script is used to add on web page to display the Yammer Follow button:

```
yam.connect.actionButton({
 container: "#Embedded-follow",
 network: "spdsuniversity.com",
 action: "follow"
});
```

Once a user has clicked the Yammer Follow button, the button's text changes to Followed, as shown in Figure 2-25.

Lorem ipsum dolor sit amet, consectetur adipiscing elit. Aliquam elit nibh, luctus ac malesuada vitae, tincidunt eu eros. Suspendisse porta gravi fermentum consequat. Curabitur consequat non odio et ornare. Phasellus non sollicitudin mauris. Ut dignissim placerat dui at porta. Aliquam ultr euismod ut mauris vitae, sodales fermentum purus.

Nam commodo ipsum ultricies lorem faucibus, eget cursus lorem elementum. Donec venenatis faucibus lorem, sit amet rutrum nibh iaculis a. Su turpis metus, fermentum non lorem ac, blandit efficitur lacus. Vivamus non faucibus quam. Nullam justo odio, convallis vel lacus id, viverra venena

Quisque non nisi mi. Nullam varius facilisis sem in feugiat. Sed vehicula orci sed dui eleifend, vitae hendrerit erat condimentum. Praesent convallis sem lacus facilisis tortor, sit amet ornare quam enim non eros. Donec pulvinar tempus orci, vitae iaculis metus rhoncus vitae. Nulla id fringilla m est. Donec mi est, pretium vel orci eget, interdum aliquam enim.

Mauris quis faucibus sem. Maecenas placerat dolor at leo volutpat fringilla. Maecenas vitae mi quis orci sollicitudin tincidunt id ut purus. Ut vel m amet. Etiam id nisi vitae ipsum consectetur scelerisque non eget erat. Nam tincidunt mauris et purus rhoncus, sed lacinia nisl convallis. Nulla lec quam sit amet pulvinar varius. Praesent ac tincidunt ipsum, et imperdiet augue. Nullam vel scelerisque neque. Cras non faucibus mi.

Curabitur elit elit, ultricies non dolor vel, volutpat sagittis quam. Aenean ultricies convallis tincidunt. Mauris posuere augue dignissim, mollis ne commodo ante. Aliquam sit amet semper magna. Morbi ac consequat quam. Curabitur ornare velit quis lectus commodo, eu cursus elit faucibus. I neque erat nec ipsum. Ut porta velit vel orci bibendum ultrices. Curabitur condimentum risus accumsan tellus mollis volutpat.

Figure 2-25. *Yammer Follow button after a user has clicked it once*

Similar to the Like button, when the Follow button is clicked, a new Yammer activity is created against the user on Yammer and is visible in the Recent Activity widget, as shown in Figure 2-26. When users mouse over it, they can see the full details, as shown in Figure 2-26.

Figure 2-26. *Yammer Recent Activity widget showing that user Alex has followed a page*

Once a user has clicked the Follow button, they can't follow it again. The only option is to unfollow it by clicking the button again, as shown in Figure 2-27.

fermentum consequat. Curabitur consequat non odio et ornare. Phasellus non sollicitudin mauris. Ut dignissim placerat dui at porta. Aliquam ut euismod ut mauris vitae, sodales fermentum purus.

Nam commodo ipsum ultricies lorem faucibus, eget cursus lorem elementum. Donec venenatis faucibus lorem, sit amet rutrum nibh iaculis a. S turpis metus, fermentum non lorem ac, blandit efficitur lacus. Vivamus non faucibus quam. Nullam justo odio, convallis vel lacus id, viverra venen

Quisque non nisi mi. Nullam varius facilisis sem in feugiat. Sed vehicula orci sed dui eleifend, vitae hendrerit erat condimentum. Praesent convall sem lacus facilisis tortor, sit amet ornare quam enim non eros. Donec pulvinar tempus orci, vitae iaculis metus rhoncus vitae. Nulla id fringilla m est. Donec mi est, pretium vel orci eget, interdum aliquam enim.

Mauris quis faucibus sem. Maecenas placerat dolor at leo volutpat fringilla. Maecenas vitae mi quis orci sollicitudin tincidunt id ut purus. Ut vel r amet. Etiam id nisi vitae ipsum consectetur scelerisque non eget erat. Nam tincidunt mauris et purus rhoncus, sed lacinia nisi convallis. Nulla le quam sit amet pulvinar varius. Praesent ac tincidunt ipsum, et imperdiet augue. Nullam vel scelerisque neque. Cras non faucibus mi.

Curabitur elit elit, ultricies non dolor vel, volutpat sagittis quam. Aenean ultricies convallis tincidunt. Mauris posuere augue dignissim, mollis ne commodo ante. Aliquam sit amet semper magna. Morbi ac consequat quam. Curabitur ornare velit quis lectus commodo, eu cursus elit faucibus. neque erat nec ipsum. Ut porta velit vel orci bibendum ultrices. Curabitur condimentum risus accumsan tellus mollis volutpat.

Figure 2-27. *Yammer Follow button giving the user the option to unfollow the followed object*

Similar to the Like button, all the actions related to the Follow button are posted on the Recent Activity widget on Yammer.

Yammer Share Button

The Yammer Share Button allows users to easily share online content with groups and coworkers on Yammer using a browser pop-up.

To place a Yammer Share button on your page, embed the following code where you want the button to appear. The button will be rendered in the element with the ID `yj-share-button`.

```
<div id="yj-share-button"></div>
```

Then place the following code at the bottom of the page before closing the </body> tag.

```
<script type="text/javascript" src="https://c64.assets-Yammer.com/assets/
platform_social_buttons.min.js">
</script>
<script type="text/javascript">yam.platform.yammerShare();</script>
```

In the following example, you will see how the Share button will appear on a Microsoft SharePoint site.

■ **Note** As Yammer keeps updating and upgrading its platform, the previous Yammer action buttons and Embed feed options may change in future. For the latest, refer to `https://developer.Yammer.com`.

EXAMPLE: ADDING A YAMMER FEED TO A MICROSOFT SHAREPOINT PORTAL PAGE

In this example, you'll add Yammer Embed and Yammer action buttons to the case study SPDSUniversity portal, which is based on Microsoft SharePoint. Embedded Yammer feeds allow users to view the Yammer feed of the All Company group and to Like specific pages and share content on Yammer.

1. To do this, go to the Yammer "All Company" group feed page.
2. Click Embed This Group In Your Site under Access Options, as shown in Figure 2-28.

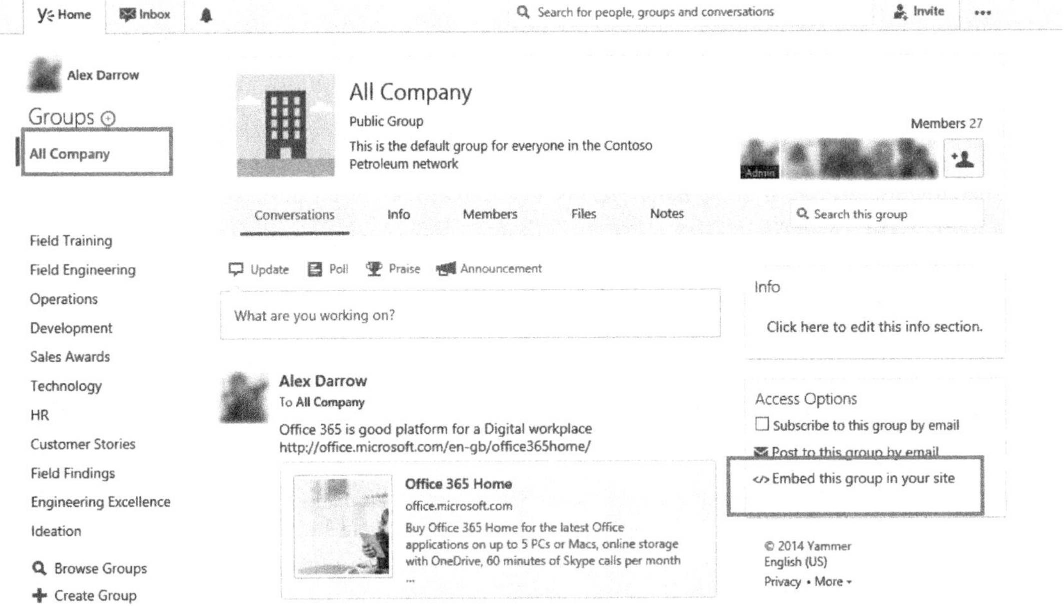

Figure 2-28. *Yammer group feed page*

3. This will open a pop-up window. Copy the script from the pop-up window shown in Figure 2-29.

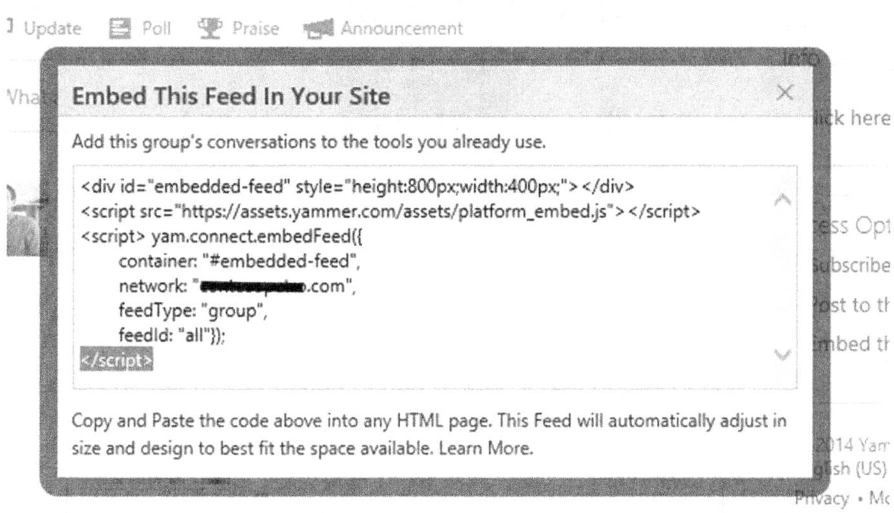

Figure 2-29. *Yammer All Company group feed script*

Copy this JS snippet to the SharePoint portal in a Script Editor web part and save the page. Once you're done, the Yammer Login button will be displayed, as shown in Figure 2-30.

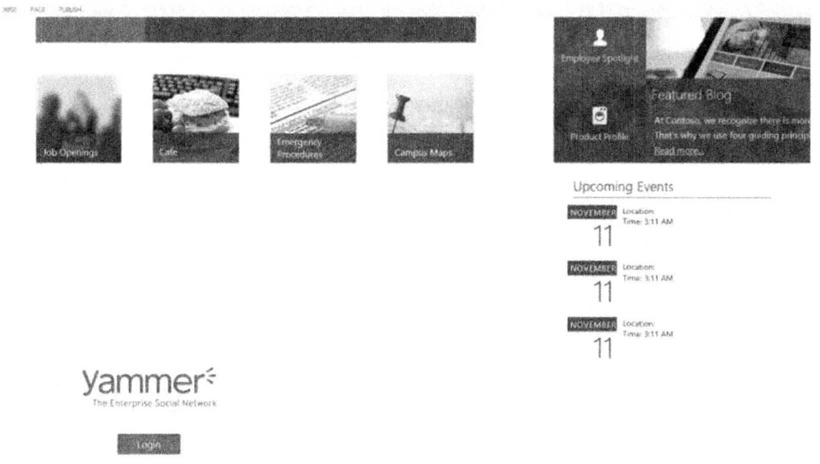

Figure 2-30. *The company portal page with Yammer Embed without a logged-in user*

Click on the Login button and enter your Yammer credentials in the pop-up window, as shown in Figure 2-31.

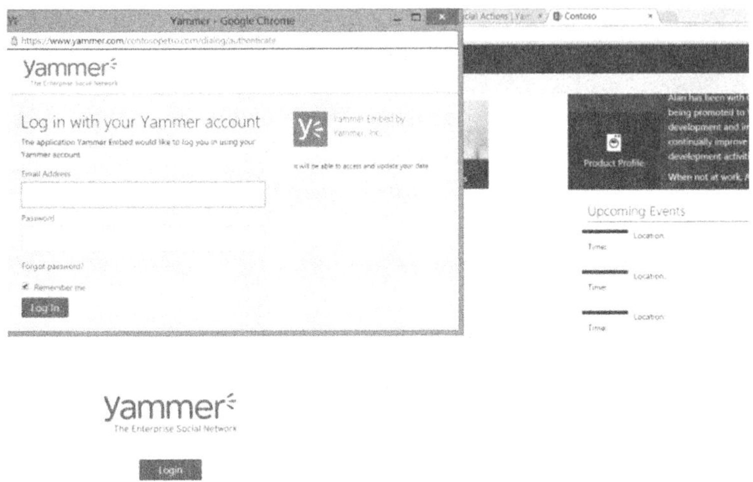

Figure 2-31. *Yammer Login pop-up window*

Once you're logged on, the pop-up window will close and you will see the Yammer feed for the "All Company" group displayed on the page (Figure 2-32).

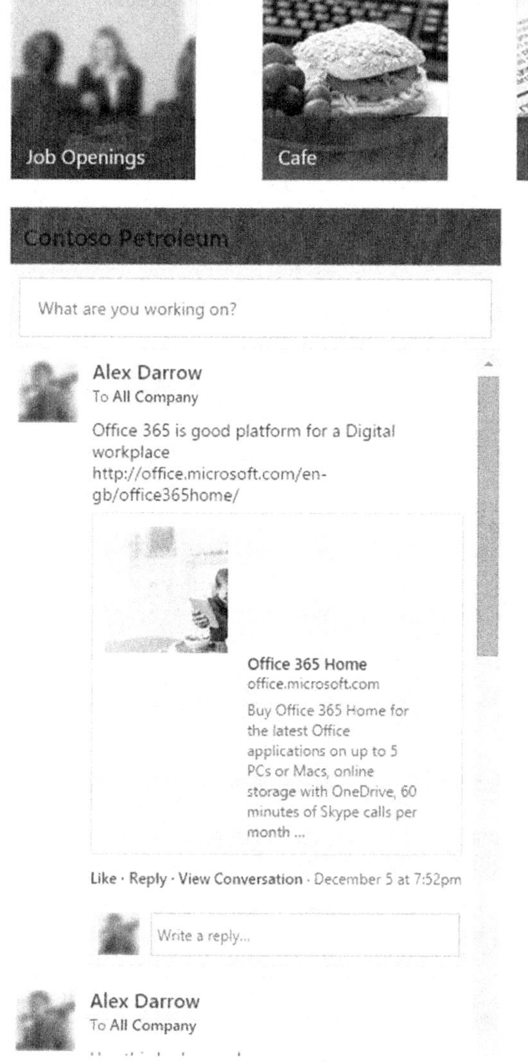

Figure 2-32. *All Company feed rendered on the page after logging in*

4. Add the Like, Follow, and Share buttons to the page.

5. Edit the web page where you want to add the Yammer action buttons and add the following snippet to the page:

```
<div><div id="Embedded-like" style="display:inline;margin:10px;"></div>
<div id="Embedded-Follow" style="display:inline;margin:10px;"></div>
<div id="yj-share-button" style="display:inline;margin:10px;"></div>

</div>
<script type="text/javascript" src="https://assets.Yammer.com/assets/
platform_Embed.js"></script>
```

```
<script type="text/javascript" src="https://c64.assets-Yammer.com/assets/
platform_social_buttons.min.js">
</script>

<script type="text/javascript">
yam.connect.actionButton({
container: "#Embedded-like",
feedType: 'open-graph',
network: "spdsuniversity.onmicrosoft.com",
action: "like",
object: {
          url: "https:/abcsite.sharepoint.com/SitePages/YammerShare.aspx",
        "title":"SPDS Scholarship News",
          type: "page"
        }
});
yam.connect.actionButton({
container: "#Embedded-Follow",
network: "spdsuniversity.onmicrosoft.com",
action: "follow",
object: {
          url: "https:// abcsite.sharepoint.com/SitePages/YammerShare.aspx",
        "title":" SPDS Scholarship News ",
          type: "page"
        }
});
yam.platform.yammerShare();
</script>
```

6. Save the page and refresh it. You will see the Yammer action buttons on the page, as shown in Figure 2-33.

Business Development Strategy

Lorem ipsum dolor sit amet, consectetur adipiscing elit. Aliquam a ultrices enim. Curabitur ut ipsum odio. Nunc blandit dictum lacinia. Quisque lacus turpis, finibus nec odio id, ullamcorper ultricies enim. Etiam euismod nunc auctor feugiat aliquam. Fusce vehicula facilisis libero, in pharetra mauris fermentum sed. Integer ut ultrices massa. Ut posuere fermentum condimentum. Nullam ultrices ipsum erat. Sed maximus magna ac tellus consectetur efficitur. Etiam in orci eu nibh lobortis molestie vel ut justo. Quisque eu dictum purus.

Sed vestibulum leo tortor. Integer sed orci augue. Sed eget venenatis neque, ac suscipit metus. Aliquam magna libero, scelerisque sit amet commodo eget, volutpat et tortor. Integer auctor nibh eu ex varius, vitae sodales odio dictum. Pellentesque bibendum libero ipsum, at euismod urna rhoncus id. Aliquam condimentum viverra ex, ut dictum tellus scelerisque posuere. Cras ornare nulla at metus fermentum, vel ullamcorper arcu porttitor. Quisque tempus lorem et odio blandit, ultricies pretium risus malesuada. Nullam quam ligula, suscipit quis nibh ac, commodo pulvinar velit. Curabitur volutpat et eros quis efficitur. Mauris sed volutpat ligula, sit amet pharetra elit. Phasellus dapibus placerat libero non dignissim.

Proin consectetur odio dui, ut elementum nibh faucibus eget. Mauris varius leo ac odio finibus, et hendrerit ante scelerisque. Nunc fringilla interdum augue quis feugiat. Curabitur et dapibus purus, sed mollis metus. Suspendisse tellus nibh, auctor id vulputate ut, ultricies sed odio. Integer sem odio, porta quis ullamcorper ut, convallis egestas odio. In hac habitasse platea dictumst.

Phasellus semper orci ac bibendum faucibus. Fusce luctus ligula a ornare viverra. Pellentesque et nibh ac tellus varius sodales non ut augue. Integer porttitor fringilla nunc quis imperdiet. Pellentesque habitant morbi tristique senectus et netus et malesuada fames ac turpis egestas. Etiam ultricies egestas enim, a fringilla magna condimentum sit amet. Donec ac risus ligula. Donec sed libero eu urna laoreet sodales. Sed vel malesuada dui. Nam fringilla mi ac sagittis laoreet.

Phasellus vel odio magna. Suspendisse blandit a dolor ut molestie. Nulla vel rutrum mauris. Vivamus efficitur turpis sodales, volutpat turpis nec, aliquam sem. Aliquam faucibus condimentum elementum. Donec ultrices augue velit. Suspendisse metus erat, tincidunt non odio id, pulvinar faucibus metus. Etiam metus est, efficitur at nulla quis, fringilla condimentum justo. Integer eu mollis arcu.

Liked
Follow
Share

***Figure 2-33.** Yammer action buttons on the company portal page*

7. When you click the Yammer Share button, you will see a pop-up window with Yammer Publisher, as shown in Figure 2-34. You can add a specific group with whom you want to share this page. Also notice the Open Graph object being created automatically by Yammer with the details of the page.

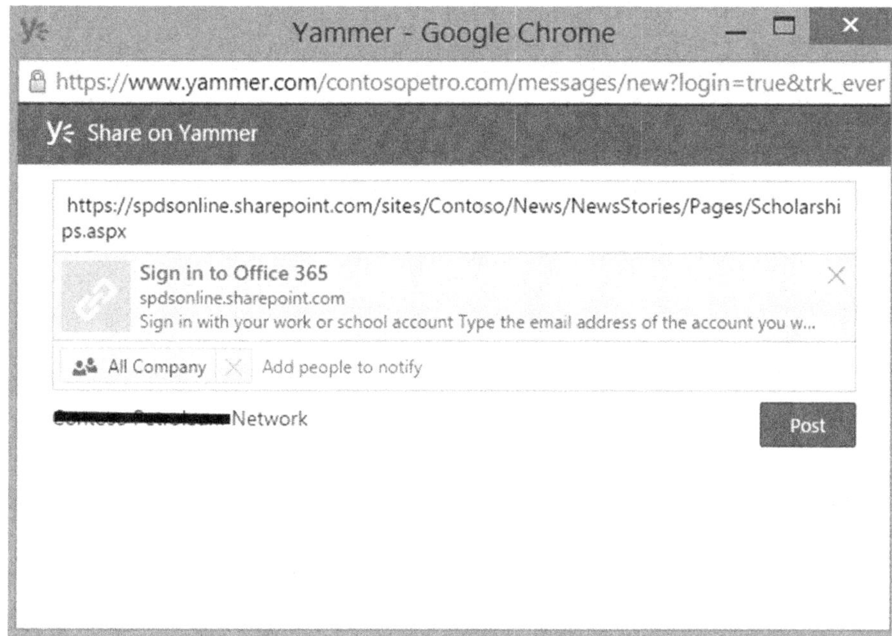

Figure 2-34. *Yammer Publisher pop-up window that appears when you click the Yammer Share button*

Similarly, you can use the Yammer Like and Follow buttons.

At this point in time, you have implemented the Yammer Embed feed and action buttons into the portal. Congratulations!

Summary

Hopefully, you are now able to use Yammer Embed in your applications. Yammer Embed feeds and Yammer action buttons provide an easy way to integrate Yammer into web applications and allow users to share application-specific updates on Yammer directly from web applications. You simply have to select the right Embed feed and action buttons based on each individual case.

CHAPTER 3

Yammer App Development Basics

Pathik Rawal

The first two chapters covered the basics of the Yammer platform, including how to use Yammer Embed in your existing business applications. Yammer Embed is a simple way to integrate your line-of-business application. The main challenge with Yammer Embed is that it does not provide deep integration between Yammer and your line-of-business applications when you want to read or write data into Yammer. Also, if you want to enable single sign-on in your business applications, that requires a deeper understanding of the Yammer platform.

The first step toward the deep integration of Yammer and your line-of-business applications is understanding the concepts surrounding a Yammer app. In this chapter, we will cover the basics of Yammer apps, including how to register your app with Yammer and how to manage your Yammer apps.

What Is a Yammer App?

Yammer apps provide a way to deeply integrate Yammer and your other line-of-business applications. As a developer, you register a Yammer app on your company's Yammer network and use Yammer APIs and SDKs to build custom applications. This provides great flexibility around how your custom applications interact with Yammer.

Let's use an example to explain the concept of the Yammer app. Suppose you are a Microsoft Dynamics CRM developer in SPDS and you want to offer an integration between Microsoft Dynamics CRM with Yammer. Business users want to be able to notify all the members of a Yammer Sales group directly from Microsoft Dynamic CRM each time a new opportunity is created. To build this feature, a deeper integration between Microsoft Dynamics CRM and Yammer is required.

The first thing you need to do is register a new Yammer app. Once your Yammer app is registered on the Yammer network, you will then use the key values provided by Yammer to develop custom applications to integrate Microsoft Dynamics CRM with Yammer.

As illustrated in Figure 3-1, the Yammer architecture allows different technology platforms to integrate with Yammer using a Yammer app.

P. Rawal and P. Rohilla, *Developing on Yammer*, DOI 10.1007/978-1-4842-0943-1_3

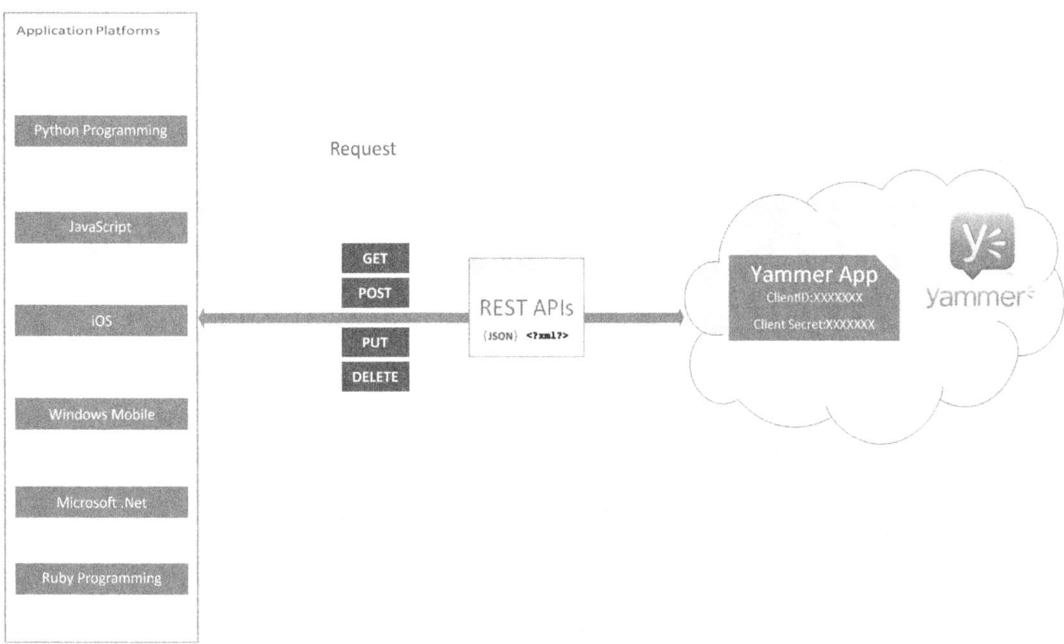

Figure 3-1. *High-Level architecture view of integrating Yammer with other platforms using a Yammer app*

Figure 3-1 gives you a high-level view of how to develop your line-of-business applications hosted on different development platforms to integrate with Yammer using Yammer apps. The key is that none of the business applications with custom code are hosted on Yammer. Rather, those applications are hosted outside of Yammer. When you write code to read and write data from Yammer, that code executes on its own hosting platform and a registered Yammer app plays an important role in providing a channel for writing or reading data from Yammer into your line-of-business applications.

As a developer, you have to register the Yammer app in your company's Yammer network to integrate with the line-of-business applications. Therefore, in the following section, we will explain how to register a Yammer app.

Registering a Yammer App

There are no restrictions on creating Yammer apps and the good thing about this is that no approvals are required to create, build, and test Yammer apps either. Users can register a new Yammer app on their Yammer home network using the Yammer web interface.

Let's start by registering a new SPDSUniversity Yammer app, which we will be using in our integration examples later in this book. The purpose of the SPDSUniversity Yammer app is to provide an integration channel between Yammer and other line-of-business applications of SPDS, which is mentioned in the case study. This Yammer app will allow business applications like the SPDSUniversity ASP.NET application, the SPDSUniversity SharePoint portal, and the SPDSUniversity Windows phone app to read and write data from Yammer. You will learn integration of all the above-mentioned line-of-business applications with Yammer in the remaining chapters.

Here are the detailed steps for registering a new Yammer app on your Yammer network.

1. Log in to the Yammer network.

2. On your Yammer home page, click on the three dots (. . .), as shown in Figure 3-2.

Figure 3-2. Creating a new Yammer app using the Yammer user interface

3. From the drop-down menu, click on Created Apps.

4. You will be presented with the Registered Applications page, as shown in Figure 3-3. It lists all your registered applications.

Figure 3-3. The list of registered applications by the logged-in user

■ **Note** If you do not see the Created Apps menu, visit `https://www.Yammer.com/client_Applications`.

5. To register a new Yammer app, click on the green Register New App button, as shown in Figure 3-3.
6. Enter the details of your new Yammer app. Figure 3-4 shows all the required fields for the SPDSUniversity Yammer app registration.

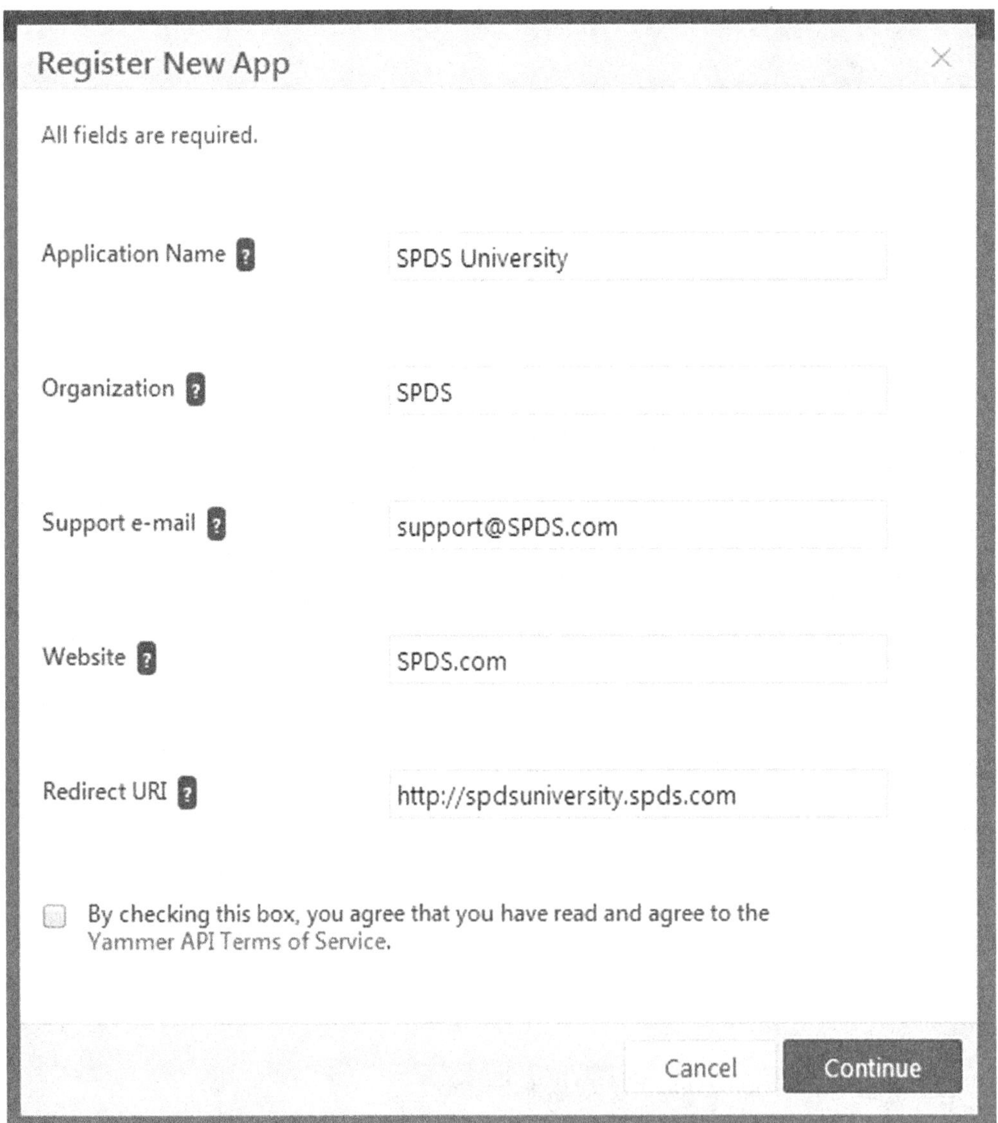

Figure 3-4. *New Yammer app registration screen*

You also have to agree on the Yammer API terms and conditions before registering your Yammer app. Table 3-1 provides a description of each field required for app registration.

Table 3-1. *Yammer App Registration Fields*

Field	Description
Application Name	The application name entered here will be the one that is used in the Yammer application directory and is visible on all Yammer activities. You can also modify the application name later by editing the Yammer App configuration details.
Organization	The name of the organization affiliated with your app. Normally your company name.
Support Email	An email address, which users of your app can contact for support.
Web Site	Your organization's web site.
Redirect URI	URL where Yammer will redirect after the OAuth2.0 authentication flow is complete. This is a requirement of the OAuth 2.0 specification and must be present for applications to be authorized by URLs. In short, it is a URL that you control and is a key part of the multi-step OAuth authentication process. As with all application URLs, this Redirect URI should use SSL to protect the authentication process. You will learn about using the Redirect URI in a Yammer authorization process in Chapter 4.

7. Click the Continue button to register the new Yammer app.

8. Once the Yammer app is successfully registered, Yammer allocates two important values—`ClientID` and `Client Secret`—to the Yammer app. These values are unique for each Yammer app and are required for OAuth authorization to Yammer from any external applications. You can view these values from the default page of the app labeled "Keys and Tokens," as shown in Figure 3-5.

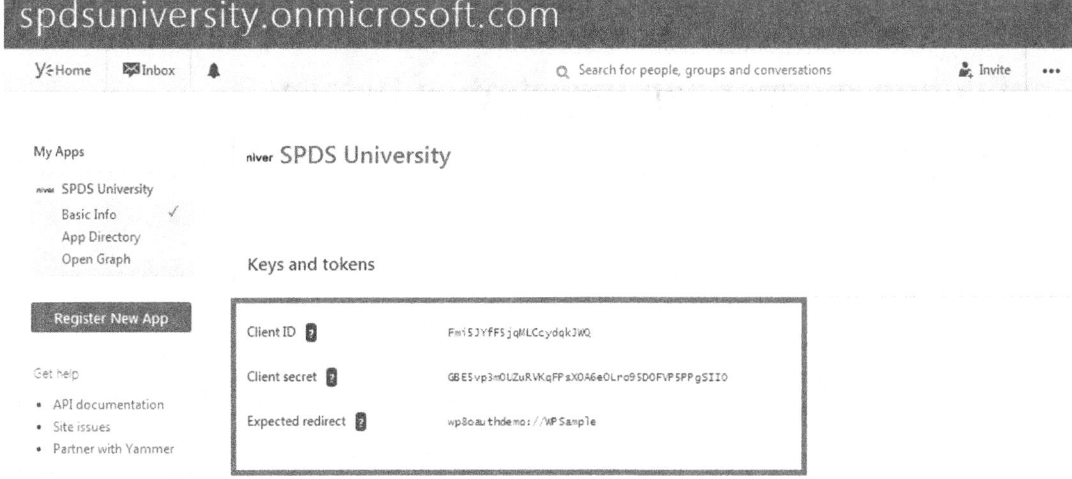

Figure 3-5. *Registered Yammer app's Keys and Tokens information*

This Yammer app is now ready for integrations with other business applications. One important point to consider here is that the SPDSUniversity Yammer app is registered under the Yammer home network.

When you register your Yammer app, it will be available only on your home network because Yammer sets the global flag to false. Apps without a global flag set are available only to the home network of the Yammer app. Developers and other users of the home network can use these local apps, but they won't be available to others outside your network until you publish them to Yammer's Global App Directory.

As shown in Figure 3-6, you can view and manage all registered apps on your home network. The user who is logged in to the system owns the listed Yammer apps.

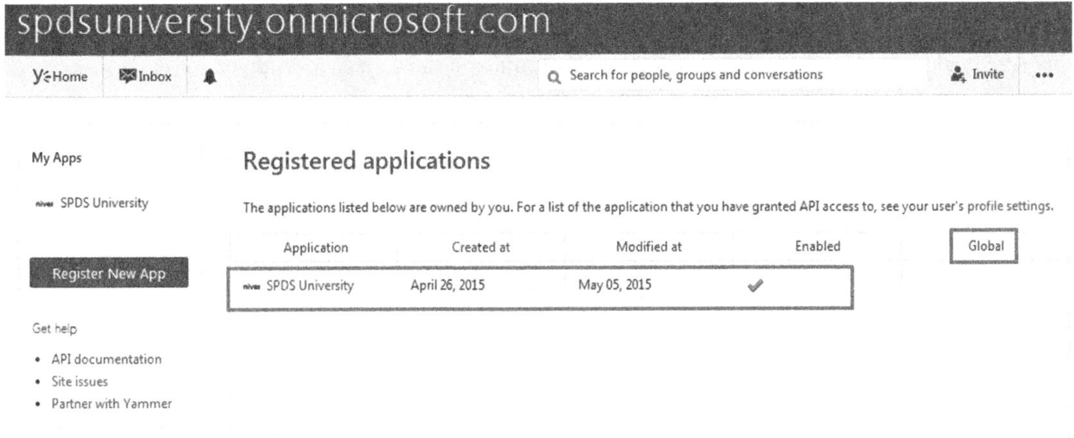

Figure 3-6. *Yammer apps under the home network*

In the next section, we will explore additional Yammer app configuration considerations using the Yammer user interface. You will also learn how to publish your Yammer app to the Global App Directory.

Configuring Yammer App Registration Details

Once your Yammer app is registered, you can configure additional information related to it. As illustrated in Figure 3-7, there are three sections—Basic Info, App Directory, and Open Graph.

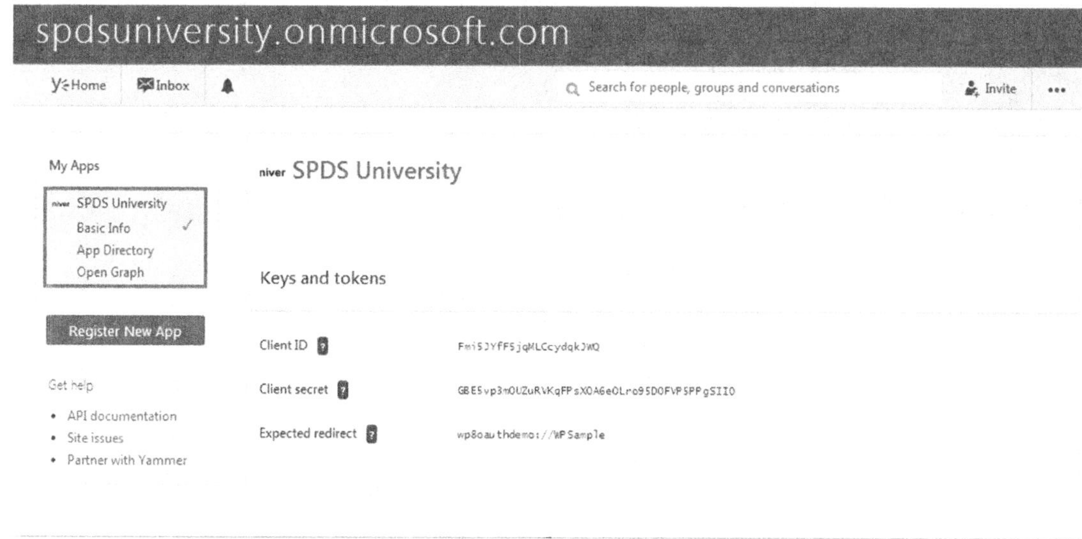

Figure 3-7. *The Yammer app's configuraiton sections*

Let's start with the Basic Info section.

Editing the Basic Info

The Basic Info link (Figure 3-8) on left side of the navigation under My App allows you as the owner of the app to edit the basic info that you entered while registering the Yammer. You can also enter additional details about the Yammer app.

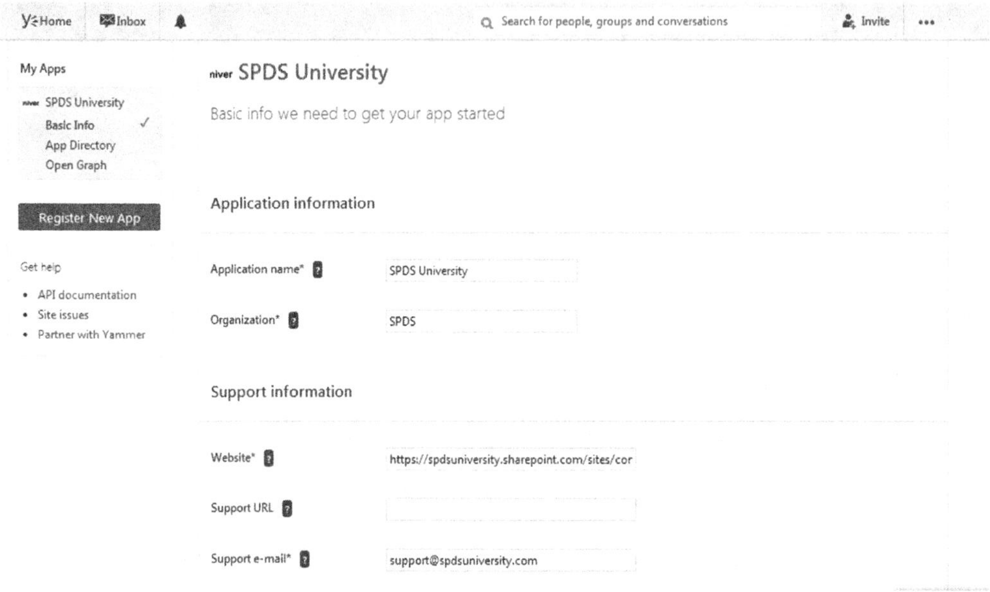

Figure 3-8. *The Yammer app's basic info*

Notice that the installation information section has some additional fields that were not presented when first registering the Yammer app. Let's examine these now.

Redirect URI and JavaScript Origins are two important properties that are used in OAuth 2.0 authentication and play important role in the entire process that makes end users' experiences easy and smooth, particularly the Redirect URI.

The Redirect URI is the URL of the site or page to redirect. Users will be redirected to the redirect URI, and generally this will be the URL of the site's home page or a landing page for the Yammer users for retrieval of access tokens. As with all application URLs, this Redirect URI should use SSL to protect the authentication process. Your Redirect URI will vary depending on how your line-of-business application is configured. Table 3-2 shows examples for static and dynamic domains.

Table 3-2. *Redirect URI Examples for Static and Dynamic Domains*

Domain Usage	Redirect URIs Example
Static domain configured for all users of the application	`https://www.application.com` `https://dev.application.com`
Dynamic subdomains for multiple users, for example, `https://[instance-name].application.com`	`https://application.com`

The second important parameter is JavaScript Origins. It is the value of the application from where you will execute the code (your application code). For the majority of cases, it is the domain address of your application that will make REST API calls to Yammer using the JavaScript SDK. The JavaScript Origin field should be updated with all the URLs if you access Yammer REST APIs from different applications. Ensure that each of these origins is configured on a new line. Whenever possible, it is best to register domains that support SSL/TLS encryption.

■ **Caution** If you do not configure JavaScript Origin for your Yammer app, it is possible that the Yammer OAuth authentication will not work.

Configuring App Directory Settings

The second set of configuration options available in the web interface relate to your app directory settings. To understand these, you first need to understand the Yammer app directory.

What Is the Yammer App Directory?

From the end user's point of view, the Yammer app directory provides an easy way to discover new Yammer apps and install them in minutes. You can also visit `https://www.Yammer.com/Apps` to view the published apps in the app directory or click the dots "..." on your Yammer page, as illustrated in Figure 3-9.

Figure 3-9. *The Yammer app directory*

Under the app directory, you can see the featured apps that Yammer shares with you, as illustrated in Figure 3-10. These apps are from different vendors who have developed generic Yammer integration apps that you can use based on available features. You can also see apps that your colleagues are using, as well as your installed apps.

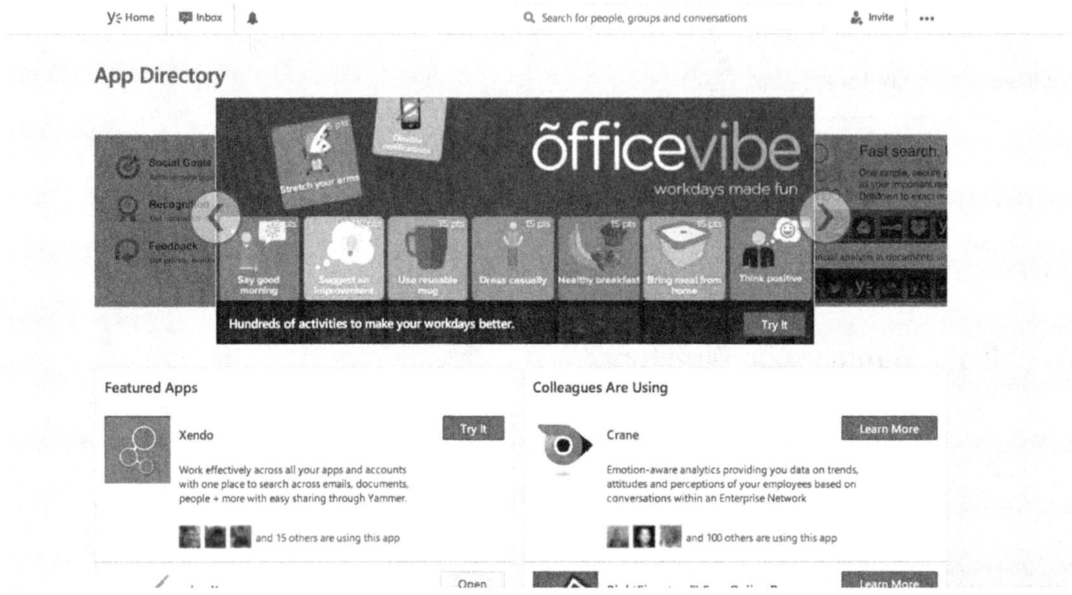

***Figure 3-10.** The Yammer app directory showing the Featured Apps, App Carousel, and Colleagues Are Using sections*

The Yammer app directory and App Carousel provides an easy way for developers to publish their Yammer apps to a wider audience if they want to develop integrations for their publicly available services. You can see apps for publicly available apps like `Sched.do` or `mindflash` in the Yammer app directory.

Configuration Options

As shown earlier in Figure 3-7, you can navigate to the App Directory configuration setting by using the app directory link on the App Configuration page.

In this section, the majority of the fields are self-explanatory. You can get further info about them by clicking the "?" button next to each field.

The first field is Category. Select a category that best applies to your Yammer app and then enter a detailed description that will help Yammer users intuit its features.

In the Installation Information section, specify the terms of service URL and private policy URL, as your Yammer app is going to be used by many users, especially if you want to make a business application (like `Sched.Do` or `mindflash.com`). In this section we specify the Redirect URI that we talked about in detail earlier in this chapter. You'll also learn more about it in Chapter 4.

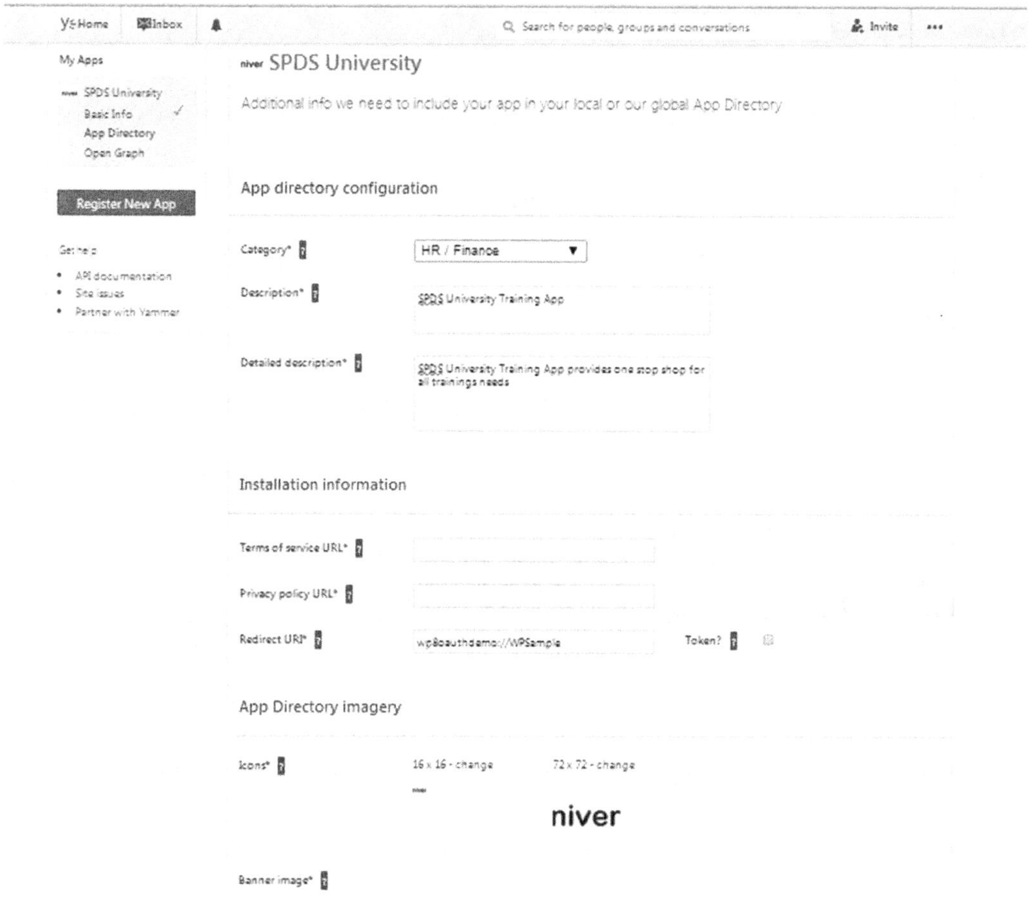

Figure 3-11. *The Yammer app's app directory configuration*

It is also useful to upload images for the Yammer app's icon, banner images, and collection of screenshots that can provide visual representation to users about your Yammer app before they actually experience it. You can add up to four screenshots in the App Directory configuration screen, as shown in Figure 3-12.

App Directory imagery

Icons* ?

16 x 16 - change

72 x 72 - change

SPDS University

Unsaved

Banner image* ?

690 x 275 - change

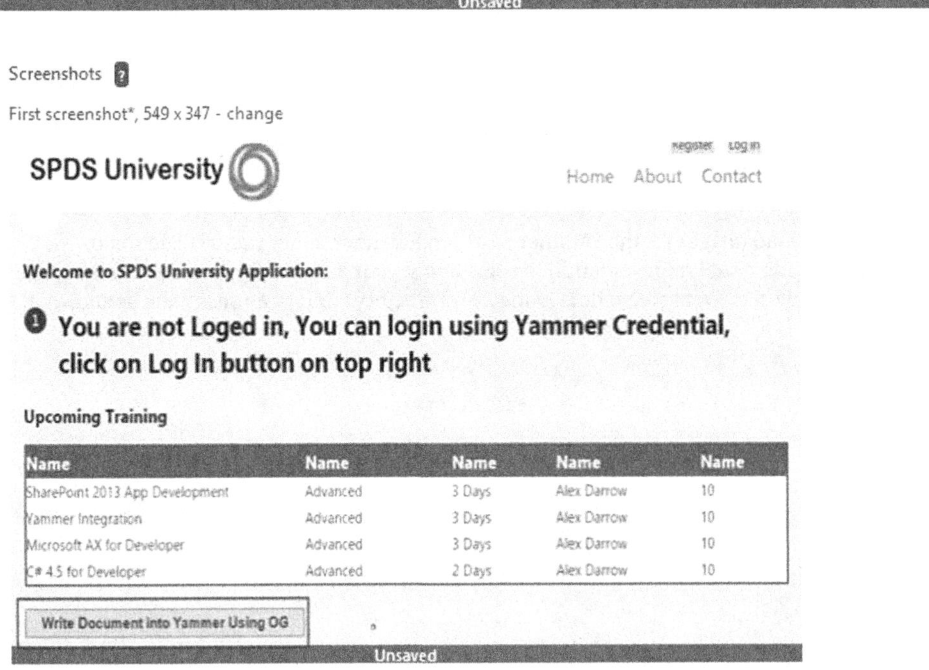

Figure 3-12. *Yammer app's app directory configuration for icons, banner images, and screenshots*

By default, when developers register their Yammer apps, it is best to do so to the home network only. To deploy a Yammer app to the Global App Directory, you need to submit your app to the Yammer support team. The Yammer support team will then contact you to ensure your app is ready to be added to the Yammer app directory. Your app can also be promoted to the Yammer App Carousel or to the featured apps, but that is based on your discussion with Yammer. Developers also have to read and sign the Yammer app directory agreement before submitting their app.

In the next section, you will learn about two different networks where you can deploy your Yammer app.

Submitting Your App to the Global App Directory

In order to deploy their Yammer apps to the Global App Directory, developers need to go through a vetting process with Yammer, and if approved, their app will be marked "Global" and will then be listed in the Global App Directory. Developers need to submit their apps by using the Yammer user interface, as shown in Figure 3-13. They do this to the Yammer support team using Yammer App's Global Directory menu on the Yammer app configuration page. Once you've submitted your app, the Yammer support team will meet with you to ensure your app is feature-ready and good enough to be added to the Yammer app directory. Before submitting your app for review, ensure that you have completed app directory configuration sections, designed your web site and landing page for the app, and prepared some marketing materials. Your app may even be promoted in the featured Yammer App Carousel or on the Yammer blog.

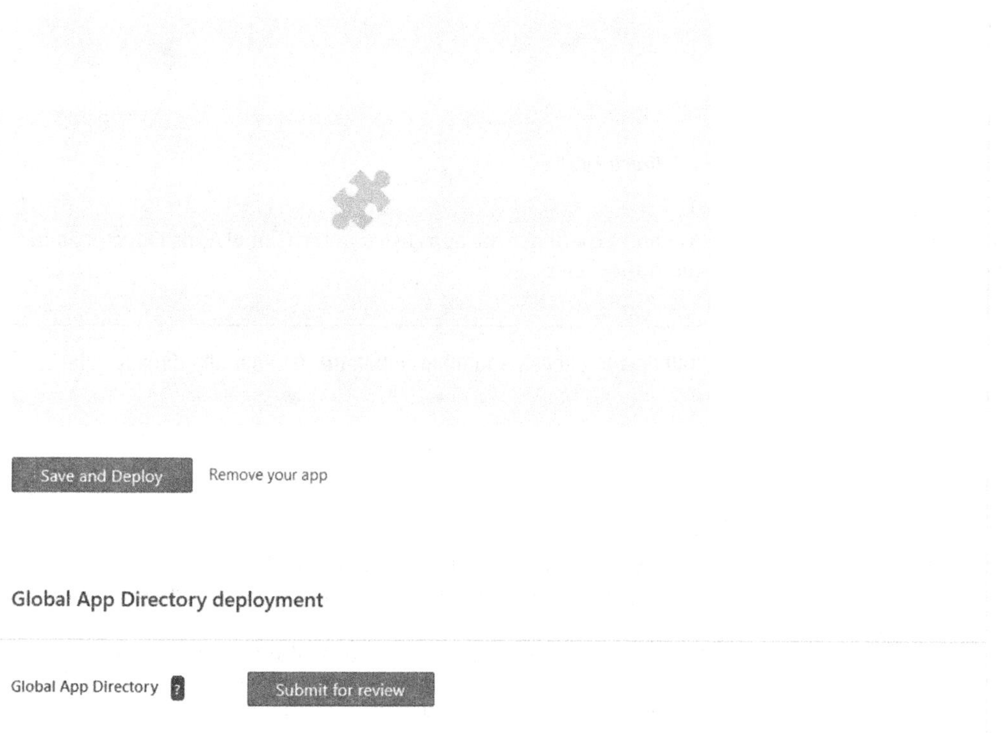

Figure 3-13. *Yammer apps in the Global directoryk*

Once your Yammer app is marked as global, it will be listed in the Global App Directory, as shown in Figure 3-14.

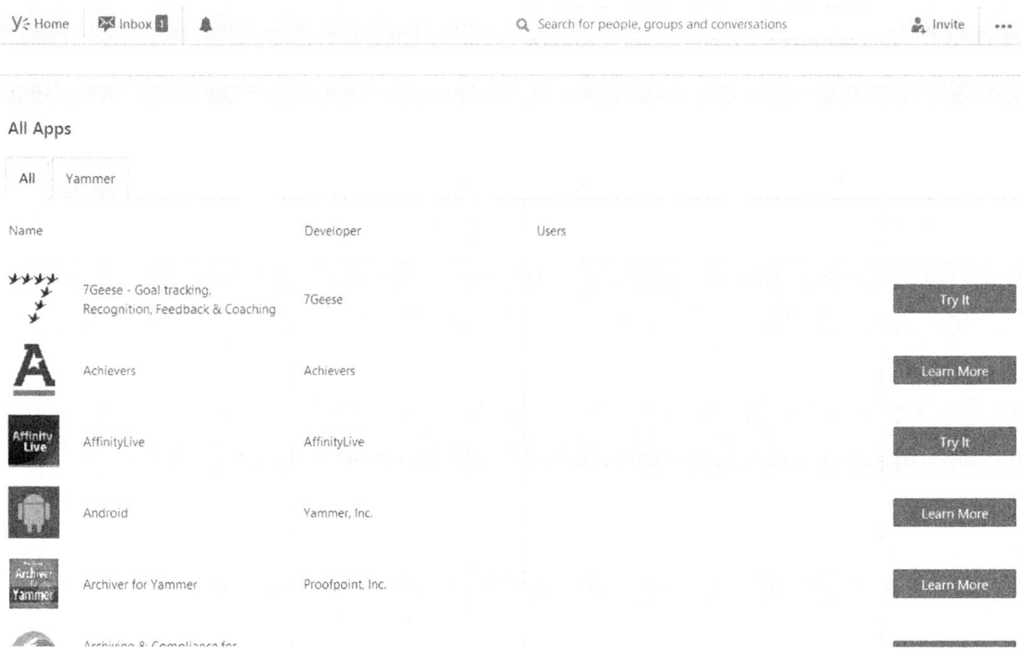

Figure 3-14. *Yammer apps in the Global directory*

Users from all networks can discover and experience the apps listed in the Global Apps Directory and can benefit from the extended functionality they offer.

■ **Note** If you want to know more about how to publish a Yammer app in the Yammer app directly, refer to `https://developer.Yammer.com`.

Configuring Open Graph

The next section on the Yammer app's configuration page is Open Graph. As mentioned in Chapter 1, Open Graph (OG) is a lightweight data integration protocol that allows developers to define an activity and post it to Yammer as an Open Graph object.

Yammer's Open Graph protocol provides many out-of-the-box objects that you can use to write data into Yammer. It also allows you to configure custom Open Graph objects and action types. The Open Graph configuration page of the Yammer app is where you can specify custom Open Graph objects and action types, as shown in Figure 3-15.

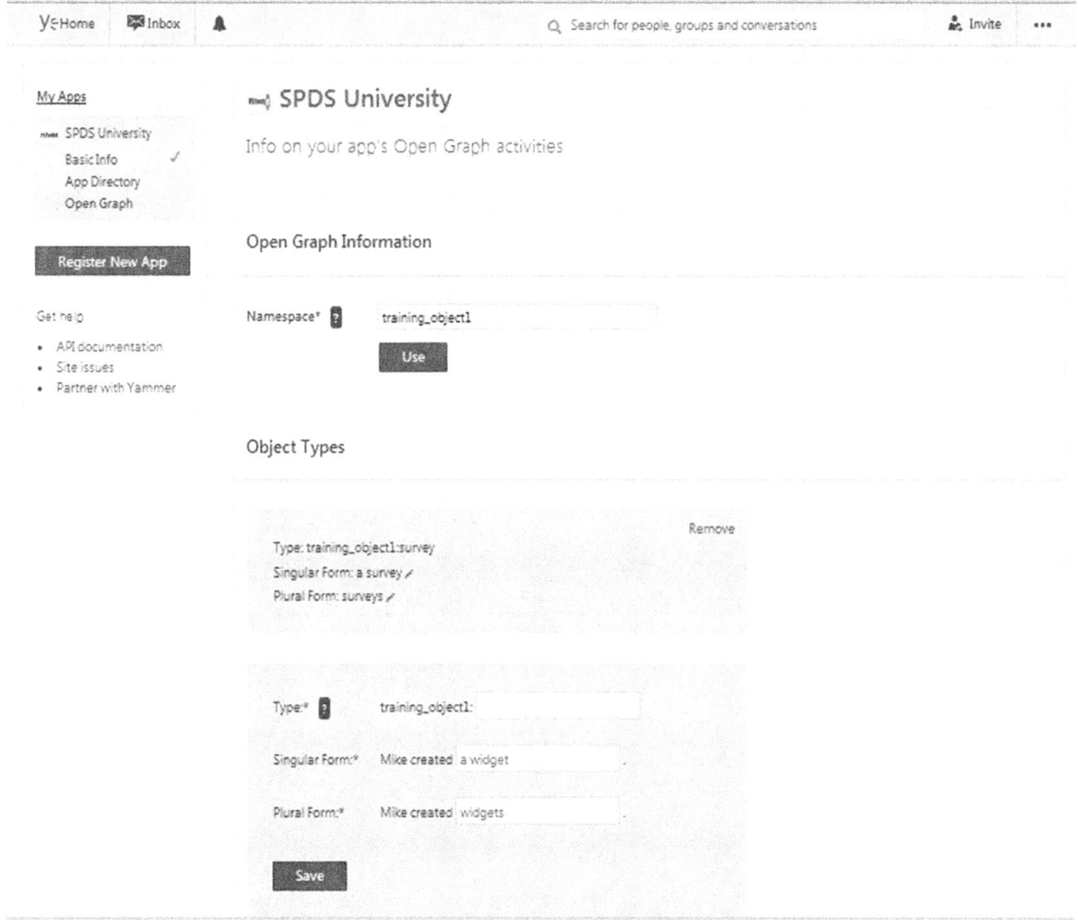

***Figure 3-15.** Yammer app's custom Open Graph object types and action types*

Chapter 5 covers the Open Graph protocol, which focuses on using the Open Graph protocol to write data into Yammer. You will learn how to create and use custom Open Graph objects in Chapter 5 as well.

Summary

In this chapter you learned about Yammer apps and the configuration of a Yammer app for the app directory. Yammer app registration is a simple process completed on the home network, whereby you can register, build, and test your apps. You also learned that from the Yammer app configuration page, you can submit your Yammer app to the Global App Directory for wider audiences.

In the next chapter, you learn how to implement Yammer authentication using the Yammer app called `SPDSUniversity` that you registered in this chapter.

CHAPTER 4

Authenticating Yammer Users

Pathik Rawal

In the previous chapter, you learned Yammer App basics, including the registration and configuration processes of Yammer apps. In this chapter, we outline the Yammer authentication process. You will become familiar with the OAuth protocol and its server-side and client-side flows. You'll also learn to tackle Yammer authentication in the exercise section of this chapter using both client-side OAuth flow and server-side OAuth flow.

In this chapter, we will cover following points

- Understand Yammer authentication
- Understand OAuth 2.0
- Understand OAuth flows
- Learn and implement server-side flow
- Learn and implement client-side flow

Understanding Yammer Authentication

The last chapter explained how to register your Yammer apps. Once your Yammer app is registered, you can implement Yammer authentication to connect your line-of-business applications with Yammer using user's Yammer credential. Yammer uses OAuth 2.0 protocol to authorize business applications in order to access its REST APIs on behalf of a user.

Yammer app authentication using OAuth 2.0 is a three-legged OAuth authorization process, as shown in Figure 4-1. In the first step, user authentication happens to ensure that the user who is accessing your application is valid. In the second step, the app authorization happens, which ensures that users allow your app to access their data. In the final step, the app authentication happens, which ensures that users are sharing their data with an authentic app and not a dubious one.

P. Rawal and P. Rohilla, *Developing on Yammer*, DOI 10.1007/978-1-4842-0943-1_4

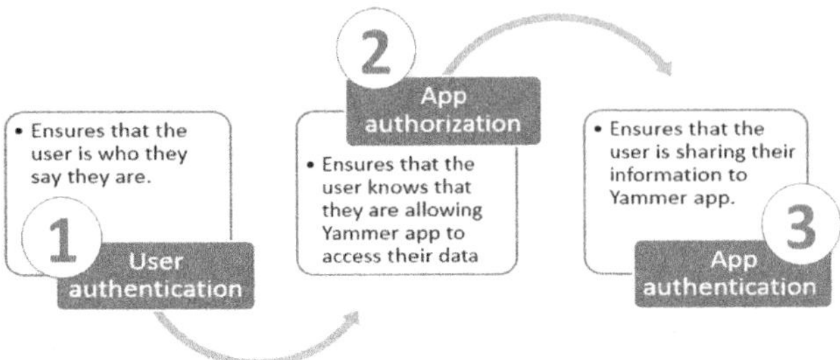

Figure 4-1. *The Yammer app authentication flow*

Once the Yammer app authentication flow is complete, your application will have all the required permissions (in the form of an access token) to update or retrieve data to Yammer on behalf of the user. If the user has admin privileges, your application can also perform administrative functionalities, such as delete a user, and so on.

What Is OAuth 2.0?

The OAuth web site defines OAuth as "An open protocol that allows secure API authorization in a simple and standard method from desktop and web applications." OAuth (Open Authorization) 2.0 is the next evolution of the open authorization protocol, which was originally created in late 2006.

OAuth 2.0 enables an external application to gain access to another application/service on behalf of a user by organizing an approval flow between users and host application/services or by allowing the external application to retrieve access on its own.

■ **Note** OAuth 2.0 requires HTTPS.

OAuth Roles

From a developer perspective, it is important to understand the different OAuth roles that are part of the Yammer's OAuth authentication process and understand how every role acts in the overall process of authentication. The four important roles are listed and described in Table 4-1.

Table 4-1. *OAuth Role Names and Descriptions*

Role	Description
Resource Owner	The Yammer user who is granting access to their Yammer profile.
Client Application	An external business application, such as the SPDSUniversity web application or a Windows mobile app.
Resource Server	A server that hosts the resources and responds to the requests of the client applications. The client application will need to present an access token to the resource server to access the resources on Yammer.
Authorization Server	A server that issues the access tokens to the client application. The access token is generated by the authorization server after successfully authenticating the resource owner.

As illustrated in Figure 4-2, multiple parties act during the Yammer OAuth authentication process. The first main role is the resource owner, which, in the Yammer world, represents a user named "Alex Darrow". Alex Darrow has a valid Yammer account. The second role is the Client Application role, which is the SPDSUniversity web application hosted on SPDS's web server. To allow users to log in to the SPDSUniversity web application using their Yammer account, the client application needs to implement Yammer's OAuth flow by implementing the "Sign In with Yammer" button on the web application login page. The third role is the Resource Server which hosts the user's data and enables REST APIs to access user's data. In our case, it is the Yammer server. The last role (but not the least) is the Authorization Server which issues access tokens to the client for accessing Alex's Yammer profile and the data hosted on the resource server.

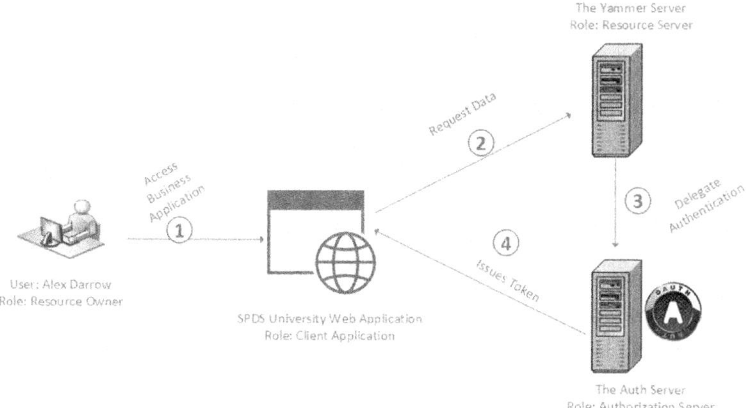

Figure 4-2. *OAuth roles*

In the next section, you will explore the benefits of OAuth 2.0. Later in this chapter, you will learn about the role of the OAuth 2.0 protocol in Yammer with different authentication flows.

Authentication on Yammer Using OAuth 2.0

The OAuth allows the developer to implement the authentication mechanism within their application in order to authenticate Yammer users. The best thing about OAuth is that it does not require users of the Yammer app to share their passwords with the Yammer app's developer. Instead using OAuth, users allow/provide external application permission to access their Yammer accounts. Yammer then provides an access token to the business application, which is used to interact with Yammer on behalf of the user(s). The access token never expires and can only be revoked by the users. You can store the access token and use it to make subsequent calls to Yammer until the user revokes the access token. Once the user revokes the access token, you need to use the OAuth flow again to obtain a new one.

OAuth is designed to use two sets of credentials, as listed in Table 4-2.

Table 4-2. *OAuth's Credential Types*

Credential Type	Description
A "client" token and secret	Authenticates an application to the provider
An "access" token and secret	Authorizes the application to access a particular set of data

When the user clicks on the "Sign In with Yammer" button in your line-of-business application page, the OAuth 2.0 authentication flow is initiated. As illustrated in Figure 4-3, an ASP.NET web application uses the "Sign In with Yammer" button. By implementing the "Sign In with Yammer" OAuth authentication in your business application, your application allows users of your application to sign in using user's Yammer credentials rather than creating/managing a new set of credential separately. In the exercise sections of this chapter, you will learn to implement the "Sign In with Yammer" button on an Microsoft ASP.NET and Microsoft SharePoint-hosted app.

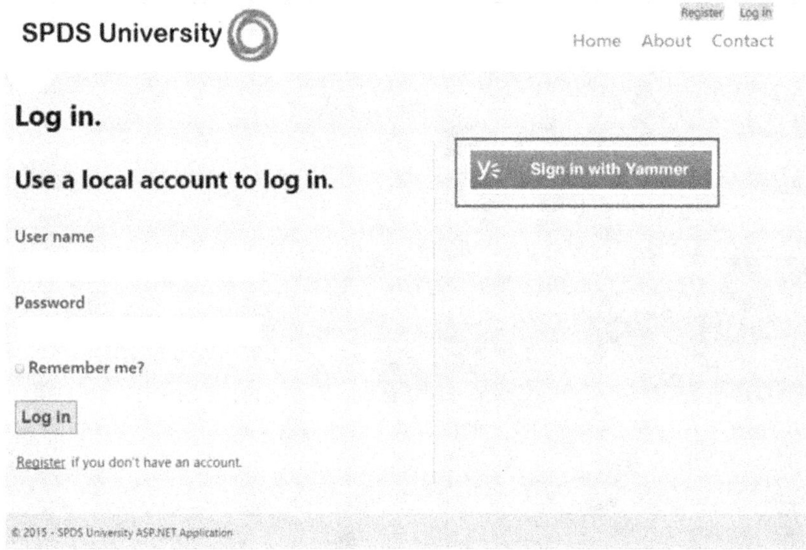

Figure 4-3. *The "Sign In with Yammer" button initiates the OAuth flow*

In the next section, you'll learn the different OAuth flows provided by OAuth authentication. Yammer supports two main OAuth flows—server-side flow and client-side flow.

PROTECTING ACCESS TOKENS

The access tokens are generated for individual users in Yammer and given to client applications when requested. The client token is generated for an indefinite time and never expires. It is recommended that the client application store the access token for each user. It is recommended that developers strongly protect the access token like any other security key or password. Developers should implement encryption in the client application to protect the access token.

Yammer Authentication Flows

The Yammer authentication that uses OAuth 2.0 involves a series of automated steps and mainly provides two different types of OAuth authentication flows, as listed in Table 4-3. In this section, we outline both flows in detail with an exercise of each flow so that you can learn to implement both OAuth flows in your line-of-business applications.

Table 4-3. *The OAuth Flows Supported by the OAuth 2.0 Protocol*

Flow	Description
Server-side	Developers can leverage the server-side flow, which is also referred to as an "authorization code grant," from line-of-business applications developed using server technologies like ASP.NET web applications.
Client-side	Developers can leverage the client-side flow, which is also referred to as an "implicit grant," from line-of-business applications developed using client-side technologies like JavaScript and HTML.

Both flows require user authentication, app authorization, and app authentication, as described in Figure 4-1. Let's explore both authentication flows and review the steps involved in both flows.

Server-Side Flow

The Yammer OAuth 2.0 endpoint supports web server applications that use programming languages and frameworks such as PHP, Java, Python, Ruby, and C#. The server-side flow requires the client application to secure the "client secret" value.

The "Sign In with Yammer" button is the simplest way to integrate an application with a Yammer app using OAuth 2.0. If your application is a web application like an ASP.NET custom web application or Microsoft SharePoint site, you can add the "Sign In with Yammer" button in HTML/ASPX code and implement redirection to the Yammer OAuth URL for authentication by using the HTML hyperlink tag or handling the Login button event in the code-behind. Later in this chapter, you'll read a step-by-step guide for implementing OAuth authentication in a SPDSUniversity training application.

The server-side flow, also known as "authorization code grant type," is the most commonly used because it is optimized for server-side applications, where source code is compiled and assemblies are deployed to the web server, and client secret confidentiality can be maintained. In the entire OAuth 2.0 flow, multiple redirection happens between the client application, the resource server, and the authorization server. So it is essential that the client application handle the redirection and communicate with the user-agent (i.e. the user's web browser).

Each step involved in the authorization code grant or server-side flow is explained in Table 4-4.

Table 4-4. Steps Invloved in Server-Side Flow

Step	Name	Description
#1	Application Request Authentication	The OAuth 2.0 authentication is initiated as soon as the user (resource owner) clicks on the "Sign In with Yammer" button. Here, the user is redirected to the OAuth 2.0 authorization endpoint.
#2	Yammer Request Credentials	Yammer then prompts the user with a login page.
#3	Yammer Request App Authorization	The OAuth process prompts the user to authorize the Yammer app.
#4	Application Receives Authorization Code	Yammer redirects the user to the app's Redirect URI with an authorization code.
#5	Application Request Access Token	The client requests a token by using `client_id`, `Client_Secretkey`, and the code.
#6	Application Receives Access Token	Based on the client app received by Yammer, Yammer sends the access token to the client application.
#7	Application makes further calls to Yammer	Using the access token, the client application can make additional calls to Yammer on behalf of the user who authorized it.

Let's explore these steps in Figure 4-4. We have three entities here and those are the end users, the external application, and Yammer. The end user is resource owner who first accesses the external application and clicks on the "Sign In with Yammer" button. Yammer then prompts the user with a login page.

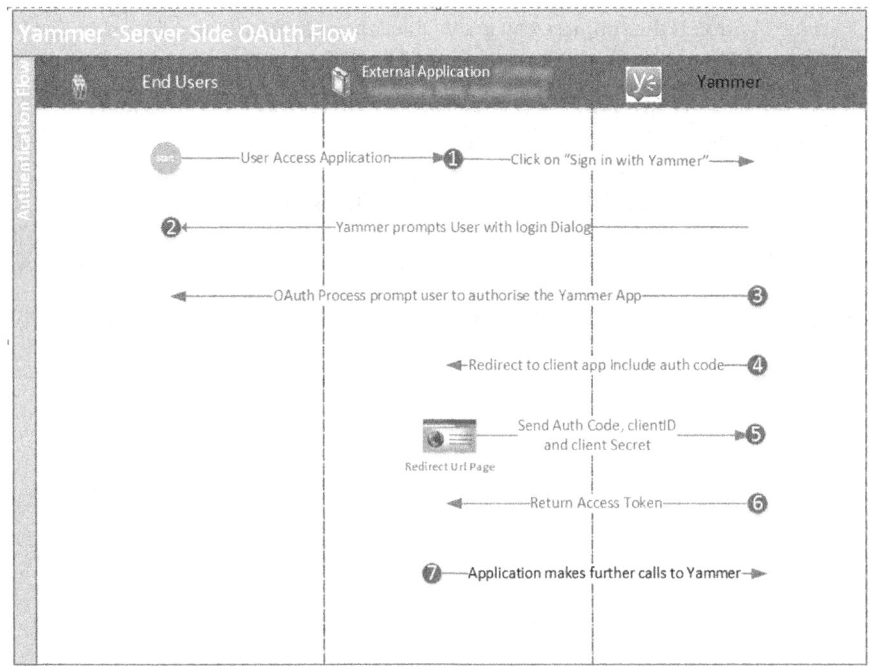

Figure 4-4. Steps invloved in server-side OAuth flow

Let's look at each of these steps in detail and explore how those parameters are passed between the client applications and Yammer's OAuth provider.

Step #1: Application Request Authentication

The authorization sequence begins when your application redirects the browser to the Yammer OAuth URL; the URL includes query parameters that indicate the type of access being requested. First, you must form the Yammer OAuth URL to initiate the flow.

Your application should redirect the user to the Yammer OAuth URL along with the Yammer app's `ClientID` and `redirect_uri` as per configuration. The OAuth URL is

```
https://www.yammer.com/dialog/oauth?client_id=[:client_id]&redirect_uri=[:redirect_uri]
```

Table 4-5 lists the query string parameters used in the Yammer OAuth URL.

Table 4-5. *Yammer OAuth URL's Query String Parameters*

Parameter	Description
`client_id`	Obtain the `Client_Id` for your Yammer app using the Yammer UI. Use the `Https://Www.Yammer.Com/Client_Applications` link for a list of registered client IDs.
`redirect_uri`	The `redirect_uri` should match the `redirect_uri` configured for your app in the Yammer platform.

For example, the OAuth URL for the SPDSUniversity web application is:

```
https://www.yammer.com/dialog/oauth?client_id=9aax1mFox7yMVBS2LpIJQ&redirect_uri=
http://localhost:54173/Default.aspx
```

To obtain the `client_id` and `redirect_uri`, navigate to your SPDSUniversity registered app in Yammer, as illustrated in Figure 4-5.

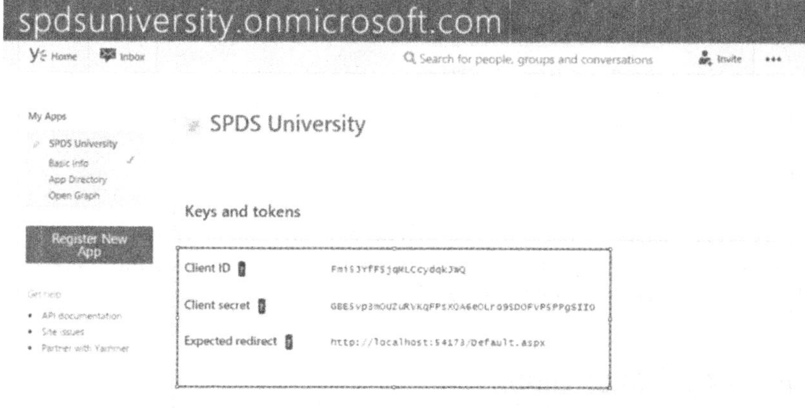

Figure 4-5. *SPDSUniversity app*

■ **Note** If your `redirect_uri` does not match the configuration of your application, then Yammer will throw an error with the description "Invalid URI".

Step #2: Server Request Credentials

The OAuth process will prompt the user with the Yammer login page, as illustrated in Figure 4-6.

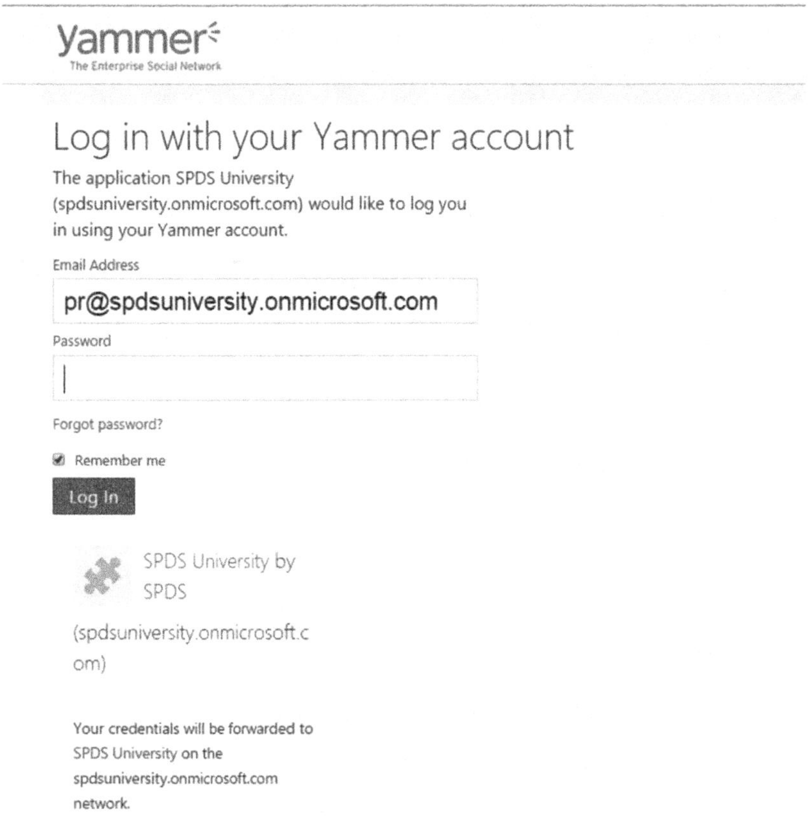

yammer
The Enterprise Social Network

Log in with your Yammer account

The application SPDS University (spdsuniversity.onmicrosoft.com) would like to log you in using your Yammer account.

Email Address

pr@spdsuniversity.onmicrosoft.com

Password

Forgot password?

Remember me

Log In

SPDS University by SPDS

(spdsuniversity.onmicrosoft.com)

Your credentials will be forwarded to SPDS University on the spdsuniversity.onmicrosoft.com network.

Figure 4-6. *Yammer login page*

This is the standard Yammer's login page. The user enters the credentials and submits the request. As you notice in Figure 4-6, the Yammer's login page displays the Yammer app name as "SPDSUniversity" and the network name on which the Yammer is registered as "SPDS".

Step #3: Server Request App Authorization

In this step, the OAuth 2.0 authentication process shows an App Authorization screen. If the user allows your Yammer app, the app will be authorized and an authorization code will be generated for the user, as shown in Figure 4-7.

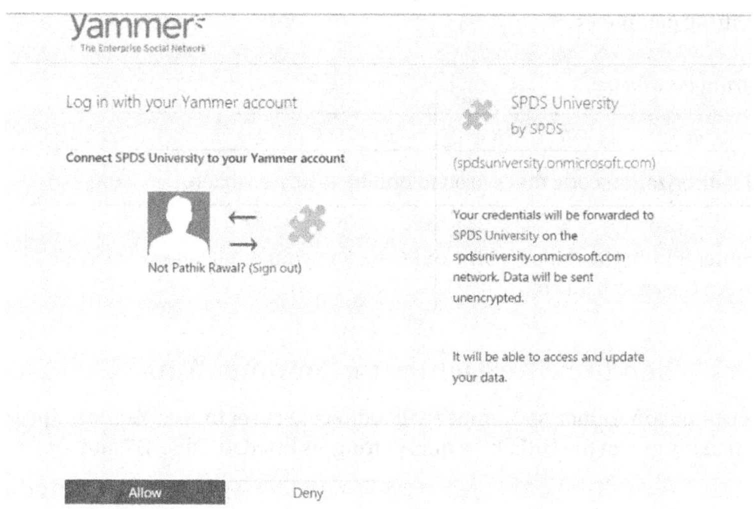

***Figure 4-7.** App authorization*

Step #4: Application Receives Authorization Code

The response will be sent to `redirect_uri`, as specified in the request URL. If the user approves the access request, the response contains an authorization code. If the user does not approve the request, the response contains an error message. The redirect URL's parameters will be different when the user allows the Yammer app than when they deny it access. Let's look at the redirect URL's parameters in each case.

Redirect URL's Parameters When the User Allows the Yammer App

In this case, the user allows the Yammer custom app to get authorization to Yammer on behalf of the user, so Yammer will redirect the user to your Yammer app's redirect URL. The code appears at the end of URL as a query string, as shown in Figure 4-8. The following is the complete URL format:

http://[:redirect_uri]?code=[:code]

***Figure 4-8.** Redirect URL when user "allows" the Yammer app*

Table 4-6 describes the query string parameter.

Table 4-6. Redirect URL's Query String Parameter

Parameter	Description
Code	Yammer-generated authorization code that's used to obtain an access token.

You can retrieve the code parameter from the redirect URL and store it in your application. The code will be used in further steps to retrieve the access token.

Redirect URL's Parameters When the User Denies the Yammer App

In this case, the user denies authorization to Yammer, so Yammer will redirect the user to your Yammer app's redirect URL with error information at the end of the URL. It's a query string, as listed in Table 4-7 and shown in Figure 4-9.

```
http://localhost:54173/Default.aspx?error=access_denied&error_description=the%20user
%20denied%20your%20request
```

Table 4-7. Redirect URL's Query String Parameters When the User Denies Access

Parameter	Description
Error	This contains an actual error, for example "Access Denied".
error_description	The description of the error, for example "The user denied your request".
invalid redirect_uri	If redirect_uri does not match your Yammer app configuration, you get the "Invalid Redirect_uri" error.

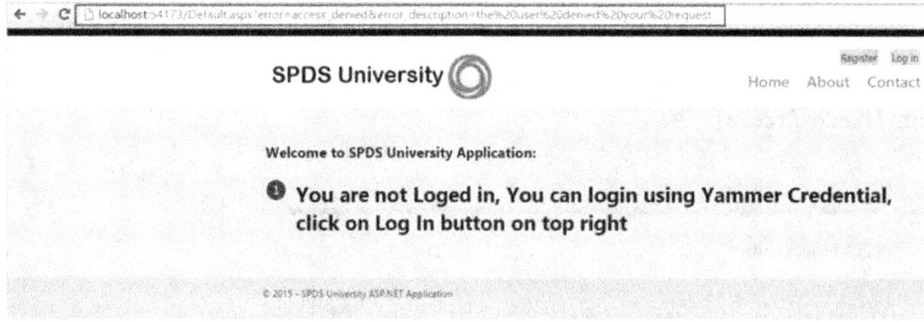
SPDS University
Register Log in
Home About Contact
Welcome to SPDS University Application:
You are not Loged in, You can login using Yammer Credential, click on Log In button on top right

Figure 4-9. Redirect URL when the user denies the Yammer app

So it's easy for your application to understand the action taken by the users. Based on the parameters, you can implement the logic to make further calls to Yammer APIs. The best way to do this is to implement the response handler code based on the user's action and then make further calls. You'll learn more about this in the exercise section of this chapter.

Step #5: Application Request Access Token

Once the application receives the authorization code from Yammer, it may exchange the authorization code for an access token and a refresh token. This request is an HTTPS POST. Table 4-8 provides the endpoint details, and the endpoint includes the parameters listed in Table 4-9.

Table 4-8. *Endpoint to Retrieve the Access Token*

Endpoint	Description
https://www.yammer.com/oauth2/access_token.json?client_id=[:client_id]&client_secret=[:client_secret]&code=[:code]	The endpoint to obtain the access token from Yammer.

Table 4-9. *The Parameters Used with the Access Token Endpoint*

Parameter	Description
Client_id	An unique ID generated by Yammer for your app.
Client_secret	An unique ID generated by Yammer for your app.
Code	The authorization code you receive after the Yammer app is authorized.

The code parameter was obtained in a previous step and the client_id and client_secret code can be configured in your application. You'll learn in the exercise of this chapter that if your line-of-business application is an ASP.NET web application, you can use Web.Config to store these IDs.

Step #6: Application Receives Access Token

Yammer's response contains an access token. The access token includes the user profile information, which can be parsed out. Developers can also store the "token," which can be used to make further calls to Yammer on behalf of the user.

The following code snippet shows the JSON response string, which contains three objects—user, access_token, and network.

```
{
  "user":
  {
    "timezone": "Hawaii",
    "interests": null,
    "type": "user",
    "mugshot_url": "https://www.yammer.com/yamage-backstage/photos/...",
    "kids_names": null,
    "settings": {
      "xdr_proxy": "https://stagexdrproxy.yammer.com"
    },
    "schools": [],
    "verified_admin": "false",
    "birth_date": "",
    "expertise": null,
    "job_title": "",
```

```
    "state": "active",
    "contact": {
      "phone_numbers": [],
      "im": {
        "provider": "",
        "username": ""
      },
      "email_addresses": [
        {
          "type": "primary",
          "address": "test@yammer-inc.com"
        }
      ]
    },
    "location": null,
    "previous_companies": [],
    "hire_date": null,
    "admin": "false",
    "full_name": "TestAccount",
    "network_id": 155465488,
    "stats": {
      "updates": 2,
      "followers": 0,
      "following": 0
    },
    "can_broadcast": "false",
    "summary": null,
    "external_urls": [],
    "name": "clientappstest",
    "network_domains": [
      "yammer-inc.com"
    ],
    "network_name": "Yammer",
    "significant_other": null,
    "id": 1014216,
    "web_url": "https://www.yammer.com/yammer-inc.com/users/...",
    "url": "https://www.yammer.com/api/v1/users/101416",
    "guid": null
  },
  "access_token": {
    "view_subscriptions": true,
    "expires_at": null,
    "authorized_at": "2011/04/06 16:25:46 +0000",
    "modify_subscriptions": true,
    "modify_messages": true,
    "network_permalink": "yammer-inc.com",
    "view_members": true,
    "view_tags": true,
    "network_id": 155465488,
    "user_id": 1014216,
    "view_groups": true,
    "token": "ajsdfiasd7f6asdf8o",
```

```
        "network_name": "Yammer",
        "view_messages": true,
        "created_at": "2011/04/06 16:25:46 +0000"
    },
    "network": {
        "type": "network",
        "header_background_color": "#0092bc",
        "community": false,
        "navigation_background_color": "#3f5f9e",
        "navigation_text_color": "#ffffff",
        "permalink": "yammer-inc.com",
        "paid": true,
        "show_upgrade_banner": false,
        "name": "Yammer",
        "is_org_chart_enabled": true,
        "id": 155465488,
        "header_text_color": "#000000",
        "web_url": "https://www.yammer.com/yammer-inc.com"
    }
}
```


The access token received from Yammer contains three main objects as listed in Table 4-10. These objects are `user`, `network`, and `access token`.

Table 4-10. *The Response Object Contains Three Main Objects*

Object	Description
`User`	Contains the user profile information like time zone, interest, job title, birth date, and so on.
`Network`	Information about the network on which your Yammer app is deployed.
`Access Token`	Contains the token with the network ID and user ID to which the token belongs.

Logically, step #6 is the end of the server-side authentication flow. You'll need to store the OAuth's access token for each user of your application and use that access token to make further calls on behalf of users to Yammer using REST APIs.

Step #7: Application Makes Further Calls to Yammer

In step #1, you learned how to obtain the access token. Once you obtain the access token, you can store it in secure manner and use it to make further calls. In Chapter 5, you'll learn how to use Open Graph to read and write data to Yammer using the access token. In Chapter 6, you'll learn to read and write data into Yammer using the Yammer REST APIs. In Chapter 7, you'll learn to read and write data into Yammer using Yammer SDKs. Given that you need an access token to make further calls to Yammer, it's very important to do Exercises 4-1 and 4-2 to obtain the access token. Exercises 4-1 and 4-2 will be used as a base for exercises you see in Chapters 5, 6, and 7.

Implementing Server-Side Flow in an ASP.NET Web Application

In the following exercise, we will implement Yammer authentication using server-side flow in an ASP.NET web application. You need to have Microsoft Visual Studio 2012 Professional, Premium, or Ultimate installed on your local computer.

EXERCISE 4-1: IMPLEMENTING SERVER-SIDE OAUTH FLOW IN AN ASP.NET WEB APPLICATION

In this exercise, we will demonstrate how to implement server-side OAuth flow in an ASP.NET web application called SPDSUniversity Training Application. We will create an ASP.NET web application and implement OAuth authentication using the Yammer app called "SPDSUniversity" that you created in Chapter 3.

Create New Project

1. Launch Microsoft Visual Studio.
2. The first screen presented to you is the Visual Studio Start page, as illustrated in Figure 4-10.

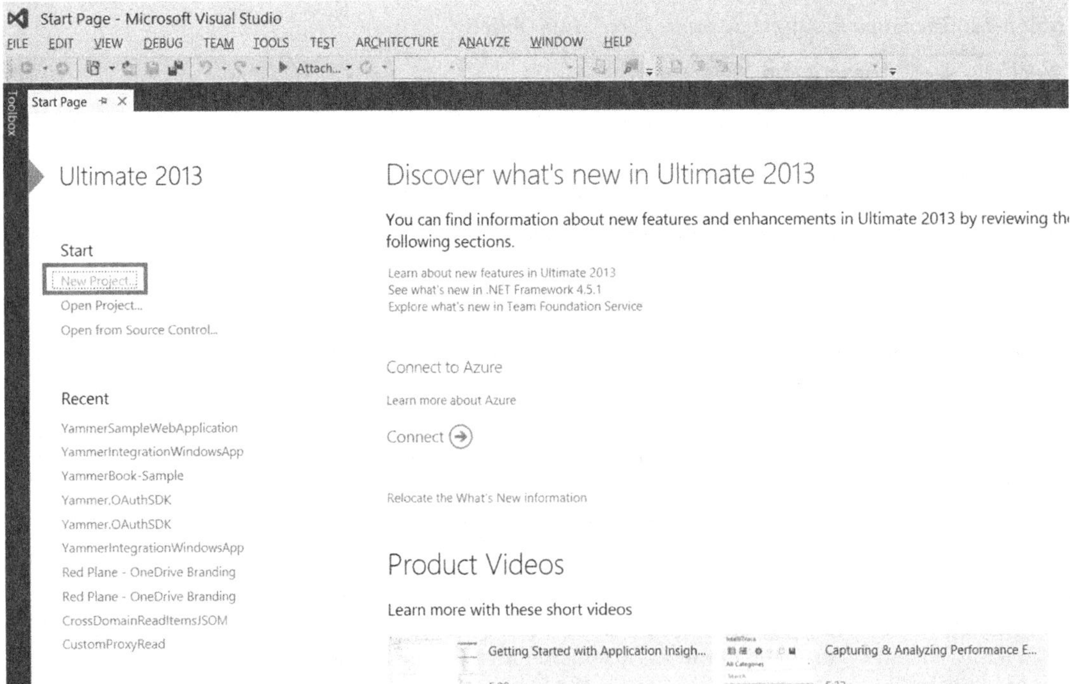

***Figure 4-10.** The Visual Studio Start page offers a quick way to get started*

3. On the left side of the start page, on the navigation pane, choose new project. Alternatively, you can use the File ➤ New Project command.

4. This brings up the New Project window. Select ASP.NET Web Forms Application. Then select Web ➤ Visual Studio 2012 ➤ ASP.NET Web Forms Application, as shown in Figure 4-11.

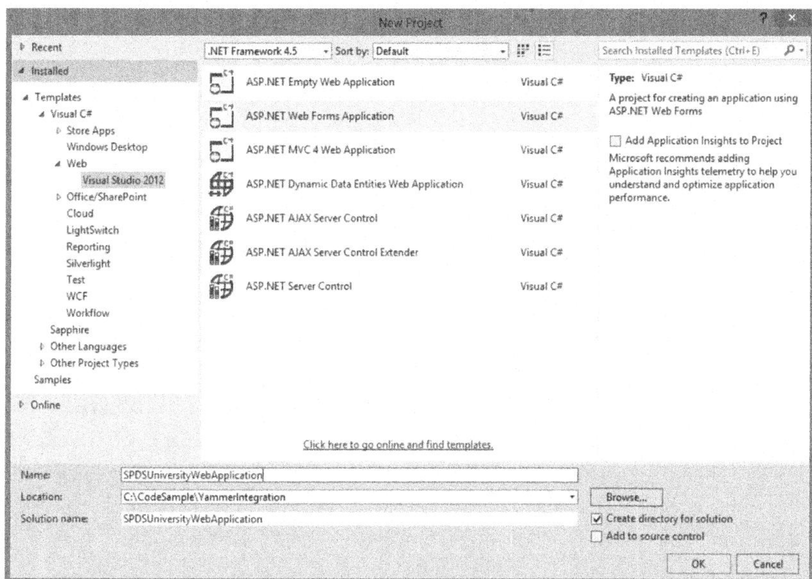

Figure 4-11. *Select the ASP.NET web application template for the new project*

5. Enter the name as "SPDSUniversityWebApplication".

6. Click OK.

7. Visual studio will create a new ASP.NET project with the `Web.config` file as part of the project, as illustrated in Figure 4-12.

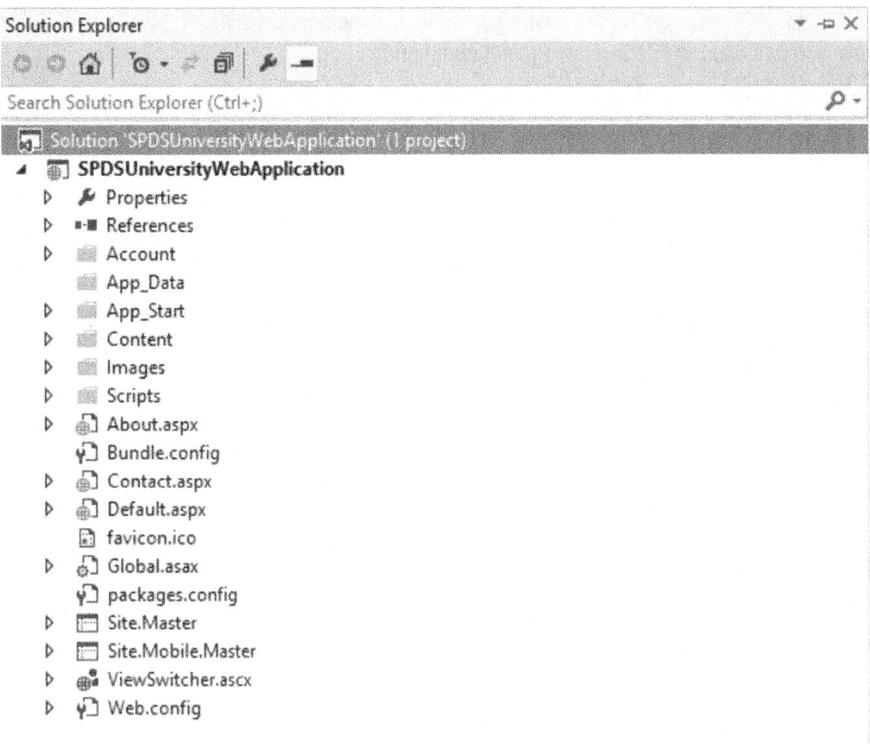

Figure 4-12. *The ASP.NET web site structure*

Add the `yammer_signin.png` and `SPDS-Uni.png` files to the `Images` folder (the `yammer_signin.png` file can be downloaded from Yammer's site and `SPDS-Uni.png` is available from the Source Code/Download area of the Apress web site at `http://www.apress.com/9781484209448`).

8. Right-click on the `Images` folder and then choose Add ➤ Existing Items. Find both images and click OK.

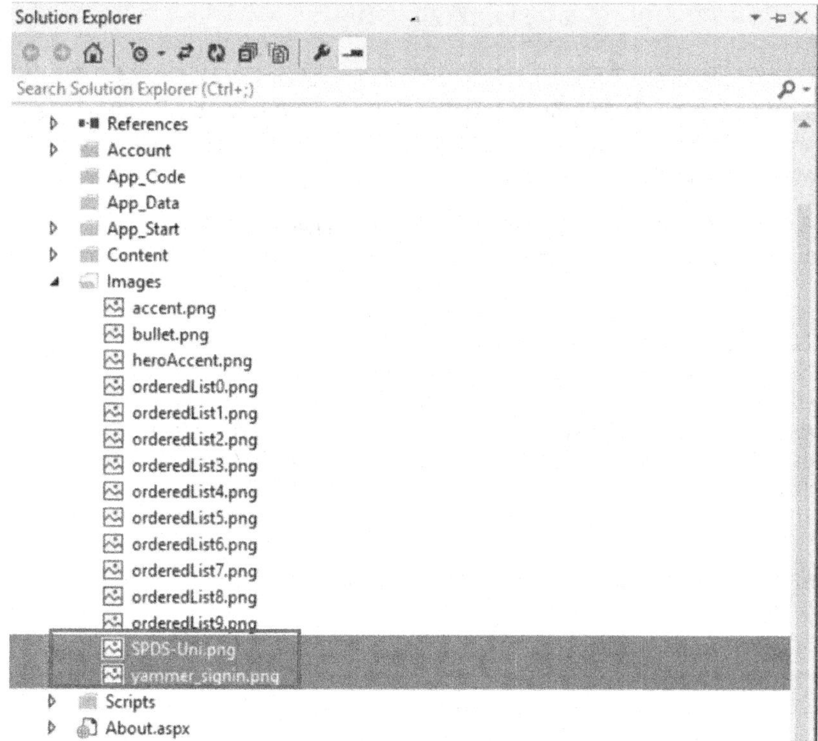

Figure 4-13. *The Yammer_signin.png and SPDS-Uni.Png files added to the Images folder*

9. Open the `Site.Master` file.
10. Replace this text in line 7:

```
<title><%: Page.Title %> - My ASP.NET Application</title>
```

with:

```
<title><%: Page.Title %> - SPDS University</title>
```

11. Replace the text in line #43:

```
<a runat="server" href="~/">your logo here</a>
```

with

```
<a runat="server" href="~/"><img src="Images/SPDS-Uni.png" /></a>
```

Configuration Values in Web.config

We will use the Web.config file to configure the Yammer App configuration values like client_id, client_secret key, and redirect_uri. These parameters are required in order to call the OAuth URLs from your ASP.NET web application. The best place to configure those parameters is in the <AppSettings> section within Web.Config.

12. Add the following code to your Web.Config file (add the code at end of the file just above </Configuration>):

```
<appSettings>
  <add key="client_id" value="Fmi5JYfF5jqMLCcydqkJWQ" />
  <add key="client_secret" value="GBE5vp3mOUZuRVKqFPsXOA6eOLro95DOFVP5PPgSIIO" />
  <add key="redirect_uri" value="http://localhost:54173/Default.aspx" />
  <add key="OAuthURL" value="https://www.yammer.com/dialog/oauth?client_id=" />
<add key="AccessTokenURL" value="https://www.yammer.com/oauth2/
access_token.json?" />
</appSettings>
```

Table 4-11 provides details about each key-value pair used in the previous code.

Table 4-11. *Key-Value Pairs Configured in Web.config*

Key	Value
client_id	Replace value with "SPDSUniversity" Yammer app's client_id.
client_secret	Replace value with "SPDSUniversity" Yammer app's client_secret.
redirect_uri	Replace value with "SPDSUniversity" Yammer app's redirect_uri.
OAuthURL	https://www.yammer.com/dialog/oauth?client_id=, we will form the complete URL in the code
AccessTokenURL	https://www.yammer.com/oauth2/access_token.json?, the OAuth's access token URL

■ **Note** When you use the Microsoft Visual Studio Development Server to run a file system web application project, by default, the development server is invoked on a randomly selected port for the localhost. You can change the port number using the project property windows in Visual Studio.

13. Navigate to https://www.yammer.com/client_applications, click on your Yammer app, and then click on the Basic Info section. You will see a screen as shown in Figure 4-14. Ensure that the redirect URI has the same value as configured in the previous Web.config file.

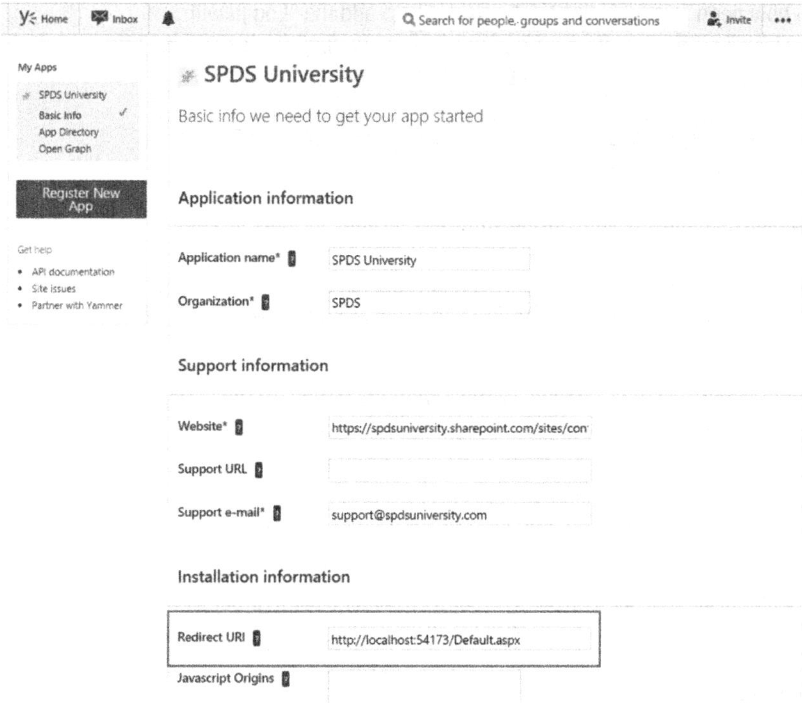

Figure 4-14. *Ensure that redirect URI is the same as the value in web.config*

Application's Home Page

14. To start designing the `default.aspx` file as the home page of your application, add the following code to `default.aspx` by opening it in the source view of Visual Studio. You need to replace the following markup in `default.aspx` with the content within `<asp:Content runat="server" ID="BodyContent" ContentPlaceHolder ID="MainContent">`:

```
<h3>Welcome to SPDS University Application:</h3>
 <ol class="round">
   <li class="one">
     <h2><asp:Label ID="lbllogin" runat="server" Text="You are not Loged in,
     You can login using Yammer Credential, click on Log In button on top
     right"></asp:Label>   </h2>
   </li>
 </ol>
 <asp:TextBox ID="txtCode" runat="server" Visible="False"></asp:TextBox>
 <asp:TextBox ID="txtaccesstoken" runat="server" Visible="false"></asp:TextBox>
```

15. Remove the following content placeholder from `Default.aspx`:

```
<asp:Content runat="server" ID="FeaturedContent" ContentPlaceHolderID=
"FeaturedContent">
```

16. Login.aspx: You now need to modify the login.aspx file to add the "Log In with Yammer" button. Open login.aspx from account/login.aspx, find <section id="socialLoginForm">, and replace it with the following code:

```
<asp:ImageButton ID="imgbtnLogin" runat="server" ImageUrl="~/Images/
yammer_signin.png" OnClick="imgbtnLogin_Click" />
```

17. Login.aspx: Remove all the validation controls from login.aspx:

```
<asp:RequiredFieldValidator runat="server" ControlToValidate="UserName"
CssClass="field-validation-error" ErrorMessage="The user name field is
required." />

<asp:RequiredFieldValidator runat="server" ControlToValidate="Password"
CssClass="field-validation-error" ErrorMessage="The password field is
required." />
```

18. Login.aspx.cs: Remove the code from Page_Load() event.

19. Login.aspx.cs: Open the code-behind file Login.aspx.cs and add the following code in the using directive. This namespace is required to write code in order to read the app settings value from the Web.config file.

```
using System.Web.Configuration;
```

20. Login.aspx.cs: Add the following code to handle the "Login In with Yammer" button event. Open the Login.aspx file in Design view and double-click on the Login button. This will open the code-behind file Login.aspx.cs.

```
/// <summary>
///
/// </summary>
/// <param name="sender"></param>
/// <param name="e"></param>
    protected void imgbtnLogin_Click(object sender, ImageClickEventArgs e)
     {
            string YammerURL = WebConfigurationManager.AppSettings["OAuthURL"]
            + WebConfigurationManager.AppSettings["client_id"] + "&redirect_
            uri=" + WebConfigurationManager.AppSettings["redirect_uri"];
             Response.Redirect(YammerURL);
      }
```

The button click event forms the OAuth URL. The final OAuth URL should be:

```
https://www.yammer.com/dialog/oauth?client_id= 9aax1mFox7yMVBS2LpIJQ&redirect_
uri=http://localhost:54173/Default.aspx"
```

Table 4-12 describes the query string parameters.

Table 4-12. *OAuth URL's Query String Parameters*

Parameter	Description
client_id	Obtain the Client_ID for the SPDSUniversity Yammer app using the Yammer UI. Use the https://www.yammer.com/client_applications link for a list of registered client IDs.
redirect_uri	The redirect_uri should match the redirect_uri configured for the SPDSUniversity app.

After forming the OAuth URL by reading values from the Web.Config file, the code calls Response.Redirect(YammerURL).

If the redirect_URI does not match the configuration of the SPDSUniversity Yammer app, Yammer will throws an error entitled "Invalid Redirect URI". So be sure that the redirect_uri matches.

Handle the Yammer's Response

Once the OAuth flow is complete, Yammer will redirect to the Redirect URI with the query string parameter, as illustrated in the following URL:

```
http://localhost:54173/Default.aspx?code=4G5y1ipTNt5nCtCw8DS1sw
```

21. Default.aspx.cs: Open the code-behind file called Default.aspx.cs and add the following code to the using directive. This namespace is required to write code in order to read app settings value from the Web.config file:

```
using System.Web.Configuration;
```

22. Default.aspx.cs: Add the following code to the Page_Load event to read the query string passed by Yammer in order to find the key "Code" and retrieve the value of the key. Once the code is retrieved, we will store it in a textbox and invoke the call to Yammer using the given code to get the access token.

```
/// <summary>
/// Page load event to check if query string contains a key called "Code"
/// </summary>
/// <param name="sender"></param>
/// <param name="e"></param>
        protected void Page_Load(object sender, EventArgs e)
        {

            string qsCode = Request.QueryString["Code"];
            if (qsCode != null)
            {
                txtCode.Text = qsCode;
                Obtain_Access_Token();
            }
            else
            {
            }
        }
```

The previous code reads the query string key "Code", if it is present, and then stores the code in a textbox and hides the Login button. Finally, we call the Obtain_Access_Token() method to obtain the access token.

Obtain the Access Token

To obtain the access token, we need to submit a GET request using an OAuth 2.0 endpoint, with these three parameters—client_id, client_secret, and code.

The complete endpoint is:

```
https://www.yammer.com/oauth2/access_token.json?client_id=[:client_id]&
client_secret=[:client_secret]&code=[:code]
```

So let's implement the code to obtain the access token.

The response you'll receive from Yammer will be in JSON or XML format based on the API endpoint you invoke. The JSON endpoint is https://www.yammer.com/oauth2/access_token.json and the XML endpoint is https://www.yammer.com/oauth2/access_token.xml. Your application should convert the given JSON string into an object. In this particular case, the response needs to be deserialized first. Then you retrieve the access token from the instance using DataContractJsonSerializer. So we will start adding few classes to help with serialize and deserialize, back and forth.

23. In Solution Explorer, right-click on References and select Add Reference. In the assemblies group of references, select the assembly called System.Runtime.Serialization.
24. In Solution Explorer, right-click on the project and select Add ➤ ASP.NET Folder ➤ App_Code. The App_Code folder is a special folder that stores classes, typed data sets, and other supporting classes for the project. The classes that are stored in App_Code are accessible throughout the application.
25. In Solution Explorer, right-click on the App_Code folder and then choose Add ➤ Class, as illustrated in Figure 4-15.

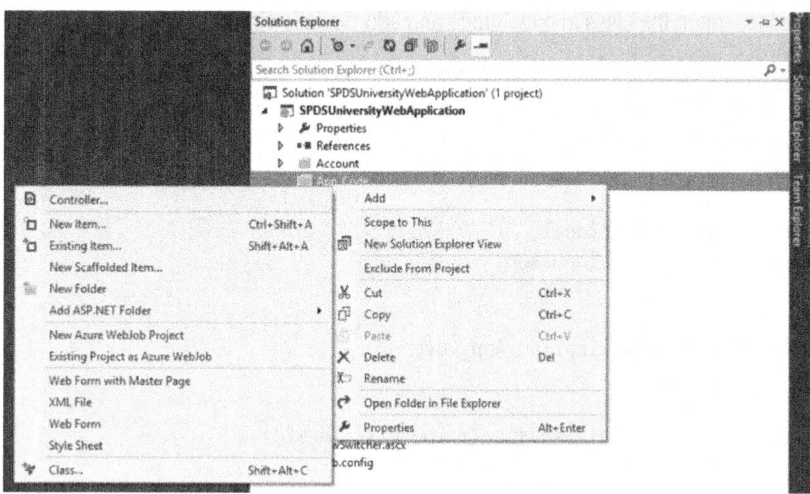

Figure 4-15. Add a new class to your web site project

26. You will be presented with a window, as illustrated in Figure 4-16, where you need to select the class template.

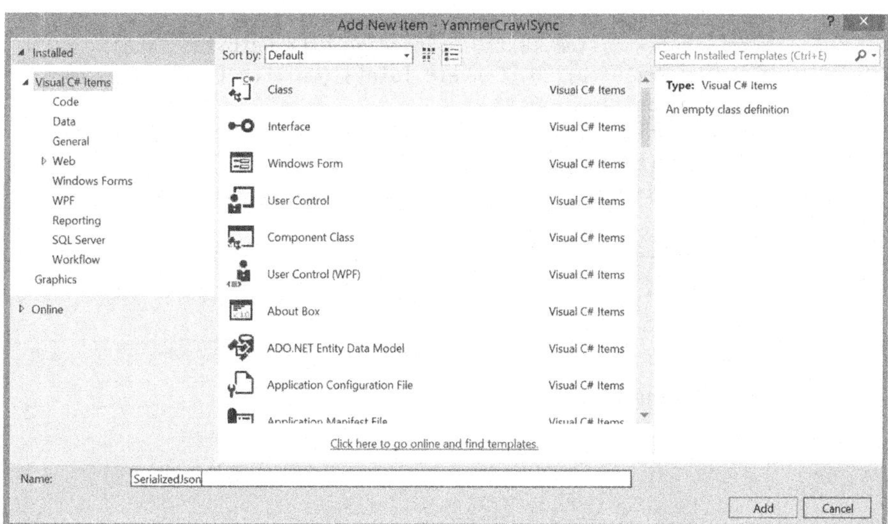

Figure 4-16. Select the class template from the available list and then enter the class name

27. Enter the name of the class as `SerializedJson`.

28. Click Add.

29. Once the class is added, open the class in code mode and add the following code snippet to the class:

```
using System;
using System.Collections.Generic;
using System.Linq;
using System.Web;
using System.Runtime.Serialization;
using System.Runtime.Serialization.Json;
using System.IO;

namespace SPDSUniversityWebApplication.App_Code
{
    [Serializable]
    public abstract class SerializedJson<T> where T : new()
    {

        public static T GetObjectInstanceFromJson(string data)
        {
            T returnInstance = default(T);

            try
            {
                MemoryStream m_stream = new MemoryStream();
                byte[] buf = System.Text.UTF8Encoding.UTF8.GetBytes(data);
                m_stream.Write(buf, 0, Convert.ToInt32(buf.Length));
                m_stream.Position = 0;
                DataContractJsonSerializer sdc_JSON_Ser = new DataContractJson
                Serializer(typeof(T));
                returnInstance = (T)sdc_JSON_Ser.ReadObject(m_stream);
            }
            catch (Exception ex)
            {

            }

            return returnInstance;
        }

    }

}
```

The `SerializedJson` class implements an abstract method called `GetObjectInstanceFromJson`, which accepts a JSON string. The method will then convert JSON to stream by using the `MemoryStream` class and then use the `DataContractJsonSerializer` class's `ReadObject` method to read the JSON into an object.

The next step is to add classes for data contracts for different objects, including for access token, user, messages, and so on, using the `DataContract` and `DataMember` attributes.

30. Add a new class called User to the App_Code folder by right-clicking on App_Code folder and choosing Add ➤ Class. Specify the name of the class as illustrated in Figures 4-14 and 4-15.

31. After the class is created, add the following code snippet for the User class.

```
using System.Collections.Generic;
using System.Linq;
using System.Web;
using System.Runtime.Serialization;
using System.Runtime.Serialization.Json;
using System.IO;
using System.Diagnostics;

namespace SPDSUniversityWebApplication.App_Code
{
    [DataContract]
    public class User : SerializedJson<User>
    {
        [DataMember(Name = "id")]
        public string UserID { get; set; }

        [DataMember(Name = "network_id")]
        public string NetworkID { get; set; }

        [DataMember(Name = "state")]
        public string AccountStatus { get; set; }

        [DataMember(Name = "job_title")]
        public string JobTitle { get; set; }

        [DataMember(Name = "expertise")]
        public string Expertise { get; set; }

        [DataMember(Name = "full_name")]
        public string FullName { get; set; }

        [DataMember(Name = "first_name")]
        public string FirstName { get; set; }

        [DataMember(Name = "last_name")]
        public string LastName { get; set; }

        [DataMember(Name = "url")]
        public string ApiUrl { get; set; }

        [DataMember(Name = "web_url")]
        public string WebUrl { get; set; }

        [DataMember(Name = "mugshot_url")]
        public string PhotoUrl { get; set; }
```

```
        [DataMember(Name = "mugshot_url_template")]
        public string PhotoTemplateUrl { get; set; }

        [DataMember(Name = "department")]
        public string Department { get; set; }

        [DataMember(Name = "contact")]
        public ContactInfo ContactInfo { get; set; }

        [DataMember(Name = "web_preferences")]
        public SettingsAndFeedsAndGroups SettingsAndFeedsAndGroups { get; set; }

        [DataMember(Name = "previous_companies")]
        public List<EmployerData> PreviousEmployers { get; set; }

        [DataMember(Name = "schools")]
        public List<YammerSchool> Schools { get; set; }

        [DataMember(Name = "stats")]
        public UserStats UserStats { get; set; }

        public User()
        {
            this.ContactInfo = new ContactInfo();
            this.SettingsAndFeedsAndGroups = new SettingsAndFeedsAndGroups();
            this.PreviousEmployers = new List<EmployerData>();
            this.Schools = new List<YammerSchool>();
            this.UserStats = new UserStats();
        }
    }

    [DataContract]
    public class UserStats
    {
        [DataMember(Name = "followers")]
        public int Followers { get; set; }

        [DataMember(Name = "following")]
        public int Following { get; set; }

        [DataMember(Name = "updates")]
        public int Updates { get; set; }
    }

    [DataContract]
    public class YammerSchool
    {
        [DataMember(Name = "degree")]
        public string Degree { get; set; }

        [DataMember(Name = "description")]
        public string Description { get; set; }
```

```
        [DataMember(Name = "end_year")]
        public string EndYear { get; set; }

        [DataMember(Name = "start_year")]
        public string StartYear { get; set; }

        [DataMember(Name = "school")]
        public string School { get; set; }
    }

    [DataContract]
    public class EmployerData
    {
        [DataMember(Name = "description")]
        public string Description { get; set; }

        [DataMember(Name = "employer")]
        public string Employer { get; set; }

        [DataMember(Name = "end_year")]
        public string EndYear { get; set; }

        [DataMember(Name = "position")]
        public string Position { get; set; }

        [DataMember(Name = "start_year")]
        public string StartYear { get; set; }
    }

    [DataContract]
    public class SettingsAndFeedsAndGroups
    {
        [DataMember(Name = "network_settings")]
        public NetworkSettings NetworkSettings { get; set; }

        [DataMember(Name = "home_tabs")]
        public List<GroupsAndFeeds> GroupsAndFeeds { get; set; }

        public SettingsAndFeedsAndGroups()
        {
            this.NetworkSettings = new NetworkSettings();
            this.GroupsAndFeeds = new List<GroupsAndFeeds>();
        }
    }

    [DataContract]
    public class GroupsAndFeeds
    {
        [DataMember(Name = "name")]
        public string Name { get; set; }
```

```
        [DataMember(Name = "select_name")]
        public string SelectName { get; set; }

        [DataMember(Name = "type")]
        public string Type { get; set; }

        [DataMember(Name = "feed_description")]
        public string Description { get; set; }

        [DataMember(Name = "ordering_index")]
        public int OrderingIndex { get; set; }

        [DataMember(Name = "url")]
        public string Url { get; set; }

        [DataMember(Name = "group_id")]
        public string GroupID { get; set; }

        [DataMember(Name = "private")]
        public bool IsPrivate { get; set; }
    }

    [DataContract]
    public class NetworkSettings
    {
        [DataMember(Name = "message_prompt")]
        public string MessagePrompt { get; set; }

        [DataMember(Name = "allow_attachments")]
        public bool AllowAttachments { get; set; }

        [DataMember(Name = "show_communities_directory")]
        public bool ShowCommunitiesDirectory { get; set; }

        [DataMember(Name = "enable_groups")]
        public bool EnableGroups { get; set; }

        [DataMember(Name = "allow_yammer_apps")]
        public bool AllowYammerApps { get; set; }

        [DataMember(Name = "admin_can_delete_messages")]
        public bool AdminCanDeleteMessages { get; set; }

        [DataMember(Name = "allow_inline_document_view")]
        public bool AllowInlineDocumentView { get; set; }

        [DataMember(Name = "allow_inline_video")]
        public bool AllowInlineVideo { get; set; }

        [DataMember(Name = "enable_private_messages")]
        public bool EnablePrivateMessages { get; set; }
```

```
    [DataMember(Name = "allow_external_sharing")]
    public bool AllowExternalSharing { get; set; }

    [DataMember(Name = "enable_chat")]
    public bool EnableChat { get; set; }
}
[DataContract]
public class ContactInfo
{
    [DataMember(Name = "has_fake_email")]
    public bool HasFakeEmail { get; set; }

    [DataMember(Name = "email_addresses")]
    public List<EmailAddresses> EmailAddresses { get; set; }

    [DataMember(Name = "phone_numbers")]
    public List<PhoneNumbers> PhoneNumbers { get; set; }

    [DataMember(Name = "im")]
    public IM IM { get; set; }

    public ContactInfo()
    {
        this.EmailAddresses = new List<EmailAddresses>();
        this.PhoneNumbers = new List<PhoneNumbers>();
        this.IM = new IM();
    }
}

[DataContract]
public class EmailAddresses
{
    [DataMember(Name = "address")]
    public string Address { get; set; }

    [DataMember(Name = "type")]
    public string Type { get; set; }

    public EmailAddresses() { }

    public EmailAddresses(string address, string type)
    {
        this.Address = address;
        this.Type = type;
    }
}

[DataContract]
public class PhoneNumbers
{
    [DataMember(Name = "number")]
    public string PhoneNumber { get; set; }
```

```
            [DataMember(Name = "type")]
            public string Type { get; set; }
        }

        [DataContract]
        public class IM
        {
            [DataMember(Name = "provider")]
            public string Provider { get; set; }

            [DataMember(Name = "username")]
            public string UserName { get; set; }
        }
    }
```

32. Add a new class called `Data` to the `App_Code` folder by right-clicking on the `App_Code` folder and choosing Add ➤ Class. Specify the name of the class as illustrated in Figures 4-14 and 4-15.

The `Data.cs` class defines two classes, `AccessToken` and `TokenResponse` by attaching `DataContractAttribute` to the classes and `DataMemberAttribute` to the members you want to serialize.

33. Replace the following code snippet in the `Data.cs`. It defines the `AccessToken` and `TokenResponse` classes.

```
using System;
using System.Collections.Generic;
using System.Linq;
using System.Web;
using System.Runtime.Serialization;
using System.Runtime.Serialization.Json;
using System.IO;
using System.Diagnostics;

namespace SPDSUniversityWebApplication.App_Code
{

    [DataContract]
    public class TokenResponse
    {
        [DataMember(Name = "user_id")]
        public string UserID { get; set; }

        [DataMember(Name = "network_id")]
        public string NetworkID { get; set; }

        [DataMember(Name = "network_permalink")]
        public string NetworkPermaLink { get; set; }

        [DataMember(Name = "network_name")]
        public string NetworkName { get; set; }
```

```
        [DataMember(Name = "token")]
        public string Token { get; set; }
    }

    [DataContract]
    public class AccessToken : SerializedJson<AccessToken>
    {
        [DataMember(Name = "access_token")]
        public TokenResponse TokenResponse { get; set; }

        [DataMember(Name = "user")]
        public User CurrentUser { get; set; }

        public AccessToken()
        {
            this.TokenResponse = new TokenResponse();
            this.CurrentUser = new User();
        }
    }
}
```

34. Add a new class called `YammerUtility` to the `App_Code` folder by right-clicking on that folder and choosing Add ➤ Class. Specify the name of the class as illustrated in Figures 4-14 and 4-15.

35. Add the following code to the `YammerUtility.cs` file.

```
using System;
using System.Collections.Generic;
using System.Linq;
using System.Web;
using System.Net;
using System.IO;

namespace SPDSUniversityWebApplication.App_Code
{
    public class YammerUtility
    {
        private static HttpWebResponse HTTPWebRes;
        private static HttpWebRequest HTTPWebReq;

        /// <summary>
        ///
        /// </summary>
        /// <param name="Url"></param>
        /// <param name="authHeader"></param>
        /// <param name="AddCookies"></param>
        /// <returns></returns>
        public static string InvokeHttpGetRequest(string Url, string
        authHeader = null, bool AddCookies = false)
        {
            string results = string.Empty;
```

```
                try
                {
                    HTTPWebReq = WebRequest.CreateHttp(Url);
                    HTTPWebReq.Method = "GET";

                    if (!string.IsNullOrEmpty(authHeader))
                        HTTPWebReq.Headers.Add("Authorization", "Bearer " +
                        authHeader);

                    HTTPWebRes = (HttpWebResponse)HTTPWebReq.GetResponse();

                    Stream dataStream = HTTPWebRes.GetResponseStream();
                    StreamReader reader = new StreamReader(dataStream);

                    results = reader.ReadToEnd();

                    reader.Close();
                }
                catch (Exception ex)
                {
                    Console.WriteLine("Error in MakeGetRequest: " + ex.Message);
                }

                return results;
            }

        }
    }
```

In the previous class definition, the `AccessToken` class contains two other objects—`TokenResponse` (defined in `Data.cs`) and `User` (defined in `user.cs`).

36. Add the method `Obtain_Access_Token()` to the `Default.aspx.cs` file.

```
    /// <summary>
            /// Obtain the access Token
            /// </summary>
            private void Obtain_Access_Token()
            {
                string accessToken = default(string);
                string AccesTokenURL = WebConfigurationManager.
                AppSettings["AccessTokenURL"] + "client_id=" +
                WebConfigurationManager.AppSettings["client_id"] + "&client_
                secret=" + WebConfigurationManager.AppSettings["client_secret"] +
                "&code=" + txtCode.Text;
                string response = SPDSUniversityWebApplication.App_Code.
                YammerUtility.InvokeHttpGetRequest(AccesTokenURL);
                if (!string.IsNullOrEmpty(response))
                {
                    SPDSUniversityWebApplication.App_Code.AccessToken jat =
                    SPDSUniversityWebApplication.App_Code.AccessToken.GetObject
                    InstanceFromJson(response);
```

```
                if (!string.IsNullOrEmpty(jat.TokenResponse.Token))
                {
                    accessToken = jat.TokenResponse.Token;
                    lbllogin.Text = "Welcome " + jat.CurrentUser.FullName;
                    txtaccesstoken.Text = accessToken;
                    Session["accesstoken"] = accessToken;
                }
            }
        }
```

We added three classes to the project. Figure 4-17 shows the class diagrams

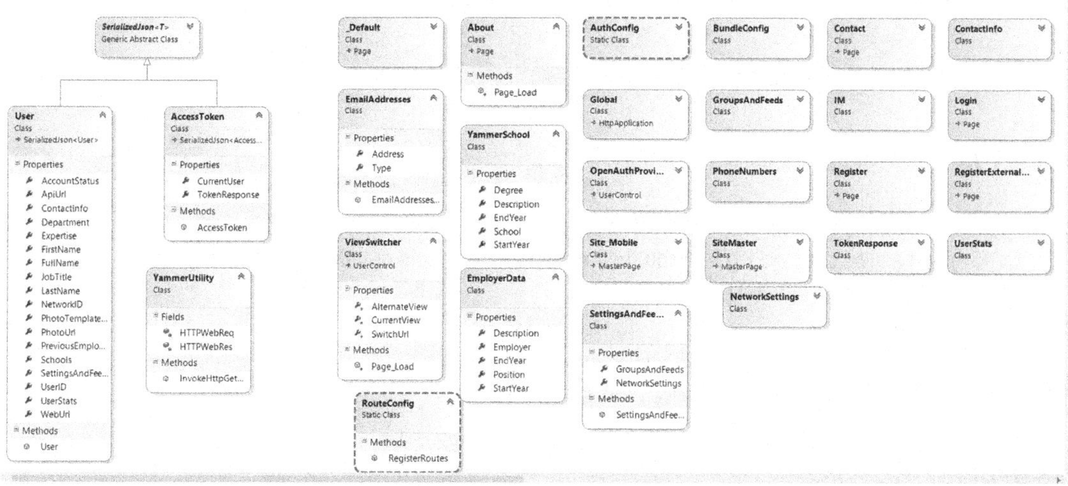

Figure 4-17. *The Yammer authentication classes*

The access token received from Yammer will be valid for a very long time, so you should save the token for a user and keep using it. For the ASP.NET application, the best approach is to store it in the cookies.

■ **Note** Once the access token expires, developers have to re-run the previous steps to generate a new code and access token. If a new access token is requested for the user who has already authorized your app, that user will not be promoted to authorize the app again.

Run the Application

37. Press F5 to execute the application. It will open in Internet Explorer with the `Default.aspx` file as the home page. The page will look similar to Figure 4-18.

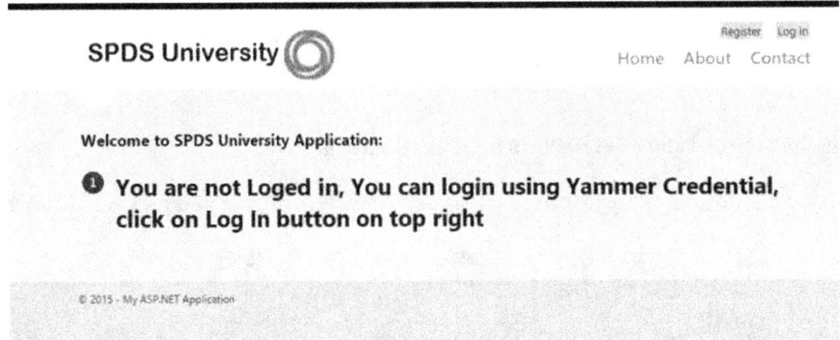

Figure 4-18. *The Default.aspx file in run mode*

38. Click on the "Log In" button, which will redirect you to the Login page. That page allows users to log in using their registered accounts or using Yammer, as illustrated in Figure 4-19.

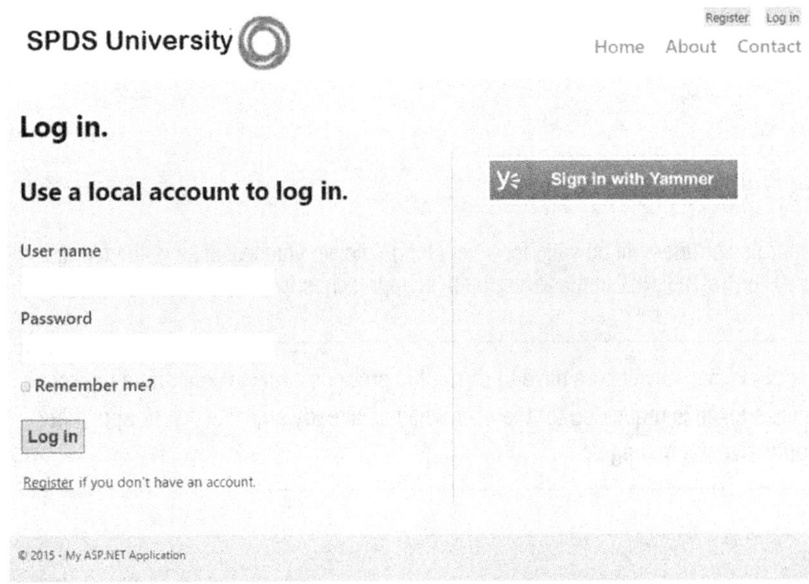

Figure 4-19. *The Login.aspx page in run mode*

39. Click on the "Sign In with Yammer" button.

40. You will be prompted with the Yammer Login page. Enter your login credentials and click "Log In," as shown in Figure 4-20.

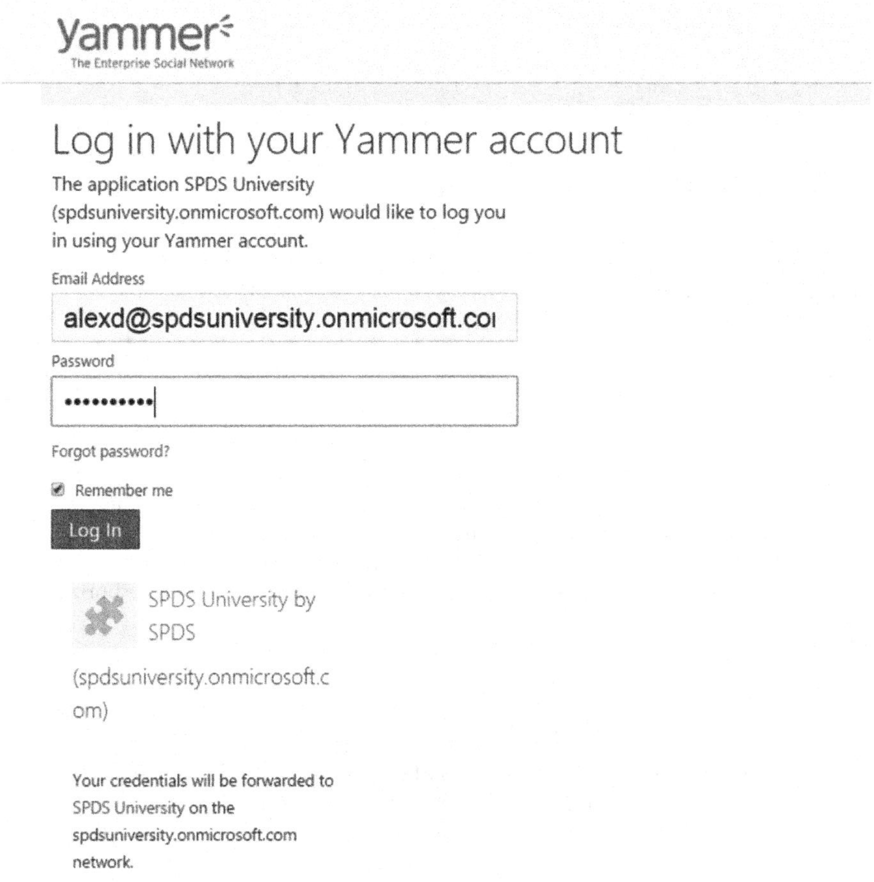

Log in with your Yammer account

The application SPDS University (spdsuniversity.onmicrosoft.com) would like to log you in using your Yammer account.

Email Address

alexd@spdsuniversity.onmicrosoft.coı

Password

••••••••••

Forgot password?

Remember me

Log In

SPDS University by SPDS

(spdsuniversity.onmicrosoft.com)

Your credentials will be forwarded to SPDS University on the spdsuniversity.onmicrosoft.com network.

Figure 4-20. *Yammer Login page*

41. You will be presented with the `Default.aspx` page showing a message, as illustrated in Figure 4-21.

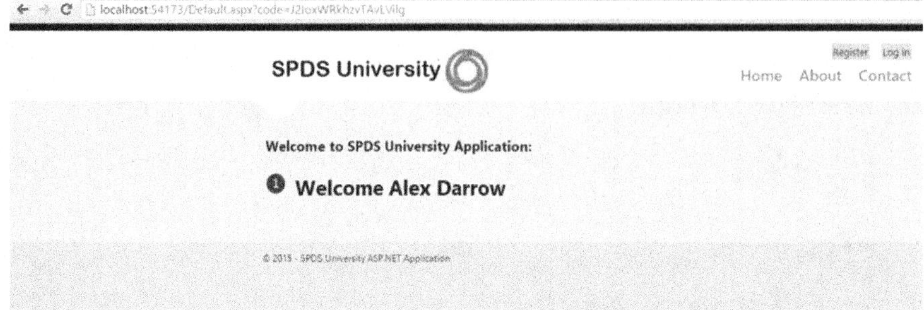

Figure 4-21. *The message after successful completion of OAuth 2.0 flow*

At this point, you have successfully implemented OAuth 2.0 server-side flow in an ASP.NET web application. In the next section, you will look at the client-side flow using a similar exercise. It will showcase the client-side flow in a Microsoft SharePoint-hosted app.

Client-Side Flow

Yammer's OAuth authentication also supports client-side flows for authentication and authorization of JavaScript-centric applications. Client-side flows are optimized for public clients, such as those implemented in JavaScript or on mobile devices, where client credentials cannot be stored.

The client-side flow is also referred as an "implicit grant," which is different from the server-side flow. In the client-side flow, the client makes a single request only to obtain the access token, as the authorization code is not required in this case.

The steps involved in an implicit grant or a client-side flow are as follows:

Step	Name	Description
#1	Application Request Authentication	The OAuth 2.0 authentication is initiated as soon as the user (resource owner) clicks on the "Sign In with Yammer" button; here, the user is redirected to the OAuth 2.0 authorization endpoint.
#2	Yammer Request Credentials	Yammer authorization server then prompts the user with a login page.
#3	Yammer Request App Authorization	The OAuth process prompts the user to authorize the Yammer app.
#4	Application Receives Access Token	Once authorized, Yammer sends the access token to the client app.

Step #1: Application Request Authentication

The authorization sequence begins when your application redirects a browser to the Yammer OAuth URL; the URL includes query parameters that indicate the type of access being requested. First, as for server-side flow, you must create the Yammer OAuth URL to initiate the flow.

Your application should redirect the user to the OAuth URL along with the Yammer app's `ClientID` and `redirect_URI` as per configuration. The OAuth URL is

```
https://www.yammer.com/dialog/oauth?client_id=[:client_id]&redirect_uri=[:redirect_uri]
&response_type=token
```

Table 4-13 lists all the parameters required in order to request the access token.

Table 4-13. *OAuth URL's Query String Parameters*

Parameter	Description
`client_id`	Obtain the `Client_ID` for your Yammer app using the Yammer UI. Use the `https://www.yammer.com/client_applications` link for list of the registered client ID.
`redirect_uri`	This `redirect_uri` should match the `redirect_uri` configured for your app in the Yammer platform.
`response_type`	The `response_type=token` parameter.

For the SPDSUniversity SharePoint-hosted app, the complete OAuth URL will look like this:

```
https://www.yammer.com/dialog/oauth?client_id=9aax1mFox7yMVBS2LpIJQ&redirect_uri=
http://localhost:54173/Default.aspx&response_type=token
```

To obtain the `client_id` and `redirect_uri`, navigate to your registered app in Yammer, as illustrated in Figure 4-22.

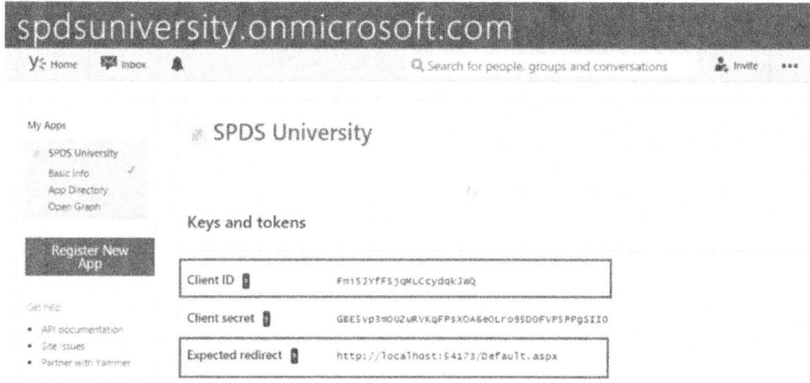

Figure 4-22. *The SPDSUniversity app's Key and Tokens Configuration*

Step #2: Server Request Credentials

The OAuth process will prompt the user with the Yammer Login window. Users then enter their credentials and submit the request, as shown in Figure 4-23.

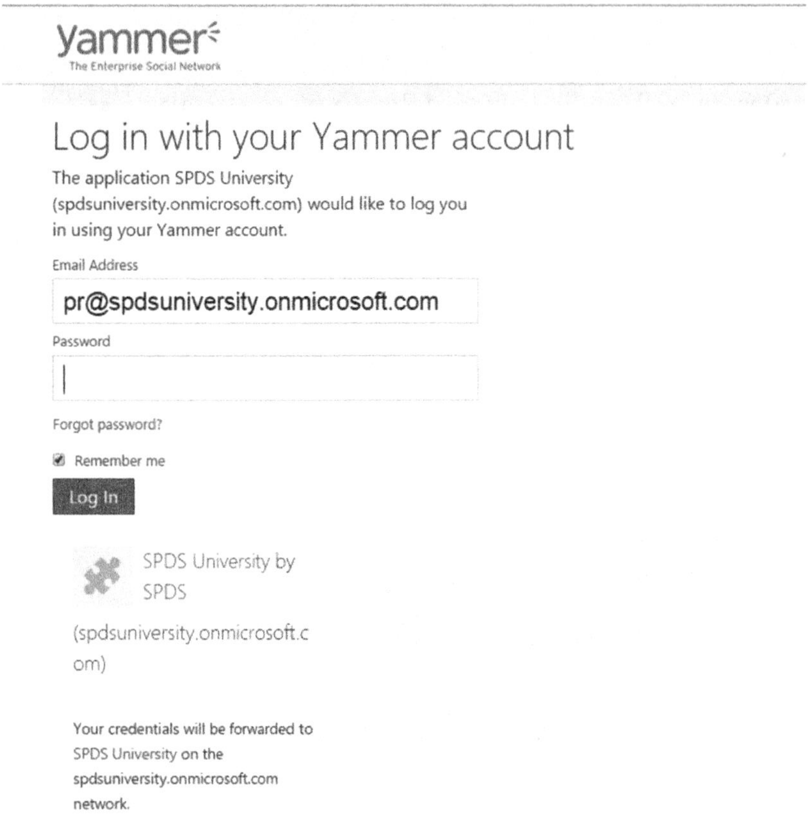

yammer
The Enterprise Social Network

Log in with your Yammer account

The application SPDS University (spdsuniversity.onmicrosoft.com) would like to log you in using your Yammer account.

Email Address

pr@spdsuniversity.onmicrosoft.com

Password

Forgot password?

Remember me

Log In

SPDS University by SPDS

(spdsuniversity.onmicrosoft.com)

Your credentials will be forwarded to SPDS University on the spdsuniversity.onmicrosoft.com network.

Figure 4-23. *Yammer Login page*

Step #3: Server Request App Authorization

In this step, the OAuth 2.0 authentication process shows an App Authorization screen, as shown in Figure 4-24. If the user has allowed your Yammer app, the app will be authorized and an access token will be generated for that user.

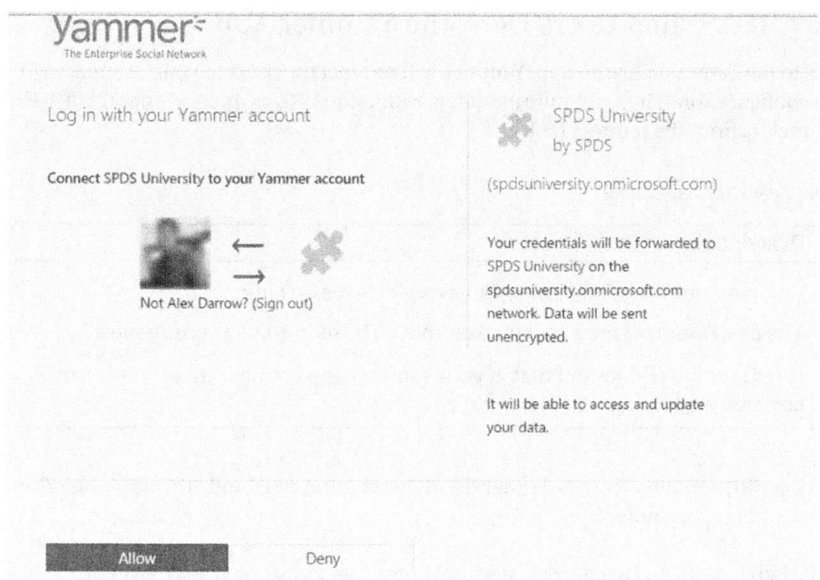

Figure 4-24. *App authorization*

Step #4: Application Receives Access Token

The response will be sent to the `redirect_uri` as specified in the request URL. If the user approves the access request, then the response contains an authorization code. If the user does not approve the request, the response contains an error message. The redirect URL's parameters will be different when the user allows the Yammer app compared to when they deny it access. Let's look at the redirect URL's parameters in each case.

Redirect URL's Parameters When Users Allow the Yammer App

Yammer will redirect the users to your Yammer app's redirect URL as per its configuration with the authorization code (parameter) as part of the URL. It's a query string and is listed in Table 4-14.

```
http://[:redirect_uri]#access_token=[:access_token]
```

Table 4-14. *OAuth URL's Query String Parameters*

Parameter	Description
`redirect_uri`	The `redirect_uri` used in the OAuth URL.
`access_token`	Yammer-generated `access_token` for the user who has authorized the app.

Redirect URL's Parameters When Users Deny the Yammer App

When the user denies access to the Yammer custom app, Yammer will redirect the users to your Yammer app's redirect URL as per its configuration. The error information is within the URL as query string. Table 4-15 lists all the query string parameters from the redirect URL.

Table 4-15. *OAuth URL's Query String Parameter*

Parameter	Description
`Error`	This contains the actual error; for example, "Access Denied".
`error_description`	The description of the error; for example, "The user denied your request".
`invalid redirect_uri`	If `redirect_uri` does not match your Yammer app configuration, you get an error entitled "Invalid Redirect_uri".

For example, the following URL contains "access denied" in the error parameter and "the user denied your request" in the error description parameter.

```
http://localhost:54173/Default.aspx?error=access_denied&error_description=the%20user%20
denied%20your%20request
```

In this section you learned about the steps involved in client-side flow, which is mainly used in business applications that use client scripting like JavaScript.

Implementing Client-Side Flow in a Microsoft SharePoint-Hosted App

In the next exercise, we will implement Yammer authentication using client-side flow in a Microsoft SharePoint-hosted app. You need to have Visual Studio 2012 Professional, Premium, or Ultimate installed on your local computer. You also need to have the Office Developer Tools for Visual Studio 2012 installed. These can be downloaded from `http://msdn.microsoft.com/en-us/office/apps/fp123627`.

EXERCISE 4-2: CLIENT-SIDE FLOW USING THE "SIGN IN WITH YAMMER" BUTTON WITH THE JAVASCRIPT SDK

In this exercise, we will create a SPDS University, Microsoft SharePoint-hosted app for Microsoft SharePoint Online. There will be a "Log In with Yammer" button on the Microsoft SharePoint App's target page.

Prerequisites for Creating a Basic Microsoft SharePoint-Hosted App

- A computer that is configured for app isolation with Microsoft SharePoint 2013 installed on it. If you're using an Office 365 Developer Site, you already have a Microsoft SharePoint 2013 environment that supports OAuth.
- Visual Studio 2012 or higher.
- Office Developer Tools for Visual Studio 2012.

Create a New Microsoft SharePoint App Project

1. Start Visual Studio by using the Run as Administrator option.
2. The first screen presented to you is the Visual Studio Start page, as illustrated in Figure 4-25.

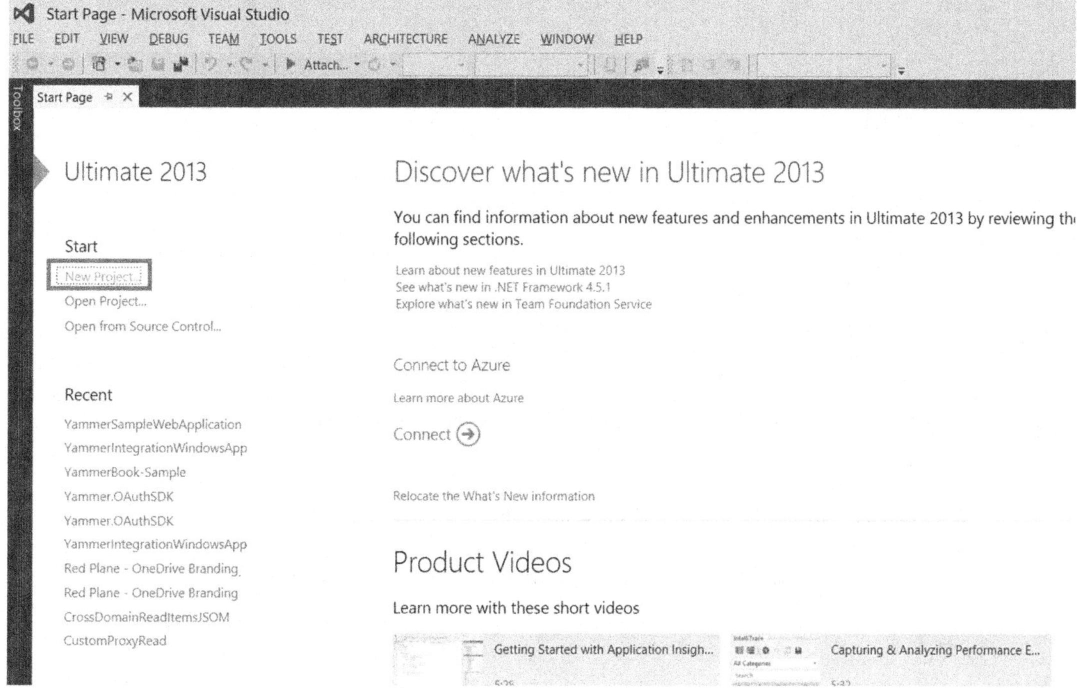

Figure 4-25. Visual Studio Start page offers a quick way to get started

3. On the left side of the start page, on the navigation pane, choose New Project. Alternatively you can use the File ➤ New Project menu command.
4. This brings up the New Project window, as illustrated in Figure 4-26. Expand the Visual C# node, expand the Office/SharePoint node, and then choose Apps ➤ App for SharePoint 2013.

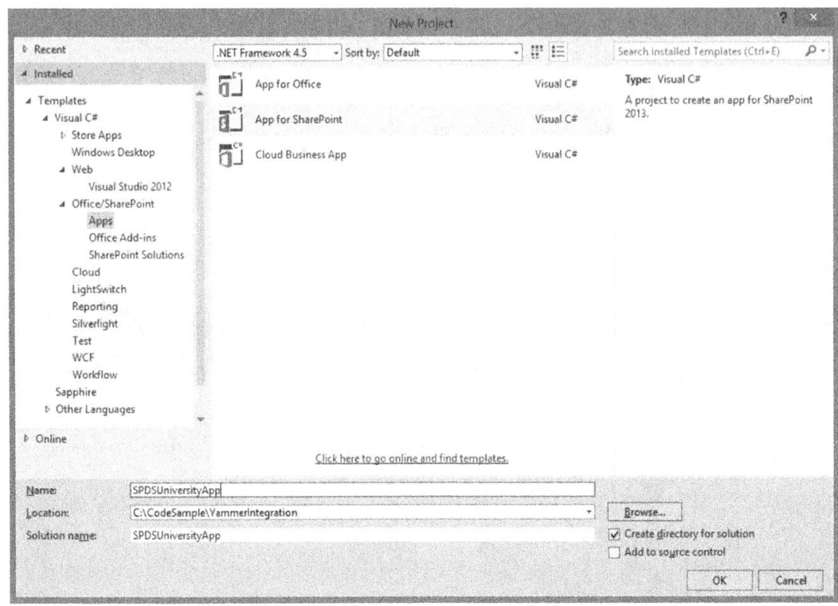

Figure 4-26. *Select the app for the SharePoint template under Office/SharePoint*

5. You will be presented with the Specify the App for SharePoint Settings window. Name your app and provide the URL of the Microsoft SharePoint 2013 site that you want to use to debug your app. Under the "How do you want to host your app for SharePoint" option, choose SharePoint-hosted. Then click the Finish button, as shown in Figure 4-27.

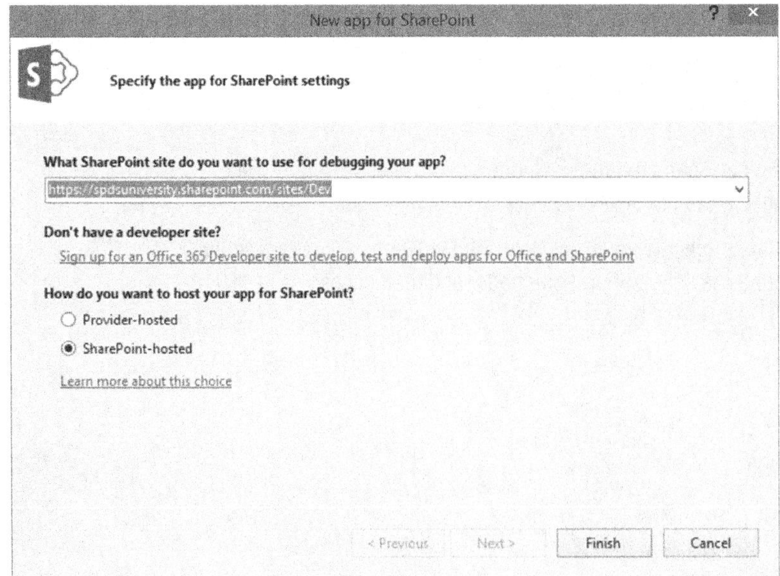

Figure 4-27. *Specify the app for the SharePoint settings and provide the URL of the SharePoint web site that you want to use for debugging*

After the wizard finishes, you should have a structure in Solution Explorer that resembles Figure 4-28. The solution comprises one App Project that contains the SharePoint-hosted app structure with an `AppManifest.xml` file.

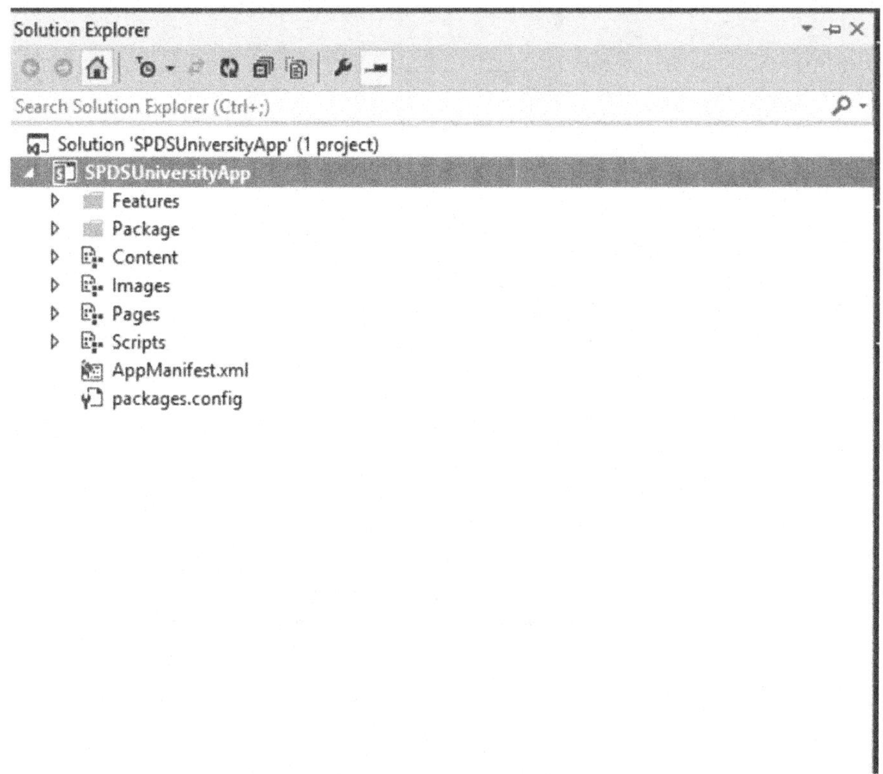

Figure 4-28. *The SharePoint-hosted app project structure*

Create Customer Ribbon Action

We will now add a new "Menu Item Custom Action" item to the SharePoint app. But first we will add a page for the custom action.

6. Right-click on the Page node in the web project and add a new page. Name the page `CustomActionTarget.aspx`, as shown in Figure 4-29.

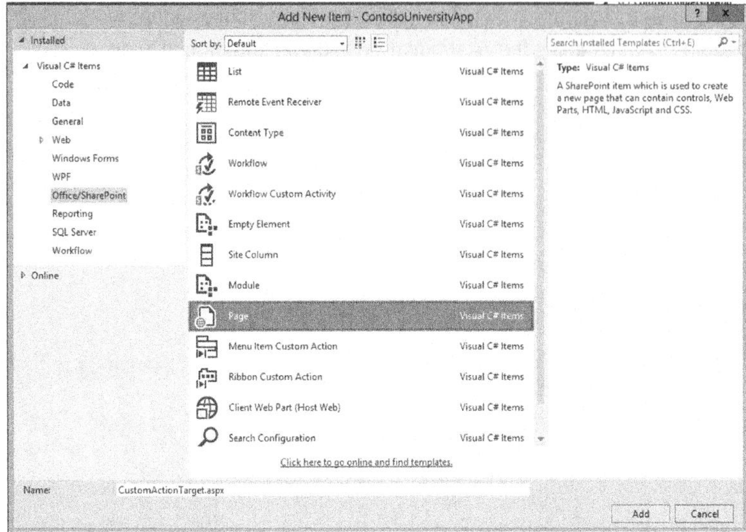

Figure 4-29. *Adding a new page to the SharePoint app project*

Add a Control "Menu Item Custom Action"

7. Right-click on the page node for the SharePoint project and add a new "Menu Item Custom Action" item. Name it `MenuItem_PosttoYammer`, as illustrated in Figure 4-30.

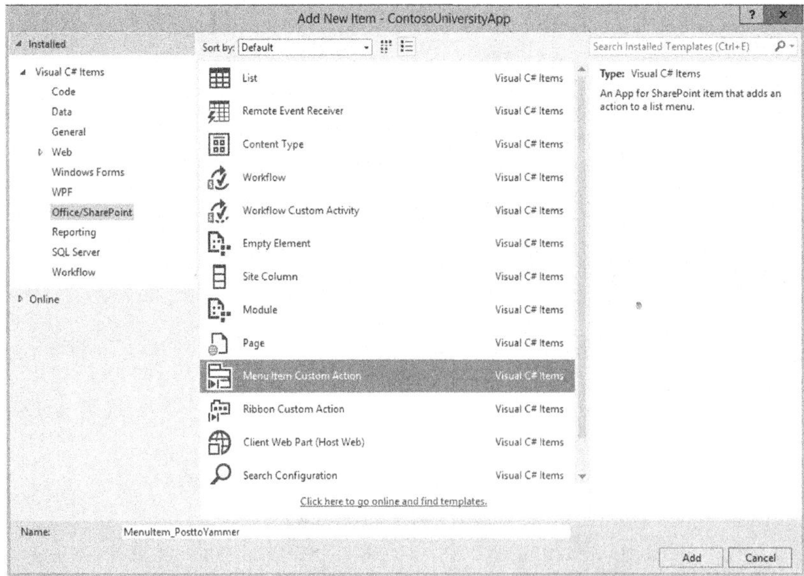

Figure 4-30. *Add a new menu item custom action to the SharePoint app project*

8. You'll be presented with the Specify the Properties to Create Custom Action Menu Item window, as illustrated in Figure 4-31. From there, you need to set the following properties for the custom action (refer to Table 4-16 for each property value).

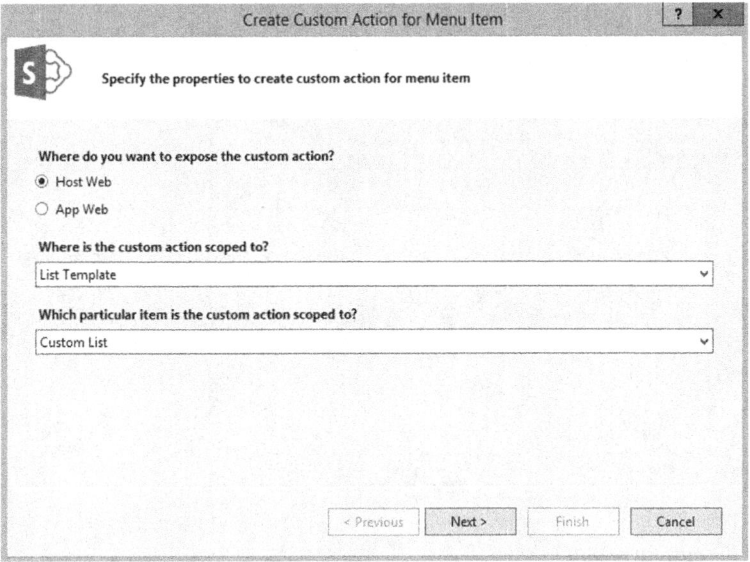

Figure 4-31. *Set the properties for the custom action*

Table 4-16. *OAuth URL's Query String Parameter*

Property Question	Answer
Where do you want to expose the custom action?	Choose Host Web
Where is the custom action scoped to?	Choose List Template
Which particular item is the custom action scoped to?	Choose Custom List
What is the text on the menu item?	Type "Invoke post to Yammer custom action"

9. You'll be presented with another window, entitled Specify the Properties to Create Custom Action Menu Item, as illustrated in Figure 4-32. From there, you need to set the following properties for the custom action (refer to Table 4-17 for property value).

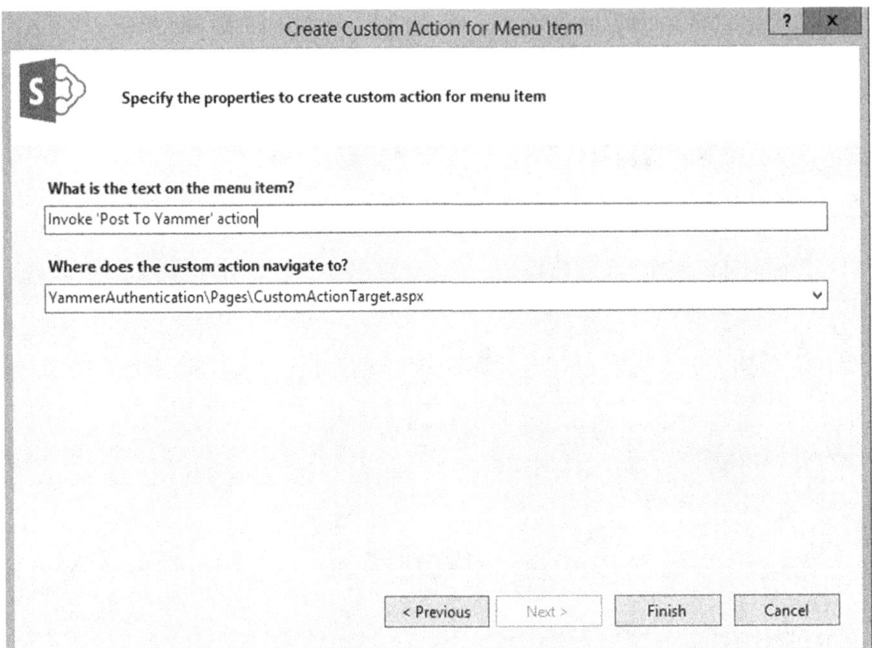

Figure 4-32. Set the properties for the custom action

Table 4-17. Specify the Properties for the Custom Action

Property Question	Answer
What is the text on the menu item?	Enter "Invoke 'Post To Yammer Action"
Where the custom action does navigates to?	Choose the CustomActionTarget.aspx which we created in previous step

10. After setting the properties for the custom action menu item, click Finish.

Visual Studio generates the following markup in the `elements.xml` file of the menu item custom action feature:

```
<?xml version="1.0" encoding="utf-8"?>
<Elements xmlns="http://schemas.microsoft.com/sharepoint/">
  <CustomAction Id="75be0d47-8c42-4f9b-afd4-7bb601ffc5e0.MenuItem_PostToYammer"
                RegistrationType="List"
                RegistrationId="100"
                Location="EditControlBlock"
                Sequence="10001"
                Title="Invoke &apos;Post To Yammer&apos; action">
    <!--
    Update the Url below to the page you want the custom action to use.
    Start the URL with the token ~remoteAppUrl if the page is in the
    associated web project, use ~appWebUrl if page is in the app project.
    -->
```

```
    <UrlAction Url="~appWebUrl/Pages/CustomActionTarget.aspx?{StandardTokens}&amp;
    SPListItemId={ItemId}&amp;SPListId={ListId}" />
  </CustomAction>
</Elements>
```

Implement the Authentication

We have all controls in the project so now we can start implementing the authentication using the JavaScript SDK. First we'll modify the `CustomActionTarget.aspx` page by adding some code in the HTML markup.

11. Add the following HTML markup to `CustomActionTarget.aspx`. Add this within the `<asp:Content ContentPlaceHolderId="PlaceHolderAdditionalPageHead" runat="server">` placeholder:

```
<script type="text/javascript" src="../Scripts/jquery-1.9.1.min.js"></script>
<script type="text/javascript" src="/_layouts/15/sp.runtime.js"></script>
<script type="text/javascript" src="/_layouts/15/sp.js"></script>
<script type="text/javascript" data-app-id="Fmi5JYfF5jqMLCcydqkJWQ"
src="https://c64.assets-yammer.com/assets/platform_js_sdk.js"></script>
```

Here you need to replace `data-app-id` with your Yammer app's ID. You need to get the client ID that was generated when you registered the app on `Yammer.com`.

The second parameter `sec` refers to the JavaScript SDK.

12. Replace the following code snippet with `ContentPlaceHolderID="PlaceHolderMain"` in the `CustomActionTarget.aspx` file:

```
<asp:Content ContentPlaceHolderId="PlaceHolderMain" runat="server">
      <div>
        <h3>Yammer Authenication Example</h3>
        <br />
        <span id="yammer-login"></span>
      </div>

      <div class="logged-in" style="display:none">
            <p>User is now signed in to the app using Yammer</p>
            <button id="disconnect" class="yj-btn yj-btn-alt">Log out from
            your Yammer account</button>
      </div>
      <div class="logged-in" style="display:none">
            <h2>Authentication Logs</h2>
            <pre id="authResult"></pre>
      </div>

</asp:Content>
```

This code will display the "Log In with Yammer" button, as illustrated in Figure 4-33. It uses an HTML `span` control with `ID="yammer-login"` to create that button.

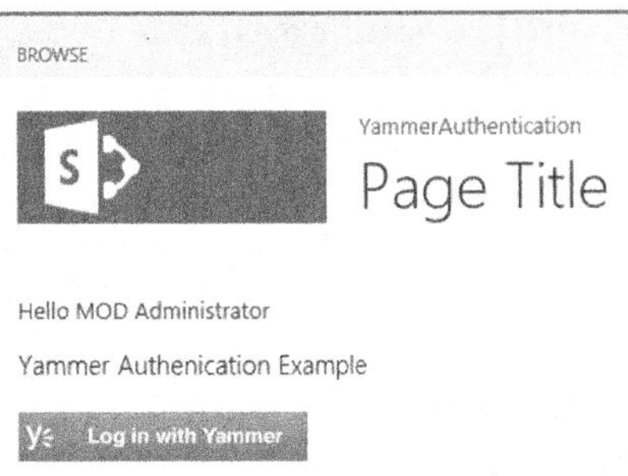

Figure 4-33. *The "Log In with Yammer" button created using the span control with Id="yammer-Login"*

13. Add the following JavaScript code to `ContentPlaceHolderID="PlaceHolderAdditionalPageHead"` of `CustomActionTarget.aspx`:

```
<script>
      yam.connect.loginButton('#yammer-login',
          function (resp) {
             if (resp.authResponse) {
                console.log(resp);
                displayAuthResult(resp);
             }
          });

      function displayAuthResult(resp) {
         document.getElementById("yammer-login").innerHTML = 'Welcome to
         Yammer!, The user ID is:  ' + resp.access_token.user_id;
        toggleLoginStatus(true);
         $('#authResult').append(' ========= <br/>');
         $('#authResult').append(' Access Token: <br/>');
         $('#authResult').append(' ========= <br/>');
         for (var field in resp.access_token) {
            $('#authResult').append(' ' + field + ': ' +
               resp.access_token[field] + '<br/>');
        }
      }

      function toggleLoginStatus(loggedIn) {
         if (loggedIn) {
            $('.not-logged-in').hide();
            $('.logged-in').show('slow');
         } else {
            $('.not-logged-in').show('slow');
            $('.logged-in').hide();
         }
      }
</script>
```

This JavaScript code on line 2 calls the yam.connect.loginButton function by passing two parameters—the selector (ID of span control "yammer-login" as a selector) and the callback function (function that will be fired after the login flow is completed). The span control <span id="yammer-login"></span> in the ContentPlaceHolderId="PlaceHolderMain" will become a standard "Log In with Yammer" button. When this button is clicked, it will initiate the Yammer client-side OAuth workflow. Once the user approves or denies the SPDSUniversity app, the OAuth callback will fire. The callback function on lines 3-8 first checks if AuthResponse is true and then calls the displayAuthResult function by passing the resp parameter. The displayAuthResult function code on line 9 changes the inner HTML of the span control to a welcome message and the user ID of the logged in user. The for loop on lines 15-18 displays all the properties of the resp.

14. The complete code of CustomActionTarget.aspx is shown in the following code snippet:

```
<%@ Page Language="C#" MasterPageFile="~masterurl/default.master"
Inherits="Microsoft.SharePoint.WebPartPages.WebPartPage, Microsoft.SharePoint,
Version=15.0.0.0, Culture=neutral, PublicKeyToken=71e9bce111e9429c" %>

<%@ Register TagPrefix="Utilities" Namespace="Microsoft.SharePoint.Utilities"
Assembly="Microsoft.SharePoint, Version=15.0.0.0, Culture=neutral,
PublicKeyToken=71e9bce111e9429c" %>
<%@ Register TagPrefix="WebPartPages" Namespace="Microsoft.SharePoint.
WebPartPages" Assembly="Microsoft.SharePoint, Version=15.0.0.0,
Culture=neutral, PublicKeyToken=71e9bce111e9429c" %>
<%@ Register TagPrefix="SharePoint" Namespace="Microsoft.SharePoint.
WebControls" Assembly="Microsoft.SharePoint, Version=15.0.0.0,
Culture=neutral, PublicKeyToken=71e9bce111e9429c" %>

<asp:Content ContentPlaceHolderID="PlaceHolderAdditionalPageHead"
runat="server">
   <SharePoint:ScriptLink Name="sp.js" runat="server" OnDemand="true"
   LoadAfterUI="true" Localizable="false" />

   <script type="text/javascript" src="../Scripts/jquery-1.9.1.min.js"></script>
<script type="text/javascript" src="/_layouts/15/sp.runtime.js"></script>
<script type="text/javascript" src="/_layouts/15/sp.js"></script>
<script type="text/javascript" data-app-id="Fmi5JYfF5jqMLCcydqkJWQ"
src="https://c64.assets-yammer.com/assets/platform_js_sdk.js"></script>

    <script>
      yam.connect.loginButton('#yammer-login',
         function (resp) {
              if (resp.authResponse) {
                  console.log(resp);
                  displayAuthResult(resp);
              }
         });
```

```
        function displayAuthResult(resp) {
            document.getElementById('yammer-login').innerHTML = 'Welcome to
            Yammer!, The user ID is:  ' + resp.access_token.user_id;
            toggleLoginStatus(true);
            $('#authResult').append(' ========= <br/>');
            $('#authResult').append(' Access Token: <br/>');
            $('#authResult').append(' ========= <br/>');
            for (var field in resp.access_token) {
                $('#authResult').append(' ' + field + ': ' +
                   resp.access_token[field] + '<br/>');
            }

        }

        function toggleLoginStatus(loggedIn) {
            if (loggedIn) {
                $('.not-logged-in').hide();
                $('.logged-in').show('slow');
            } else {
                $('.not-logged-in').show('slow');
                $('.logged-in').hide();
            }
        }

    </script>

    </asp:Content>
    <asp:Content ContentPlaceHolderId="PlaceHolderMain" runat="server">
       <div>
          <h3>Yammer Authenication Example</h3>
          <br />
          <span id="yammer-login"></span>
      </div>

       <div class="logged-in" style="display: none">
              <h2>Authentication Logs</h2>
              <pre id="authResult"></pre>
          </div>

    </asp:Content>
```

Run the Solution

15. You can run this app now and see that Visual Studio deploys the app to your site. To deploy it from Visual Studio, select Deploy from the project's context menu, as illustrated in Figure 4-34.

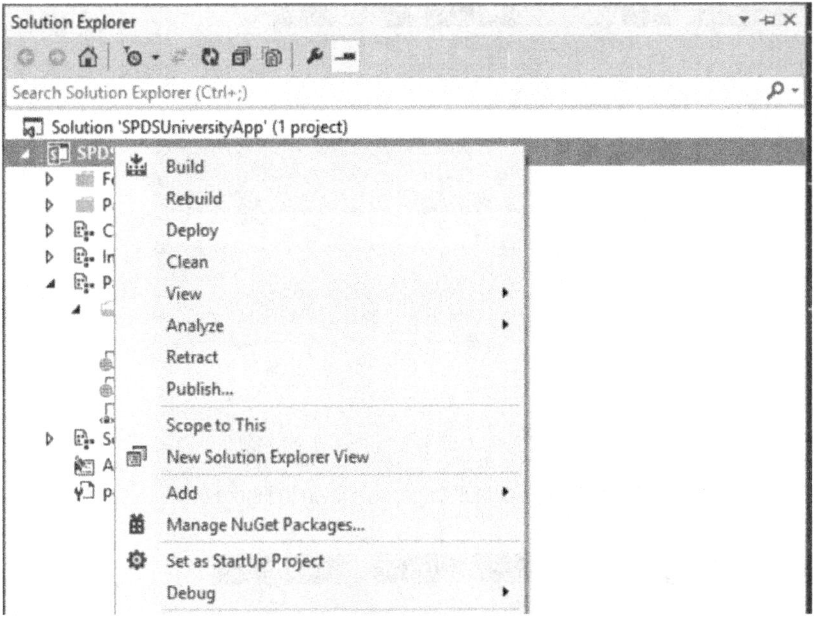

Figure 4-34. *Visual Studio's deploy solution*

16. Visual Studio will deploy the solution to the SharePoint Online site. In the first step, it will prompt you to log in to your SharePoint Online site, enter your Office 365 credentials, and click on Sign In, as shown in Figure 4-35.

Figure 4-35. *Log in to the Office 365 site*

17. You will be prompted to authorize the app. Click on the Trust It button and Visual Studio will deploy the app in the target site, as shown in Figure 4-36.

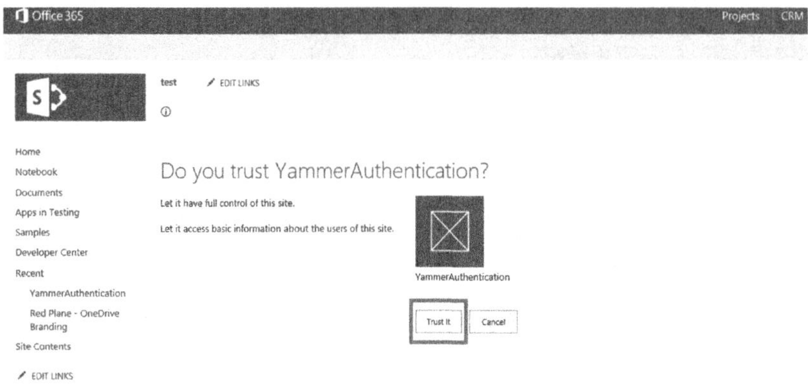

Figure 4-36. *SharePoint prompts you to authorize the app*

18. You will be presented with the SharePoint app's default page, as shown in Figure 4-37.

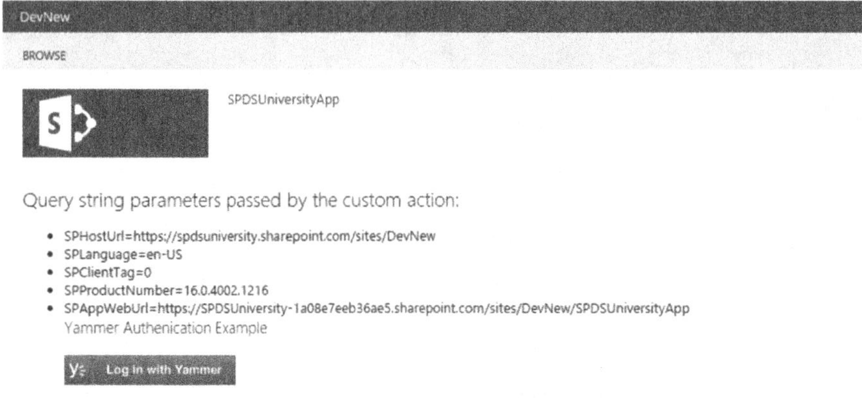

Figure 4-37. *The app's default page*

19. Now click on the "Log In with Yammer" button. You will be prompted with the Yammer Login screen, as illustrated in Figure 4-38.

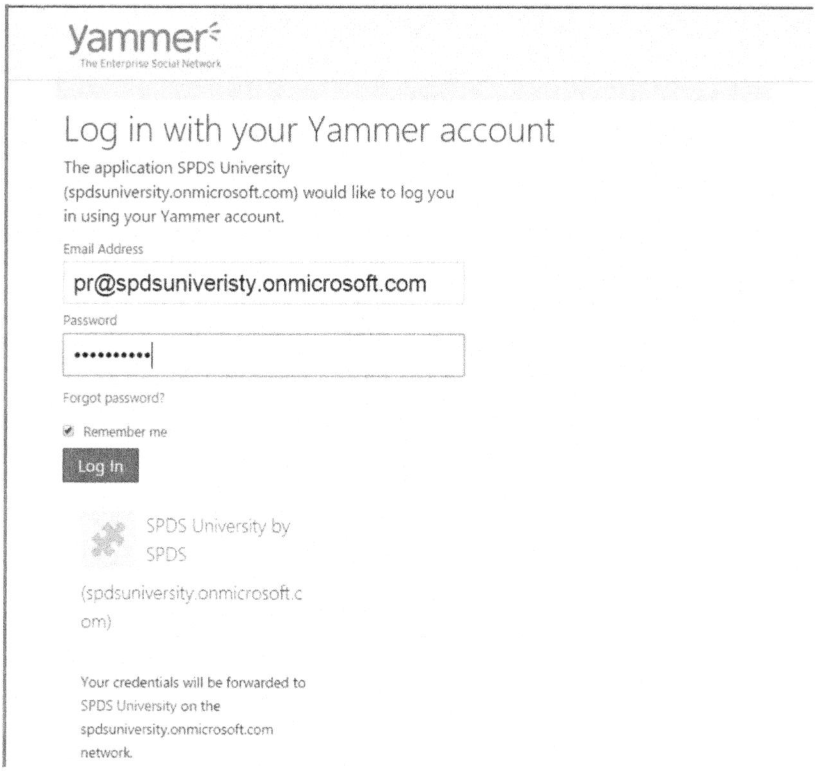

Figure 4-38. *Clicking on the "Log In with Yammer" button opens the Yammer Login page*

After you log into Yammer using your Yammer credentials, Yammer will return to the callback function you have written in the `Default.aspx` function. In this case it is the inline callback function that checks if `resp.authResponse` is not null. If it is not null, that means the user is already logged into Yammer. The code then displays the fields available in `access_token`—`user_id`, `network_id`, `network_permalink`, `network_name`, `token`, `view_members`, `view_groups`, `view_message`, `view_subscriptions`, `modify_subscriptions`, `modify_message`, `view_tags`, `created_at`, `authorized_at`, and `expires_at`, as shown in Figure 4-39.

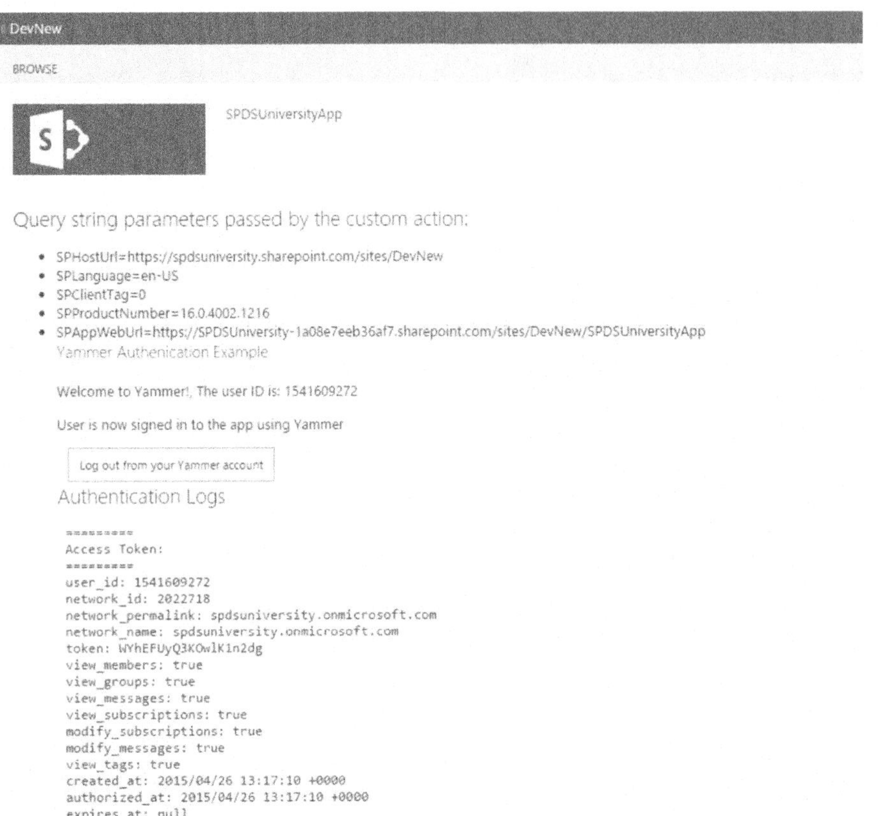

Figure 4-39. *CustomActionTarget.aspx displays the fields from access_token after the user logs in successfully*

At this point, you have successfully implemented OAuth 2.0 client-side flow in a SharePoint-hosted app.

Summary

By now you are aware of Yammer apps and understand the authorization process on Yammer for integration with your business applications. Examples provided in this chapter have given you a kick-start to enable Yammer integration in your business applications. In Chapters 5, 6, and 7, you'll learn advanced Yammer integration concepts using different technologies like Open Graph and REST APIs.

CHAPTER 5

Writing Data into Yammer with Open Graph

Pathik Rawal

In Chapters 1-4, we covered an introduction to Yammer, explained the Yammer platform, discussed the Yammer apps, and explored how to implement authentication on Yammer. We hope you read those chapters fully and understood the concepts of using Yammer apps for integration with external applications.

In this chapter, you will learn how to write data from your business applications into Yammer using the Open Graph protocol. This chapter covers:

- Introduction to Enterprise Social Graph
- The Open Graph Protocol
- Lab exercise on how to create custom Open Graph objects
- Lab exercise on how to write data from an ASP.NET web application into Yammer using an Open Graph activity

Introduction to Enterprise Social Graph

Yammer Enterprise Social Graph (AKA Enterprise Social Graph) is an adoption of the Open Graph Protocol that provides capabilities to establish the connection between employees, content, and data from different line-of-business applications. Figure 5-1 is a visual representation of Enterprise Social Graph. Implementing Enterprise Social Graph in business applications improves information sharing and allows users to get updated information related to business processes and make quicker decisions, thus improving productivity.

P. Rawal and P. Rohilla, *Developing on Yammer*, DOI 10.1007/978-1-4842-0943-1_5

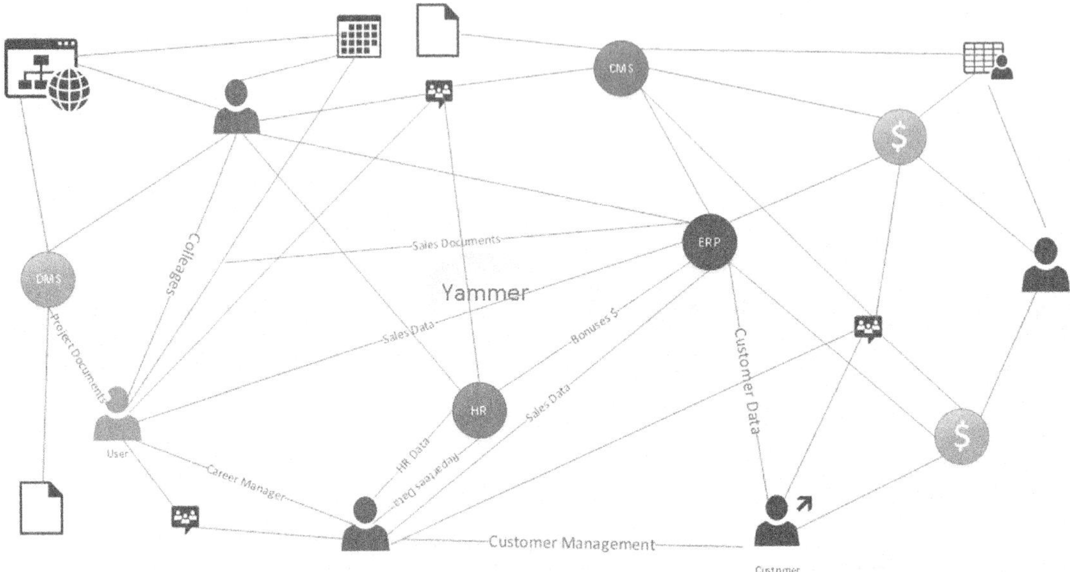

Figure 5-1. *Line-of-business applications and Yammer integration using Enterprise Social Graph*

Today's business applications maintain lots of data about business processes and employees. For example, a CRM application manages customers and prospects information, while a SharePoint site manages the product catalogues. But this setup does not provide a seamless access for employees and creates silos of information about customers and products in two different applications. Using Yammer Enterprise Social Graph, you can establish a connection between customers and the products the company wants to sell. Creating the Enterprise Social Graph—"a single mapping of Actions and objects they encounter at work," which will allow employees to understand more easily how information flows from different business processes.

Before exploring the technical aspects, let's look at an example in an organization. In SPDS University web application, the company's training manager creates training schedules that he wants to share with all the employees. This is achieved by Yammer's Enterprise Social Graph, which uses the Recent Activity widget to display the latest updates, as illustrated in Figure 5-2.

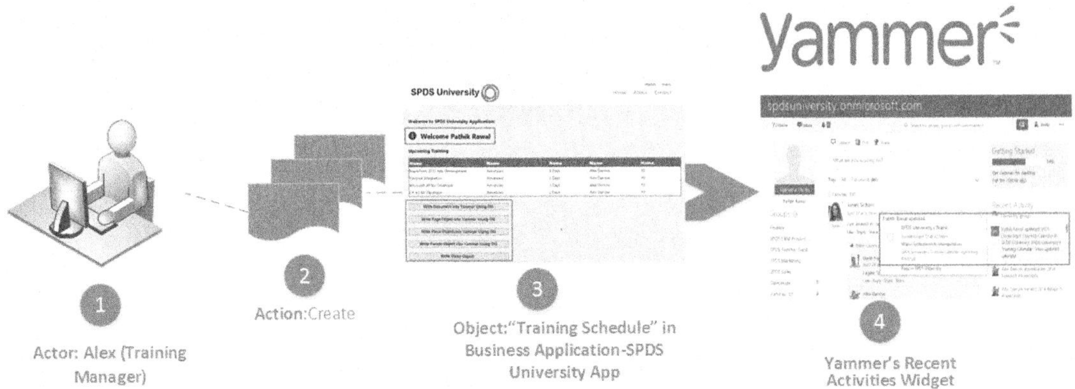

Figure 5-2. *Line-of-business application using Enterprise Social Graph to share information in real-time*

In Yammer Enterprise Social Graph, the "actors" are users, the "actions" are what users are working on, and the "objects" are applications used by users or the output created by users. The mapping shows how these three interact. The mappings derived using Enterprise Social Graph, as illustrated in Figure 5-2, are as follows:

1. **Actor**: Alex, the Training Manager, plans to share the "training schedule" with others using the SPDS University web application on an ASP.NET platform. The SPDS University web application is integrated into Yammer using the Enterprise Social Graph.
2. **Action**: Alex takes an action by creating a training schedule.
3. **Object**: A new "training schedule" object is created in the SPDS University web application hosted on ASP.NET.
4. Enterprise Social Graph creates a new activity on Yammer in the Recent Activity section.

Using Yammer, this mapping can be presented in a meaningful way using the Recent Activities widget so that users can discover information easily, as illustrated in Figure 5-2.

You'll learn more about the Recent Activities widget later in this chapter.

■ **Note** Enterprise Social Graph is similar to Facebook's social graph. Facebook's social graph connects people to people, photos, places, events, music, games, work, education, or universities; for example, "A user is watching (Action) the FIFA world cup final (an event)." Facebook records the actions of users and stores them into Open Graph as stories. These stories then can be shared on the user's newsfeed so that other users can discover information and collaborate easily.

Open Graph Protocol

As mentioned in the introduction, Yammer Enterprise Social Graph is an implementation of Open Graph (`http://ogp.me/`), and it's important for you to know what Open Graph is and how it can be used for Yammer integration with business applications.

Open Graph (OG) is a lightweight social data integration protocol that allows developers to define an activity and post it to Yammer as an Open Graph object. Open Graph provides:

- APIs to write data (activities) into Yammer on behalf of users from line-of-business applications
- Rich metadata around an object (page objects, place objects, person objects, and so on) that is uniquely identified by an URL
- Integration of business data into Yammer Enterprise Social Graphs
- Provision to configure custom Open Graph Objects that provide richer activities in terms of custom objects well suited for line-of-business applications

In other words, Open Graph is a strongly typed API consisting of objects and actions. Objects are the "nouns" or targets for actions taken by people in your app. For example, Anne Wallace uploaded the Microsoft Dynamics CRM 2015 User Guide to the SPDSUniversity app. The activity you write using Open Graph is displayed in the Recent Activity widget, as illustrated in Figure 5-3.

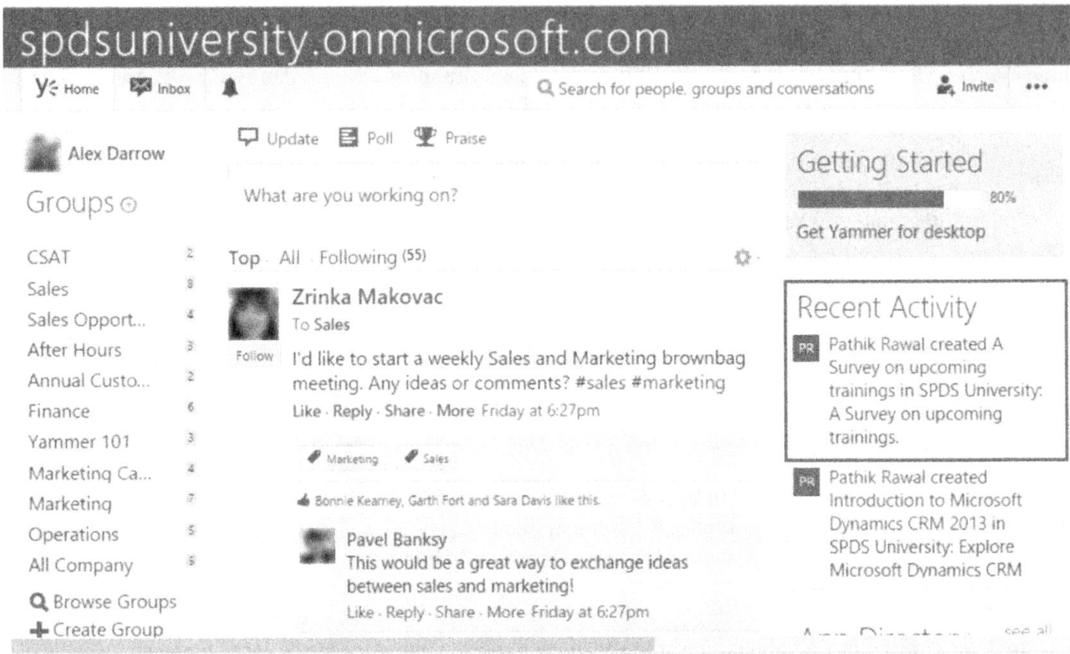

***Figure 5-3.** Enterprise Social Graph activities displayed in the Recent Activity widget*

■ **Tip** For general details on Open Graph outside of Yammer's implementation, check out `http://ogp.me/`.

When Open Graph activity is created and posted on Yammer, it's actual implementation is a JSON object that's posted to Yammer using a Yammer REST API. You will learn later in this chapter how to create Open Graph activities and post them on Yammer from external applications. Let's first explore how Open Graph activity is visualized on Yammer.

As of now, there are two ways that Open Graph activity is visualized on Yammer:

- Recent Activity widget
- Open Graph Activity Details page (OG Details page)

Both of these features are interlinked, where the Recent Activity widget gives users an overview of the activity and the OG Details page provides the details of the activity and related actions taken by users. Let's look at the details of each of these features.

Recent Activity Widget

The Recent Activity widget displays the most important activities on Yammer. Yammer's out-of-the-box features also use the Recent Activity widget to post people's latest activities. People's most important or latest updates are posted automatically to the Recent Activity stream, which is illustrated in Figure 5-4. This stream shows the activities of different users:

- Tyler Chessman has joined the network
- Dorena Paschke is now following David
- Dorena Paschke is now following Molly Dempsey

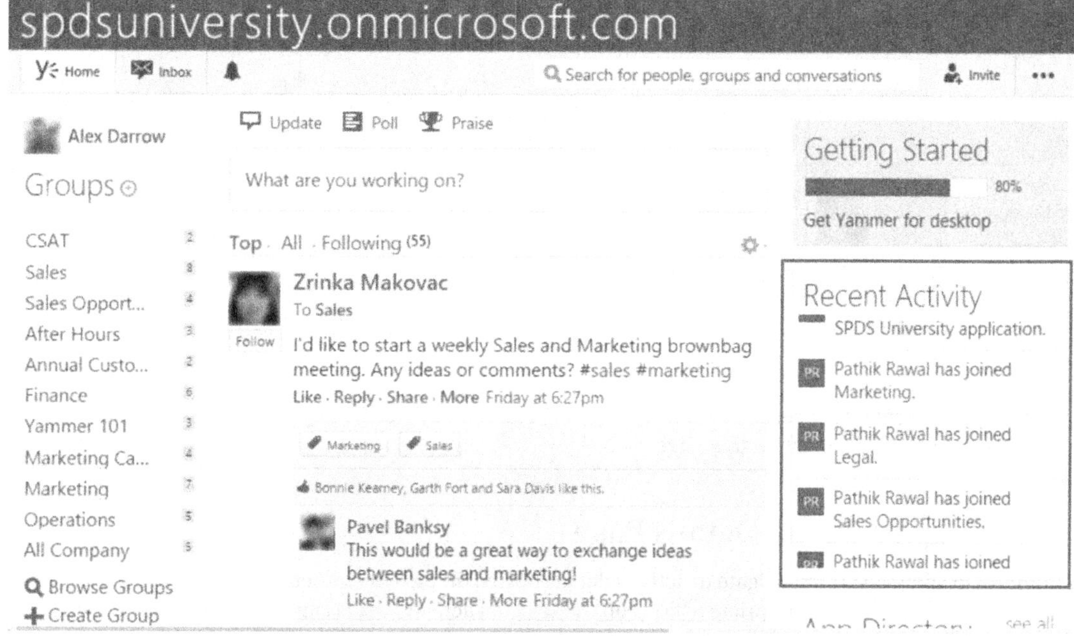

***Figure 5-4.** Yammer Recent Activity widget shows all the important activities on Yammer*

As mentioned, the Recent Activity widget can also be used by Open Graph to post the updates or actions taken in business applications. Figure 5-5 illustrates an activity that shows that Alex has viewed the Microsoft Dynamics CRM 2015 User Guide document and another post shows that Alex has downloaded the Microsoft Dynamics CRM 2015 User Guide document. In both cases, Anne was working on SharePoint and predefined integration points allowed updates to be shared on Yammer.

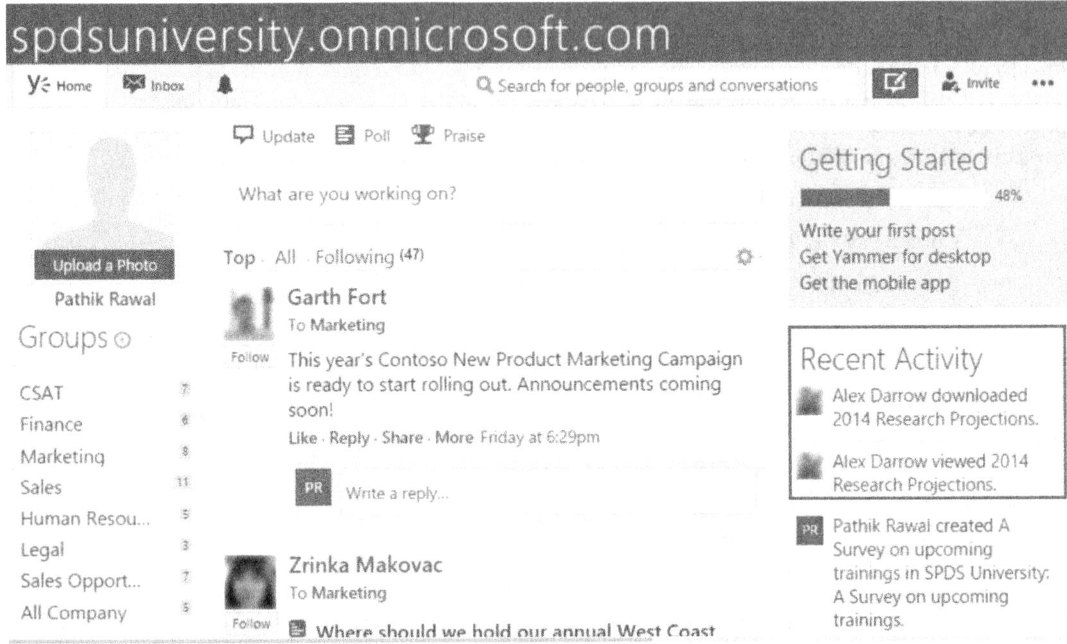

Figure 5-5. *Yammer Recent Activity widget also shows the important activities of a user from external applications*

The Recent Activity widget is linked to the Open Graph Activity Details page. The next section discusses how the activity details appear on that page.

Open Graph Activity Details Page

Yammer also allows users to navigate to activity details posted on the Recent Activity widget, where they can then collaborate and take appropriate actions on the selected activity. Users can comment on an activity, share the activity with others, create an announcement, praise someone, or create a poll. As illustrated in Figure 5-6, Alex Darrow has commented on Anne Wallace's activity, which is about an active document on SharePoint.

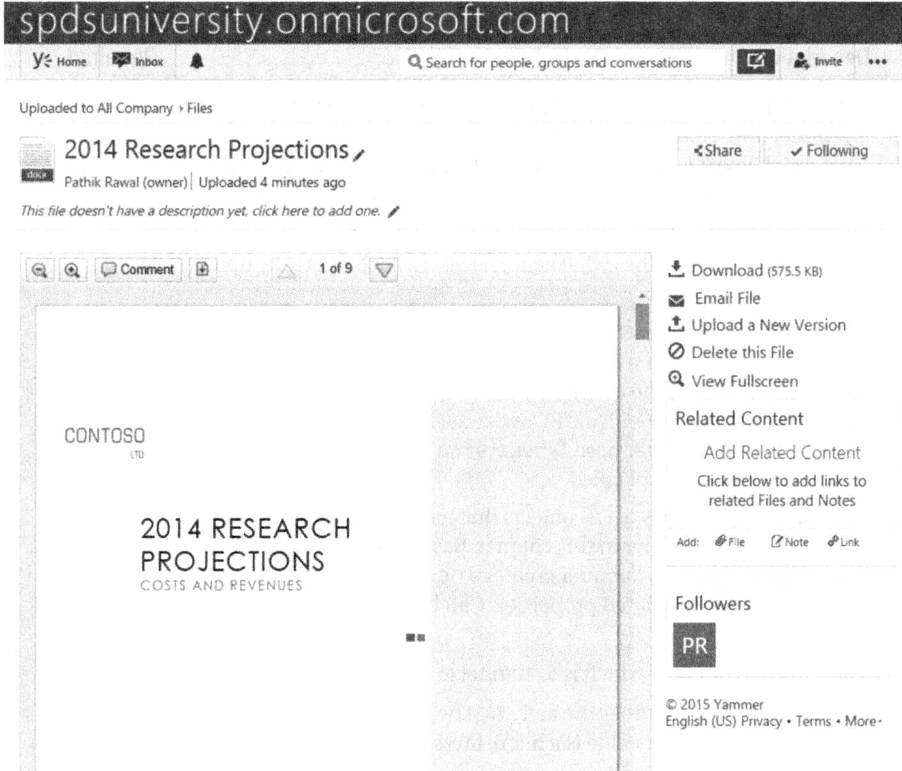

Figure 5-6. *Yammer Open Graph Activity Detail page*

So, hopefully you now understand the concept of Open Graph. Let's start with the technical aspects of Open Graph. First we explain the format used by Open Graph for creating an activity and the schema for posting Open Graph activity on Yammer. Then we will learn about the Yammer REST API endpoint used to deliver the Open Graph activity on Yammer with different examples.

Format of Open Graph Activity

Open Graph supports a standard format for Open Graph activity that developers should know how to write data into Yammer using the Open Graph protocol. Open Graph supports the following JSON format for integration:

```
<Actor> <Action> <Object> on <App Name>:<Message>
```

`Action` and `Object` are the main building blocks of an Open Graph activity. Actions are the Yammer actions that the user can perform, like creating files, deleting objects, liking, following, and so on. Objects are the nouns on which actions can be performed, like page, document, place, person, and so on.

Table 5-1. *Elements Specified in Open Graph Object Format*

Activity Elements	Description	Required
Actor	A user object represents the Yammer user who performs an action in a Yammer app. Here, the actor is the main character of an activity post to whom the post is delivered, along with others (depending on the delivery rules). If the actor is missing from the OG object, no post will be created on Yammer.	Yes
Action	It's the verb that describes what action is taken, such as create, update, delete, follow, and like.	Yes
Object	Also known as an Open Graph object (OG object). It represents a Yammer object such as a Page, Place, Person, Team, and Project, etc. This is the key of the activity on which action is taken and it's distinctively identified with a URL and associated title, which is displayed in the Yammer post. Whenever an activity is created, the Object value must be specified. There are various types of OG objects that have different properties. These are explained later in this chapter. Based on each object, which is sent with an activity, Yammer creates a new object if it does not exist and displays the associated properties. Can be a title of page, map of location, etc.	Yes
App Name	The name of your app, which is a channel to write data into Yammer.	Yes
Message	The message that describes the activity. The max length is 200 characters. The default value is a blank message.	Optional
User	A collection of user objects to whom the activity will be delivered or notify users who are part of the activity. Default is blank.	Optional

To understand Open Graph format, let's look at the following example. In Figure 5-7, the Open Graph object is a page named "New CRM Training" posted on Yammer using an the SPDSUniversity app by a user (actor) named Garret Vargas with the Create action.

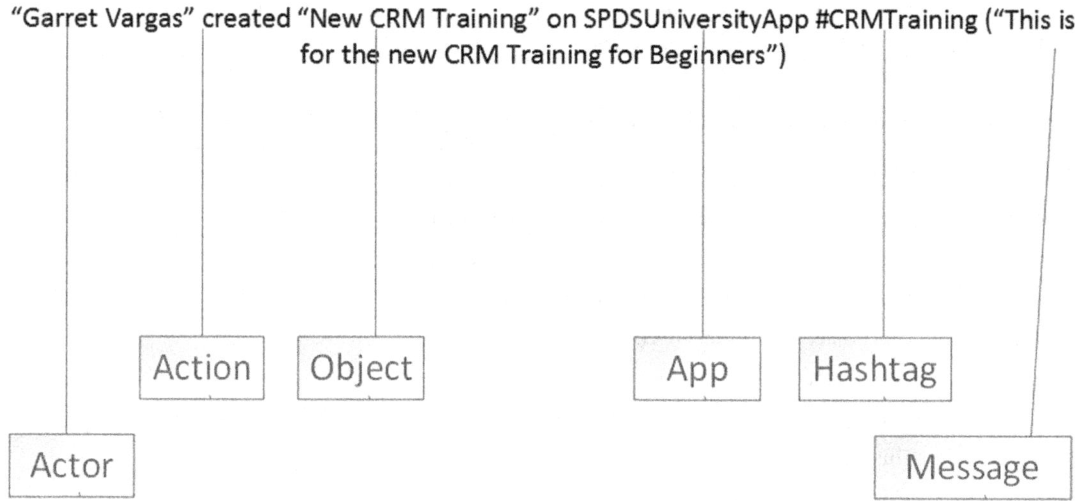

Figure 5-7. An example of Open Graph using the standard format

Now that you know the format of an Open Graph activity, let's look at the different schema of objects used to create and post an Open Graph activity on Yammer.

Open Graph Activity Objects Schema

Open Graph provides a very rich set of schemas. Open Graph supports built-in objects and actions, and developers can define custom objects and actions based on the requirements. In this section, we will explain the different supported object types, object attributes, supported actions on objects, and delivery rules that you can apply while creating a Yammer Open Graph activity from your line-of-business applications.

Supported Object Types

Let's look at the different supported object types in an Open Graph activity. Table 5-2 lists all supported object types.

Table 5-2. Supported Objects and Descriptions in an Open Graph Activity

Object	Description
page (default)	Represents a page in Yammer. You can refer to an external page that's hosted outside of Yammer. Yammer renders the page in Activity Detail view. The page object is the default object.
Place	This object type represents a place, such as a venue, a business, a landmark, or any other location that can be identified by longitude and latitude. This is useful when you're posting an activity related to events, parties, conferences, and so on, and you want to share the accurate location with users on Yammer. For example, for next company event, you want to share the extract map location. You can post this location on Yammer with an Open Graph object.
Person	This object type represents a person. It can be used when recognizing a colleague or informing others about someone using OG object.

There are additional Open Graph object types as mentioned in Table 5-3, and they can be used in similar ways as the standard supported object types.

Table 5-3. *Additional Objects Types and Descriptions in Open Graph Activity*

Object	Description
`Department`	This object type represents the user's department.
`Team`	This object type represents the user's hierarchy team.
`Project`	This object type represents the project.
`Folder`	This object type represents a folder within Yammer.
`File`	This object represents a file that can be a document, image, and so on.
`Document`	This object represents a document such as a PDF, word document, and so on.
`Image`	This object type represents an image object.
`Audio`	This object type represents an audio file.
`Video`	This object type represents a video file.

Open Graph Object Attributes

In the previous section, we learned that the object is an important component of Open Graph. The object supports multiple properties or attributes for different kinds of objects. These attributes provide information about the object that you are specifying in the Open Graph activity. So, it's ideal to specify as many attributes as you can specify when posting an Open Graph activity from your application.

For example, when you're sharing the latest news page on Yammer from your portal using the Open Graph protocol, you can specify the Title and Description as attributes of the page's object in an Open Graph activity. This will be displayed in Yammer's Recent Activity widget. Table 5-4 lists all standard attributes for an Open Graph object.

Table 5-4. *Open Graph Object's Attributes*

Object Attribute	Description
`URL`	Canonical URL of the object. This attribute is used as an ID of the object that uniquely identifies the object in the graph. (Required)
`Title`	Title of the object as it should appear in stories. (Optional)
`Type`	Reference to associated `OpenGraphObjectType`. (Optional)
`Image`	Thumbnail image that represents the object. (Optional)
`Description`	Description of the object in one or two sentences. (Optional)
`Site Name`	If the object you are creating is part of another object in the hierarchy (like a page object (child) in a site object or parent), this attribute is used as the name of the overall object. (Optional)
`Locale`	This attribute is used to specify the locale. This locale should be in the format `language_TERRITORY`. The default is `en_US`. (Optional)

Supported Actions on Object

Actions are the verb performed on the objects. With Yammer Open Graph objects, you must specify actions associated with an object. Table 5-5 describes the actions.

Table 5-5. *Supported Actions on Object*

Action	Description
Create	To create a new object.
Update	To update an existing object.
Delete	To delete an object.
Follow	To select the Follow tag on existing object.
Like	To select the Like tag on an existing object.

Apart from these standard actions, Yammer allows you to create custom actions as per your requirements. Later in this chapter, we will explain how to create custom actions associated with an object. Before that, let's look at different delivery rules that can be associated with an Open Graph activity.

Delivery Rules

The Open Graph object also supports adding delivery rules to the Open Graph activity. The delivery rules enable developers to target the recipients for the activity. Suppose you want to ensure that the activity you are posting is visible to specific users on Yammer. You can use the `private: true` parameter with an additional `user:` element to specify your target recipients.

The `private` parameter can be used to target the activity to certain recipients. By default, the `private` parameter is false but you can set it to true. In that case, the activity will be delivered only to the target users included in the activity "users" list and to the actor of the activity. Table 5-6 lists two important parameters for specifying a delivery rule for an activity.

Table 5-6. *Delivery Rules Parameter of an Activity*

Parameter	Description
`private:false` (default)	Activity will be delivered to everyone.
`private:true`	Activity will be delivered to target recipient specified by the `users:` element in the JSON string.

So far we have seen all the built-in objects defined by Yammer that are available globally (to all Yammer apps). However, you may wish to create a custom object that's more suitable for your line-of-business application.

Before exploring the Open Graph activity delivery REST endpoint, let's discuss the custom objects and actions.

Custom Objects and Actions

Open Graph enables developers to create custom objects and actions for a particular Yammer app. The custom objects and action TYPES you create are scoped to your Yammer app only. For example, the SPDSUniversity app may want to create `training_object:training_material` or `training_object:survey` objects to create richer activities.

Custom objects are very useful when you want to provide a reference to business processes associated with activities. For example, you are planning to integrate between Yammer and the company's CRM application and there is a need to post new sales opportunities to the Sales group on Yammer so that every Sales team member is notified. For this, you can create a custom Open Graph object in Yammer called `Opportunity` and post the information via the CRM application using the Yammer custom Open Graph object.

Later in this chapter (in Exercise 5-1), we will explain the custom activity implementation for the Yammer SPDSUniversity app.

You have learned about the Open Graph activity schema, but in order to post activities on Yammer, you need to understand the REST endpoint-related Open Graph activity. In next section. let's look at REST endpoint, which is used to deliver Open Graph activities to Yammer from line-of-business applications.

Delivery: The Open Graph Activity REST Endpoint

In order to post custom Open Graph objects as activities on Yammer, you need an endpoint that can do this. Yammer exposes a REST API endpoint that allows users to post or deliver activities on Yammer.

The REST API endpoint is:

```
https://www.yammer.com/api/v1/activity.json
```

In order to use this REST API endpoint, you need to create a JSON payload for the Open Graph activity. The OAUTH access token is then sent as the "bearer" in the "authorization" request handler and the content type is specified as `application/Json` in the request body. Figure 5-8 shows the request header as a JSON payload with a bearer token.

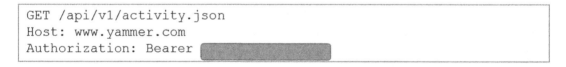

***Figure 5-8.** Request header with bearer token for an Open Graph activity endpoint*

■ **Note** To learn more about the "bearer" token, refer to `http://tools.ietf.org/html/draft-ietf-oauth-v2-bearer-23`.

Let's now look at different examples of creating an Open Graph activity.

Open Graph Implementation Examples

The following examples show how to create JSON for different types of Open Graph activities, which you can then use from line-of-business applications while posting data to Yammer.

Single Activity with Object Types and Actions as a JSON String (Public Object)

The following shows the JSON code for the Training Calendar activity created by Alex Darrow on the SPDSUniversity app. It includes the message, "Hi all, the training schedule is now available!"

```
{
"activity":{
"actor":{"name":"Pathik Rawal",
"email":"pr@spdsuniversity.onmicrosoft.com"},
"action":"create",
"object": {
"url":"https://spdsuniversity.sharepoint.com/sites/SPDS/Lists/Modern%20Calendar/calendar.
aspx ",
"title":"SPDS University's Training Calendar"
},
"message":"SPDS University's Training Calendar- View updated calendar!",
}
}
```

The activity is then posted on Yammer, as shown in Figure 5-9.

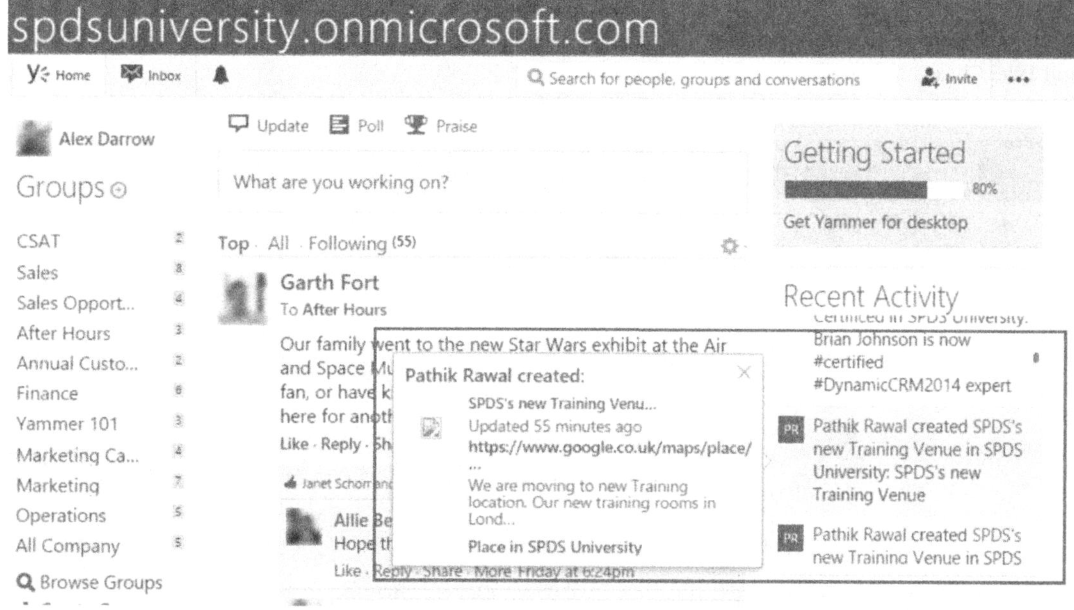

Figure 5-9. *Open Graph activiy delivered as a public post and visible to all in the Recent Activity widget*

Single Activity with Delivery Rules (Private Object)

We look at the previous example again, but this time the target recipients are specified with the `user:` element so that activities are visible to specified users only:

```
{
"activity":{
"actor":{"name":"Pathik Rawal",
"email":"pr@spdsuniversity.onmicrosoft.com"},
"action":"create",
"object": {
"url":"https://spdsuniversity.sharepoint.com/sites/SPDS/Lists/Modern%20Calendar/calendar.
aspx ",
"title":"SPDS University's Training Calendar"
},
"private":"true",
"message":"SPDS University's Training Calendar- View updated calendar!",
"users":[
  {"name":"Anne Wallace", "email":"annw@spdsuniversity.onmicrosoft.com"},
  {"name":"Tyler Chessman", "email":"tylerc@spdsuniversity.onmicrosoft.com"}
 ]
}
}
```

The activity is then posted on Yammer, as shown in Figure 5-10, and it will be visible to Anne Wallace and Tyler Chessman only.

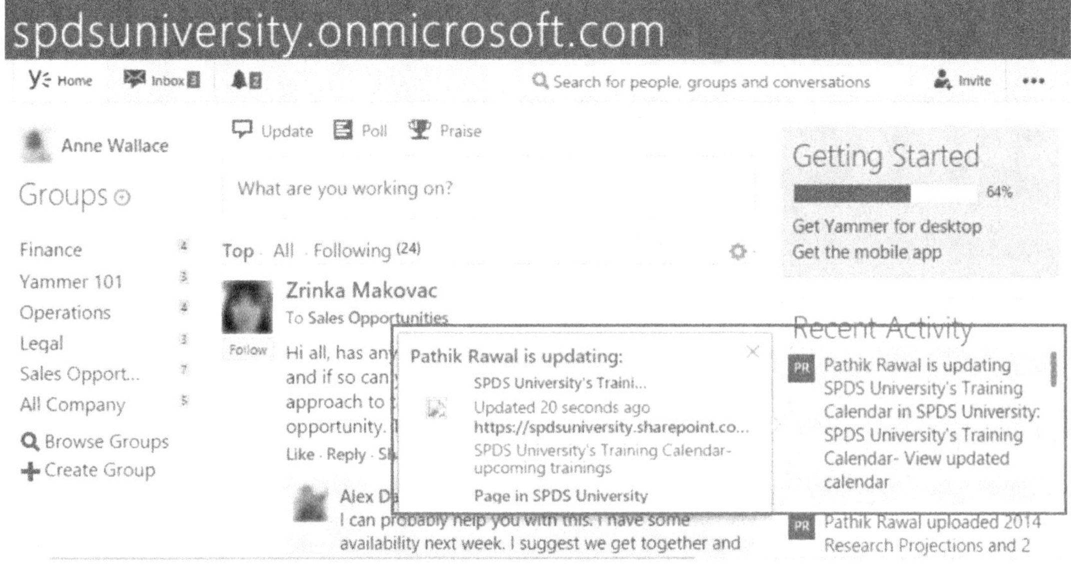

Figure 5-10. *Open Graph activity delivered as private and visible to Anne Wallace and Tyler Chessman only*

Multiple Activities

Yammer also allows developers to deliver multiple activities in one batch. When developers wrap multiple activities in one batch, this will prevent the client application from hitting the rate limit of the Yammer API. You will learn more about rate limits in Chapter 6. The following JSON code shows multiple activities wrapped in one batch:

```
{
"activity":{
"actor":{"name":"Pathik Rawal",
"email":"pr@spdsuniversity.onmicrosoft.com"},
"action":"create",
"object": {
"url":"https://spdsuniversity.sharepoint.com/sites/SPDS/Lists/Modern%20Calendar/calendar.
aspx ",
"title":"SPDS University's Training Calendar"
},
"message":"SPDS University's Training Calendar- View updated calendar!",
}
{
"activity":{
"actor":{"name":"Pathik Rawal",
"email":"pr@spdsuniversity.onmicrosoft.com"},
"action":"create",
"object": {
"url":"https://spdsuniversity.sharepoint.com/sites/SPDS/Lists/Modern%20Calendar/calendar.
aspx ",
"title":"SPDS University's Training Calendar"
},
"private":"true",
"message":"SPDS University's Training Calendar- View updated calendar!",
"users":[
  {"name":"Anne Wallace", "email":"annw@spdsuniversity.onmicrosoft.com"},
  {"name":"Tyler Chessman", "email":"tylerc@spdsuniversity.onmicrosoft.com"}
 ]
}
}
```

Case Study: Open Graph in the SPDSUniversity App

Finally it's time to do lab exercises to learn how to integrate line-of-business application with Yammer using Open Graph. In the first exercise, you learn how to create custom objects and actions in Yammer for the SPDSUniversity line-of-business application. In Exercise 5-2, you learn how to integrate ASP.NET web applications into Yammer using the Open Graph protocol.

Exercise 5-1 takes you through the process of creating objects and actions on an object.

EXERCISE 5-1: CREATE CUSTOM OPEN GRAPH OBJECTS FOR THE SPDSUNIVERSITY APP

In this exercise you learn to create Open Graph's custom objects. First take a look at Table 5-7, which describes custom objects and their actions used in this exercise.

Table 5-7. *Open Graph's Custom Objects and Actions*

Namespace	Object Types	Action Types
`training_object`	Seminar	Present: is creating Past: created
	Survey	Present: is creating Past: created
	training_material	Present: is creating Past: created
	training_monthly_calendar	Present: is creating Past: created
	training_video	Present: is creating Past: created

We will create the objects mentioned in Table 5-7 using the Yammer user interface. Let's start:

1. Navigate to `https://www.yammer.com/client_applications`.
2. Alternatively, you can navigate to the registered apps using the Ellipsis button (...) and then choose Created Apps from drop-down menu, as illustrated in Figure 5-11.

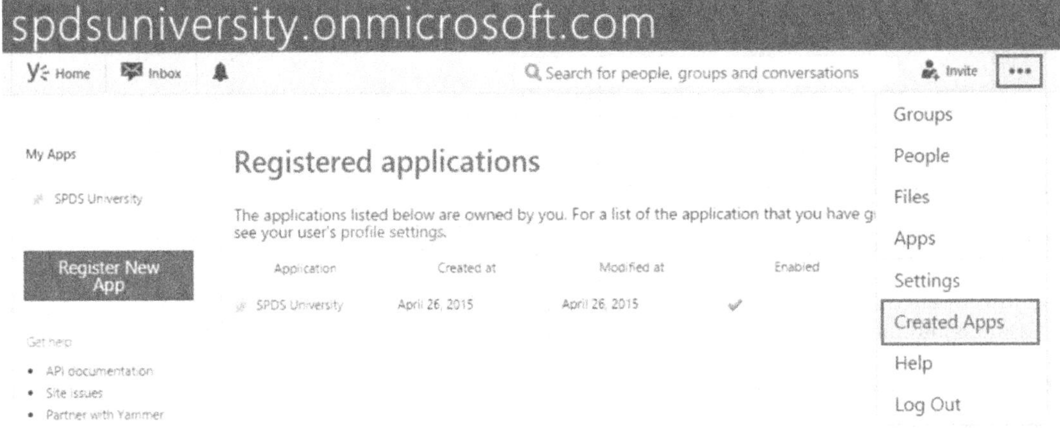

Figure 5-11. *Registered Applications view*

3. Click on the SPDSUniversity app from the Registered Application screen.
4. From the Yammer App configuration page, click on Open Graph on the left side of the screen.

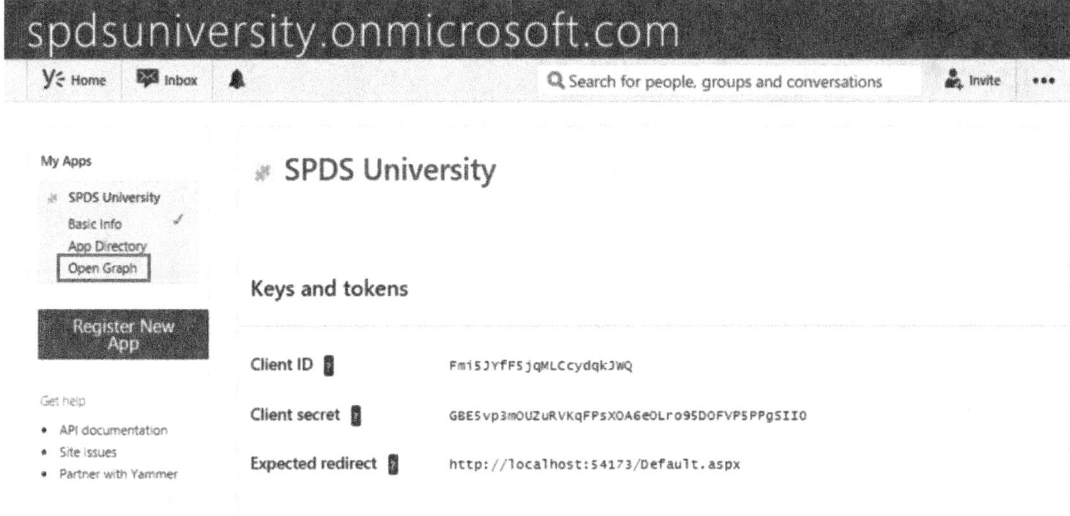

Figure 5-12. Yammer App configuration page

5. You will be presented with the screen shown in Figure 5-13. Enter `training_object` for the namespace of the custom Open Graph object.

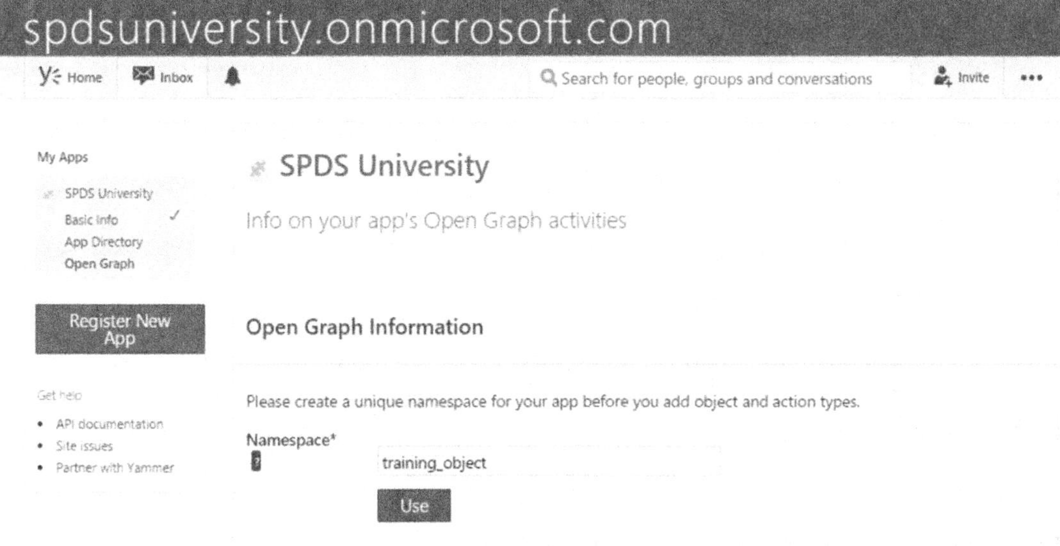

Figure 5-13. The Yammer app's Open Graph page to configure namespace

6. After entering the namespace, we will configure the object type called `seminar`. In the Type textbox, enter `seminar`. In the singular form, enter `a seminar` and the plural form should be `seminars`. Finally, click on Save.

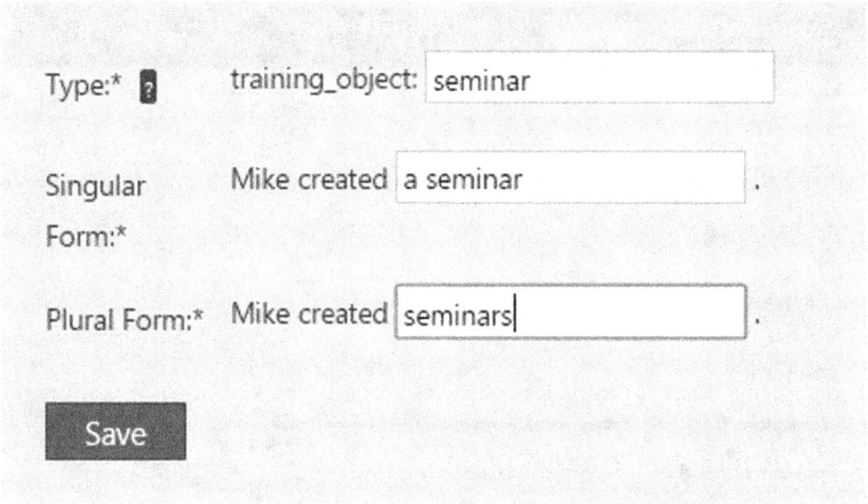

Figure 5-14. *The Yammer app's Open Graph types*

7. Configure the object type called `survey`. In the Type textbox, enter `survey`, and in singular form, enter `a survey`. The plural form should be `surveys`. Finally, click on Save.

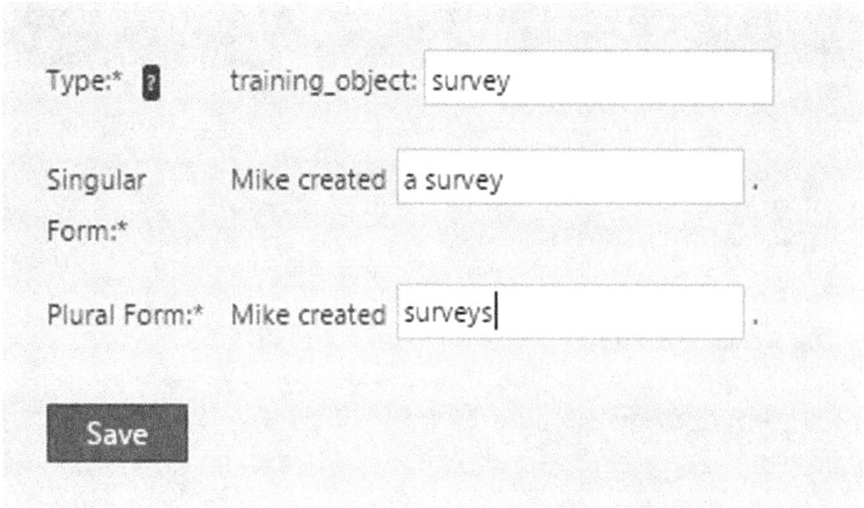

Figure 5-15. *The Yammer app's Open Graph type definitions*

8. Now you'll configure the object type called `training_material`. In the Type textbox, enter `training_material`. In the singular form, enter `a training material`. The plural form should be `training materials`. Then click on Save.

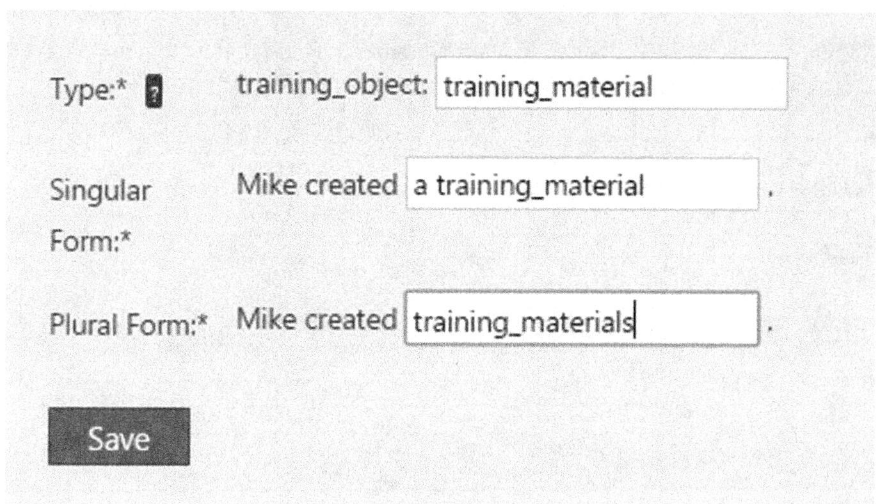

Figure 5-16. *The Yammer app's Open Graph type definitions*

9. In this step, you'll configure the object type called `training_monthly_calendar`. In the Type textbox, enter `a training monthly calendar`. In the singular form, enter `a training monthly calendar`. The plural form should be `training monthly calendars`. Then click on Save.

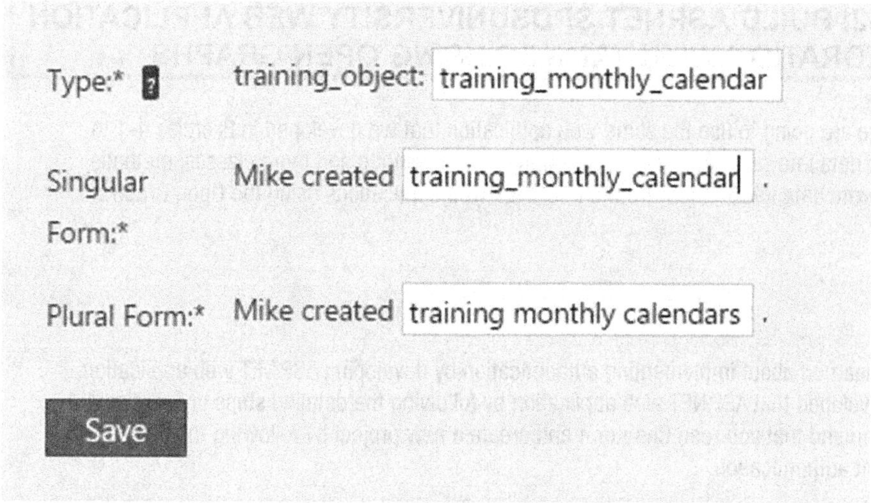

Type:* training_object: training_monthly_calendar

Singular Form:* Mike created training_monthly_calendar .

Plural Form:* Mike created training monthly calendars .

Save

Figure 5-17. *The Yammer app's Open Graph type definitions*

10. Now configure the object type called `training_video`, In the Type textbox, enter `training_video`. In the singular form, enter `a training video`. The plural form is `training videos`. Then click on Save.

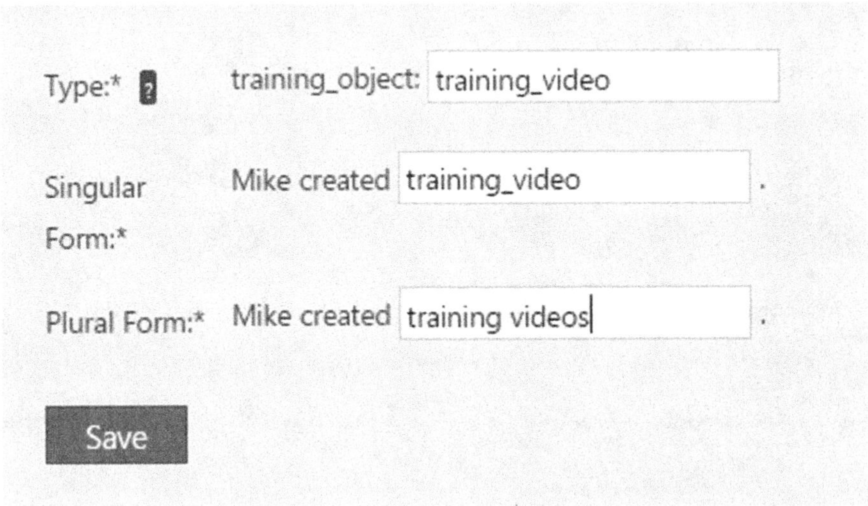

Figure 5-18. *The Yammer app's Open Graph types definitions*

At this point of time, you have successfully configured the Open Graph custom objects for the Yammer app called SPDSUniversity. We will use those objects in the next exercise to write data into Yammer's activity.

EXERCISE 5-2: BUILD ASP.NET SPDSUNIVERSITY WEB APPLICATION INTEGRATION WITH YAMMER USING OPEN GRAPHS

In this exercise, we are going to use the same web application that we developed in Exercise 4-1 to implement writing data into Yammer using Open Graph. We are going to add more classes, methods, and UI control to write data into Yammer from an ASP.NET web applications using the Open Graph protocol.

Open the Existing Project

In Chapter 4, you learned about implementing authentication by developing ASP.NET web application. If you have not developed that ASP.NET web application by following the detailed steps in Exercise 4-1, we strongly recommend that you read Chapter 4 and create a new project by following the step-by-step guide to implement authentication.

1. Launch Microsoft Visual Studio and open the existing project that you created in Exercise 4-1. The structure of the project should look like Figure 5-19.

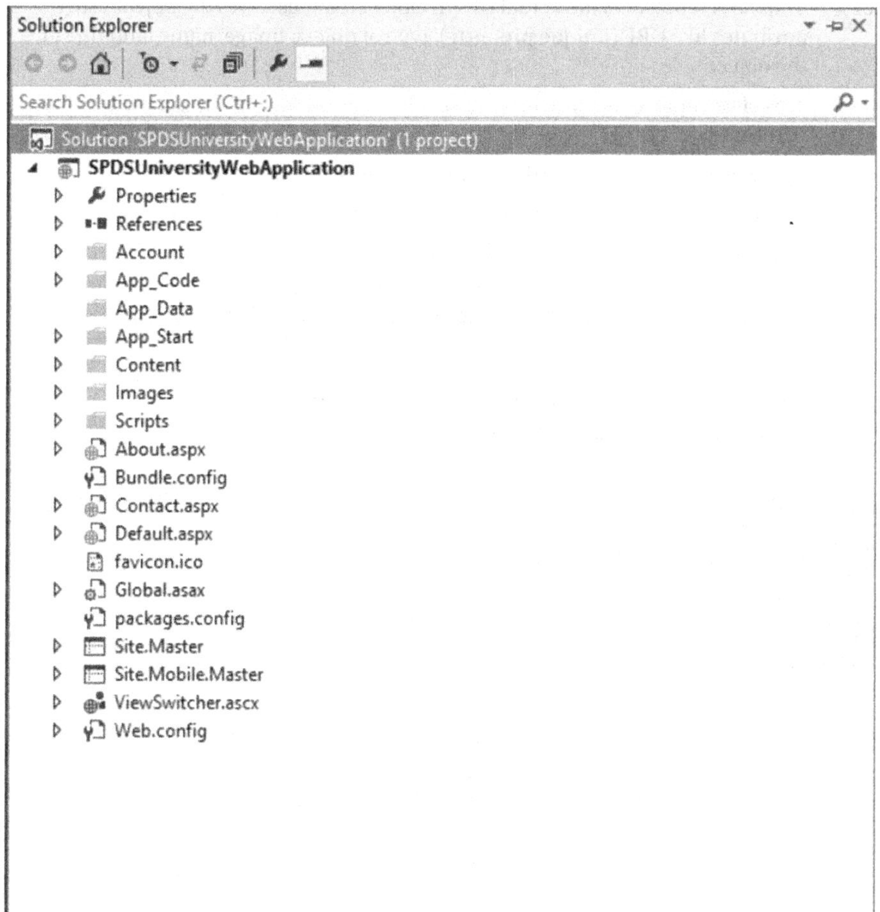

Figure 5-19. *Existing ASP.NET web application project structure developed in Exercise 4-1*

Classes for Yammer Activity

Yammer REST APIs exchange data using XML (Extensible Mark-Up Language) and JSON (JavaScript Object Notation) textual data formatting. When you make a request to Yammer, Yammer responds by returning XML or JSON data, depending on which data format you request. You can then parse that data and go joyfully on your programming way. We'll write a bunch of .NET classes that we can use to serialize and deserialize back and forth. Let's take a look at a few classes required at this stage.

Table 5-8. .NET Classes to Write Data into Yammer Using Open Graph

Class	Description
OG_GraphObj_Instance	This class represents the actual Graph Object that describes the object using attributes like URL (unique property), type of object, image, name, and title of the object.
OG_Actor	This class represents the actor—a user who acts on the object, using attributes name and email.
OG_Activity	This class represents the activity with attributes for actor and action.
OG_GraphObj	This class represents the activity object and a function to convert the object into a string.
YammerUtility	We have already designed this class in a previous chapter and we going to add few methods to this class to enhance the functionality of our web applications.

2. `OG_GraphObj_Instance.cs`: Add a class to the `App_Code` folder and name it `OG_GraphObj_Instance.cs`, as illustrated in Figure 5-20.

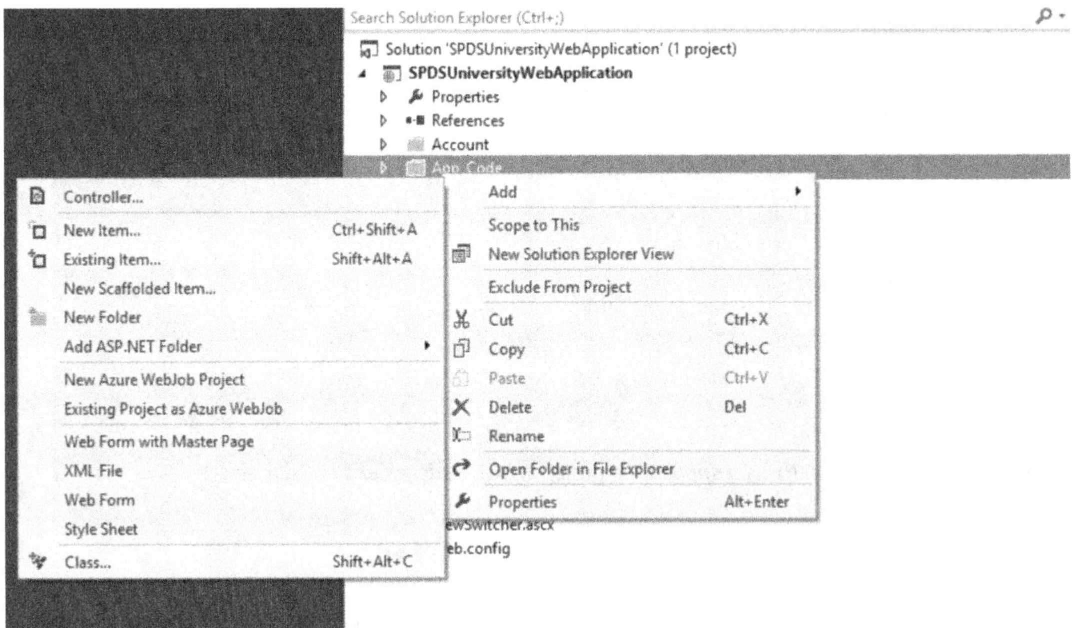

Figure 5-20. Add a new class to the project

3. Open the class file and add the following code to the class. This class defines properties such as URL, Type, Title, Image, and Description for the Open Graph object.

```
using System;
using System.Collections.Generic;
using System.Linq;
using System.Web;
using System.Xml.Serialization;
using System.Diagnostics;
using System.Runtime.Serialization;
using System.Runtime.Serialization.Json;

namespace SPDSUniversityWebApplication.App_Code
{
    /// <summary>
    /// This class represents the actual Graph Object which
    describes the object using attributes
    /// like URL (Unique property), type of object, image, name and
    title of the object
    /// </summary>
    [DataContract]
    public class OG_GraphObj_Instance
    {
        [DataMember(Name = "url")]
        public string Url { get; set; }

        [DataMember(Name = "type")]
        public string Type { get; set; }

        [DataMember(Name = "title")]
        public string Title { get; set; }

        [DataMember(Name = "image")]
        public string Image { get; set; }

        [DataMember(Name = "description")]
        public string Description { get; set; }
    }

}
```

An Open Graph object is the key piece of any activity. It represents an entity instance in your app, such as an URL, Title, Page, Place, Person, Team, Project, and Folder, and so on.

Table 5-9. *OG_GraphObj_Instance Class's Attributes*

Property	Description
URL	This URL property represents the URL of the object, such as the URL of the document path or the web URL.
Type	The type represents the object type, such as document, page, and link.
Title	The title property represents the title that will be shown in the recent activity widget.
Image	Represents an image that can be associated with an object.
Description	Represents the details description for the object.

4. `OG_Actor.cs`: Add another class to the `App_Code` folder and name it `OG_Actor.cs`. After that, open the class file and add the following code to the class. This class represents an actor, which defines properties such as name and email.

```
using System;
using System.Collections.Generic;
using System.Linq;
using System.Web;
using System.Runtime.Serialization;
using System.Runtime.Serialization.Json;
using System.IO;
using System.Xml.Serialization;
using System.Diagnostics;

namespace SPDSUniversityWebApplication.App_Code
{
    /// <summary>
    /// This class represents the Actor, user who acts on the
    object, using attributes name and email
    /// </summary>
    [DataContract]
    public class OG_Actor
    {
        [DataMember(Name = "name")]
        public string Name { get; set; }

        [DataMember(Name = "email")]
        public string Email { get; set; }

        public OG_Actor() { }

        public OG_Actor(string name, string email)
        {
            this.Name = name;
            this.Email = email;
        }
    }
}
```

The actor class defines the properties listed in Table 5-10.

Table 5-10. *OG_Actor Class's Attributes*

Property	Description
Name	This property represents the Yammer's username
Email	This property represents the Yammer user email as per the Yammer account.

5. OG_Activity.cs: Add another class to the App_Code folder and name it OG_Activity.cs. Open the class file and add the following code to the class. This class represents the actual Yammer activity that defines properties such as an instance of OG_Actor, an instance of OG_GraphObj_Instance, and a list object for users, messages, and actions such as create, update, delete, like, and follow.

```
using System;
using System.Collections.Generic;
using System.Linq;
using System.Web;
using System.Runtime.Serialization;
using System.Runtime.Serialization.Json;
using System.IO;
using System.Xml.Serialization;
using System.Diagnostics;

namespace SPDSUniversityWebApplication.App_Code
{
    /// <summary>
    /// Summary description for YammerOG_Activity
    /// </summary>
    [DataContract]
    public class OG_Activity
    {
        [DataMember(Name = "actor")]
        public OG_Actor Actor { get; set; }

        [DataMember(Name = "action")]
        public string Action { get; set; }

        [DataMember(Name = "object")]
        public OG_GraphObj_Instance Object { get; set; }

        [DataMember(Name = "message")]
        public string Message { get; set; }

        [DataMember(Name = "private")]
        public bool Private { get; set; }
```

```
        [DataMember(Name = "users")]
        public List<OG_Actor> Users { get; set; }

        public OG_Activity()
        {
            this.Actor = new OG_Actor();
            this.Object = new OG_GraphObj_Instance();
            this.Users = new List<OG_Actor>();
            this.Private = false;
        }
    }
}
```

Table 5-11. *OG_Activity Class's Attributes*

Property	Description
`Action`	This property represents the action on an object, such as Create, Update, Delete, Like, and Follow.
`Message`	This property represents the message for the activity post, such as "This is for the new sales proposal".
`Private`	This property represents the visibility of the pot, whether you want to mark it as private or public.
`Users`	This property represents the user collection object in which more users can be added to the activity who will be notified when this activity is posted.
`Actor`	This property represents a user who performing the activity.
`Object`	The object property represents the `OG_GraphObj_Instance`, which is described in the `OG_GraphObj_Instance.css` class, which contains properties like URL, Title, Description, Image, and the types.

6. `OG_GraphObj.cs`: Finally, add a class to the `App_Code` folder and name it `OG_GraphObj.cs` to the project and add the following code to the class file:

```
using System;
using System.Collections.Generic;
using System.Linq;
using System.Web;
using System.Runtime.Serialization;
using System.Runtime.Serialization.Json;
using System.IO;
using System.Xml.Serialization;
using System.Diagnostics;

namespace SPDSUniversityWebApplication.App_Code
{
    /// <summary>
    /// This class represents the Activity Object and a function to
convert object into string
```

```
    /// </summary>
    [DataContract]
    public class OG_GraphObj
    {
        [DataMember(Name = "activity")]
        public OG_Activity Activity { get; set; }

        public OG_GraphObj()
        {
            this.Activity = new OG_Activity();
        }

        public override string ToString()
        {
            string jsonData = string.Empty;

            try
            {
                DataContractJsonSerializer ys = new DataContractJson
                Serializer(typeof(OG_GraphObj));
                MemoryStream msBack = new MemoryStream();
                ys.WriteObject(msBack, this);
                msBack.Position = 0;
                StreamReader sr = new StreamReader(msBack);
                jsonData = sr.ReadToEnd();

                //replace \\ with / as in jsonData
                jsonData = jsonData.Replace("\\/", "/");
            }
            catch (Exception ex)
            {
                Debug.WriteLine("An Error occurred in serializing
                into string: " + ex.Message);
            }

            return jsonData;
        }
    }
}
```

7. `YammerUtility.cs`: This sample application has a class (`YammerUtility.cs`) that contains all common methods to support the integration. Open `YammerUtility.cs`.

8. Add the following namespace in the `YammerUtility.cs` file:

```
using System.Text;
```

9. Add the following to the class named `PostRequesttoYammer` in `YammerUtility.cs`:

```
/// <summary>
///
/// </summary>
/// <param name="postBody"></param>
/// <param name="url"></param>
/// <param name="authHeader"></param>
/// <param name="contentType"></param>
/// <returns></returns>
public static string PostRequesttoYammer(string postBody, string url,
string authHeader = null, string contentType = null)
{
    string results = string.Empty;

    try
    {

        HTTPWebReq = WebRequest.CreateHttp(url);
        HTTPWebReq.Method = "POST";

        if (!string.IsNullOrEmpty(authHeader))
            HTTPWebReq.Headers.Add("Authorization",
            "Bearer " + authHeader);

        byte[] postByte = Encoding.UTF8.GetBytes(postBody);

        if (string.IsNullOrEmpty(contentType))
            HTTPWebReq.ContentType = "application/
            x-www-form-urlencoded";
        else
            HTTPWebReq.ContentType = contentType;

        HTTPWebReq.ContentLength = postByte.Length;
        Stream postStream = HTTPWebReq.GetRequestStream();
        postStream.Write(postByte, 0, postByte.Length);
        postStream.Close();

        HTTPWebRes = (HttpWebResponse)HTTPWebReq.GetResponse();
        postStream = HTTPWebRes.GetResponseStream();
        StreamReader postReader = new StreamReader(postStream);

        results = postReader.ReadToEnd();

        postReader.Close();
        postStream.Close();
    }
    catch (Exception ex)
    {
    }

    return results;
}
```

This method takes four parameters, as described in Table 5-12.

Table 5-12. *PostRequesttoYammer Method's Parameters*

Property	Description
postBody	The actual body of the post. For Open Graph, the string should be in the <Actor> <Action> <Object> on <App Name>: <Message> format.
url	The endpoint URL of the Yammer API. In this case, it is `https://www.yammer.com/api/v1/activity.json`.
authHeader	The access token received so the user can make subsequent calls.
contentType	The content type HTTP web request object. In this case, it's `application/x-www-form-urlencoded`.

Posting Object Type: Document

`Default.aspx`: You have added all the necessary classes to the `App_Code` folder, so now it's time to add the user interface to the web page. This includes adding a button to the `default.aspx` page, which will include an `on click` event to trigger the method to write data into Yammer using Open Graph.

10. In the `App_Data` folder, add the following XML and name it `Courses.xml`:

```
<?xml version="1.0" encoding="utf-8" ?>
<Courses>
  <Course>
    <Name>SharePoint 2013 App Development</Name>
    <Level>Advanced</Level>
    <Duration>3 Days</Duration>
    <Trainer>Alex Darrow</Trainer>
    <Noofseats>10</Noofseats>
  </Course>
  <Course>
    <Name>Yammer Integration</Name>
    <Level>Advanced</Level>
    <Duration>3 Days</Duration>
    <Trainer>Alex Darrow</Trainer>
    <Noofseats>10</Noofseats>
  </Course>
  <Course>
    <Name>Microsoft AX for Developer</Name>
    <Level>Advanced</Level>
    <Duration>3 Days</Duration>
    <Trainer>Alex Darrow</Trainer>
    <Noofseats>10</Noofseats>
  </Course>
  <Course>
```

```
    <Name>C# 4.5 for Developer</Name>
    <Level>Advanced</Level>
    <Duration>2 Days</Duration>
    <Trainer>Alex Darrow</Trainer>
    <Noofseats>10</Noofseats>
  </Course>
</Courses>
```

11. Add the following `<div>` control in `Default.aspx`, just after `</ol>`.

```
<div id="CourseDiv" runat="server">
        <h3>Upcoming Training </h3>
        <p>
            <asp:XmlDataSource ID="XmlDataSourceCourse"
            runat="server" DataFile="~/App_Data/Courses.xml"></
            asp:XmlDataSource>

            <asp:GridView ID="GridView1" runat="server" XPath="/
            Employees/Employee" DataSourceID="XmlDataSourceCourse"
                AutoGenerateColumns="False" HeaderStyle-
                BackColor="#3AC0F2" HeaderStyle-ForeColor="White"
                BackColor="White" BorderColor="#336666"
                BorderStyle="Double" BorderWidth="3px"
                CellPadding="4" GridLines="Horizontal"
                Height="124px" Width="985px">
                <Columns>
                    <asp:TemplateField HeaderText="Name"
                     HeaderStyle-Width="50">
                        <ItemTemplate>
                            <%# XPath("Name") %>
                        </ItemTemplate>

<HeaderStyle Width="50px"></HeaderStyle>
                    </asp:TemplateField>
                    <asp:TemplateField HeaderText="Name"
                    HeaderStyle-Width="50">
                        <ItemTemplate>
                            <%# XPath("Level") %>
                        </ItemTemplate>

<HeaderStyle Width="50px"></HeaderStyle>
                    </asp:TemplateField>
                    <asp:TemplateField HeaderText="Name"
                    HeaderStyle-Width="50">
                        <ItemTemplate>
                            <%# XPath("Duration") %>
                        </ItemTemplate>
```

```
<HeaderStyle Width="50px"></HeaderStyle>
                    </asp:TemplateField>
                    <asp:TemplateField HeaderText="Name"
                    HeaderStyle-Width="50">
                        <ItemTemplate>
                            <%# XPath("Trainer") %>
                        </ItemTemplate>

<HeaderStyle Width="50px"></HeaderStyle>
                    </asp:TemplateField>
                       <asp:TemplateField HeaderText="Name"
                       HeaderStyle-Width="50">
                        <ItemTemplate>
                            <%# XPath("Noofseats") %>
                        </ItemTemplate>

<HeaderStyle Width="50px"></HeaderStyle>
                    </asp:TemplateField>

                </Columns>
                <FooterStyle BackColor="White" ForeColor="#333333" />

                <HeaderStyle BackColor="#336666" ForeColor="White"
                Font-Bold="True"></HeaderStyle>
                <PagerStyle BackColor="#336666" ForeColor="White"
                HorizontalAlign="Center" />
                <RowStyle BackColor="White" ForeColor="#333333" />
                <SelectedRowStyle BackColor="#339966" Font-
                Bold="True" ForeColor="White" />
                <SortedAscendingCellStyle BackColor="#F7F7F7" />
                <SortedAscendingHeaderStyle BackColor="#487575" />
                <SortedDescendingCellStyle BackColor="#E5E5E5" />
                <SortedDescendingHeaderStyle BackColor="#275353" />
            </asp:GridView>
        </p>

    </div>
```

12. Add the following key in `<AppSettings>` in the `web.config` file.

```
<add key="activityURL" value="https://www.yammer.com/api/v1/activity.json" />
```

13. Add the following HTML markup for a button in the `Default.aspx` file.

```
<table>
    <tr><td><asp:Button ID="btnWriteDataOG" CssClass="button" runat="server"
OnClick="btnWriteDataOG_Click" Text="Write Document into Yammer Using OG"
Width="363px" /></td></tr>
</table>
```

The button will look like the one shown in Figure 5-21.

Name	Name	Name	Name	Name
SharePoint 2013 App Development	Advanced	3 Days	Alex Darrow	10
Yammer Integration	Advanced	3 Days	Alex Darrow	10
Microsoft AX for Developer	Advanced	3 Days	Alex Darrow	10
C# 4.5 for Developer	Advanced	2 Days	Alex Darrow	10

Figure 5-21. *The Write Document button*

14. `Default.aspx.cs`: You will now add the code in the code-behind file `Default.aspx.cs`, which is a button's click event handler code to create the Open Graph object by using the classes you created in the previous steps. The following code creates an object of the class `OG_GraphObj` and assigns values to properties like actor, message, and actions. The next few lines create an instance of the class `YammerGraphObjectInstance`, which is used to specify the URL property, the title of the activity, the description of the activity, including an image and type of object (document).

```
/// <summary>
        /// Event Handler to write Document object
        /// </summary>
        /// <param name="sender"></param>
        /// <param name="e"></param>
        protected void btnWriteDataOG_Click(object sender, EventArgs e)
        {
            SPDSUniversityWebApplication.App_Code.OG_GraphObj
            yammergraphobject = new SPDSUniversityWebApplication.
            App_Code.OG_GraphObj();
```

```
    yammergraphobject.Activity.Actor = new
    SPDSUniversityWebApplication.App_Code.OG_Actor("Pathik
    Rawal", "pr@spdsuniversity.onmicrosoft.com");
    yammergraphobject.Activity.Message = "Learn the sales
    process in Microsoft Dynamics CRM.";
    yammergraphobject.Activity.Action = "create";

    SPDSUniversityWebApplication.App_Code.OG_
    GraphObj_Instance yammergraphobjectinst = new
    SPDSUniversityWebApplication.App_Code.OG_GraphObj_
    Instance();

    yammergraphobjectinst.Url = "https://
    spdsuniversity.sharepoint.com/_layouts/15/
    WopiFrame.aspx?sourcedoc=%7B7614951D-3C30-
    4924-B815-1354570EE805%7D&file=2014%20Expenses.
    xlsx&action=default";
    yammergraphobjectinst.Title = "Microsoft Dynamics CRM
    2015 User Guide";
    yammergraphobjectinst.Description = "Microsoft Dynamics
    CRM 2015 User Guide";
    yammergraphobjectinst.Image = "https://www.yammer.com/
    api/v1/uploaded_files/29860625/version/28812608/preview/
    UAPP_LOGO.png";
    yammergraphobjectinst.Type = "document";

    yammergraphobject.Activity.Object = yammergraphobjectinst;

    string postData = yammergraphobject.ToString();
    string activityURL = WebConfigurationManager.
    AppSettings["activityURL"];
    string response = SPDSUniversityWebApplication.App_Code.
    YammerUtility.PostRequesttoYammer(postData, activityURL,
    txtaccesstoken.Text.ToString(), "application/json");

}
```

When the page is posted to Yammer using Open Graph, the post will look like Figure 5-22, showing the Recent Activity view.

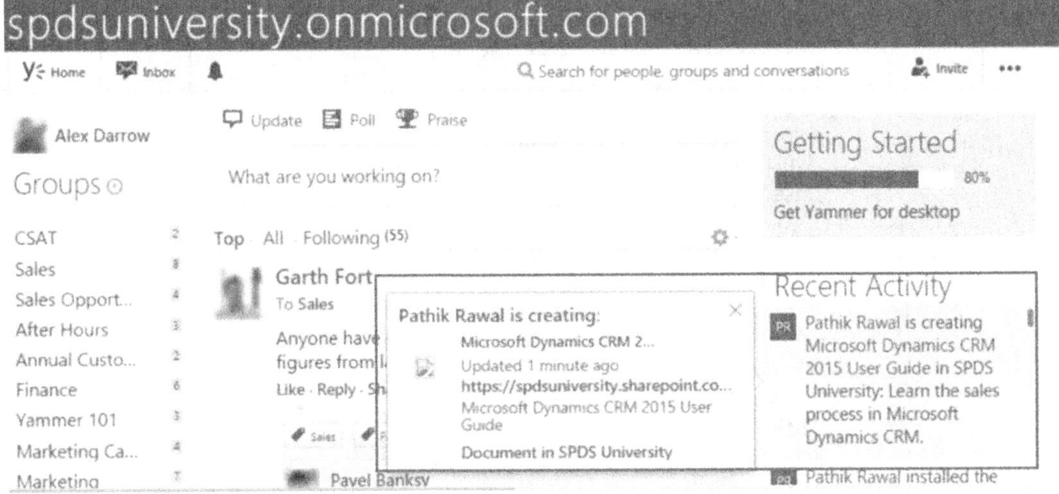

Figure 5-22. *Document Object activity on Yammer*

Posting Object Type: Page

The Page Object type represents a web page that can be posted as an object into Yammer using the Open Graph. The important object attributes for page are URL of the Page, Title, and Description, Image, and Type.

Action type: Create, Update, and Delete can be used on object page. Use the right action term provided in the code snippet (such as `action: create`, `action: update`, and `action: delete`).

15. Add the Write Page Object into Yammer Using OG button to the markup in `Default.aspx` below the button control in the previous step.

```
<tr><td><asp:Button ID="btnWriteDataOGPage" runat="server"
OnClick="btnWriteDataOGPage_Click" Text="Write Page Object into
Yammer Using OG" Width="363px" /></td></tr>
```

The button will look like the one shown in Figure 5-23.

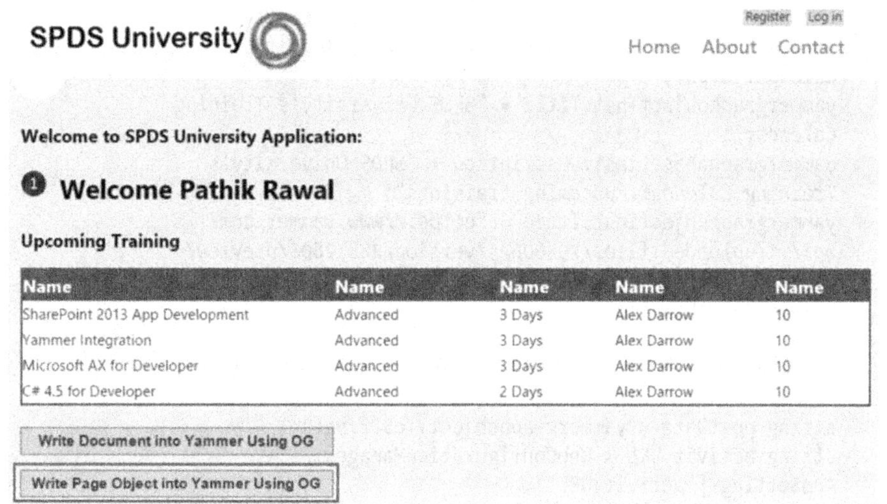

Figure 5-23. *The Write Page Object button*

16. Add a button click event in `Default.aspx.cs`. Add the following code to `Default.aspx.cs`:

```
/// <summary>
        /// Write a Page Object into Yammer.
        /// </summary>
        /// <param name="sender"></param>
        /// <param name="e"></param>
        protected void btnWriteDataOGPage_Click(object sender,
        EventArgs e)
        {
            SPDSUniversityWebApplication.App_Code.OG_GraphObj
            yammergraphobject = new SPDSUniversityWebApplication.
            App_Code.OG_GraphObj();

            yammergraphobject.Activity.Actor = new
            SPDSUniversityWebApplication.App_Code.OG_Actor
            ("Pathik Rawal", "pr@spdsuniversity.onmicrosoft.com");
            yammergraphobject.Activity.Message = "SPDS University's
            Training Calendar- View updated calendar";
            yammergraphobject.Activity.Action = "create";

            SPDSUniversityWebApplication.App_Code.OG_GraphObj_Instance
            yammergraphobjectinst = new SPDSUniversityWebApplication.
            App_Code.OG_GraphObj_Instance();
```

```
        yammergraphobjectinst.Url = "https://spdsuniversity.
        sharepoint.com/sites/SPDS/Lists/Modern%20Calendar/
        calendar.aspx";
        yammergraphobjectinst.Title = "SPDS University's Training
        Calendar";
        yammergraphobjectinst.Description = "SPDS University's
        Training Calendar- upcoming trainings";
        yammergraphobjectinst.Image = "https://www.yammer.com/
        api/v1/uploaded_files/29860625/version/28812608/preview/
        UAPP_LOGO.png";
        yammergraphobjectinst.Type = "page";

        yammergraphobject.Activity.Object = yammergraphobjectinst;

        string postData = yammergraphobject.ToString();
        string activityURL = WebConfigurationManager.
        AppSettings["activityURL"];
        string response = SPDSUniversityWebApplication.App_Code.
        YammerUtility.PostRequesttoYammer(postData, activityURL,
        txtaccesstoken.Text.ToString(), "application/json");

    }
```

Table 5-13. *Object Attribute for a Page Object*

Object Attribute	Description
`Title`	This property represents the title of the page.
`URL`	This property represents the URL of the page.
`Image`	Thumbnail image displayed as a title.
`Description`	Page description.

When the page is posted to Yammer using Open Graph, the post will look as shown in Figure 5-24, the Recent Activity view.

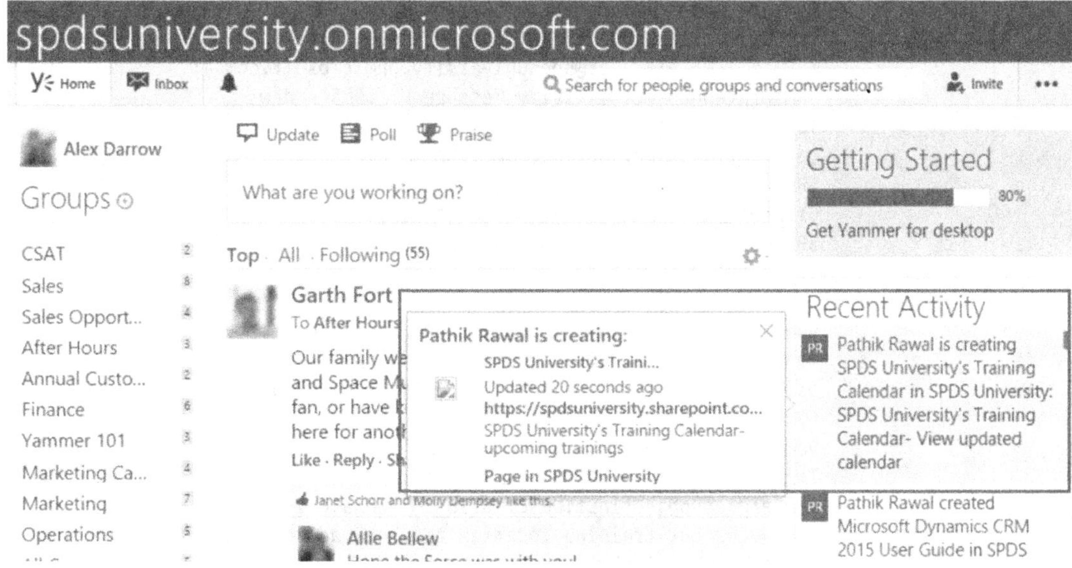

***Figure 5-24.** Page Object activity on Yammer*

Posting Object Type: Place

The Page Object type represents a place that can be posted as an object into Yammer using Open Graph. This object type represents a place—such as a venue, a business, a landmark, or any other location—that can be identified by longitude and latitude.

17. Add the Write Place Object into Yammer Using OG button markup in `Default.aspx`, below the button you added in the previous step.

```
<tr><td><asp:Button ID="btnWriteDataOGPlace" runat="server"
OnClick="btnWriteDataOGPlace_Click" Text="Write Place Object into
Yammer Using OG" Width="363px" /></td></tr>
```

18. Add a button click event in `Default.aspx.cs`. Add the following code to `Default.aspx.cs`.

```
/// <summary>
        ///  Write a Place Object into Yammer.
        /// </summary>
        /// <param name="sender"></param>
        /// <param name="e"></param>
        protected void btnWriteDataOGPlace_Click(object sender,
        EventArgs e)
        {
            SPDSUniversityWebApplication.App_Code.OG_GraphObj
            yammergraphobject = new SPDSUniversityWebApplication.
            App_Code.OG_GraphObj();
```

```
        yammergraphobject.Activity.Actor = new
        SPDSUniversityWebApplication.App_Code.OG_Actor
        ("Pathik Rawal", "pr@spdsuniversity.onmicrosoft.com");
        yammergraphobject.Activity.Message = "SPDS's new
        Training Venue";
        yammergraphobject.Activity.Action = "create";
        SPDSUniversityWebApplication.App_Code.OG_
        GraphObj_Instance yammergraphobjectinst = new
        SPDSUniversityWebApplication.App_Code.OG_
        GraphObj_Instance();

        yammergraphobjectinst.Url = "https://www.google.co.uk/
        maps/place/Oxford+St,+London/@51.5154003,-0.1412821,17z/
        data=!3m1!4b1!4m2!3m1!1s0x48761ad554c335c1:0xda2164b934c
        67c1a?hl=en";
        yammergraphobjectinst.Title = "SPDS's new
        Training Venue";
        yammergraphobjectinst.Description = "We are in process
        of moving our training location to a new address in the
        heart of the city";
        yammergraphobjectinst.Image = "https://www.yammer.com/
        api/v1/uploaded_files/29860625/version/28812608/preview/
        UAPP_LOGO.png";
        yammergraphobjectinst.Type = "place";
        yammergraphobject.Activity.Object =
        yammergraphobjectinst;
        string postData = yammergraphobject.ToString();
        string activityURL = WebConfigurationManager.
        AppSettings["activityURL"];
        string response = SPDSUniversityWebApplication.App_Code.
        YammerUtility.PostRequesttoYammer(postData, activityURL,
        txtaccesstoken.Text.ToString(), "application/json");

    }
```

Table 5-14. *Object Attribute for a Place Object*

Object Attribute	Description
`Title`	This property represents the title of the place.
`URL`	This property represents the URL of the place, possibly the maps in Google.
`Image`	Thumbnail image displayed as a title.
`Description`	Page description.

When the place is posted to Yammer using Open Graph, the post will look like Figure 5-25, which shows the activity details view. Figure 5-26 shows the Activity Details page.

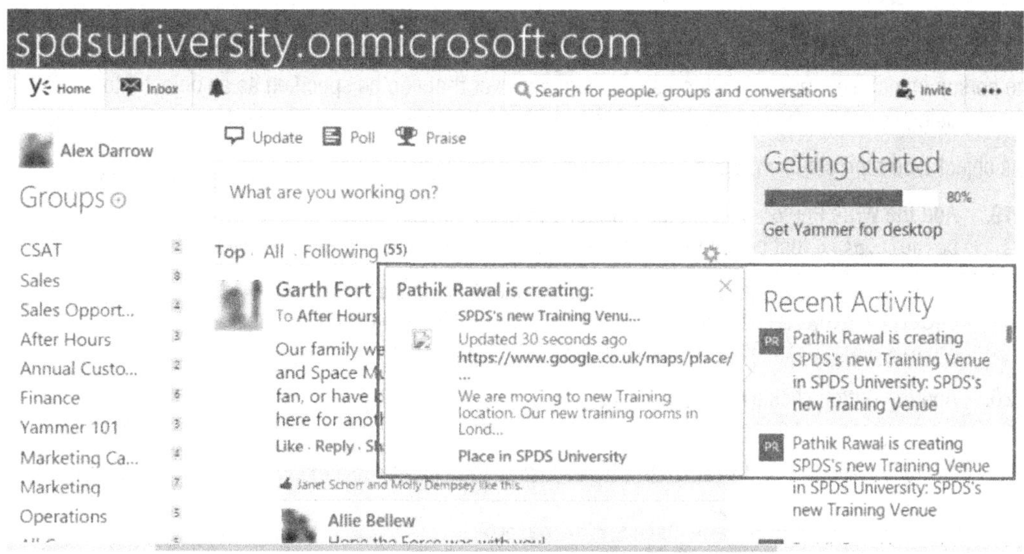

Figure 5-25. *Yammer Open Graph activity showing a place object*

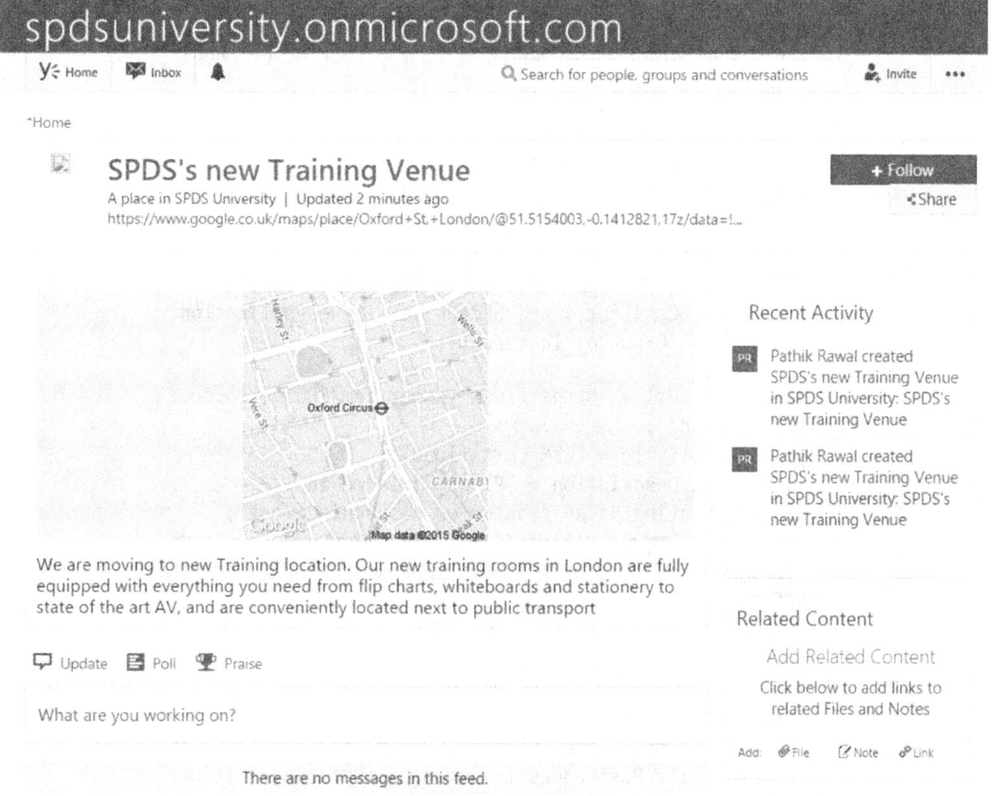

Figure 5-26. *Yammer Open Graph activity showing a place object in detail view*

Posting Object Type: Person

The person object type represents a person or Yammer user that can be specified as an object into Yammer using Open Graph.

This object type represents a person.

19. Add the Write Person Object into Yammer Using OG button markup in `Default.aspx`, just below the button markup you added in the previous step.

```
<tr><td><asp:Button ID="btnWriteDataOGPerson" runat="server"
OnClick="btnWriteDataOGPerson_Click" Text="Write Person Object
into Yammer Using OG" Width="363px"  /></td></tr>
```

20. Add the button click event in `Default.aspx.cs`.

```
/// <summary>
        /// Write Data into Yammer using object type Person
        /// </summary>
        /// <param name="sender"></param>
        /// <param name="e"></param>
        protected void btnWriteDataOGPerson_Click(object sender,
        EventArgs e)
        {
            SPDSUniversityWebApplication.App_Code.OG_GraphObj yOG_obj
            = new SPDSUniversityWebApplication.App_Code.OG_GraphObj();

            yOG_obj.Activity.Actor = new
            SPDSUniversityWebApplication.App_Code.OG_Actor("Pathik
            Rawal", "pr@spdsuniversity.onmicrosoft.com");
            yOG_obj.Activity.Message = "Brian Johnson is now
            #certified  #DynamicCRM2014 expert ";
            yOG_obj.Activity.Action = "create";
            SPDSUniversityWebApplication.App_Code.OG_GraphObj_
            Instance yOGobjInst = new SPDSUniversityWebApplication.
            App_Code.OG_GraphObj_Instance();

            yOGobjInst.Url = "https://www.yammer.com/SPDSpetro.com/
            users/brianj";
            yOGobjInst.Title = "CRM Certificed";
            yOGobjInst.Description = "Please join me in
            conguratulating Brian Johnson on his achievement";
            yOGobjInst.Image = "https://www.yammer.com/api/v1/uploaded_
            files/29860625/version/28812608/preview/UAPP_LOGO.png";
            yOGobjInst.Type = "person";
            yOG_obj.Activity.Object = yOGobjInst;
            string postData = yOG_obj.ToString();
            string activityURL = WebConfigurationManager.
            AppSettings["activityURL"];
            string response = SPDSUniversityWebApplication.App_Code.
            YammerUtility.PostRequesttoYammer(postData, activityURL,
            txtaccesstoken.Text.ToString(), "application/json");

        }
```

When the person object is posted to Yammer using Open Graph, the post will look as illustrated in Figure 5-27, which shows the activity details view. Figure 5-28 shows the Activity Details page.

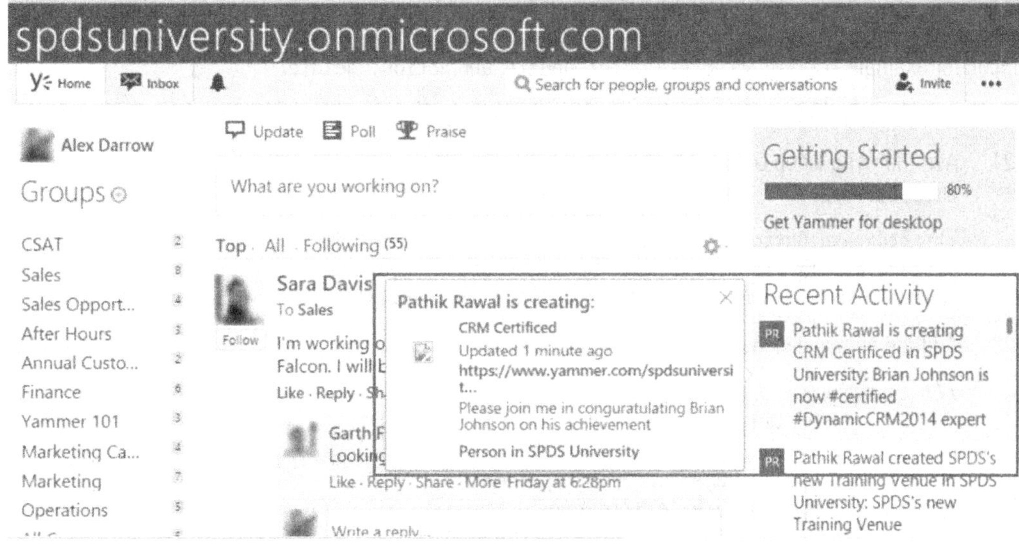

Figure 5-27. *Yammer Open Graph activity showing a person object*

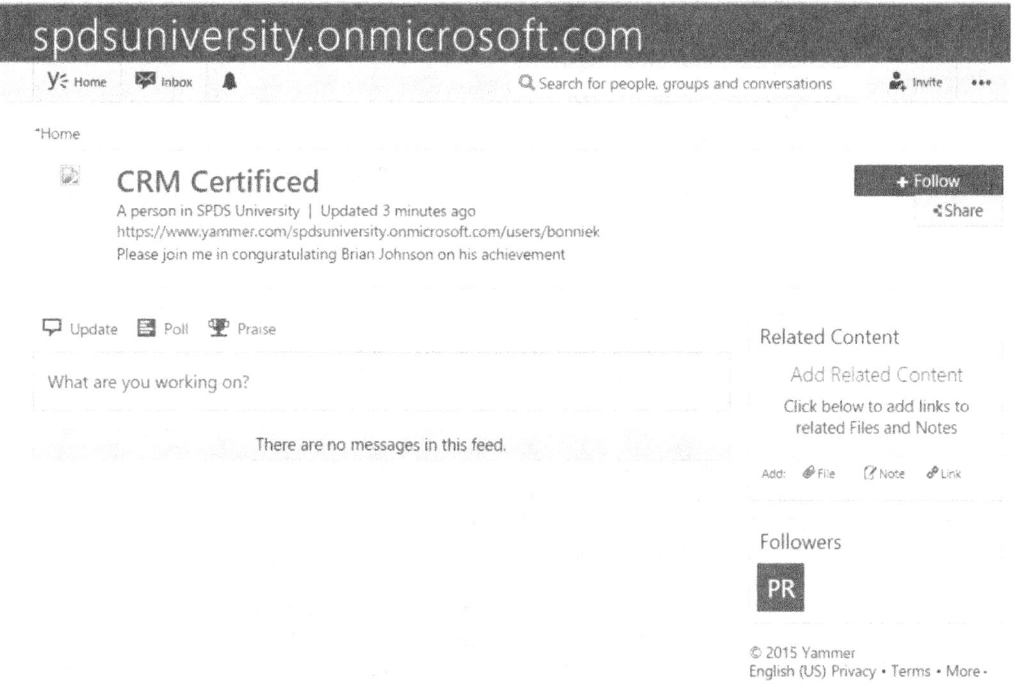

Figure 5-28. *Yammer Open Graph activity showing a person object in detail view*

Posting Object Type: Videos

Similar to the page object, the video object type represents a video file that can be posted to Yammer using Open Graph.

Action type: `create`, `update`, and `delete` can be used. Use the right action term provided in the code snippet; for example `action: create`, `action: update`, and `action: delete`.

This object type represents a video object.

21. Add the Write Video Object into Yammer Using OG button to the markup in `Default.aspx`.

```
<tr><td><asp:Button ID="btnWriteDataOGVideo" class="btn btn-
primary btn-lg" runat="server" OnClick="btnWriteDataOGVideo_Click"
Text="Write Video Object  " Width="363px" /></td></tr>
```

22. Add the button click event in `Default.aspx.cs`.

```
/// <summary>
        /// Posting a Video using Open Graph
        /// </summary>
        /// <param name="sender"></param>
        /// <param name="e"></param>
        protected void btnWriteDataOGVideo_Click(object sender,
        EventArgs e)
        {
            SPDSUniversityWebApplication.App_Code.OG_GraphObj
            yOG_obj = new SPDSUniversityWebApplication.App_Code.
            OG_GraphObj();

            yOG_obj.Activity.Actor = new
            SPDSUniversityWebApplication.App_Code.OG_Actor
            ("Pathik Rawal","pr@spdsuniversity.onmicrosoft.com");
            yOG_obj.Activity.Message = "Explore Microsoft Dynamics
            CRM more deeply-Introduction to Microsoft Dynamics CRM
            2013 .";
            yOG_obj.Activity.Action = "create";
            SPDSUniversityWebApplication.App_Code.OG_
            GraphObj_Instance yammergraphobjectinst = new
            SPDSUniversityWebApplication.App_Code.OG_GraphObj_
            Instance();

            yammergraphobjectinst.Url = "http://video.ch9.ms/
            ch9/62c8/87663cbb-5485-4264-b23d-371d2b7362c8/
            IntroToDynamicsCRM2013M02.mp3";
            yammergraphobjectinst.Title = "Introduction to Microsoft
            Dynamics CRM 2013";
            yammergraphobjectinst.Description = "Find out about
            accounts and contacts (and the relationship between
            them), activities, Yammer, views, importing data, and
            processes..";
```

```
        yammergraphobjectinst.Image = "https://www.yammer.com/
        api/v1/uploaded_files/29860625/version/28812608/preview/
        UAPP_LOGO.png";
        yammergraphobjectinst.Type = "video";

        yOG_obj.Activity.Object = yammergraphobjectinst;
        string postData = yOG_obj.ToString();
        string activityURL = WebConfigurationManager.
        AppSettings["activityURL"];
        string response = SPDSUniversityWebApplication.App_Code.
        YammerUtility.PostRequesttoYammer(postData, activityURL,
        txtaccesstoken.Text.ToString(), "application/json");

    }
```

When the video object is posted to Yammer using Open Graph, the post will show the video icons illustrated in Figure 5-29, which shows the activity details view. Figure 5-30 shows the Activity Details page.

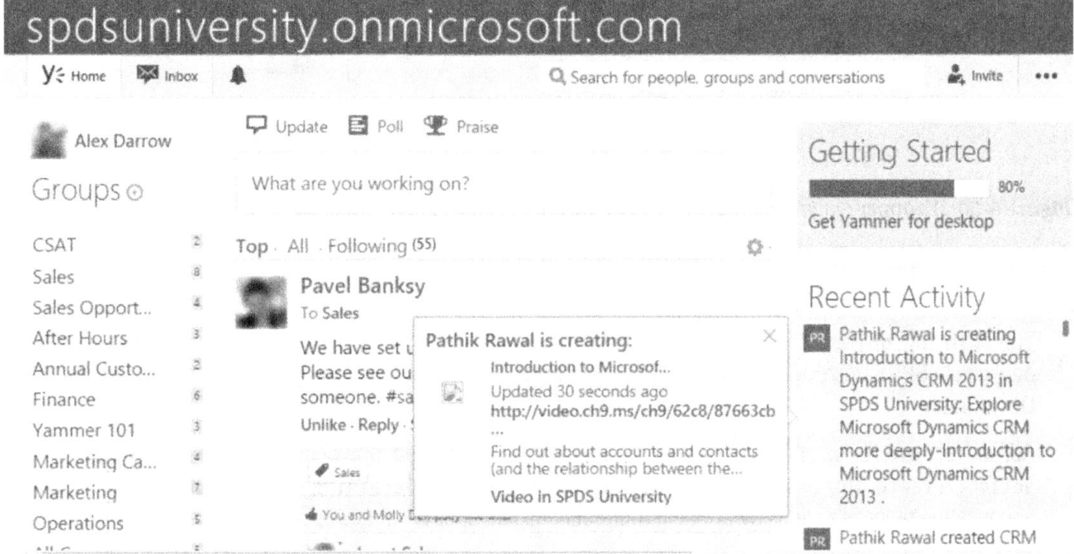

Figure 5-29. *Yammer Open Graph activity showing a video object*

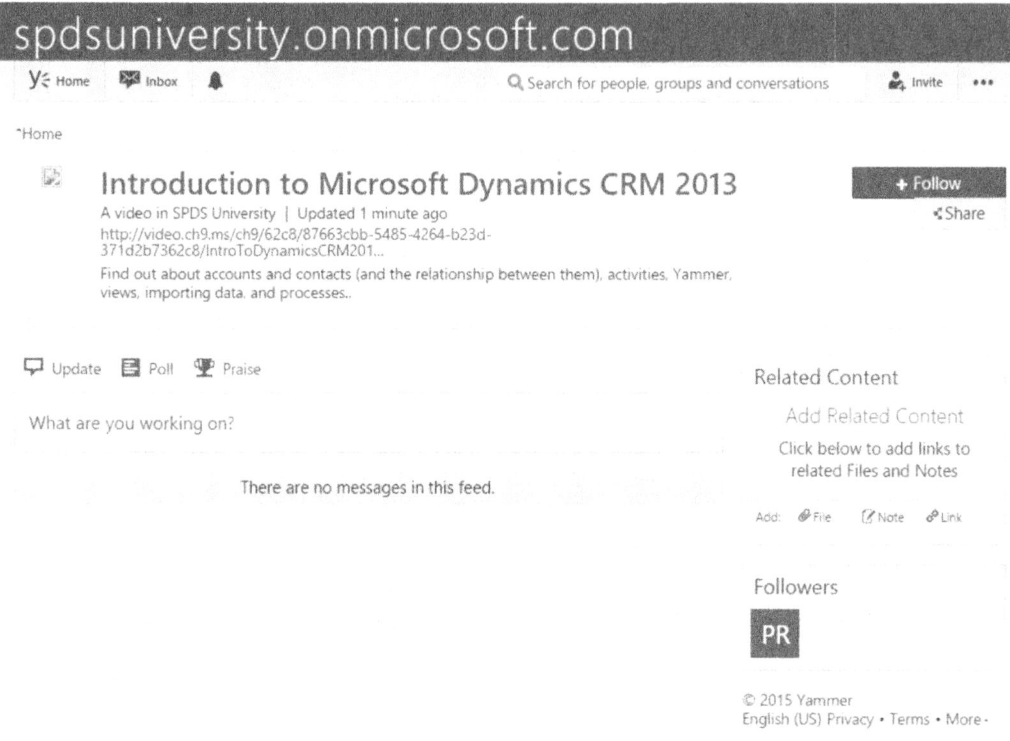

Figure 5-30. *Yammer Open Graph activity showing a video object in detail view*

Posting Custom Object Type: Training Object

The `training_object` object type is custom object that represents a training object for the web application SPDS University web application, which can be posted as an object into Yammer using Open Graph.

Action type: `create` can be used. Use the right action term provided in the code snippet; for example `action: create`. This exercise only defines the `create` action for `training_object`, but you can enhance the object's actions by creating more actions like `update` and `delete`.

This object type represents a video object.

23. Add the Write Training Object into Yammer Using OG button markup in `Default.aspx`.

```
<tr><td>
<asp:Button ID="btnWriteDataOG_Custom" runat="server"
OnClick="btnWriteDataOGCustom_Click" Text="Write Custom
(trainingobject) Object into Yammer Using OG" Width="573px" />
</td></tr>
```

24. Add the button click event in `Default.aspx.cs`.

```
/// <summary>
        /// Writing to Yammer using Open Graph's Custom Objects
        /// </summary>
        /// <param name="sender"></param>
        /// <param name="e"></param>
        protected void btnWriteDataOGCustom_Click(object sender,
        EventArgs e)
        {
            SPDSUniversityWebApplication.App_Code.OG_GraphObj
            yOG_obj = new SPDSUniversityWebApplication.App_Code.
            OG_GraphObj();

            yOG_obj.Activity.Actor = new
            SPDSUniversityWebApplication.App_Code.OG_Actor
            ("Pathik Rawal","pr@spdsuniversity.onmicrosoft.com");
            yOG_obj.Activity.Message = "A Survey on upcoming
            trainings.";
            yOG_obj.Activity.Action = "create";
            SPDSUniversityWebApplication.App_Code.OG_
            GraphObj_Instance yammergraphobjectinst = new
            SPDSUniversityWebApplication.App_Code.OG_GraphObj_
            Instance();

            yammergraphobjectinst.Url = "http://localhost:43615/
            Survey.aspx";
            yammergraphobjectinst.Title = "A Survey on upcoming
            trainings";
            yammergraphobjectinst.Description = "A survey on
            upcoming trainings";
            yammergraphobjectinst.Image = "https://www.yammer.com/
            api/v1/uploaded_files/29860625/version/28812608/preview/
            UAPP_LOGO.png";
            yammergraphobjectinst.Type = "training_object:survey";

            yOG_obj.Activity.Object = yammergraphobjectinst;
            string postData = yOG_obj.ToString();
            string activityURL = WebConfigurationManager.
            AppSettings["activityURL"];
            string response = SPDSUniversityWebApplication.App_Code.
            YammerUtility.PostRequesttoYammer(postData, activityURL,
            txtaccesstoken.Text.ToString(), "application/json");

        }
```

When the custom object is posted to Yammer using Open Graph, the post will look like Figure 5-31, which shows the activity details view. Figure 5-32 shows the Activity Details page.

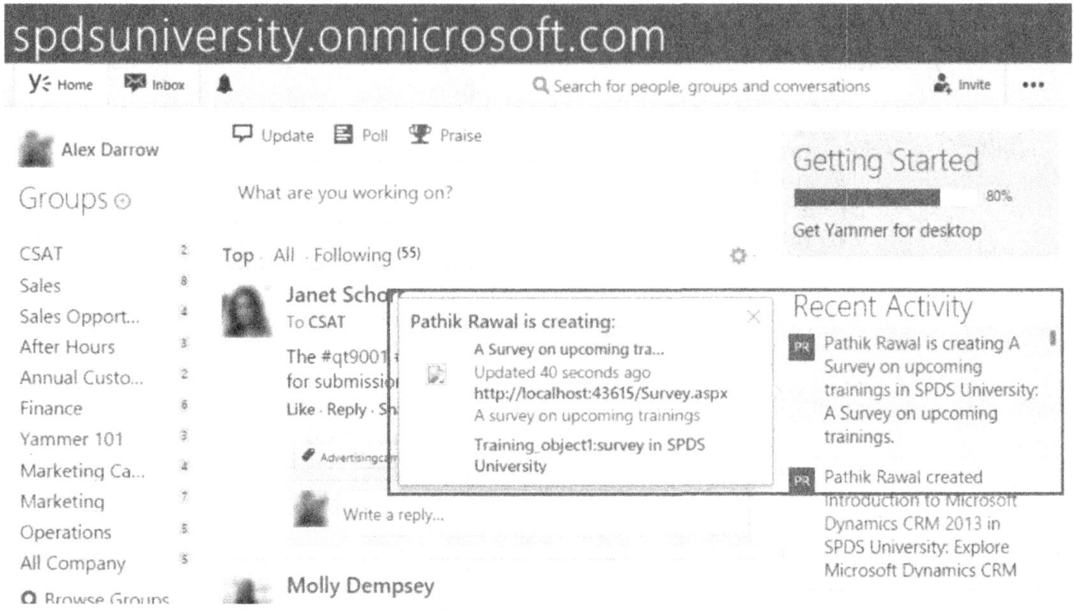

Figure 5-31. *Yammer Open Graph activity showing a custom object*

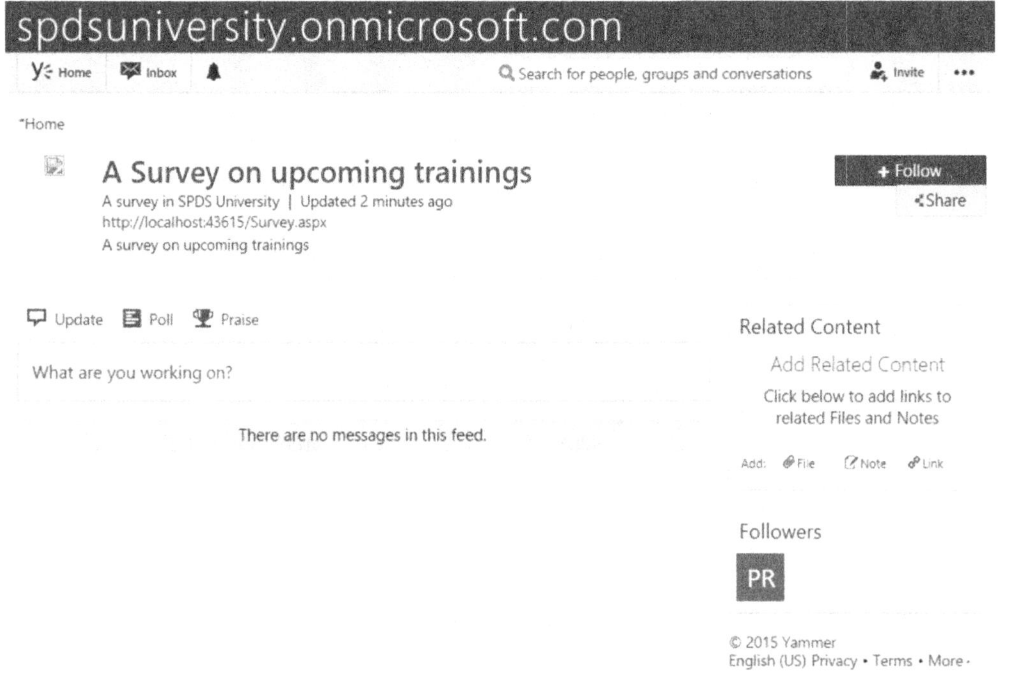

Figure 5-32. *Yammer Open Graph activity showing a custom object in detail view*

25. Default.aspx. The complete default.aspx code is as follows:

```
<%@ Page Title="Home Page" Language="C#" MasterPageFile="~/Site.
Master" AutoEventWireup="true" CodeBehind="Default.aspx.cs" Inherits
="SPDSUniversityWebApplication._Default" %>

<asp:Content runat="server" ID="BodyContent" ContentPlaceHolderID=
"MainContent">
    <h3>Welcome to SPDS University Application:</h3>
    <ol class="round">
        <li class="one">
            <h2>
                <asp:Label ID="lbllogin" runat="server" Text="You
                are not Loged in, You can login using Yammer
                Credential, click on Log In button on top right">
                </asp:Label>
            </h2>
        </li>
    </ol>
    <div id="CourseDiv" runat="server">
        <h3>Upcoming Training </h3>
        <p>
            <asp:XmlDataSource ID="XmlDataSourceCourse"
            runat="server" DataFile="~/App_Data/Courses.xml">
            </asp:XmlDataSource>

            <asp:GridView ID="GridView1" runat="server" XPath="/
            Employees/Employee" DataSourceID="XmlDataSourceCourse"
                AutoGenerateColumns="False" HeaderStyle-
                BackColor="#3AC0F2" HeaderStyle-ForeColor="White"
                BackColor="White" BorderColor="#336666"
                BorderStyle="Double" BorderWidth="3px"
                CellPadding="4" GridLines="Horizontal"
                Height="124px" Width="985px">
                <Columns>
                    <asp:TemplateField HeaderText="Name"
                    HeaderStyle-Width="50">
                        <ItemTemplate>
                            <%# XPath("Name") %>
                        </ItemTemplate>

<HeaderStyle Width="50px"></HeaderStyle>
                    </asp:TemplateField>
                    <asp:TemplateField HeaderText="Name"
                    HeaderStyle-Width="50">
                        <ItemTemplate>
                            <%# XPath("Level") %>
                        </ItemTemplate>
```

```
<HeaderStyle Width="50px"></HeaderStyle>
                    </asp:TemplateField>
                    <asp:TemplateField HeaderText="Name"
                    HeaderStyle-Width="50">
                        <ItemTemplate>
                            <%# XPath("Duration") %>
                        </ItemTemplate>

<HeaderStyle Width="50px"></HeaderStyle>
                    </asp:TemplateField>
                    <asp:TemplateField HeaderText="Name"
                    HeaderStyle-Width="50">
                        <ItemTemplate>
                            <%# XPath("Trainer") %>
                        </ItemTemplate>

<HeaderStyle Width="50px"></HeaderStyle>
                    </asp:TemplateField>
                       <asp:TemplateField HeaderText="Name"
                       HeaderStyle-Width="50">
                        <ItemTemplate>
                            <%# XPath("Noofseats") %>
                        </ItemTemplate>

<HeaderStyle Width="50px"></HeaderStyle>
                    </asp:TemplateField>

                </Columns>
                <FooterStyle BackColor="White" ForeColor="#333333" />

                <HeaderStyle BackColor="#336666" ForeColor="White"
                Font-Bold="True"></HeaderStyle>
                <PagerStyle BackColor="#336666" ForeColor="White"
                HorizontalAlign="Center" />
                <RowStyle BackColor="White" ForeColor="#333333" />
                <SelectedRowStyle BackColor="#339966" Font-
                Bold="True" ForeColor="White" />
                <SortedAscendingCellStyle BackColor="#F7F7F7" />
                <SortedAscendingHeaderStyle BackColor="#487575" />
                <SortedDescendingCellStyle BackColor="#E5E5E5" />
                <SortedDescendingHeaderStyle BackColor="#275353" />
            </asp:GridView>
        </p>
```

```
    </div>
    <table>
        <tr><td> <asp:Button ID="btnWriteDataOG" CssClass="button"
        runat="server" OnClick="btnWriteDataOG_Click" Text="Write
        Document into Yammer Using OG" Width="363px" /></td></tr>
         <tr><td> <asp:Button ID="btnWriteDataOGPage" runat="server"
         OnClick="btnWriteDataOGPage_Click" Text="Write Page Object
         into Yammer Using OG" Width="363px"/></td></tr>
        <tr><td><asp:Button ID="btnWriteDataOGPlace" runat="server"
        OnClick="btnWriteDataOGPlace_Click" Text="Write Place Object
        into Yammer Using OG" Width="363px" /></td></tr>
         <tr><td><asp:Button ID="btnWriteDataOGPerson" runat="server"
         OnClick="btnWriteDataOGPerson_Click" Text="Write Person
         Object into Yammer Using OG" Width="363px"  /></td></tr>
          <tr><td><asp:Button ID="btnWriteDataOGVideo"
          class="btn btn-primary btn-lg" runat="server"
          OnClick="btnWriteDataOGVideo_Click" Text="Write Video
          Object " Width="363px" /></td></tr>
           <tr><td><asp:Button ID="btnWriteDataOGImage"
           runat="server" OnClick="btnWriteDataOGImage_Click"
           Text="Write Image Object into Yammer Using OG"
           Width="363px" /></td></tr>
         <tr><td><asp:Button ID="btnWriteDataOG_Custom"
         runat="server" OnClick="btnWriteDataOGCustom_Click"
         Text="Write Custom (trainingobject) Object into Yammer
         Using OG" Width="573px" /></td></tr>

    </table>

    <asp:TextBox ID="txtCode" runat="server" Visible="False">
    </asp:TextBox>
    <asp:TextBox ID="txtaccesstoken" runat="server"
Visible="false"></asp:TextBox>

</asp:Content>
<asp:Content ID="Content1" runat="server" ContentPlaceHolderID="Head
Content">
    <style type="text/css">
        .auto-style1 {
            width: 100%;
        }
    </style>
</asp:Content>
```

26. Here is the `Default.aspx.cs`'s `page_load` event code:

```
/// <summary>
        /// Page load event to check if query string contains a key
        called "Code"
        /// </summary>
        /// <param name="sender"></param>
        /// <param name="e"></param>
        protected void Page_Load(object sender, EventArgs e)
        {

            string qsCode = Request.QueryString["Code"];
            if (qsCode != null)
            {
                txtCode.Text = qsCode;
                Obtain_Access_Token();
            }
            else
            {
                CourseDiv.Visible = false;
                btnWriteDataOG.Visible = false;
                btnWriteDataOGPage.Visible = false;
                btnWriteDataOGPlace.Visible = false;
                btnWriteDataOGPerson.Visible = false;
                btnWriteDataOGVideo.Visible = false;
                btnWriteDataOG_Custom.Visible = false;

            }
        }
```

27. Here is the `Default.aspx.cs`'s `Obtain_Access_Token` method:

```
/// <summary>
        /// Obtain the access Token
        /// </summary>
        private void Obtain_Access_Token()
        {
            string accessToken = default(string);
            string AccesTokenURL = WebConfigurationManager.
            AppSettings["AccessTokenURL"] + "client_id=" +
            WebConfigurationManager.AppSettings["client_id"]
            + "&client_secret=" + WebConfigurationManager.
            AppSettings["client_secret"] + "&code=" + txtCode.Text;
            string response = SPDSUniversityWebApplication.App_Code.
            YammerUtility.InvokeHttpGetRequest(AccesTokenURL);
            if (!string.IsNullOrEmpty(response))
            {
                SPDSUniversityWebApplication.App_Code.AccessToken
                jat = SPDSUniversityWebApplication.App_Code.
                AccessToken.GetInstanceFromJson(response);
```

```
                if (!string.IsNullOrEmpty(jat.TokenResponse.Token))
                {
                    accessToken = jat.TokenResponse.Token;
                    lbllogin.Text = "Welcome " + jat.CurrentUser.
                    FullName;
                    txtaccesstoken.Text = accessToken;
                }
            }
        }
```

■ **Note** To learn more about JSON for JavaScript and .NET, visit `https://msdn.microsoft.com/en-us/library/bb299886.aspx`.

Run Application

1. In Visual Studio, click on the Debug button, as illustrated in Figure 5-33. Then select your desired browser from the drop-down menu.

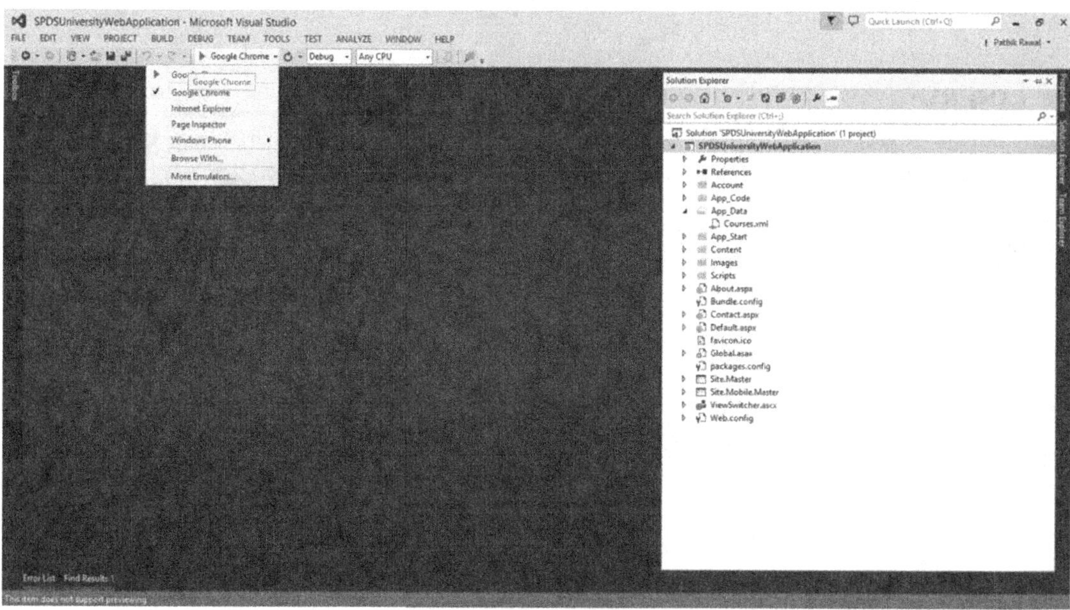

Figure 5-33. *Visual Studio's debug application feature*

2. You will be presented with the screen shown in Figure 5-34. Click on the Log In button.

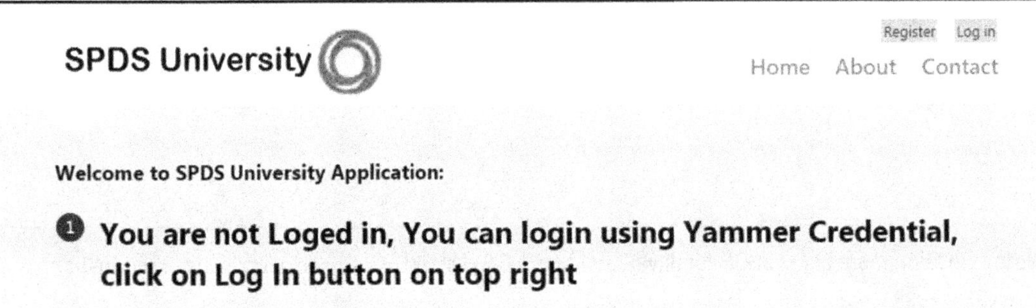

Figure 5-34. *SPDS University's home page*

3. You will be presented with a Login screen as illustrated in Figure 5-35. Our SPDS University web Application provides the "Sign In with Yammer" button. Click on it.

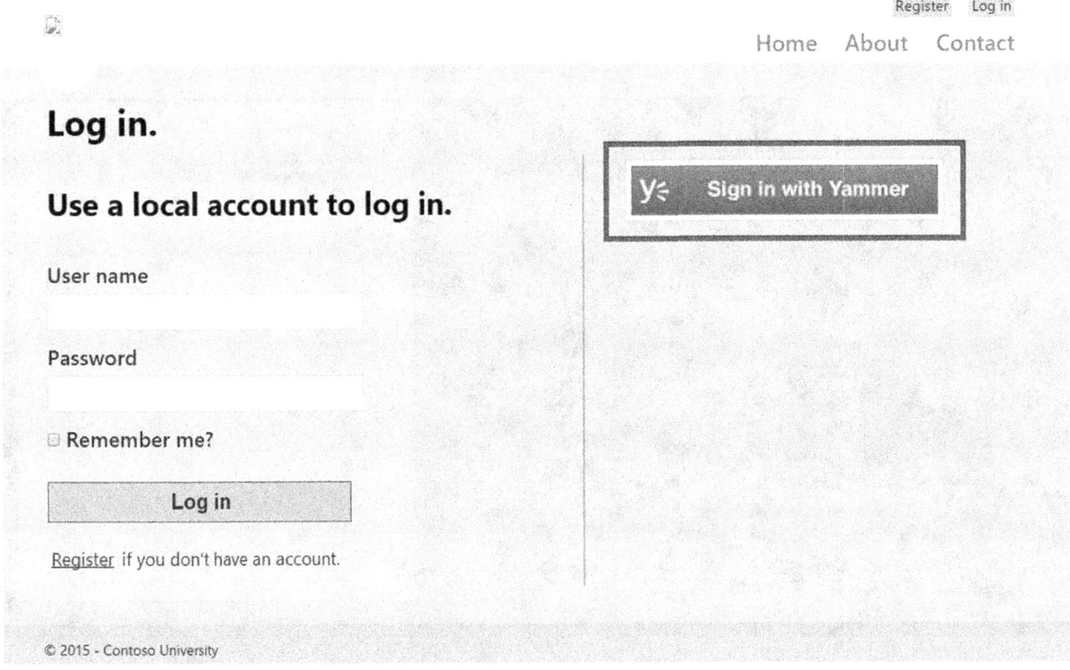

Figure 5-35. *SPDS University's Login page*

4. Yammer will present the Login page, shown in Figure 5-36.

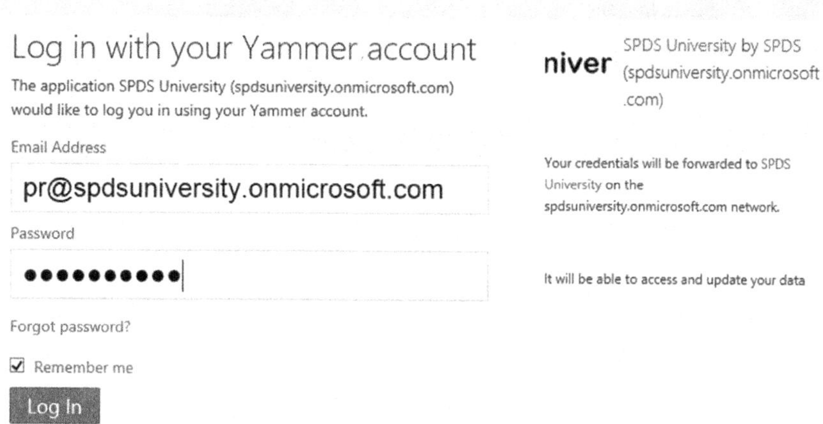

Figure 5-36. Yammer's Login page

5. Yammer will redirect users to the redirect_uri with code in the URL as a query string parameter, as illustrated in Figure 5-37. The home page also displays the Welcome <<User name>> message. The <<User Name>> is retrieved from the access token response in the Obtain_Access_Token() method.

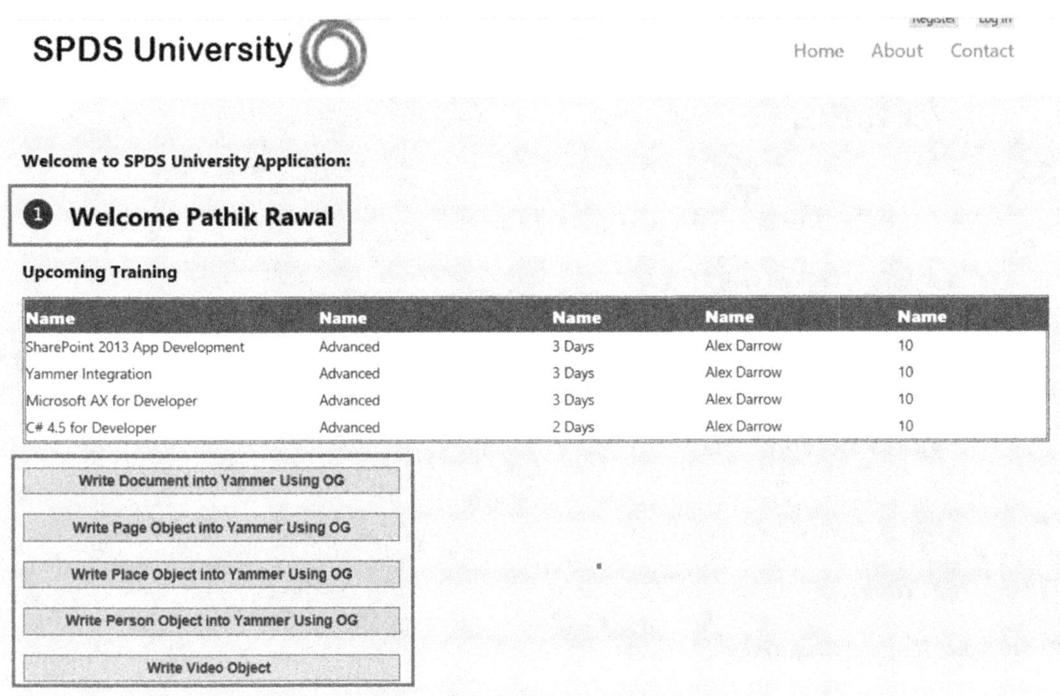

Figure 5-37. *SPDS University home page*

At this point of time, you have implemented how to write data into Yammer using Open Graph out-of-the-box and created custom objects for the Yammer app SPDSUniversity as a ASP.NET web application.

We hope using these exercises you can now use Yammer Open Graph to provide integration with your external applications. This could be your existing sales, HR, operations, or internal learning applications, which can be integrated into Yammer to allow employees to see appropriate updates and take quick actions as required to complete the tasks.

Summary

This chapter covered an introduction to the Enterprise Yammer Social Graph and explained the Open Graph activity format and schema. You also learned how to use Open Graph to integrate external applications into Yammer. You saw some examples of posting data to Yammer from external applications using the Open Graph activities.

In Chapter 6, we will explain the integration of line-of-business applications using Yammer REST APIs.

CHAPTER 6

Integration Using Yammer Rest APIs

Pryank Rohilla

In Chapter 5, we explained how to use Yammer Open Graph API to bring information stored in different business applications into Yammer and allow users to discover data from other applications and see the full view in a structured manner. This is all good, but it provides only one-way integration—from your business applications to Yammer. What if you want to integrate Yammer data into your business applications and make your applications more social and able to share content? The Yammer REST APIs provide this capability.

In this chapter, we will explain Yammer REST APIs, which allow developers to access Yammer data from line-of-business applications running on different platforms. Yammer's REST APIs allow inbound and outbound flow of messages. This chapter covers:

- Explanation of REST
- Introduction to Yammer's REST APIs
- Yammer features that can be accessed using REST APIs from line-of-business applications
- Yammer's REST service endpoints details
- Lab exercise using the SPDS University application to see how to access data from Yammer and write data into Yammer using Yammer's REST API endpoints

REST

As per Wikipedia, "Representational State Transfer (REST) is a software architecture style consisting of guidelines and best practices for creating scalable web services".

REST relies on stateless, client-server, cacheable HTTP channel and is a lightweight alternative to using web services or RPC. RESTs benefits include:

- It's platform independent
- It's programming-language independent
- Can be used when firewalls exist
- REST services use HTTP as main communication channel and have a uniform interface where resources are identified as URIs. This allows easy implementation of REST endpoints.

P. Rawal and P. Rohilla, *Developing on Yammer*, DOI 10.1007/978-1-4842-0943-1_6

Any service based on the REST protocol is called a RESTful service. In a RESTful application, REST-enabled resources are maintained in an accessible data store. When a request is sent to a RESTful application to perform an action (create, retrieve, delete, or update), the RESTful application performs the operation and provides a response, as shown in Figure 6-1. All RESTful applications use HTTP requests to post and get data.

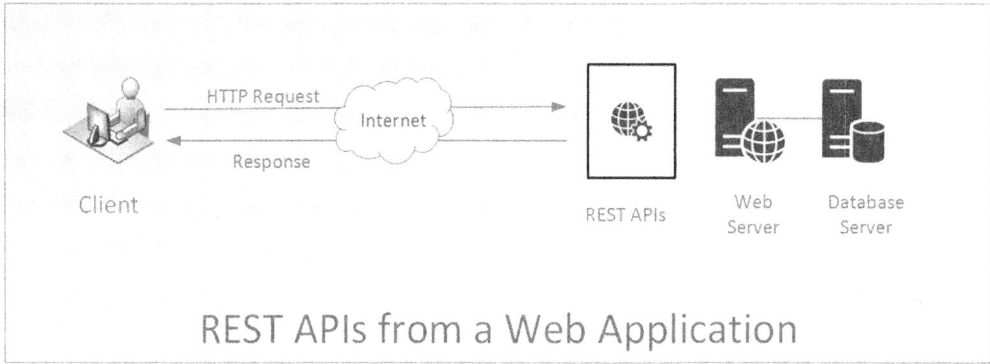

Figure 6-1. *Client web application communication with web server using REST API over an HTTP channel*

As all REST API resources have unique HTTP-accessible URIs, REST enables data caching and is optimized to work with the distributed infrastructure. For more information about REST, you may find the following third-party references useful:

- Wikipedia (`http://en.wikipedia.org/wiki/REST`) provides a good overview of REST
- HTTP 1.1 method definitions (`http://www.w3.org/Protocols/rfc2616/rfc2616-sec9.html`); includes a specification for `GET`, `POST`, `PUT`, and `DELETE`

Yammer REST APIs

Like other social networking applications Yammer has provided REST APIs to develop custom integrations with business applications. Yammer REST APIs are most common way to integrate your line-of-business applications with Yammer and enables you to add social features to virtually any type of business application within your organization.

Yammer REST API is the lowest-level API provided by Yammer and enables developers to build both client and server applications. In this chapter, we will go through all the available Yammer REST endpoints and try to explain them in a manner that will allow you to implement integrations with your business applications. First, let's look at the main features of Yammer APIs.

Yammer REST API Features

Before you develop integrations with Yammer REST APIs, it's useful to know about various features provided by them. Here are the main features of using Yammer REST APIs:

- The REST API is available for any platform that can make HTTP calls over SSL. Current supported platforms are Ruby, Python, JavaScript, iOS, .NET, and Windows Phone.
- Yammer APIs mainly support JSON (JavaScript Object Notation), but it also supports XML format for many APIs.

- Developers simply need to create HTTP requests going to Yammer and process the JSON returned from Yammer in response on their business applications.
- Using Yammer REST APIs, you can work on different Yammer objects, including messages, users, groups, and so on.
- Yammer REST APIs enable developers to access Yammer's data using simple HTTP methods like `GET` and `POST`.

■ **Note** As Yammer keeps adding new features, we suggest you review the latest API reference on the Yammer Developer Network for the currently supported API set (`https://developer.yammer.com`).

What You Can Do with Yammer REST APIs

As mentioned, Yammer REST APIs help you develop and add social features to your business application, and you can easily post messages or activity updates from any platform. Here are some useful examples of what you can do.

- **Bring Yammer's social experience to your business applications.**
  - You can use REST APIs to view, create, edit, or delete messages on Yammer.
  - You can use Yammer REST APIs to append or delete attachments or topics to messages or message threads.
  - You can provide and manage subscriptions to Yammer topics, discussion threads, and users from business applications.
  - You can use Yammer REST APIs to view organizational charts and relationships.
  - You can add or remove relationship between users.
  - You can send email invites to users who have not joined Yammer using REST APIs.
- **Search Yammer content from other applications.**
  - Using Yammer REST APIs, you can search for Yammer data directly from your business applications.
  - You can use the Yammer autocomplete feature in your business applications.
- **Meet compliance needs.**
  - Yammer also provides a data export API, which can help IT administrators archive Yammer Network content and be compliant with an organization's rules and legal requirements.
- **Monitor Yammer usage.**
  - You can use data export to do reporting on Yammer content, provide useful insight on adoption, and help measure ROI from the Yammer investment.

Before You Start Using the Yammer REST APIs

Before you start using the Yammer REST endpoints, it is important to familiarize yourself with the high-level requirements.

- Authentication on Yammer
- User privileges

Let's explore why these are required.

Authentication on Yammer

Just like any enterprise application, before requesting Yammer data, any request to access Yammer data must be authorized by the authenticated user. This authorization is done using the Yammer Authentication model based on the OAuth2.0 protocol, which we covered in detail in Chapter 4. As you know when you do user authentication, Yammer provides an access token that's linked to the authorized user. Developers should send an authorization header with the access token to make sure the request to POST/GET/DELETE using the Yammer REST API is authenticated by Yammer.

The format of the authentication header is:

```
Authorization: Bearer [Access Token]
```

Any operation that modifies the Yammer data can be performed only by the user who owns that data. It's important to understand that the user's access token much be strongly protected when used with REST APIs. If a security breach occurs, an attacker can post and read messages to/from Yammer. So, you need to use measures like encryption, permission, and least privilege policy to protect the user authorization access tokens in your business applications.

User Privileges

Your enterprise Yammer network has three types of users and each user type has a different set of permissions on Yammer. As a developer, you should consider which accounts are used while doing integration using Yammer REST APIs.

The different user types are described in Table 6-1.

Table 6-1. *Yammer User Account Types and Privileges*

User Account Type	Privileges
User	Read own messages Post messages Delete own messages
Admin	All User permissions and change some admin settings
Verified Admin	All User permissions and delete any Yammer message or file Read any content in private Yammer groups. Acquire access tokens for impersonation. Export all Yammer network content.

Getting Started with Yammer REST APIs

Yammer REST APIs are useful wrappers that speed up the development of your applications. There are different Yammer REST APIs for different Yammer objects:

- Messages
- Users
- Groups
- Relationships
- Notifications
- Suggestions
- Subscriptions
- Autocomplete
- Search
- Networks

Yammer API Operations

Table 6-2 provide the available HTTP methods that can be used for invoking Yammer resources.

Table 6-2. *Yammer API Operations*

HTTP Method	Description	REST HTTP Mapping
`GET`	Get a specific Yammer resource	`GET` on Yammer REST API endpoint
`POST`	Update an existing resource or create a new one	`POST` on Yammer REST API endpoint, where you pass in data associated with a related resource
`DELETE`	Delete a specific resource	`DELETE` on Yammer REST API endpoint, where you specify the resource to be deleted

The operations that are supported for the different types of resources are summarized in Table 6-3.

Table 6-3. *Operations Supported for the Yammer Resources*

	GET	POST	DELETE
Messages	✓	✓	✓
Topics	✓	×	×
Groups	×	✓	✓
Users	s✓	✓	✓
Relationships	✓	✓	×
Notifications	✓	×	×
Suggestions	✓	×	✓
Subscriptions	✓	✓	✓
Autocomplete	✓	×	×
Search	✓	×	×
Invitations	×	✓	×
Network	✓	×	×
Dataexport	✓ (Verified admin only)	×	×

There are few other considerations you should know about when implementing Yammer REST APIs in your applications:

- **Admin actions**: When you plan to use administrative Yammer API for actions like adding or deleting Yammer users, you should only use authorization access tokens from a Yammer-verified admin user.
- **Versioning**: The Yammer API version is visible in the URL of the REST API endpoints. For example, `/api/v1`. As per the Yammer guidelines, there could be additional elements added to output from endpoints. When elements are added or removed a new version of the API is typically released.
- **Calling styles**: There are several ways to invoke the API from your business applications.
    - Using a REST endpoint directly
    - Using a REST endpoint from JavaScript (no server-side code required)
    - Using a server-side application (explained later in the SPDSUniversity application exercise)
    - Using REST endpoints directly. You need to specify Yammer actions using the HTTP verbs `POST`, `GET`, `PUT`, or `DELETE`. The Yammer resource is specified by a unique URI:

      `https://www.yammer.com/api/v1/users.json`

- **REST from JavaScript**: Developers can invoke the Yammer REST API from JavaScript using the callback query parameter and a callback function. This allows developers to write rich applications without need to write server-side code:

```
function PostYammerMessage(val) {
   var msg = document.getElementById('msgtxt').value;
   var groupID = "71618329";
    if(msg == ""){
     alert ("Message cannot be empty!");
     return false;
    }

 yam.platform.request(
   {
    url: "https://api.yammer.com/api/v1/messages.json"
    , method: "POST"
    , data: {
     "body" : msg,
     "group_id" : groupID
    }
    , success: function (msg) { alert("Yammer message Post was Successful!"); }
    , error: function (msg) { alert("Yammer Post failed"); }
    }
    )
 }
```

In the previous code, the `PostYammerMessage()` function accepts a message and then posts the request to Yammer's messages REST endpoint to a Yammer group.

Later in this chapter, we will explain the use of REST endpoints using an example. But before that, you need to understand the basics of the different Yammer REST endpoints.

REST Endpoints

Let's go through all the available endpoints and explore how to use them in your application.

■ **Note** Yammer provides a full list of the latest APIs and a new interface (API Explorer) to try the APIs endpoints. For full details, go to `https://developer.yammer.com/`.

The API references used in this book are from `https://developer.yammer.com/`.

Messages

All posted Yammer messages are displayed as feeds and messages are grouped into threaded conversations, as shown in Figure 6-2. Using Yammer REST APIs, you can post a message to Yammer, reply to a post, follow a post, share a post, delete a post, email a Yammer message, and do many other operations.

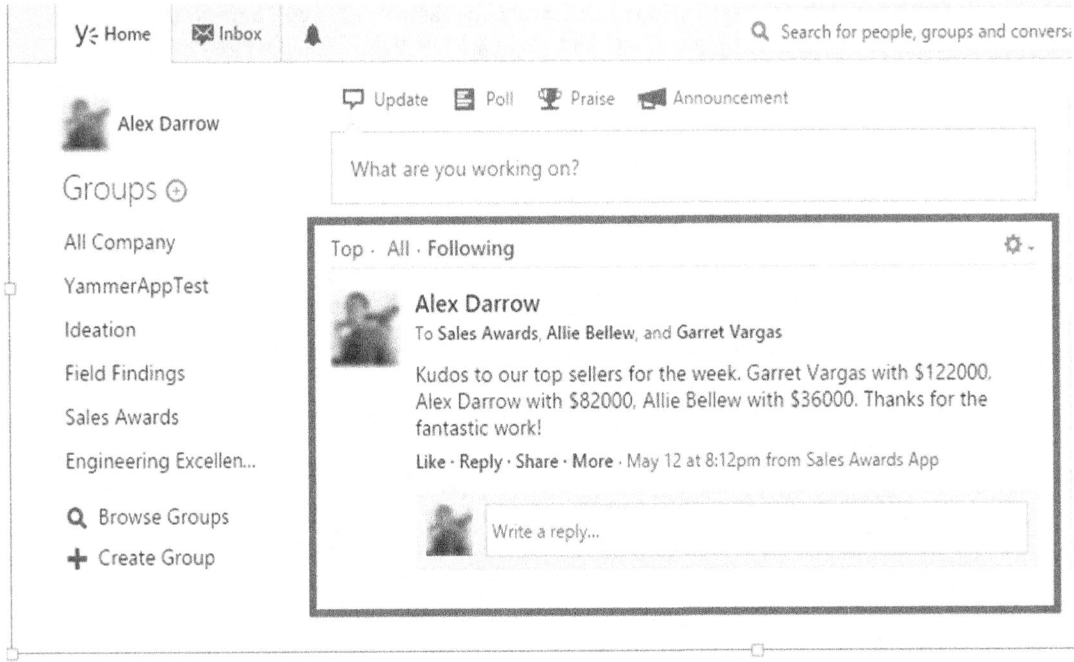

Figure 6-2. *Yammer messages*

Yammer has provided many APIs to view and retrieve messages. Yammer's feed is the information hub, and it provides three feed views that users can toggle among, as highlighted in Figure 6-3.

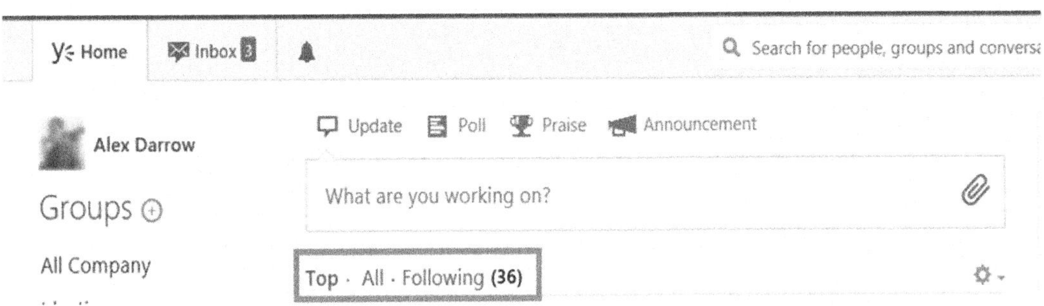

Figure 6-3. *Yammer's feed section*

As shown in Figure 6-3, the three view options are Top, All, and Following. The Top view shows the conversations most relevant to user, based on what that user subscribes to and her interactions with the Yammer network content. The All view renders all the conversations to which that Yammer user has access within his Yammer network, and the Following view displays messages that users actively subscribe to. This includes conversations that the user's followers have participated in or liked, conversations that have been tagged with a Yammer topic that users follow, and conversations that have been posted in one of the user's Yammer groups.

Retrieve All Public Messages

You use the `message.json` REST API endpoint to get all the public messages and conversations in the user's Yammer network. This is linked to the All view in the Yammer web interface.

Endpoint:

```
https://www.yammer.com/api/v1/messages.json
```

Or:

```
https://www.yammer.com/api/v1/messages.xml
```

Table 6-4 lists the required parameters.

Table 6-4. *Yammer Messages REST API Parameters*

Parameter	Type	Description	Example
`older_than:`	integer	Retrieve messages that are older than the specific message ID. Good for displaying messages in paging format on your application.	`https://www.Yammer.com/api/v1/messages.json?older_than=426` This will show you messages prior to message ID 426. If you have added the `limit` parameter, you'll get only 10 messages. So you will get 10 messages prior to 426.
`newer_than:`	integer	Retrieve messages that are newer than the specific message ID. Good when you want to get the latest messages after you got an initial set of messages.	`https://www.Yammer.com/api/v1/messages.json?newer_than=426` This will show you messages from 426 and, based on the limit, a total number of messages you want to see for any given request.
`threaded:`	Boolean (true/ false)	If this parameter is set to `true`, Yammer retrieves only the first message in a given thread of discussion.	`https://www.Yammer.com/api/v1/messages.json?threaded=true`
`Limit`	integer	Retrieve specified number of messages	`https://www.Yammer.com/api/v1/messages.json?limit=5` Only five messages will be returned by Yammer.

Later in this chapter, you will go through a detailed exercise on how to retrieve messages from Yammer using the SPDSUniversity business application case study.

Other Message REST APIs Used to GET Yammer Messages

Table 6-5 lists the related RESTful APIs used to `GET` messages from different feeds on Yammer, such as `my_feed.json`, which is the user's feed, `algo.json`, which is the algorithmic feed, and `following.json`, which is the feed the resource users are following.

Table 6-5. *Yammer Messages REST API Endpoints*

Endpoint (HTTP Method: GET)	Description
`https://www.yammer.com/api/v1/messages/my_feed.json` or `https://www.yammer.com/api/v1/messages/my_feed.xml`	Provides an endpoint for a Yammer user's feed, based on the Following and Top conversations.
`https://www.yammer.com/api/v1/messages/algo.json` or `https://www.yammer.com/api/v1/messages/algo.xml`	Endpoint to get the Top conversations
`https://www.yammer.com/api/v1/messages/following.json` or `https://www.yammer.com/api/v1/messages/following.xml`	This endpoint shows the messages feed for a user who is following and is shown in the Following view, including people, groups, and topics that the user is following
`https://www.yammer.com/api/v1/messages/sent.json` or `https://www.yammer.com/api/v1/messages/sent.xml`	Use this endpoint to get messages sent by a user
`https://www.yammer.com/api/v1/messages/private.json` or `https://www.yammer.com/api/v1/messages/private.xml`	This endpoint provides output for any private messages received by the user
`https://www.yammer.com/api/v1/messages/received.json` or `https://www.yammer.com/api/v1/messages/received.xml`	Use this endpoint to get all the messages received by a user.

All the previously mentioned endpoints use the same parameters as mentioned in Table 6-4.

Manipulating/Updating Messages REST API

Yammer's REST APIs provide a simple way to post messages to Yammer. You can use the same APIs to post your message to the whole company, broadcast to everyone in the network, post to a specific group, send a private message, add topics, and so on.

In order to post messages to Yammer, you need different IDs like a Group ID, User ID, Message ID, and Feed ID. You can use the `GET` method of `message.json` to retrieve the IDs of different objects. Tables 6-6 and 6-7 list the endpoints and their related parameters.

Table 6-6. *Yammer POST Messages REST API Endpoints*

Endpoint (HTTP Method: POST)	Description
`https://www.yammer.com/api/v1/messages.json` OR `https://www.yammer.com/api/v1/messages.xml`	To POST a message

Table 6-7. *Yammer POST Messages REST API Parameters*

Parameter	Type	Example
Body: The message as string	string	String data = "group_id=4659506" + "&body=" + "Greeting, This is my first post";
Group_ID: The ID of the target group to which this message is to be posted	integer	String data = "group_id=4659506" + "&body=" + "Greeting, This is my first post";
Replied_to_id: The message ID this is in response to	integer	String data = "replied_to_id=433483891" + "&body=" + "Greeting, This is my first post";
Direct_to_id: Sends a private message to a user indicated by the user ID	integer	String data = "direct_to_id=1522209393" + "&body=" + "Greeting, this is private message";
broadcast: The broadcast-=true is used to broadcast the message to all Yammer users on a particular network. For the broadcast=true parameter, the Yammer admin user's access token should be used	Boolean	String data = "broadcast=" + "&body=" + "Greeting, this is private message";
topicn: Specifies the topics in the message. Can use topic1 through topic20.		String data = "group_id=4659506&body= A message with Topic" + "&topic1=" + "YammerBook!!"

Here's an example:

```
function postAMessage() {
    var testMessage = { "body": "Hello Test, have you seen this" + location.href };
    yam.platform.request({
        url: "messages.json",
        method: "POST",
        data: testMessage,
        success: function (msg) {
            console.log("Message Posted Successfully");
        },
        error: function (msg) {
            console.log("Message Posting Error: " + msg.statusText);
        }
    });
}
```

Other parameters for the POST message Open Graph (OG) object parameter include:

- og_<property>: This parameter is required if your message contains an Open Graph (OG) object as an attachment.
- og_fetch (true/false): If this parameter is set to true, Yammer will get all the available Open Graph parameters for a specified page URL.

If you want to delete a message that contains an OG object, you need to specify the og_url parameter. Along with this there are other optional parameters specified in Table 6-8. Refer to the Open Graph site for the latest details (http://ogp.me/).

Table 6-8. *Yammer POST Messages REST API Additional Parameters for OG Objects*

Parameter	Description
og_url	This is required and must be a canonical URL of the Object Graph object, which can be used as a permanent ID. For example: https://myblog/book/title123
og_title	Title of the Open Graph object. This will be displayed in a message. For example: The Book
og_image	URL of a thumbnail image that you want to add to represent the OG object.
og_description	Description of the OG object.
og_object_type	The type of your object. For example: audio.song. Also note, depending on the type, there may be other required properties. Check the Open Graph documentation (https://developer.yammer.com/v1.0/docs/schema).
og_site_name	A unique value to relate objects from a common domain, for example, Yammer Blog.
og_meta	Use this parameter to specify additional information for custom rendering.
og_fetch	Get Open Graph object attributes from the Internet (default: false).

Delete a Posted Message from Your Business Application

You can remove a message from your application using Yammer. Table 6-9 provides the endpoint details.

Table 6-9. *Yammer's Delete a Message REST API Endpoint*

Endpoint (HTTP Method: DELETE)	Parameters
https://www.yammer.com/api/v1/messages/[:id]	[:id] is the message id to be deleted. Note that in order to delete the message, it must be added/edited on Yammer by current user.

Note Yammer DELETE requests should be specified with query string parameters. If your app does not support the HTTP DELETE method, try HTTP POST with the parameter _method=DELETE.

Adding an Attachment to a Message

You can easily add an attachment file to a message from your application. Again, the Yammer message must be related to the current user.

Table 6-10. *Yammer REST API Endpoints to Add an Attachement to a POST Message*

HTTP Method Endpoint	Description	Parameter
(HTTP method: POST) `https://www.yammer.com/api/v1/pending_attachments`	Use this endpoint to create a new pending attachment.	Attachment: Use HTTP multipart request to upload attachments with Yammer Message
(HTTP method: DELETE) `https://www.yammer.com/api/v1/pending_attachments/[:id]`	To delete a pending attachment.	Attachment: Use HTTP multipart request to specify attachments that you want to delete from a Yammer message.

Emailing Messages to Yammer

Using Yammer REST API, you can programmatically send a copy of any message in Yammer as email to a currently logged in user. Figure 6-4 shows how the message will appear in email.

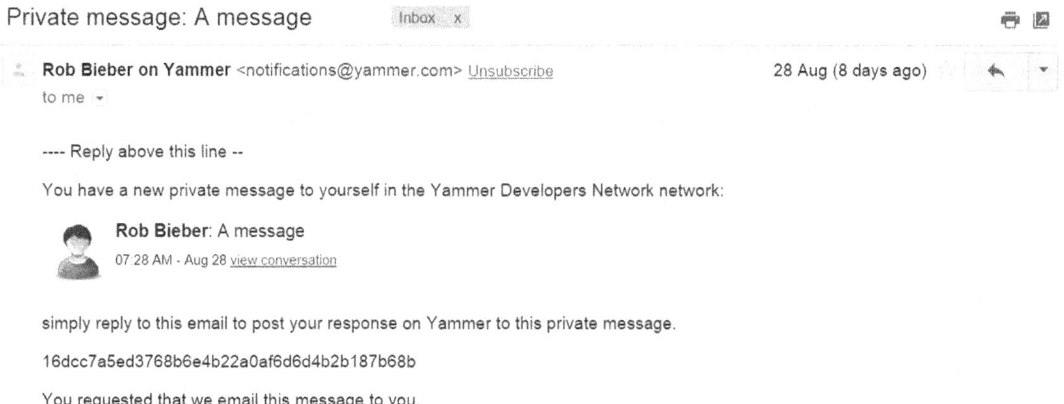

Figure 6-4. *A copy of private message sent as an email*

Table 6-11 provides the endpoints and the parameters for emailing a message.

Table 6-11. *Yammer REST API Endpoint to Add an Attachement to a Message POST*

Endpoints (HTTP Method: POST)	Parameter
`https://www.yammer.com/api/v1/messages/email`	`message_id`: The ID of the message to be sent as email.

Example:

```
https://www.yammer.com/api/v1/messages/email?message_id=436054827
```

Viewing a Thread

This endpoint (Table 6-12) is used to get the Yammer conversation thread of a message.

Table 6-12. *Yammer REST API Endpoint to view a Yammer Converation Thread*

Endpoints (HTTP Method: POST)	Parameter
JSON: `https://www.yammer.com/api/v1/threads/[:id].json` XML: `https://www.yammer.com/api/v1/threads/[:id].xml`	`threadId`: The ID of the message to be sent as email.

Examples:

`https://www.yammer.com/api/v1/threads/436054827.json`

`https://www.yammer.com/api/v1/threads/436054827.xml.`

Figure 6-5 shows how the XML looks in Yammer conversation thread output. You can see that the output type is `thread` and determine which group it is related to.


```
This XML file does not appear to have any style information associated with it. The document tree is shown below.

▼<response>
  ▼<url>
      https://www.yammer.com/api/v1/messages/in_thread/436054827
    </url>
  ▼<web-url>
      https://www.yammer.com/yammerdevelopersnetwork/threads/436054827
    </web-url>
    <type>thread</type>
    <id>436054827</id>
    <thread-starter-id>436054827</thread-starter-id>
    <group-id>39121</group-id>
    <topics/>
    <privacy>public</privacy>
    <direct-message>false</direct-message>
    <has-attachments>false</has-attachments>
  ▼<stats>
      <updates>1</updates>
      <shares>0</shares>
      <first-reply-id nil="true"/>
      <first-reply-at nil="true"/>
      <latest-reply-id>436054827</latest-reply-id>
      <latest-reply-at>2014-09-04T15:42:49Z</latest-reply-at>
    </stats>
  ▼<attachments-meta>
      <more-files>false</more-files>
      <more-images>false</more-images>
    </attachments-meta>
    <attachments/>
  ▼<references>
    ▼<reference>
        <type>group</type>
        <id>39121</id>
        <full-name>Yammer API user group</full-name>
        <name>yammerapiusergroup1</name>
```


Figure 6-5. *The XML output of the Yammer conversation thread view*

Liking a Message

Yammer provides many different uses of the Like button; for example, people can use the Like button when they prefer a post and feel it is informative.

Yammer provides REST APIs (Table 6-13) to programmatically mark a message as Liked by the current user. Chapter 7 provides a step-by-step guide on how to implement this feature in your line-of-business applications.

Table 6-13. *Yammer REST API Endpoints to Posting a Like on Yammer*

Endpoints (HTTP Method: POST)	Parameter
`https://www.yammer.com/api/v1/messages/liked_by/current.json?message_id=[:id]`	`message_id`: The ID of the message to mark as liked by the logged-in user.

You can also use the Yammer Like button as shown in Chapter 2 with the Yammer Embed functionality. Example:

```
https://www.yammer.com/api/v1/messages/liked_by/current.json?message_id=436054827
```

Unlike a Message

Yammer provides REST APIs (Table 6-14) to programmatically unmark a message liked by current users. Chapter 7 provides a step-by-step guide on how to implement this feature in your line-of-business applications. The implementation remains the same as you saw in previous examples. The only difference is the method type. Instead of using `POST`, you use `DELETE`.

Table 6-14. *Yammer REST API Endpoint to Delete a Like on Yammer*

Endpoints (HTTP Method: DELETE)	Parameter
`https://www.yammer.com/api/v1/messages/liked_by/current.json?message_id=[:id]`	`message_id`: The ID of the message to unmark the liked message.

Example:

```
https://www.yammer.com/api/v1/messages/liked_by/current.json?message_id= 436054827
```

Yammer Topics

Yammer Topics provides a better way to organize your messages around specific subjects. The user who is posting or editing a message can add topics it and this will allow users to view all the messages posted using the same topics. Users can follow topics. Once a user follows a topic, any posts that contain the topic name will appear in the user's MyFeed.

If you want to show the trending topics or get all the Yammer posts by topic, the following Yammer REST endpoints (Table 6-15) can be useful.

Table 6-15. *Yammer REST API Endpoint for Topics*

Endpoints	Description	Parameter
POST `https://www.yammer.com/api/v1/topics/[:id].json`	To create a TOPIC on Yammer You can use all other parameters like posting to a group to reply to an existing message or to add topics. Example: String data =`"group_id=4659506&body=A message with Topic" + "&topic1=" + "YammerBook!!"`	Topic: integer 1 to 20: The ID of the message to mark as liked by the current user. Body: String The actual message
GET JSON: `https://www.yammer.com/api/v1/topics/[:id].json` or XML: `https://www.yammer.com/api/v1/topics/[:id].xml`	If you know the topic ID and want to retrieve all users who have used that topic. Example: `https://www.yammer.com/api/v1/topics/1788026.json`	Id: The ID of the topic to be used/followed by users in your network.

GET
`https://www.yammer.com/api/v1/messages/about_topic/[:id].json`
or
`https://www.yammer.com/api/v1/messages/about_topic/[:id].xml`
	If you know the topic ID, you can retrieve all messages that have the specified topic or hashtag.
	Example:
	`https://www.yammer.com/api/v1/messages/about_topic/1788026.json`
		Id: The ID of the topic to used/followed by users in your network.

Yammer Users

In Yammer, users are the key player of any social platform. Performing user management in Yammer through your line-of-business applications is as important as managing users of your sites. You can view all the users in the network and see their profiles, who they following, and so on, using the Yammer web interface (Figure 6-6).

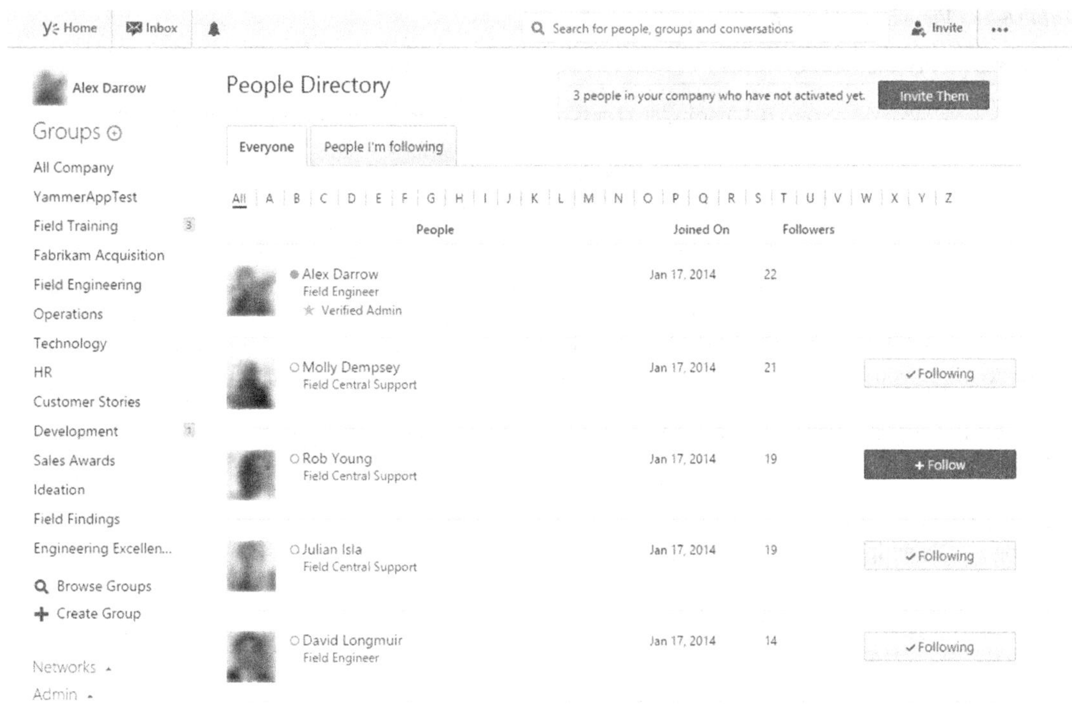

Figure 6-6. *Yammer people*

Yammer has provided a REST endpoint to work on the user object in different manners:

- Get all users on a given network for your internal analysis or audit.
- Engage users on an internal application by showing their Yammer profile info on business applications.
- Make applications more social by adding details of messages liked by users, topics specified by users, and group membership of users.
- Update information about users from business applications.
- Suspend or delete a user.
- Delete messages directly from business applications behalf of a user.
- Search users on Yammer by email address and share their Yammer profiles in business applications.
- Show relationships between users and show the org chart of the current user in business applications.

Table 6-16 lists the APIs available from Yammer related to user objects.

Table 6-16. View Data About the Current User

Endpoints (HTTP Method: GET)	Parameter
https://www.yammer.com/api/v1/users/current.json or https://www.yammer.com/api/v1/users/current.xml	This endpoint does not require a parameter.

The best way to view data about a particular user in XML or JSON is to use the browser window and retrieve the user's data. You can get the user ID from previous examples and form the URL as https://www.yammer.com/api/v1/users/current.xml or https://www.yammer.com/api/v1/users/current.json.

Type the URL in the browser to retrieve the XML, as shown in Listing 6-1 for user ID 1510462475. You will notice when you get the details of the user that you get full profile information, number of followers, number of people followed by the user, the user type, user permissions, different feeds of the user (home, company, and all), number of messages liked by the user, sites bookmarked by the user, and other related details.

Listing 6-1. View any user's data by using the user's ID. You can also retrieve the user's data in JSON format by using a JSON endpoint instead of the XML one


```
<response>
<type>user</type>
<id>1541217186</id>
<network-id>2022718</network-id>
<state>active</state>
<guid nil="true"/>
<job-title>Marketing Assistant</job-title>
<location>U.S.</location>
<significant-other>Janet</significant-other>
<kids-names>Charlie, Donna</kids-names>
<interests>
Running, Yoga, Cooking, Creative Writing, Digital Cameras
</interests>
<summary>
I have been at SDPS for five years as a Marketing assistant. I like to help marketing teams
in effective campaigns.
</summary>
<expertise>
Marketing Communication, Creative Writing, Product Vision, Consumer Advocate, Market
Analysis
</expertise>
<full-name>Alex Darrow</full-name>
<activated-at>2015-04-23T18:05:54Z</activated-at>
<show-ask-for-photo>false</show-ask-for-photo>
<first-name>Alex</first-name>
<last-name>Darrow</last-name>
<network-name>spdsuniversity.onmicrosoft.com</network-name>
<network-domains>
<network-domain>spdsuniversity.onmicrosoft.com</network-domain>
</network-domains>
<url>https://www.yammer.com/api/v1/users/1541217186</url>
```

```
<web-url>
https://www.yammer.com/spdsuniversity.onmicrosoft.com/users/alexd
</web-url>
<name>alexd</name>
<mugshot-url>
https://mug0.assets-yammer.com/mugshot/images/48x48/tFGfQ6ktQDj9szvM2mjpTdgZ2XGRCMJQ
</mugshot-url>
<mugshot-url-template>
https://mug0.assets-yammer.com/mugshot/images/{width}x{height}/
tFGfQ6ktQDj9szvM2mjpTdgZ2XGRCMJQ
</mugshot-url-template>
<birth-date/>
<timezone>Pacific Time (US & Canada)</timezone>
<external-urls/>
<admin>false</admin>
<verified-admin>false</verified-admin>
<can-broadcast>false</can-broadcast>
<department>Sales and Marketing</department>
<email>alexd@spdsuniversity.onmicrosoft.com</email>
<can-create-new-network>true</can-create-new-network>
<can-browse-external-networks>true</can-browse-external-networks>
<previous-companies>
<previous-company>
<employer>SPDS</employer>
<position>Product Manager</position>
<description>Responsible for new product design</description>
<start-year>2010</start-year>
<end-year>2012</end-year>
</previous-company>
</previous-companies>
<schools>
<school>
<school>Univeristy of Maine, Penn State University</school>
<degree>BSc, MA, Business Communication</degree>
<description>
Course requirements and Online Media Communications electives
</description>
<start-year>2004</start-year>
<end-year>2008</end-year>
</school>
</schools>
<contact>
<im>
<provider/>
<username/>
</im>
<phone-numbers>
<phone-number>
<type>work</type>
<number>+1 858 555 0110</number>
</phone-number>
```

```
<phone-number>
<type>mobile</type>
<number>+1 858 555 0109</number>
</phone-number>
</phone-numbers>
<email-addresses>
<email-address>
<type>primary</type>
<address>alexd@spdsuniversity.onmicrosoft.com</address>
</email-address>
</email-addresses>
<has-fake-email>false</has-fake-email>
</contact>
<stats>
<following>5</following>
<followers>3</followers>
<updates>0</updates>
</stats>
<settings>
<xdr-proxy/>
</settings>
<web-preferences>
<absolute-timestamps>false</absolute-timestamps>
<threaded-mode>true</threaded-mode>
<network-settings>
<message-prompt>What are you working on?</message-prompt>
<allow-attachments>true</allow-attachments>
<show-communities-directory>true</show-communities-directory>
<allow-notes>true</allow-notes>
<allow-yammer-apps>true</allow-yammer-apps>
<enable-groups>true</enable-groups>
<admin-can-delete-messages>false</admin-can-delete-messages>
<allow-inline-document-view>true</allow-inline-document-view>
<allow-inline-video>true</allow-inline-video>
<enable-private-messages>true</enable-private-messages>
<allow-external-sharing>true</allow-external-sharing>
<enable-chat>true</enable-chat>
</network-settings>
<enter-does-not-submit-message>true</enter-does-not-submit-message>
<preferred-my-feed>algo</preferred-my-feed>
<prescribed-my-feed>algo</prescribed-my-feed>
<sticky-my-feed>false</sticky-my-feed>
<enable-chat>true</enable-chat>
<dismissed-feed-tooltip>false</dismissed-feed-tooltip>
<dismissed-group-tooltip>false</dismissed-group-tooltip>
<dismissed-profile-prompt>false</dismissed-profile-prompt>
<dismissed-invite-tooltip>false</dismissed-invite-tooltip>
<dismissed-apps-tooltip>false</dismissed-apps-tooltip>
<dismissed-invite-tooltip-at nil="true"/>
<dismissed-browser-lifecycle-banner nil="true"/>
<make-yammer-homepage>true</make-yammer-homepage>
```

```
<locale>en-US</locale>
<yammer-now-app-id>42686</yammer-now-app-id>
<has-yammer-now>false</has-yammer-now>
<has-mobile-client>false</has-mobile-client>
</web-preferences>
<follow-general-messages>false</follow-general-messages>
</response>
```


Figure 6-7 shows the sample JSON output of the current user using the REST APIs.

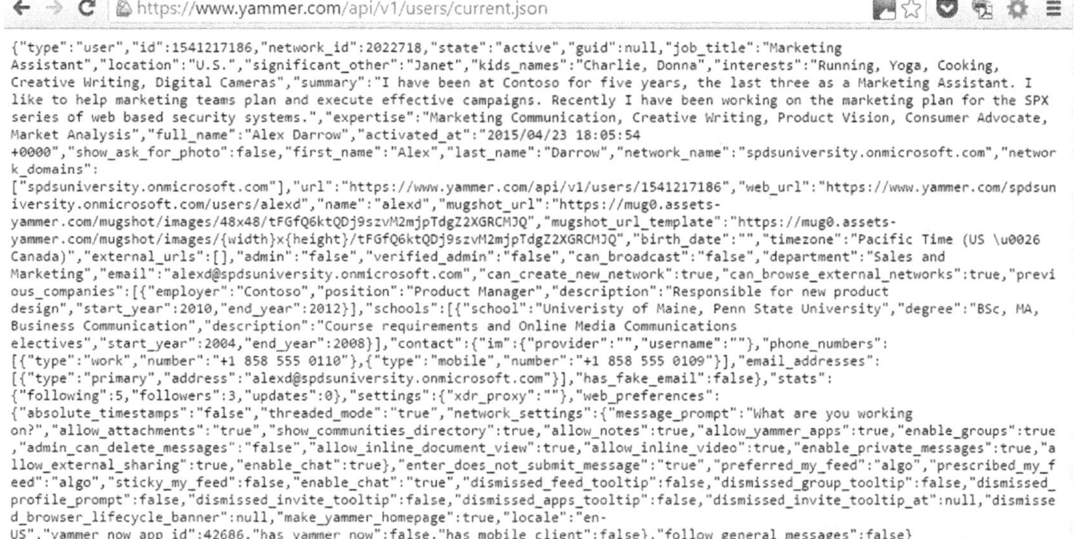

Figure 6-7. *Sample JSON output of current user using the REST APIs*

Retrieve All Users

You can use Yammer's REST API endpoints (Table 6-17) to retrieve all users in a Yammer network. These endpoints support parameters for paging, sort_by, and so on, as listed in Table 6-18.

Table 6-17. *Yammer REST API Endpoint for Getting Users*

Endpoints (HTTP Method: GET)	Description	Parameter

`https://www.yammer.com/api/v1/users.json`
or
`https://www.yammer.com/api/v1/users.xml`
	Retrieve all users in a Yammer network	This endpoint does not require a parameter

`https://www.yammer.com/api/v1/users/[:id].json`
or
`https://www.yammer.com/api/v1/users/[:id].xml`
	View data about any user	ID: User ID of Yammer network

`https://www.yammer.com/api/v1/users/by_email.json?email=user@domain.com`
or
`https://www.yammer.com/api/v1/users/by_email.xml?email=user@domain.com`
	Retrieve user's data about any user using an email ID
	Example:
	`https://www.yammer.com/api/v1/users/by_email.xml?email=alexd@spds.com`
	or `https://www.yammer.com/api/v1/users/by_email.json?email=alexd@spds.com`
		Email: Email ID if existing Yammer user on your Yammer network

`https://www.yammer.com/api/v1/users/in_group/:Group_Id.json`
or
`https://www.yammer.com/api/v1/users/in_group/:Group_Id.xml`
	Get users in a group	`groupId`: Add a group specified by the numeric string ID

Table 6-18. *Query String Parameters for Retrieving Users*

Parameter	Description
`page`	Pagination to 50 users will be shown per page from the Yammer network
`letter`	Retrieve users whose username starts with a given letter
`sort_by=[ messages | followers ]`	The default behavior for sorting messages while retrieving is alphabetically You can use this parameter to sort number of messages the user has posted or followers of the users
`reverse=TRUE`	Should be used with `sort_by` to reverse the sorting order
`Delete=True`	You can suspend user account by passing `Delete=true` as a parameter Note: This can cause the user Yammer account to be deleted and you'll have to contact admin to get it reinitiated.

You can specify the query string parameters listed in Table 6-18.

Create a User

You can create a user using the REST endpoints in Table 6-19.

Table 6-19. *Yammer REST API Endpoints for Creating Users*

REST Endpoint (HTTP Method: POST)	Description	Parameter
POST `https://www.yammer.com/api/v1/users.json`	Use this API to provision a new user. For this endpoint the current user must be a verified Yammer Network admin.	email: Mixed Email for new user `full_name`: Mixed Full name of user
PUT `https://www.yammer.com/api/v1/users/[:id].json`	To update information about an existing Yammer user.	`user_id`: Integer User id specified by the numeric string ID `job_title`: Mixed updated job title

Additional parameters are supported for creating or updating users:

```
email (required for creating a new user), full_name, job_title, department_name, location,
im_provider, im_username, work_telephone, work_extension, mobile_telephone, external_
profiles, ignificant_other, kids_names, interests, summary, expertise, education[] (school,
degree,description,start_year,end_year) - accepts multiple attributes i.e. education[]=UCLA,
BS,Economics,1998,2002&education[]=USC,MBA,Finance,2002,2004, previous_companies[] (company,
position,description,start_year,end_year) - accepts multiple attributes i.e. previous_
companies[]=Geni.com,Engineer,2005,2008
```

Groups REST APIs

As you know, Yammer uses the concept of groups. Groups are a great way to reach a specific audience in your network, such as a specific department in your company like HR or IT. Yammer groups can be private or public. Figure 6-8 shows how Yammer messages, users, and groups are linked.

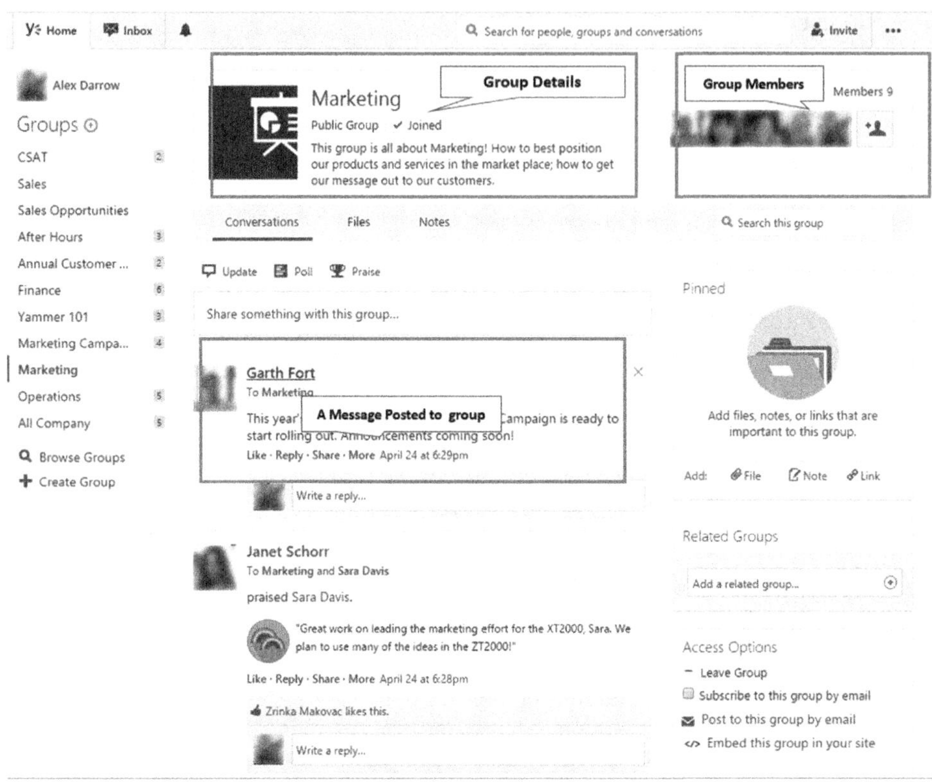

Figure 6-8. *Yammer groups*

Yammer REST APIs (Table 6-20) allow developers to integration these groups by joining a new group or leaving existing groups.

Table 6-20. *Yammer REST API Endpoints for Groups*

Endpoints	Description	Parameter
GET `https://www.yammer.com/api/v1/group_memberships.json?group_id=[:id]`	To get the current user to join the specified group in `group_id` Example: `https://www.yammer.com/api/v1/group_memberships.json?group_id=4695277`	`group_id`: The ID of the group to join
DELETE `https://www.yammer.com/api/v1/group_memberships.json?group_id=[:id]`	Similar to the join the group, you can use this functionality to leave the group. You will need to specify the `group_id` by the numeric string ID. Example: `https://www.yammer.com/api/v1/group_memberships.json?group_id=4695277`	`group_id`: The ID of the group you're leaving

Relationships

Microsoft introduced the org chart in the My Profile section of SharePoint 2010. It's a very nice feature that provides a visual org chart. Yammer provides a very similar org chart, as shown in Figure 6-9.

Figure 6-9. *Organization chart example on Yammer*

By using REST APIs, developers can manipulate the org chart.

Use the REST endpoints listed in Table 6-21 to view or manipulate the Yammer org chart.

Table 6-21. *REST Endpoints Points Top View or Manipulate Organization Chart*

REST Endpoint	Description	Parameters
`GET https://www.yammer.com/api/v1/relationships.json`	View existing chart relationship	`user_id`: Integer (user ID of user who is not the currently logged-in user) `subordinate`: Email addresses of users who are in relation to user, so are added to the user org chart. All three (subordinate, superior, and colleague) can be passed in one request and can be passed multiple times. `id`: Integer The user ID of the user you want to remove relationship in organization chart. Must be combined with type.
`POST https://www.yammer.com/api/v1/relationships.json`	Add an org chart relationship. You have to specify a `user_id` if the user is not the current user for whom the relationship is being added. Specify [subordinate | superior | colleague] to create the relationship	`user_id`: Integer To view or edit the relationships of a user who is different than the currently logged-in user. `Subordinate`: Email addresses values of users who are in relation to user, so add them to the user org chart. All three (subordinate, superior, and colleague) can be passed in one request and can be passed multiple times. `id`: Integer The user ID of the user you want to remove relationship in organization chart Must be combined with type.

To delete existing relationships from the user organization chart, use the endpoints listed in Table 6-22.

Table 6-22. *REST Endpoints to Delete Members from an Organization Chart*

Endpoint (HTTP Method: DELETE)	Description	Parameters

`https://www.yammer.com/api/v1/relationships/[:id].json?type=[relationship_type]`	Deletes the relationship between users by `relationship_type`. You have to specify a user ID for whom the relationship is deleted.	`user_id`: integer
		To view/edit the relationships of a user other than the current user.
		`[ subordinate | superior | colleague ]=email_address string`
		Specify email addresses of the other users (colleagues, superior, and subordinate) to add them to the org chart.
		`Id`: Integer
		Pass the user ID of the user for whom you want to remove relationship
		`type=relationship_type string`
		Specify each for subordinate, superior, and colleague in the `DELETE` requests for which you want to remove the relationship.

Yammer Notifications

Yammer Notifications (Figure 6-10) are a quick way to let people know when some actions are being performed related to them. Yammer notifies users of each interaction the users are a part of on the Yammer network via notification bar, email, SMS, or IM.

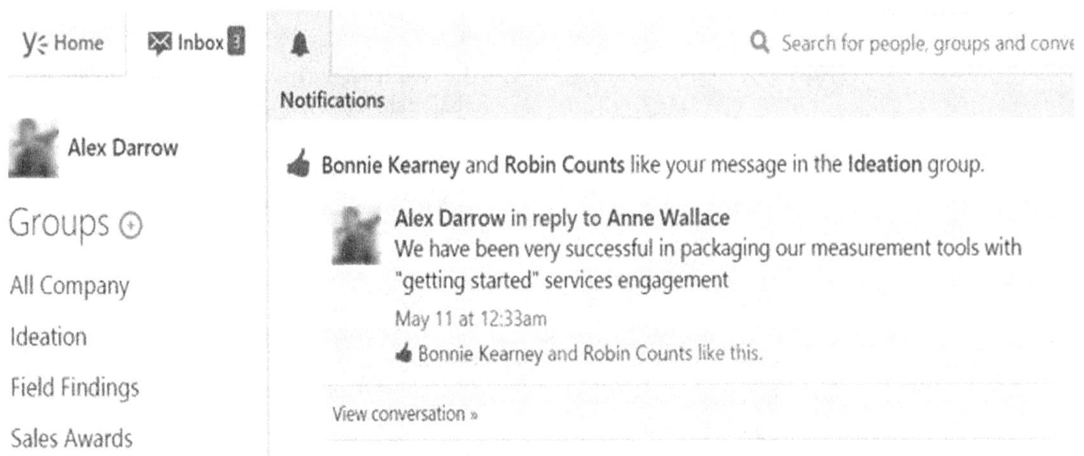

Figure 6-10. *Yammer's notification center*

Yammer REST APIs provide an easy way to retrieve notifications for a particular user so that user can take immediate required actions or reciprocate.

Table 6-23 shows the endpoint for getting the notifications feed for the currently logged-in user.

Table 6-23. *REST Endpoint to Get Notification Feed for Current User*

Endpoint (HTTP Method: GET)	Description
`https://www.yammer.com/api/v1/streams/notifications.json`	This endpoint is used to get the Yammer notifications feeds for the current user.

Yammer Suggestions

Yammer suggests users join similar group (Suggested Groups) or follow similar people (Suggested People) in the same network. This helps users expand their social circles. Figure 6-11 shows the suggestion process on a Yammer web interface.

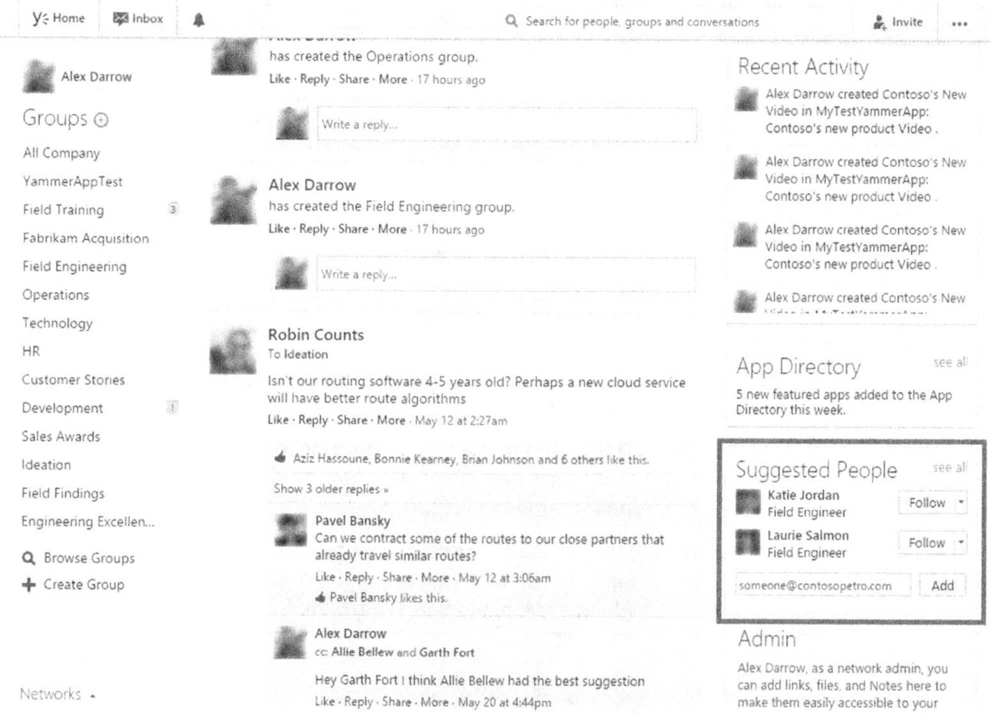

Figure 6-11. *Yammer's suggested people to follow*

Similarly, developers can use the available REST API endpoints to provide suggestions to users based on certain application types that they work on regularly (Table 6-24). This allows users to find relevant messages more quickly and collaborate with teams and share information.

Table 6-24. *REST Endpoints to Show suggested groups to join and suggested user to follow*

Endpoint (HTTP Method: GET)	Description	Parameters
`https://www.yammer.com/api/v1/suggestions.json`	This endpoint is used to provide a list of suggested Yammer groups that the current user can join.	Limit: To get the specified number of suggestions.

Subscription REST APIs

When you follow or subscribe to other users in your network, all the Yammer messages will also appear in your Yammer feed. Let's consider an example—you are working on a project and you follow other project members who are also on Yammer network. Each time a new post is submitted by other users, all these posts appear in your feeds, providing you with an easy way to get insight. Yammer REST APIs provide an endpoint to retrieve subscriptions (Table 6-25) or manage the subscriptions by following or unfollowing actions of the `POST` method.

Table 6-25. *REST Endpoints to Manage Scubscriptions*

Endpoint	Description
`GET https://www.yammer.com/api/v1/subscriptions/to_user/[:id].json`	Use this endpoint to determine if the current user is subscribed to another user specified by the user `id`. If the current user is not following the specified user, the REST endpoint returns HTTP 404.
`GET https://www.yammer.com/api/v1/subscriptions/to_thread/[:id].json`	Use this endpoint to determine if as a user you are subscribed to a discussion thread based on the thread ID. If the current user is not following the specified discussion thread, the REST endpoint returns HTTP 404.
`GET https://www.yammer.com/api/v1/subscriptions/to_topic/[:id].json`	This allow you to check the subscription for a particular topic. It takes the topic ID as a parameter. If the topic is not followed error 404 is returned.
`POST https://www.yammer.com/api/v1/subscriptions`	This endpoint is used to subscribe to a user or a Yammer topic. It supports the `target_type` and `target_id` parameters, which are explained in Table 6-26.
`DELETE https://www.yammer.com/api/v1/subscriptions`	This endpoint is used to unsubscribe to a user or a Yammer topic. It supports the `target_type` and `target_id` parameters, which are explained in Table 6-26.

Table 6-26. *Parameters for REST Endpoints for Manging Subsriptions*

Parameter	Description
`target_type`	Used with `target_id` and allows you to specify a user or tag a current user to support subscribe and unsubscribe.
`target_id`	Yammer object ID to which the current user will subscribe or unsubscribe.

AutoComplete

Autocomplete suggests to the users prepopulated values as the users type in the word. As you start typing the name of a user or group in Yammer, it will try to autocomplete your entry. It will show you similar usernames or group names in drop-down list.

Autocomplete is a useful feature when users are composing a new Yammer message from their application and want to add a group, user, or topic. As soon as you start typing the name of user/group/topic, Yammer starts giving you suggestions based on its existing values.

For example, if the user is typing a new message to all the trainers in a company from an internal training application and want to recognize a trainer on new training calendar, they can start typing "Hello @Al". When the user pauses, they are prompted with the username Alex to complete what they are typing. Table 6-27 lists the REST endpoints related to autocomplete.

Method: `GET`

Endpoint: `https://yammer.com/api/v1/autocomplete/ranked`

Table 6-27. *Parameters for REST Endpoints Related to Autocomplete*

Parameter	Type	Description
`Prefix`	string	Specified text for getting the output of the fields in the specified models. (Users, group, topic, etc.). For example, the prefix text "al" will return results for models that have fields beginning with "al".
`models=modelName:count`	string	Specify comma-separated values of models that can be searched on and a count of results should be returned for each model. Format supported is: `modelName1:count1, modelName2:count2`. `countn` is an integer and model `Name` can be one of the following: • user • group • topic • file • page (note) • open_graph_object • department • external_network • domain For example: the parameter *models=user:2,group:2,topic:2* would return autocomplete six results for users, groups, and topics.

We will show you how to use autocomplete with REST API endpoints in the exercise later in this chapter.

■ **Tip** When using the Autocomplete REST endpoint, avoid excessive network activity and ensure your application adheres to the rate limits. As of now, Yammer Autocomplete has a maximum of five words per search.

We also suggest that as a developer you use caching mechanisms to cache the Yammer returned results to improve the performance of the application for autocomplete. Users will sometimes start to type text and then press Delete or Backspace. Use the cache results for the same prefix rather sending multiple requests.

Invitations REST APIs

The invitations REST APIs (Table 6-28) give developers the ability to send email to users who have not joined the Yammer network programmatically. The Yammer admin can invite people outside your organization, but if the person (who inviting users) is not the Yammer admin, only the official company domain's email addresses will be allowed.

Table 6-28. *REST Endpoints to Invite Users*

REST Endpoint (POST)	Description	Parameters
`https://www.yammer.com/api/v1/invitations.json`	Use this endpoint to send an email invitation to join the Yammer network.	`Email`: A valid email address. Supports inviting multiple users.

Search REST APIs

Yammer's another cool feature is search, which allows developers to use REST API to search users, groups, and messages that match the search string programmatically.

The search endpoint (Table 6-29) returns a list of messages, users, topics, and groups that match the user's search query.

Table 6-29. *Search Related REST Endpoints*

REST Endpoint (GET)	Description	Parameters
`https://www.yammer.com/api/v1/search.json`	The search endpoint returns a list of messages, users, topics, and groups that match the search query text.	Search: String In the search query, Yammer fetches all results that match the search query. Page: Integer Output is restricted to 20 results count per given object type for each page. Along with the results, you get the total count of results with each query. For example, `Page=1` (the default) will return items 1-20, `page=2` will return items 21-30, and so on, depending on the results. `num_per_page`: Integer This parameter limits the count of results of per object type per page. By default, its 20 maximum results.

The return JSON contains the following objects

- Messages
- Groups
- Topics

- Uploaded files
- Pages
- Praises

Later in the training web application exercise, you will see how to include search results from Yammer using the REST APIs.

Yammer Networks

Yammer provides two types of networks—the internal network and external network (Figure 6-12). An internal network, also known as a home network, is private to an organization and only for its internal employees.

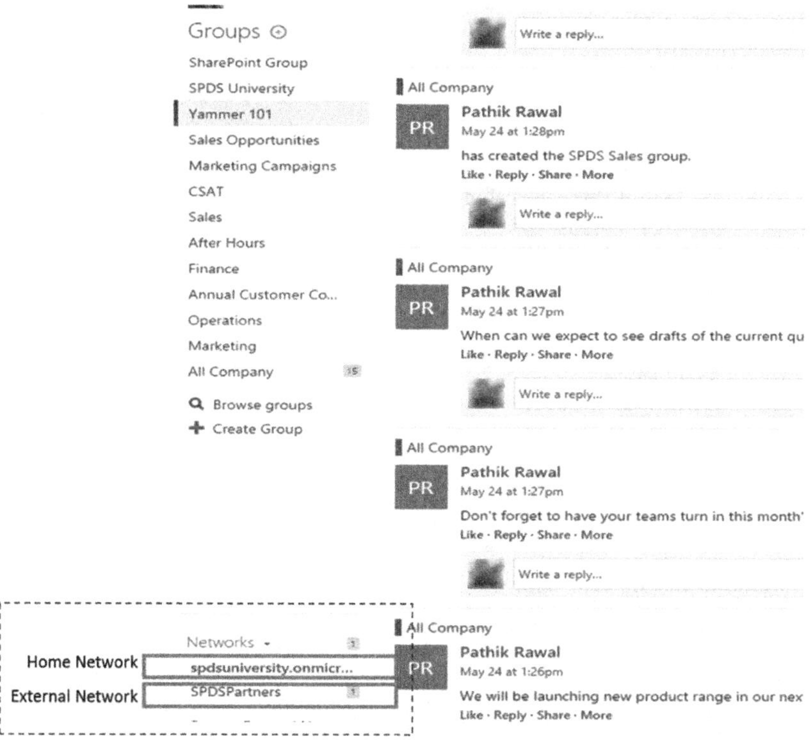

***Figure 6-12.** Yammer networks*

An external network is a separate extension of your home network where organizations can invite users from outside their organization, such as partners, vendors, and so on. While external networks can accommodate users with different email domains, access is invite-only based on users invited by the home network.

The network endpoint (Table 6-30) allows users to select different Yammer networks. The network permalink in indicated in the URL `https://www.yammer.com/network_permalink/resource_path`.

Table 6-30. REST Endpoints to Get a List of Networks for the User

REST Endpoint (GET)	Description	Parameters
`https://www.yammer.com/api/v1/networks/current.json`	Gets a list of Yammer networks for the current user using this REST endpoint. It also supports `Include_suspended` for networks where the user account is in the suspended state.	`include_suspended=TRUE` This field is optional and gets a list of Yammer networks where the user is suspended. `exclude_own_messages_from_unseen=TRUE` Excludes the messages of users from an unseen count. This field is optional.

There are different OAuth tokens when you make REST API requests from your application for each user per network.

Return JSON contains the following properties:

`Name`	`is_org_chart_enabled`
`Permalink`	`is_group_enabled`
`Web_URL`	`is_chat_enabled`
`show_upgrade_banner`	`is_translation_enabled`
`header_background_color`	`profile_fields_config`
`header_text_color`	`unseen_message_count`
`navigation_background_color`	`preferred_unseen_message_count`
`navigation_text_color`	`private_unseen_thread_count`
`paid`	`inbox_unseen_thread_count`
`moderated`	`is_primary`
`created_at`	`unseen_notification_count`
`enable_job_title`	`enable_mobile_phone`
`enable_work_phone`	

For an example, follow these steps:

1. Open a browser windows and log in to Yammer.
2. Open another tab in the same browser window and type `https://www.yammer.com/api/v1/networks/current.json`.

The REST API request will return the following JSON detailing lists of Yammer networks of which the current user is a member.

Return value:


```
{"type":"network","id":54605,"name":"Yammer Developers Network","community":true,"permalink"
:"yammerdevelopersnetwork","web_url":"https://www.yammer.com/yammerdevelopersnetwork",
"show_upgrade_banner":false,"header_background_color":"#F7CC65","header_text_
color":"#000000","navigation_background_color":"#292929","navigation_text_color":"#FFFFFF
","paid":true,"moderated":true,"is_org_chart_enabled":false,"is_group_enabled":true,"is_
chat_enabled":true,"is_translation_enabled":true,"created_at":"2009/07/02 22:33:32
+0000","profile_fields_config":{"enable_job_title":true,"enable_work_phone":false,"enable_
mobile_phone":false},"unseen_message_count":1,"preferred_unseen_message_count":1,"private_
unseen_thread_count":0,"inbox_unseen_thread_count":0,"is_primary":false,"unseen_
notification_count":1}]
```

This covers the main Yammer REST API endpoints. You can refer to these endpoints based on your integration requirements. There are few additional APIs we will talk in this chapter, but first let's look at how to view Yammer's REST endpoint output.

Yammer Output in a JSON/XML Viewer

As mentioned, the output of the REST API comes in two formats—JSON and XML. You can retrieve the output of the REST API using the browser. While working with JSON, you may need a JSON viewer.

First we will retrieve the JSON by using the REST APIs. To do this, open Internet Explorer or any other browser (see Figure 6-13).

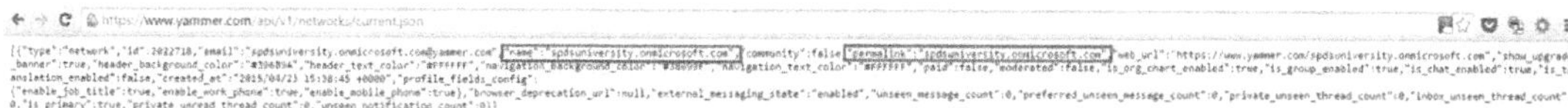

Figure 6-13. *JSON showing current user membership to different Yammer networks*

Type this URL in the address bar: `https://www.yammer.com/api/v1/messages.json`.

You will be prompted with the screen shown in Figure 6-14.

Figure 6-14. *Using Internet Explorer to retrieve a message*

If you use Chrome, the JSON will be rendered in the browser window, which you can copy directly. You can save the JSON on your local system or open the JSON in a tool like Notepad.

The next step is to use the online JSON viewer. There are many JSON viewers available. The one used in this book is `jsonviewer.stack.hu`. Open a browser and type in the URL: `http://jsonviewer.stack.hu/`.

You will be presented with the screen shown in Figure 6-15.

Figure 6-15. *Open/save JSON output*

Now click on the Text tab and copy and paste the JSON you retrieved in previous step. Alternatively, you can use the Load JSON Data button to supply an URL and the viewer will load the JSON from that resource.

After pasting in the JSON, click on the Viewer tab (Figure 6-16). You will be presented with the screen shown in Figure 6-17. Clicking on Viewer changes the mode of the viewer. You can expand or collapse the JSON tree on the left side to view the name and the values on the right side.

Figure 6-16. *Using the JSON viewer, you can copy the JSON and use a viewer to view the JSON object*

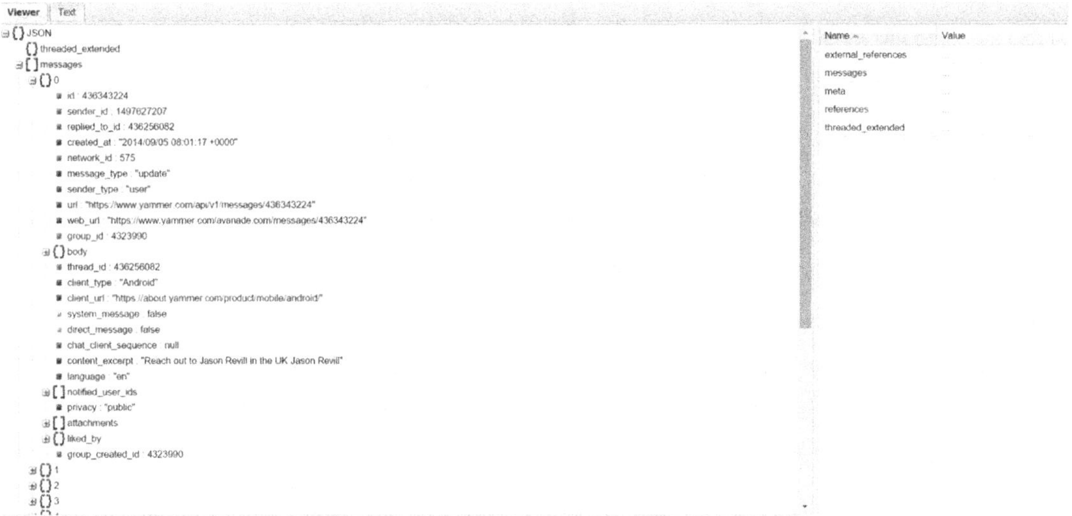

Figure 6-17. *The JSON object viewer window*

In order to view the output in the XML, change the REST APIs endpoint URL by changing the .JSON to .XML. For example, from `https://www.yammer.com/api/v1/messages.xml` (Figure 6-17), type the XML URL in the browser window. The browser will render the output XML file shown in Figure 6-18.

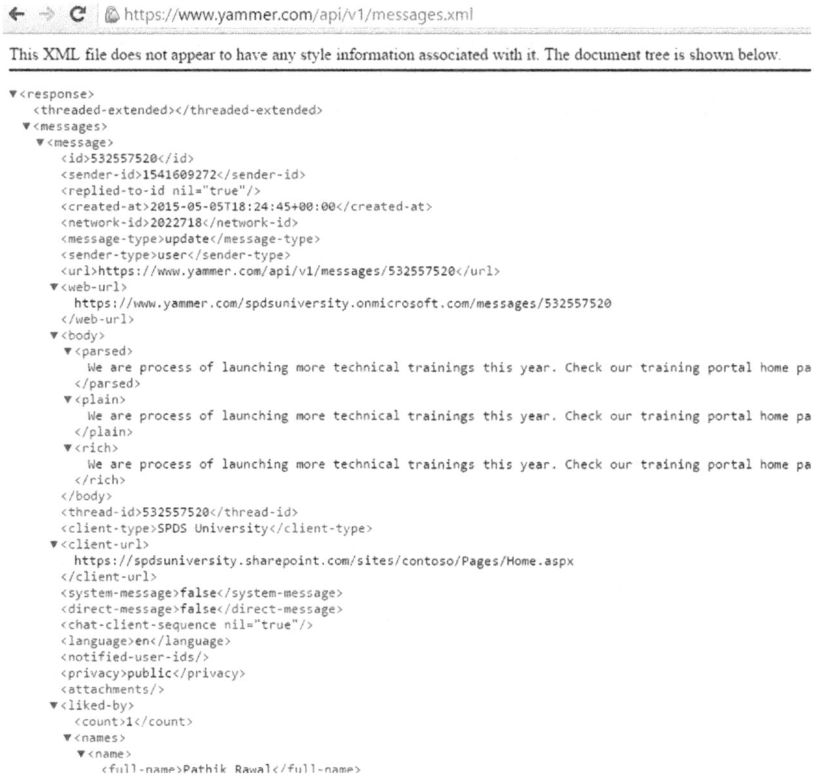

https://www.yammer.com/api/v1/messages.xml

This XML file does not appear to have any style information associated with it. The document tree is shown below.


```
▼<response>
  <threaded-extended></threaded-extended>
  ▼<messages>
    ▼<message>
      <id>532557520</id>
      <sender-id>1541609272</sender-id>
      <replied-to-id nil="true"/>
      <created-at>2015-05-05T18:24:45+00:00</created-at>
      <network-id>2022718</network-id>
      <message-type>update</message-type>
      <sender-type>user</sender-type>
      <url>https://www.yammer.com/api/v1/messages/532557520</url>
    ▼<web-url>
        https://www.yammer.com/spdsuniversity.onmicrosoft.com/messages/532557520
      </web-url>
    ▼<body>
      ▼<parsed>
          We are process of launching more technical trainings this year. Check our training portal home pa
        </parsed>
      ▼<plain>
          We are process of launching more technical trainings this year. Check our training portal home pa
        </plain>
      ▼<rich>
          We are process of launching more technical trainings this year. Check our training portal home pa
        </rich>
      </body>
      <thread-id>532557520</thread-id>
      <client-type>SPDS University</client-type>
    ▼<client-url>
        https://spdsuniversity.sharepoint.com/sites/contoso/Pages/Home.aspx
      </client-url>
      <system-message>false</system-message>
      <direct-message>false</direct-message>
      <chat-client-sequence nil="true"/>
      <language>en</language>
      <notified-user-ids/>
      <privacy>public</privacy>
      <attachments/>
    ▼<liked-by>
        <count>1</count>
      ▼<names>
        ▼<name>
            <full-name>Pathik Rawal</full-name>
```


Figure 6-18. *The XML is parsed by Internet Explorer*

The previous methods to view output from REST endpoints are helpful for debugging and validating purposes when developing integrations.

Now, let's look at additional REST endpoints provided by Yammer for administration and analysis purposes.

Data Export

■ **Note** This option is for verified Yammer Admin users only.

The Yammer REST API for data export contains the raw data you would use to perform social mining on the enterprise.

Developers and Yammer administrators can use the available reporting tools to use data exports from Yammer to get reporting models for data visualizations. Developers can use Microsoft Excel and Power BI to get these detailed reports. This helps your organization start analyzing the information contained in Yammer, identify key trends/insights, and use those trends/insights to become a more responsive organization.

■ **Tip** There are MSDN blogs which provides details how to use standard data exports from Yammer and convert them into detailed reporting models with rich data visualizations.

Yammer exports include the following list of elements:

- Admins
- Files
- Groups
- Messages
- Networks
- Pages
- Topics
- Users

Using Data Export APIs, you can automate the process of getting regular reports. The data export is a .ZIP file that includes messages, users, topics, and groups that are exported in separate .CSV files. This contains complete details of each data type, such as message ID, timestamps, participants, group names, topic IDs, user IDs, usernames, and so on.

The Files and Notes folders will be exported in folders that are separated from your Yammer network. Notes will be exported in the .HTML format. Note that data exports will only return Files and Notes created or modified during the time mentioned in the data export request.

Yammer (`https://developer.yammer.com/v1.0/docs/data-export-api`) has provided good guidance on Yammer Data Export using the Yammer Data Export API and a script for your Yammer network admin

Method: `GET`

Endpoint: `https://www.yammer.com/apa/v1/export`

Yammer REST APIs Rate Limits

When you develop business applications integrations that use Yammer REST APIs, you may run into a situation where you are notified that you have been rate limited. This means the business application has tried to get information from Yammer too many times. Yammer limits the number of times you can call REST APIs in a given timeframe. When this limit is exceeded, Yammer returns the status code `429(Too Many Requests)`. So when you're designing the integrations with Yammer, you have to consider these rate limits.

Yammer enforces the rate limit per user, per Yammer app. Table 6-31 lists the different rate limits.

Table 6-31. *Yammer REST Endpoint Rate Limits*

Yammer Resource	Limit
Messages	In 30 seconds you can make only 10 requests
Autocomplete	In 10 seconds you can make only 10 requests
Notifications	In 30 seconds you can make only 10 requests
All Other Resources	In 10 seconds you can make only 10 requests

■ **Note** Note that these rate limits are subject to change. For the latest, check `https://developer.yammer.com`.

All rate limits are independent of each other. For example, your application can make 10 messages and 10 notifications separately in the same 30 seconds.

There are certain guidelines that you need to adhere to make sure your application is not blocked due to rate limits.

- Do not exceed one poll per minute when polling for messages using the Yammer REST APIs.
- Try to limit the frequency of checking new messages from your application. This impacts the message's latency.
- As autocomplete objects are designed to provide instant response for a user as they start typing the text, the Yammer REST APIs allow more frequent polling.

Now that you understand the concepts and details of the Yammer REST APIs, it is important that you can implement them properly. The following exercise will help you adopt Yammer REST APIs in your real world integration scenarios. In the next section, we will cover an exercise on implementing the Yammer REST endpoints.

Yammer REST Endpoint in Practice

EXERCISE 6-1: ASP.NET SPDSUNIVERSITY WEB APPLICATION INTEGRATION WITH YAMMER USING REST APIS

In this exercise, you are going to use the same web application developed in Chapter 4, Exercise 4-1 to implement writing and reading data from Yammer using Yammer RESTful APIS. You are going to add classes, methods, and UI controls to write data into Yammer from an ASP.NET web application using Yammer REST APIs.

Open the Existing Project

In Chapter 4, you learned about implementing authentication by developing a ASP.NET web application. If you have not developed that ASP.NET web application by following the detailed steps in Exercise 4-1, we strongly recommend you read Chapter 4 and create a new project by following step-by-step guide.

1. Launch Microsoft Visual Studio and open the project created in Exercise 4-1. The structure of the project should look like Figure 6-19.

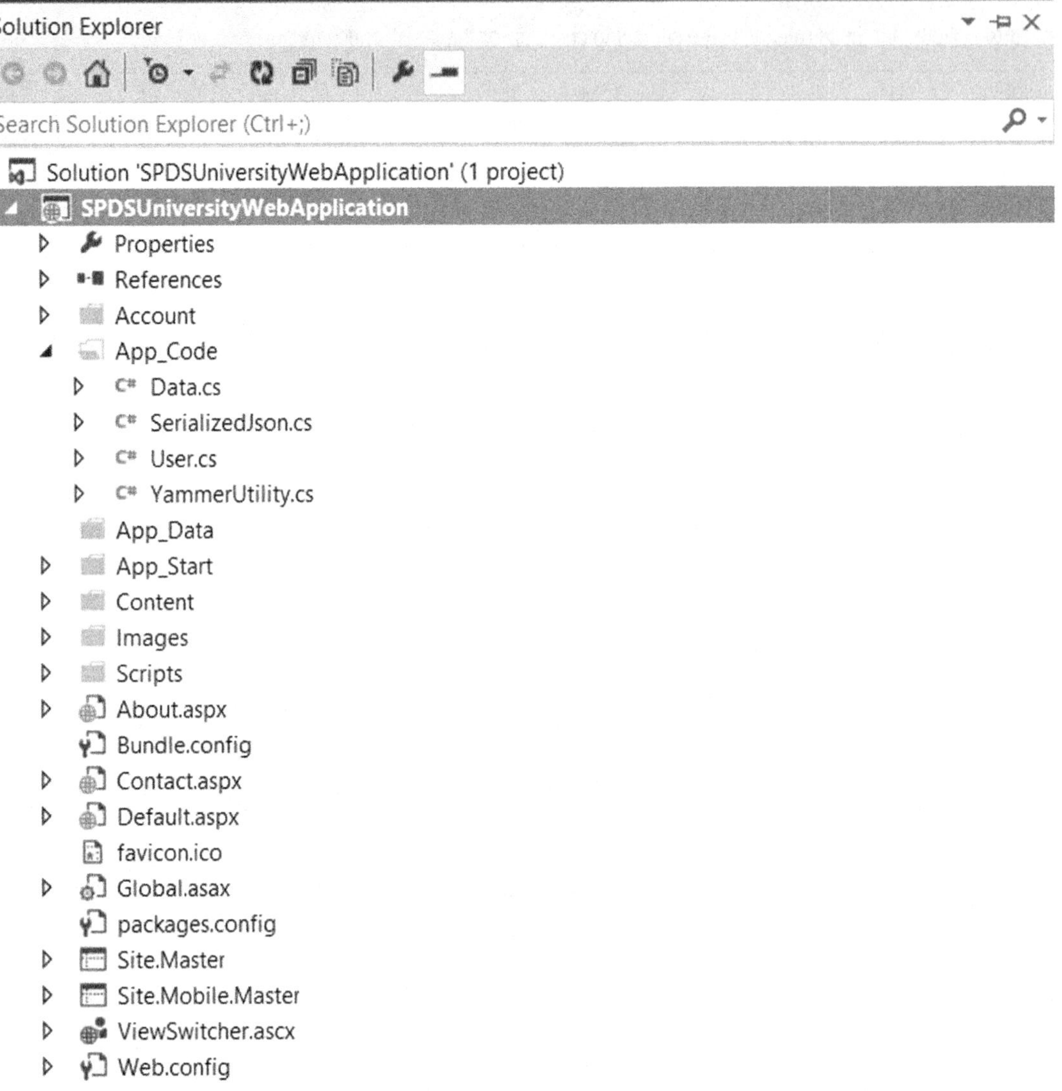

Figure 6-19. *Existing ASP.NET web application project structure developed in Exercise 4-1*

The solution developed in Exercise 4-1 implements the authentication and stores the access token in a textbox that will be used to make further calls to Yammer.

Post a Message

The actual fun of working with Yammer data begins in this section. You will start by posting a message to Yammer from the SPDSUniversity web application.

2. Open the `YammerUtility.cs` and add the following code to the `using` directive:

```
using System.Web.Configuration;
```

3. You need to add a method to the `YammerUtility.cs` class. The method is a generic PostRequesttoYammer method. Add the following code to the `YammerUtility.cs` class.

```
/// <summary>
        /// PostRequesttoYammer
        /// </summary>
        /// <param name="Body"></param>
        /// <param name="url"></param>
        /// <param name="authHeader"></param>
        /// <param name="contentType"></param>
        /// <returns></returns>
        public static string PostRequesttoYammer(string Body, string url,
        string authHeader = null, string contentType = null)
        {
            string results = string.Empty;

            try
            {

                HTTPWebReq = WebRequest.CreateHttp(url);
                HTTPWebReq.Method = "POST";

                //if an authHeader was provided, add it as a Bearer token to
                the request
                if (!string.IsNullOrEmpty(authHeader))
                    HTTPWebReq.Headers.Add("Authorization", "Bearer " +
                    authHeader);

                byte[] postByte = Encoding.UTF8.GetBytes(Body);

                if (string.IsNullOrEmpty(contentType))
                    HTTPWebReq.ContentType = "application/x-www-form-
                    urlencoded";
                else
                    HTTPWebReq.ContentType = contentType;

                HTTPWebReq.ContentLength = postByte.Length;
                Stream RequestStream = HTTPWebReq.GetRequestStream();
                RequestStream.Write(postByte, 0, postByte.Length);
                RequestStream.Close();
```

```
                HTTPWebRes = (HttpWebResponse)HTTPWebReq.GetResponse();
                RequestStream = HTTPWebRes.GetResponseStream();
                StreamReader streamReader = new StreamReader(RequestStream);

                results = streamReader.ReadToEnd();

                streamReader.Close();
                RequestStream.Close();
            }
            catch (Exception ex)
            {
                Console.WriteLine("Error has occured in PostRequesttoYammer:
                " + ex.Message);
            }

            return results;
        }
```

This method takes four parameters—body, endpoint, authheader, and content type. The body is the message to be posted, URL is the endpoint of the Yammer REST API, and authheader is simply a bearer (an access token) received from OAuth. Finally you have the content type value.

4. Now add the endpoint URL to the web.config file. Add the following code to <AppSetting>:

```
<add key="Messageendpoint" value="https://www.yammer.com/api/v1/
messages.json" />
```

On the Default.aspx page, you will add some static content for demonstration purposes. Here we will add the upcoming trainings details.

5. Add the following HTML markup to Default.aspx in <asp:Content runat="server" ID="BodyContent" ContentPlaceHolderID="MainContent">:

```
<table class="table" id="tblupcoming" border="1" runat="server" style="border-
style: solid;border-width:medium">

                <tr>
                    <th class="auto-style7" scope="col">
                        Course
                        Name</th>
                    <th class="auto-style6" scope="col">
                        Level</th>
                    <th class="auto-style5" scope="col">
                        Type</th>
                    <th class="auto-style4" scope="col">
                        Seats Available</th>

                </tr>
```

```
        <tr class="row1">
            <td class="auto-style7">
                SharePoint 2013</td>

            <td class="auto-style6">
                Level 300</td>
            <td class="auto-style5">

                Online</td>
            <td class="auto-style4">
              5</td>
        </tr>

     <tr class="row2">
            <td class="auto-style7">
                Microsoft Dynamic 2014 Advanced
            </td>

            <td class="auto-style6">
                Level 300</td>
            <td class="auto-style5">

                In Person</td>
            <td class="auto-style4">
                10</td>
        </tr>
    <tr class="row1">
            <td class="auto-style7">
             Office 365 Ignite Training
            </td>

            <td class="auto-style6">
                Level 300</td>
            <td class="auto-style5">

                In Person</td>
            <td class="auto-style4">

                10</td>
        </tr>

     <tr class="row1">
            <td class="auto-style7" colspan="4">
                  <asp:Button ID="btnPost" runat="server" Text="Post
                  Upcoming Trainings on Yammer" Width="514px"
                  OnClick="btnPost_Click" />
            </td>
        </tr>

</table>
```

```
<asp:TextBox ID="txtCode" runat="server" Visible="False"></asp:TextBox>
<asp:TextBox ID="txtaccesstoken" runat="server" Visible="false">
</asp:TextBox>

<asp:Label ID="lblMessage" runat="server" ForeColor="#FF3300" Text=" ">
</asp:Label>
<br />
```

6. Add the following code to the `Page_Load` event to hide the table when the page loads. Note that you need to add just two lines of code, as highlighted, which is `tblupcoming.Visible = true` and `tblupcoming.Visible = false`. You add these to the **if** and **else** blocks, as the rest of code already exists:

```
/// <summary>
        /// Page load event to check if query string contains a key called
        "Code"
        /// </summary>
        /// <param name="sender"></param>
        /// <param name="e"></param>
        protected void Page_Load(object sender, EventArgs e)
        {

            string qsCode = Request.QueryString["Code"];
            if (qsCode != null)
            {
                txtCode.Text = qsCode;
                Obtain_Access_Token();
tblupcoming.Visible = true;
            }
            else
            {
tblupcoming.Visible = false;
            }
        }
```

7. Add the following code button event handler code to `Default.aspx.cs`:

```
/// <summary>
        /// Post to Yammer Button's Click event
        /// </summary>
        /// <param name="sender"></param>
        /// <param name="e"></param>
        protected void btnPost_Click(object sender, EventArgs e)
        {
            //Get the current URL of the Page
            string url = HttpContext.Current.Request.Url.AbsoluteUri;
            //Read the Message endpoint from web.config file
             string Messageendpoint = WebConfigurationManager.AppSettings["Mes
             sageendpoint"];
```

```
        ///Construct the messagebody
         string Messagebody = "group_id=4966305" + "&body=Hi All, We have
         seats available for upcoming trainings, Kindly self-nominate
         before the registration deadline. View all training using the
         following link: " + url;

        //call the YammerUtlity's PostRequesttoYammer methis passing the
        message, endpoint and the access token stored in a textbox
        string response = SPDSUniversityWebApplication.App_Code.
        YammerUtility.PostRequesttoYammer(Messagebody, Messageendpoint,
        txtaccesstoken.Text);

        if(!string.IsNullOrEmpty(response))
        {
            lblMessage.Text = "Message posted";
        }

    }
```

The "Post Upcoming Trainings to Yammer" button's click event first gets the current page URL, then it gets the message endpoint from the `web.config` file, followed by the code to construct the message body. It finally invokes the `YammerUtility`'s `PostRequesttoYammer` method. The post targets a specific group, which is mentioned in the `POST` body with a tag `group_id=4966305`.

Run the Application

Let's see this application in action now. You can use Visual Studio to debug and run the application.

8. Click on the Debug button using the Google Chrome option, as shown in Figure 6-20.

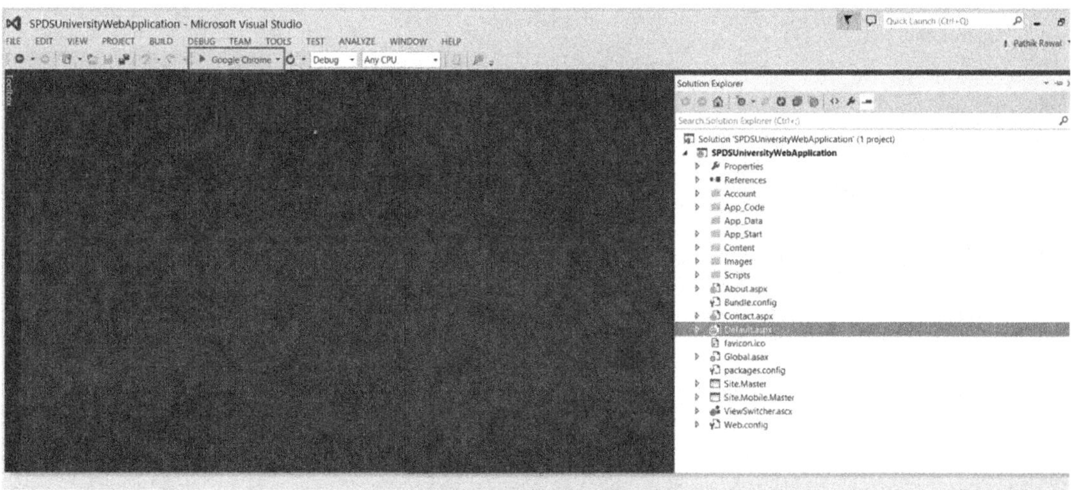

Figure 6-20. *Run the application using Debug in Google Chrome or in the browser of your choice*

9. You will be presented with the screen shown in Figure 6-21, where you see a message saying, "You are not logged in..." Click on the Log In button on the top-right side of the screen.

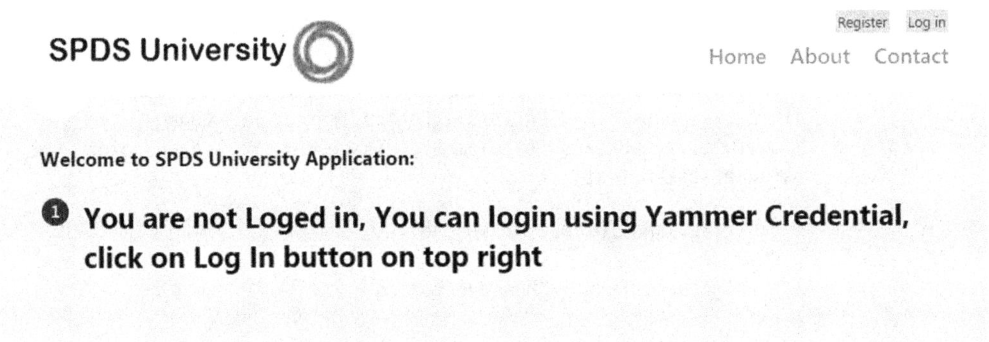

Figure 6-21. *SPDS University web application's home page*

10. You will be presented with the login page shown in Figure 6-22. Click on the "Sign In with Yammer" button, which implements the OAuth authentication.

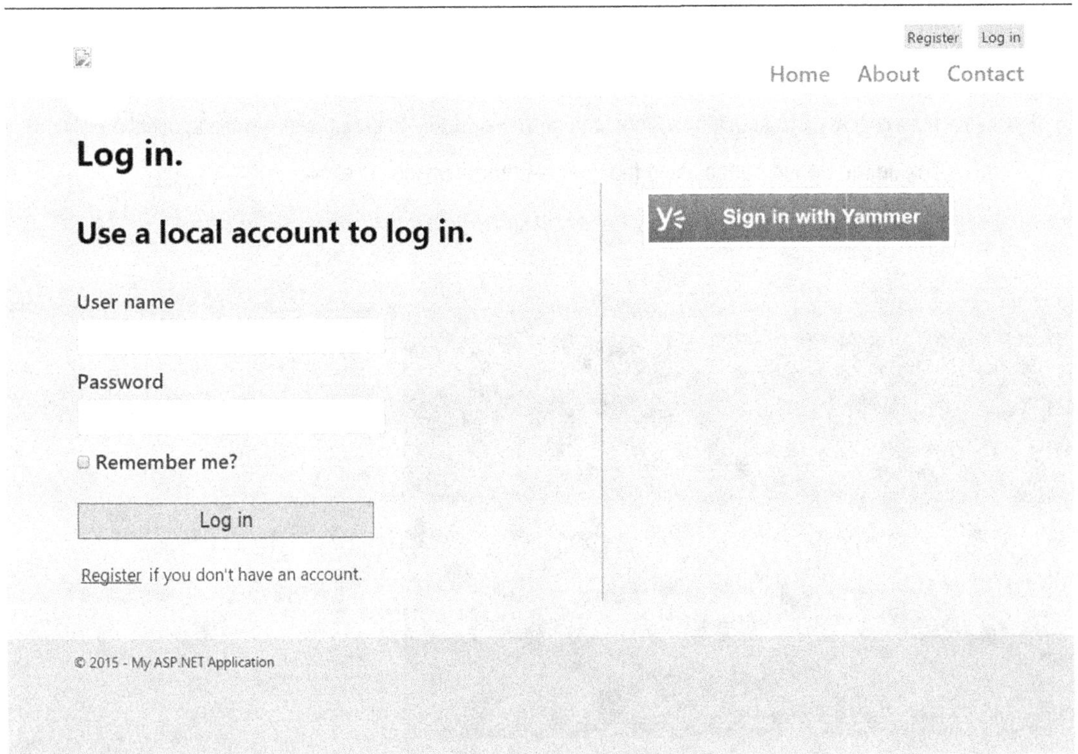

Figure 6-22. *SPDS University web application's login page with a "Sign In with Yammer" button*

11. You will be presented with the Yammer login page. Enter your credentials and click Log In, as shown in Figure 6-23.

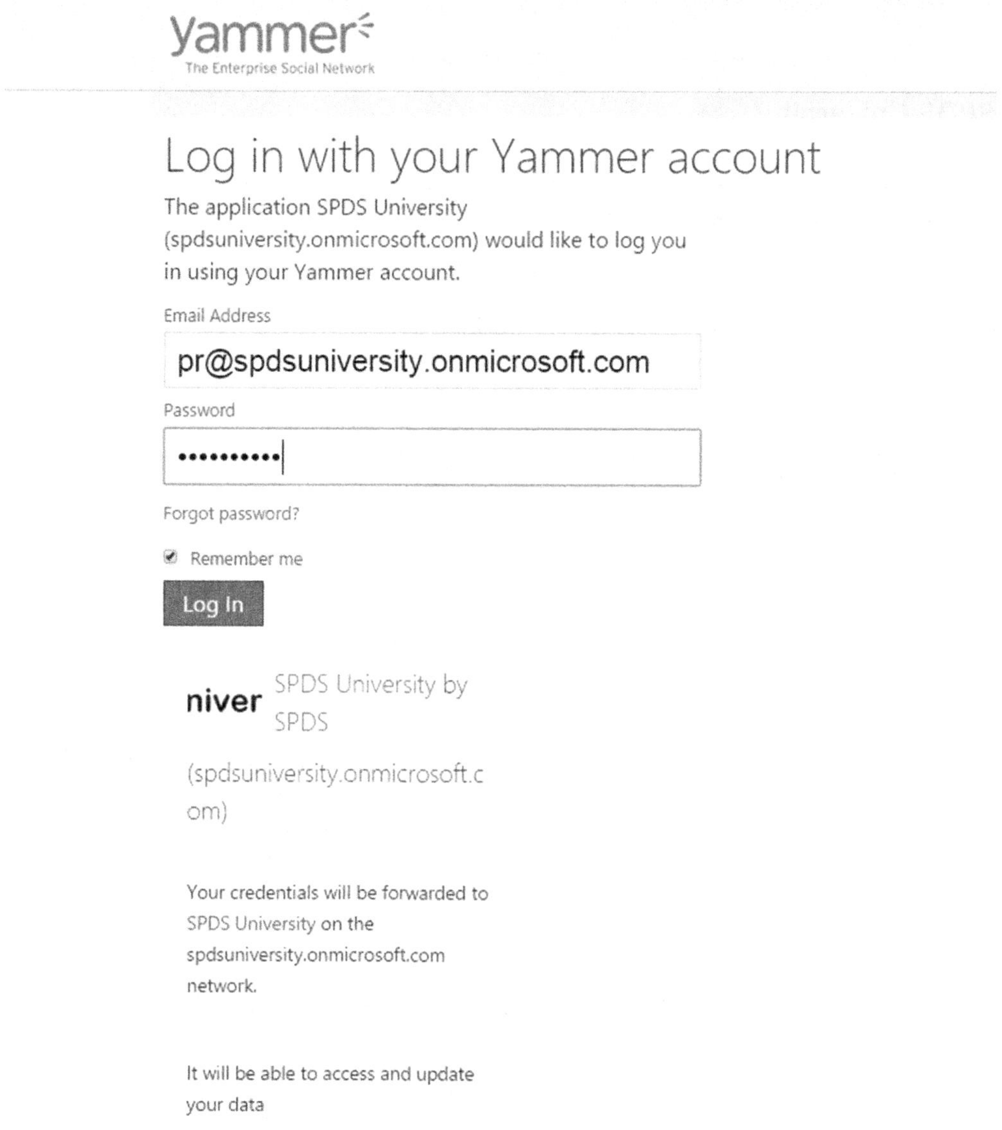

Log in with your Yammer account

The application SPDS University (spdsuniversity.onmicrosoft.com) would like to log you in using your Yammer account.

Email Address

pr@spdsuniversity.onmicrosoft.com

Password

••••••••••

Forgot password?

Remember me

Log In

niver SPDS University by SPDS

(spdsuniversity.onmicrosoft.com)

Your credentials will be forwarded to SPDS University on the spdsuniversity.onmicrosoft.com network.

It will be able to access and update your data

Figure 6-23. *Yammer's Login page*

12. Next you will be presented with the home page of the SPDSUniversity application, with upcoming training details as shown in Figure 6-24. To demonstrate the messaging posting from this application to Yammer, click on the "Post Upcoming Trainings on Yammer" button.

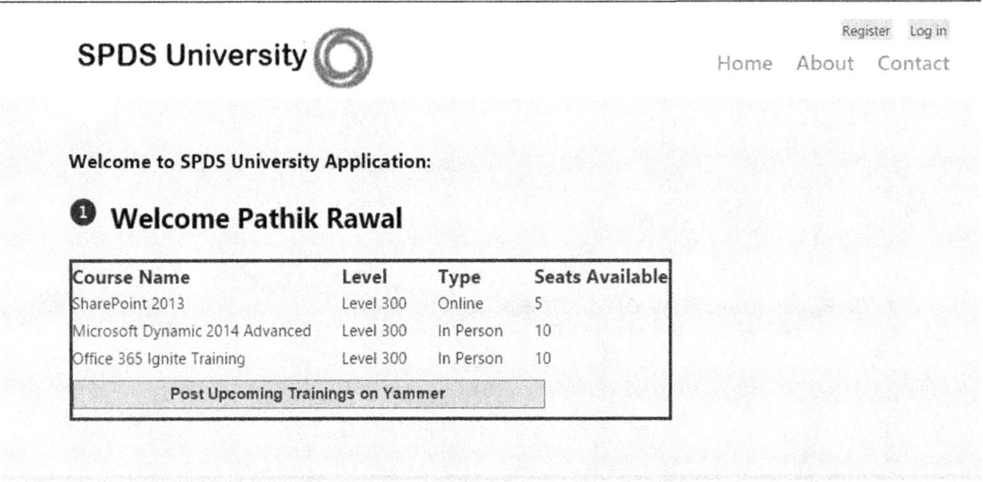

Figure 6-24. *SPDS University home page with a "Post Upcoming Trainings on Yammer" button*

13. After you click on the "Post Upcoming Trainings on Yammer" button, your message will be posted on Yammer (Figure 6-25).

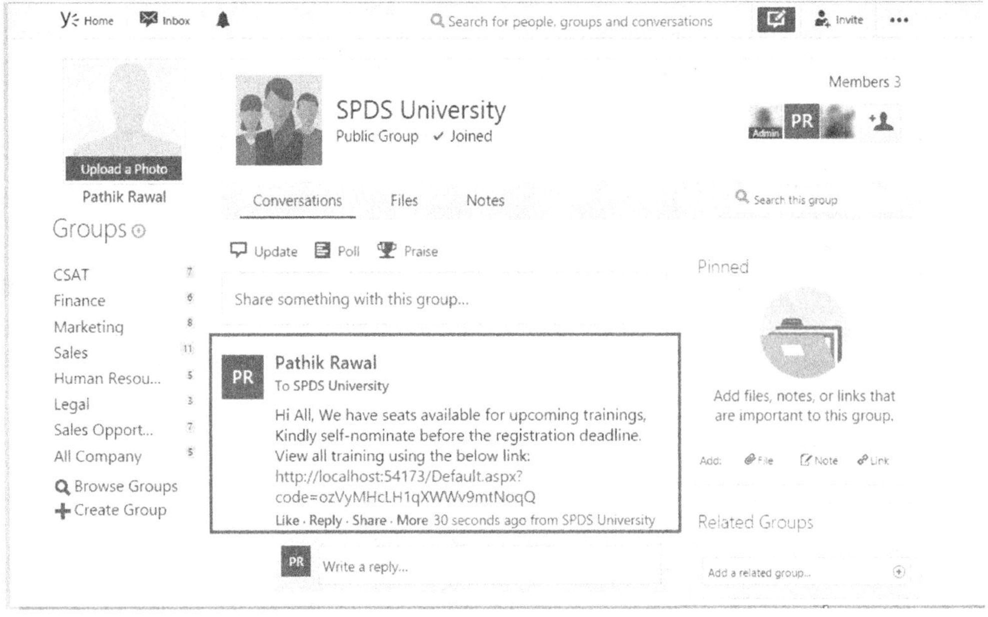

Figure 6-25. *The message is posted on Yammer*

Retrieve Messages Using the Message API

Next you can retrieve all messages using message RESTful APIs. We will add a new web form to the ASP.NET project and will implement an ASP.NET grid control to display messages retrieved from Yammer.

14. Add a new web form to the project by right-clicking on the project in the Solution Explorer and choosing Add ➤ New Item.

15. You will be presented with another window. Enter the name of the web form as YammerMessage and click OK.

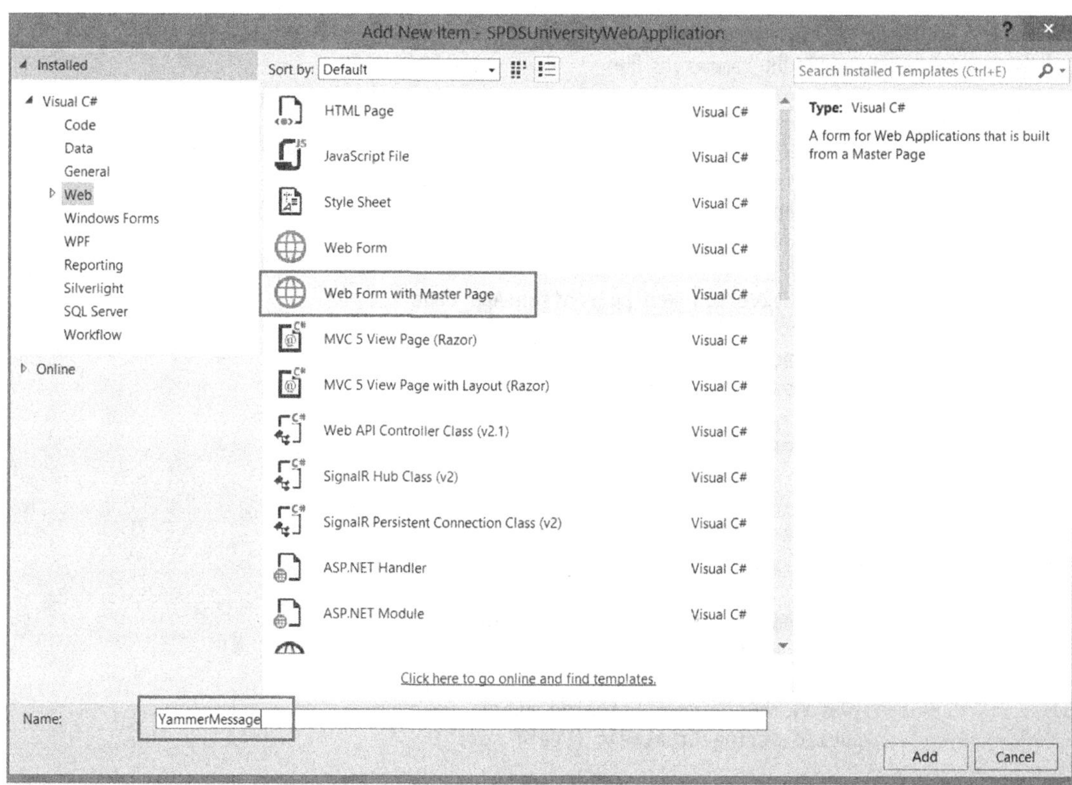

Figure 6-26. Add a web form to the project

You are now going to add a Grid View control to the new page. This grid will render the posts retrieved from Yammer.

16. Add the following code to YammerMessage.aspx within <asp:Content runat="server" ID="BodyContent" ContentPlaceHolderID="MainContent">:

```
<div>
    <asp:GridView ID="grdYammerMessage" runat="server"
    AutoGenerateColumns="false">
<Columns>
```

```
                <asp:BoundField DataField="id" HeaderText="Post ID" />
                <asp:BoundField DataField="weburl" HeaderText="URL" />
                <asp:BoundField DataField="ContentExcerpt" HeaderText=
                "Post Body" />
                   <asp:BoundField DataField="YammerPostLikedBy.Count"
                   HeaderText="Number of Likes" />

            </Columns>
        </asp:GridView>

    </div>
```

17. Add a class called `YammerMessage.cs` to the `App_code` folder and then add the following code to the `Yammer.cs` file:

```
using System;
using System.Collections.Generic;
using System.Linq;
using System.Web;
using System.Runtime.Serialization;

namespace SPDSUniversityWebApplication.App_Code
{
    [DataContract]
    public class YammerPost
    {
        [DataMember(Name = "id")]
        public string ID { get; set; }

        [DataMember(Name = "sender_id")]
        public string SenderID { get; set; }

        [DataMember(Name = "replied_to_id")]
        public string RepliedToID { get; set; }

        [DataMember(Name = "created_at")]
        public string CreatedAt { get; set; }

        [DataMember(Name = "network_id")]
        public string NetworkID { get; set; }

        [DataMember(Name = "message_type")]
        public string MessageType { get; set; }

        [DataMember(Name = "sender_type")]
        public string SenderType { get; set; }

        [DataMember(Name = "url")]
        public string Url { get; set; }

        [DataMember(Name = "web_url")]
        public string WebUrl { get; set; }
```

```
    [DataMember(Name = "group_id")]
    public string GroupId { get; set; }

    [DataMember(Name = "body")]
    public YammerPostContent MessageContent { get; set; }

    [DataMember(Name = "rich")]
    public YammerPostContent MessageContent1 { get; set; }

    [DataMember(Name = "thread_id")]
    public string ThreadID { get; set; }

    [DataMember(Name = "client_type")]
    public string ClientType { get; set; }

    [DataMember(Name = "client_url")]
    public string ClientUrl { get; set; }

    [DataMember(Name = "system_message")]
    public bool SystemMessage { get; set; }

    [DataMember(Name = "direct_message")]
    public bool DirectMessage { get; set; }

    [DataMember(Name = "chat_client_sequence")]
    public string ChatClientSequence { get; set; }

    [DataMember(Name = "content_excerpt")]
    public string ContentExcerpt { get; set; }

    [DataMember(Name = "language")]
    public string Language { get; set; }

    [DataMember(Name = "privacy")]
    public string privacy { get; set; }

    [DataMember(Name = "group_created_id")]
    public string group_created_id { get; set; }

    [DataMember(Name = "liked_by")]
    public YammerPostLikedBy YammerPostLikedBy { get; set; }

    public YammerPost()
    {

        this.MessageContent = new YammerPostContent();
    }
}
```

```
[DataContract]
public class YammerPostContent
{
    [DataMember(Name = "parsed")]
    public string ParsedText { get; set; }

    [DataMember(Name = "plain")]
    public string PlainText { get; set; }

    [DataMember(Name = "rich")]
    public string RichText { get; set; }

}

[DataContract]
public class YammerPostLikedBy
{
    [DataMember(Name = "count")]
    public int Count { get; set; }

    [DataMember(Name = "names")]
    public List<YammerLikedbyNames> Names { get; set; }

}

[DataContract]
public class YammerLikedbyNames
{
    [DataMember(Name = "full_name")]
    public string FullName { get; set; }

    [DataMember(Name = "permalink")]
    public string Permalink { get; set; }

    [DataMember(Name = "user_id")]
    public int Userid { get; set; }

    [DataMember(Name = "network_id")]
    public int Networkid { get; set; }

}

[DataContract]
public class YammerPosts: SerializedJson<YammerPosts>
{
    [DataMember(Name = "messages")]
    public List<YammerPost> Posts { get; set; }
```

```
            public YammerPosts()
            {
                this.Posts = new List<YammerPost>();
            }
        }
    }
```

This code contains the main classes listed in Table 6-32.

Table 6-32. *Login Function Parameters*

Name	Type	Description
YammerPost	Class	Instance of Yammer post with properties like message ID, message body, liked by count and names.
YammerPostContent	class	This class contains the actual message body in pursed text, plain text, and rich text.
YammerPostLikedBy	Class	This class contains properties like count and object of the YammerLikedbyNames class.
YammerLikedbyNames	Class	This class contains the names object with properties like by name, user_id, and network_id.
YammerPosts	Class	Yammer Post's collection object, which contains the YammerPost object.

18. Open the YammerMessage.aspx.cs file and add the following code to the using directive:

```
using System.Web.Configuration;
```

19. The final code for post retrieval is to be added to the YammerMessage.aspx.cs file. This is a Load_YammerPost function, which will be invoked from the Page_load event.

```
/// <summary>
        /// Load_YammerPost method invokes YammerUtility.InvokeHttpGetRequest
        and then the response is SerializedJson
        /// </summary>
        private void Load_YammerPost()
        {
            string response = default(string);
            //Read the Message endpoint from web.config file
            string Messageendpoint = WebConfigurationManager.AppSettings
            ["Messageendpoint"];

            //call the YammerUtlity's PostRequesttoYammer methis passing the
            message, endpoint and the access token stored in a textbox
            if (Session["accesstoken"] != null)
            {
                response = SPDSUniversityWebApplication.App_Code.
                YammerUtility.InvokeHttpGetRequest(Messageendpoint,
                Session["accesstoken"].ToString());
```

```
                SPDSUniversityWebApplication.App_Code.YammerPosts allposts =
                SPDSUniversityWebApplication.App_Code.YammerPosts.GetObjectIns
                tanceFromJson(response);

                grdYammerMessage.DataSource = allposts.Posts;
                grdYammerMessage.DataBind();
            }

        }
```

This method first retrieves the message endpoint from the `web.config` file, then it invokes the `YammerUtility.InvokeHttpGetRequest` method by passing the message endpoint and access token stored in the session variable. The JSON response is then serialized and the object is used as the data source of the grid control.

20. Now add markup for the button control in the `Default.aspx` file, next to the "Post Upcoming Trainings on Yammer" cell:

```
<asp:Button ID="btnPostView" runat="server" Text="Retrieve all Post from
Yammer" Width="514px" OnClick="btnPostView_Click" />
```

21. Finally, add the click event for the "Retrieve all Post from Yammer" button you added in the previous step.

```
/// <summary>
/// Post to Yammer Button's Click event
/// </summary>
/// <param name="sender"></param>
/// <param name="e"></param>
protected void btnPostView_Click(object sender, EventArgs e)
{
     Response.Redirect("YammerPost.aspx");
}
```

Run the Application

Let's see this application in action now. You can use Visual Studio to debug and run the application.

22. Click on the Debug button using Google Chrome, as shown in Figure 6-5, and then click on the Log In button on the top-right, as shown in Figure 6-6. Follow the login process.

23. After you are successfully logged into the application, you will see the home page shown in Figure 6-27.

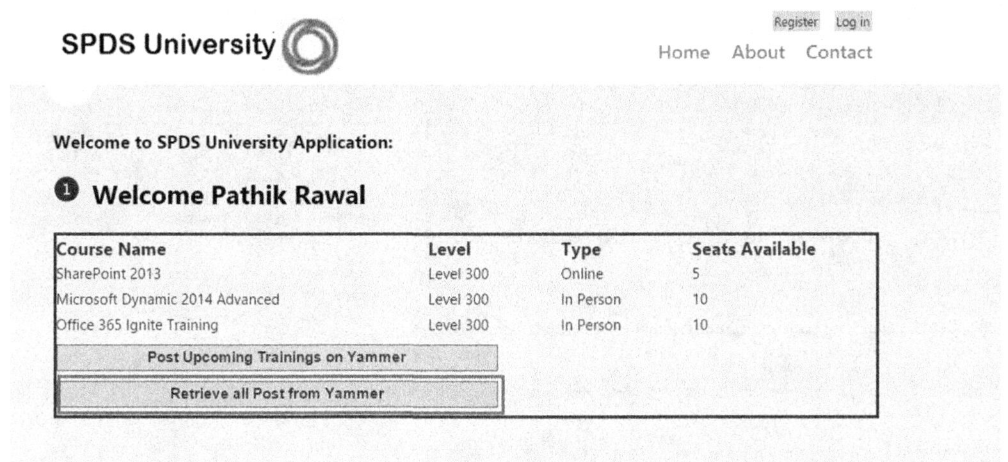

Figure 6-27. *SPDS University home page with the "Retrive All Post from Yammer" button*

24. You will be presented with a screen as shown in Figure 6-28. The page uses an ASP.NET grid control to show you all the message retrieved from Yammer. It displays four properties—`message_Id` (as the post ID), the web URL of the message, the message body as Post Body, and number of likes for that particular message.

Register Log in

Home About Contact

Post ID	URL	Post Body	Number of Likes
532401400	https://www.yammer.com/spdsuniversity.onmicrosoft.com/messages/532401400	Hi All, We have seats available for upcoming trainings, Kindly self-nominate before the registration deadline. View all training using the below link: http://localhost:54173/Default.aspx?code=ozVyMHcLH1qXWWv9mtNoqQ	0
531942523	https://www.yammer.com/spdsuniversity.onmicrosoft.com/messages/531942523	has created the SPDS University group.	0
528964955	https://www.yammer.com/spdsuniversity.onmicrosoft.com/messages/528964955	(Senior Sales Manager) has #joined the spdsuniversity.onmicrosoft.com network. Take a moment to welcome P.	0
528613275	https://www.yammer.com/spdsuniversity.onmicrosoft.com/messages/528613275	Yes! Garth Fort, I'll put time on your calendar tomorrow. cc: Garth Fort	0
528613259	https://www.yammer.com/spdsuniversity.onmicrosoft.com/messages/528613259	Robin Counts, do you know if it will be available in the next few weeks? cc: Robin Counts	0
528613235	https://www.yammer.com/spdsuniversity.onmicrosoft.com/messages/528613235	Will the XT2000 be available for a demo in the next few weeks?	0
528613221	https://www.yammer.com/spdsuniversity.onmicrosoft.com/messages/528613221	Prior to that meeting, let's review the updated figures on how much has been spent on the campaign and how we're targeting potential customers.	0
528613191	https://www.yammer.com/spdsuniversity.onmicrosoft.com/messages/528613191	Molly Dempsey we will be presenting our European Expansion Dashboard to our marketing vendor (Kari) later this week.	1
528613169	https://www.yammer.com/spdsuniversity.onmicrosoft.com/messages/528613169	Thanks. Lets meet today	0
528613157	https://www.yammer.com/spdsuniversity.onmicrosoft.com/messages/528613157	I have the overview from our last meeting. I will post it on the Marketing Campaign site. #xt2000 #marketingcampaign	0
528613109	https://www.yammer.com/spdsuniversity.onmicrosoft.com/messages/528613109	Anyone have any new information on the XT2000 marketing campaign?	1

Figure 6-28. *SPDS University home page with the "Retrive all Post from Yammer" button*

In this section, we show you how to retrieve messages from Yammer using the REST APIs. In the next section, you will see more REST APIs in action.

Search Yammer Using REST APIs

25. You will now add the endpoint URL to the `web.config` file. Add the following code to `<AppSetting>` (you can do it only to a shared resource):

```
<add key="Searchendpoint" value="https://www.yammer.com/api/v1/search.json" />
```

26. Add markup for the button control in the `Default.aspx` file next to the "Post Upcoming Trainings on Yammer" cell:

```
<tr class="row1">
                <td class="auto-style7" colspan="2">
                    <asp:Button ID="btnSearch" runat="server" Text="Search On
                    Yammer" Width="514px" OnClick="btnSearch_Click" />
```

```
                </td>
            <td class="auto-style7" colspan="2">
                     </td>
            </tr>
```

27. Add the click event for the “Retrieve all Post from Yammer” button you added in the previous step.

```
/// <summary>
/// Search Button Event
/// </summary>
/// <param name="sender"></param>
/// <param name="e"></param>
protected void btnSearch_Click(object sender, EventArgs e)
{
    Response.Redirect("YammerSearch.aspx");
}
```

28. Add a new web form to the project by right-clicking on the project in the Solution Explorer and choosing Add ➤ New Item.

29. You will be presented with another window, as shown in Figure 6-29. Enter the name of the web form as `YammerSearch` and click OK.

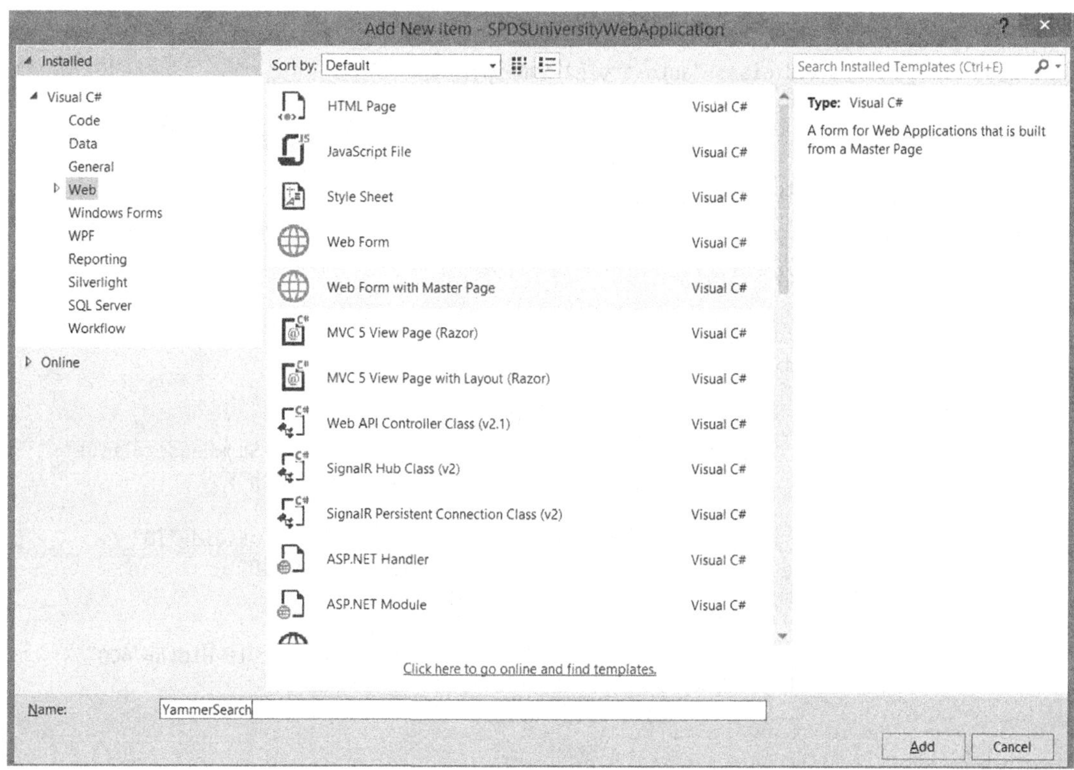

Figure 6-29. Add a web form to the project to implement Yammer Search using REST API

30. Replace `ContentPlaceHolderID="MainContent"` with the following code.

```
<asp:Content ID="Content3" ContentPlaceHolderID="MainContent" runat="server">
    <table class="auto-style1">
        <tr>
            <td class="auto-style2">Seach keyword</td>
            <td>
                <asp:TextBox ID="txtSearch" runat="server" Width="590px">Enter
                seach keyword</asp:TextBox>
            </td>
        </tr>
        <tr>
            <td class="auto-style2">Pages </td>
            <td>
                <asp:TextBox ID="txtPages" runat="server" Width="590px">Enter
                number of pages</asp:TextBox>
            </td>
        </tr>
        <tr>
            <td class="auto-style2">Search items/Page</td>
            <td>
                <asp:TextBox ID="txtItems" runat="server" Width="590px">Enter
                items per page</asp:TextBox>
            </td>
        </tr>
        <tr>
            <td class="auto-style2"> </td>
            <td>
                <asp:Button ID="btnsearch" runat="server" OnClick="btnsearch_
                Click" Text="Search Now" />
            </td>
        </tr>
<tr>
            <td>

            </td>
            <td>

                 <asp:GridView ID="grdYammerMessage"
                 AutoGenerateColumns="false" runat="server" ShowHeader="true"
                 Width="100%" BorderWidth="2" GridLines="Both">
                    <Columns>
                        <asp:BoundField HeaderText="ID"  DataField="ID" />
                         <asp:BoundField HeaderText="SenderID"
                         DataField="SenderID" />
                         <asp:BoundField HeaderText="Message"
                         DataField="ContentExcerpt" HeaderStyle-Width="600" />
                         <asp:BoundField HeaderText="WebUrl"
                         DataField="WebUrl" />
```

```
                    </Columns>
                </asp:GridView>
            </td>
        </tr>
    </table>
</asp:Content>
```

This code adds three input textboxes (the search keyword, the number of result pages, and the search items per page) and the button to invoke the search APIs.

31. Open the `YammerSearch.aspx.cs` file and add the following code to the `using` directive:

```
using System.Web.Configuration;
```

32. Add the search button click event to `YammerSearch.aspx.cs`.

```
/// <summary>
        /// Search Button event
        /// </summary>
        /// <param name="sender"></param>
        /// <param name="e"></param>
        protected void btnsearch_Click(object sender, EventArgs e)
        {
            string response = default(string);
            //Read the Message endpoint from web.config file
            string Messageendpoint = WebConfigurationManager.
            AppSettings["Searchendpoint"] + "?search=" + txtSearch.Text +
            "&page=" + txtPages.Text + "&num_per_page=" + txtItems.Text;

            //call the YammerUtlity's PostRequesttoYammer methis passing the
            message, endpoint and the access token stored in a textbox
            if (Session["accesstoken"] != null)
            {
                response = SPDSUniversityWebApplication.App_Code.
                YammerUtility.InvokeHttpGetRequest(Messageendpoint,
                Session["accesstoken"].ToString());

                SPDSUniversityWebApplication.App_Code.SearchResults results =
                SPDSUniversityWebApplication.App_Code.SearchResults.GetObjectI
                nstanceFromJson(response);

                grdYammerMessage.DataSource = results.Results.Posts;
                grdYammerMessage.DataBind();

            }

        }
```

33. Add a new class to the project and name it `SearchResults.cs`. Then add the following code to the class:

```
using System;
using System.Collections.Generic;
using System.Linq;
using System.Web;
using System.Runtime.Serialization;

namespace SPDSUniversityWebApplication.App_Code
{
    [DataContract]
    public class SearchResults : SerializedJson<SearchResults>
    {
        [DataMember(Name = "messages")]
        public YammerPosts Results { get; set; }

    }

}
```

That's it from search. The class object will be used to store the converted JSON response (the serialized object). The exercise uses a minimum of object properties from JSON. You can add more properties in the class to convert the entire JSON object into a C# object.

Run the Application

Let's see this feature of the application in action now. You can use Visual Studio to debug and run the application.

34. Click on the debug button using the Google Chrome option, as shown in Figure 6-5. Then click on the Log In button at the top right, as shown in Figure 6-6. Follow the login process.

35. After you have successfully logged into the application, you will see home page shown in Figure 6-30.

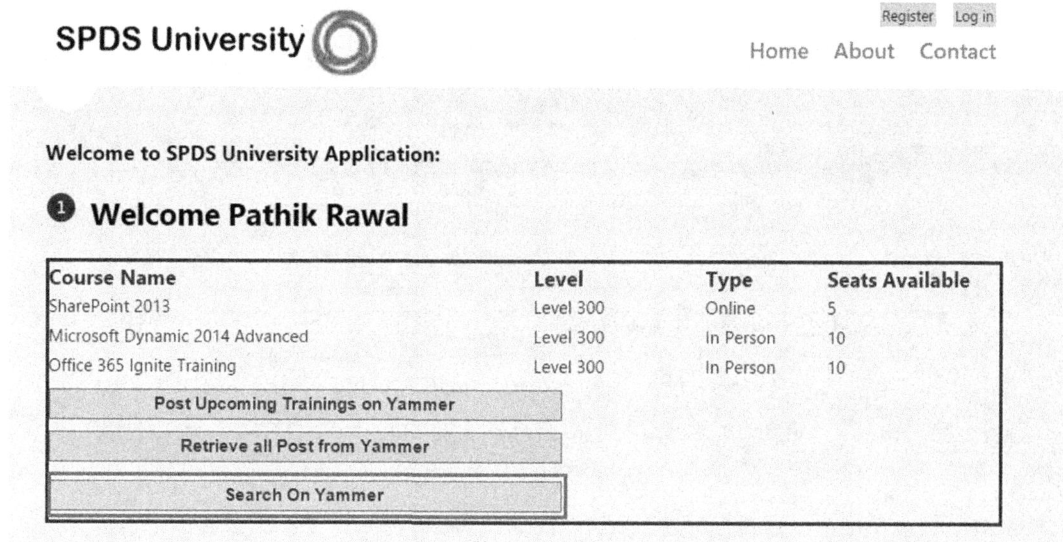

Figure 6-30. *SPDSUniversity home page with the "Search on Yammer" button*

36. You'll be presented with a search page, as shown in Figure 6-31. This page allows users to enter the search keyword and the number of pages and items per page. Click on the Search on Yammer button now.

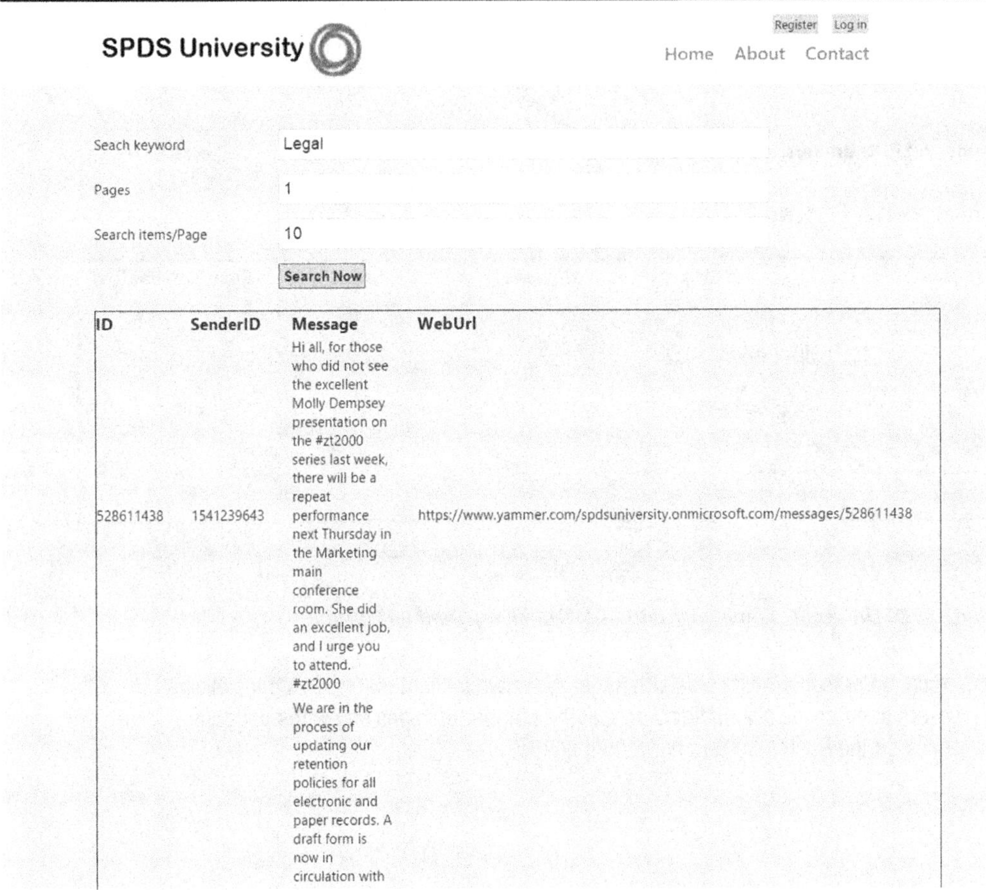

Figure 6-31. Search page with three textboxes as per the search API parameters and the result

The page uses an ASP.NET grid control to show the result retrieved from Yammer. It displays four properties—message_Id (as Post ID), the web URL of the message, the message body as the post body, and the sender ID for that particular message. For demonstration purposes, a simple grid is used to display the result. You can add more features to display other properties and allow users to navigate to actual data pages.

In this exercise, you learned to implement Yammer REST APIs to post a massage, retrieve Yammer posts, and search the API in action. You should be able to call other REST APIs in a similar way.

It's not possible to create exercises for all endpoints in this book, so we expect you to look at your business case and adopt appropriate endpoints per your business needs.

Summary

Yammer REST API are one of the easiest and most comprehensive ways to do integrations with business applications. As a developer, you need to understand the architecture of Yammer REST API endpoints and the important requirements to start using Yammer REST services endpoints. You should also follow the best practices and rate limits when using Yammer REST APIs for creating objects in Yammer. In the following chapter, we will cover the different Yammer SDKs and use them to integrate with HTML-based business applications.

CHAPTER 7

Building Social Apps Using Yammer JavaScript SDK

Pathik Rawal

In the last chapter, you learned about the Yammer REST web service interface and learned how to use Yammer REST APIs in your business applications. In this chapter, you will learn about the Yammer SDKs released by Yammer. Yammer has released the following SDKs specifically for developers to build on the Yammer platform:

- JavaScript SDK
- Windows Phone 8 SDK
- .NET SDK
- iOS SDK
- Ruby
- Python

Yammer SDKs are open source code, which enables you to access Yammer APIs from various technology platforms. Yammer SDKs enable developers to include Yammer authentication and integrate Yammer data into their business applications using client-side and server-side code.

In this chapter, we're going to use Yammer's JavaScript SDK to integrate Yammer with HTML-based enterprise business applications.

Note SDK (Software Development Kit) is a programming kit that includes platform APIs, programming tools, and help documentation that allows developers to develop applications for a specific platform.

P. Rawal and P. Rohilla, *Developing on Yammer*, DOI 10.1007/978-1-4842-0943-1_7

Introduction to the JavaScript SDK

Let's start working with Yammer's JavaScript SDK. The Yammer JavaScript SDK allows developers to integrate Yammer into JavaScript-enabled applications using its rich set of functions for adding social plugins, making API calls, and implementing the Yammer login. The JavaScript SDK provides the following features:

- Enables developers to authenticate users with OAuth 2.0 client-side flow
- Enables developers to use Yammer login in line-of-business applications to authenticate users
- Makes it easy to call into Yammer's API to integrate business applications with Yammer
- Makes it easy to call into Yammer's Open Graph and leverage social graphs

JavaScript SDK includes a rich set functions that allow developers to integrate line-of-business applications with Yammer.

Before we implement the Yammer JavaScript SDK, let's explore the setup that's required to use the SDK for integrations and learn how to configure authentication to Yammer from a business application using Yammer's JavaScript SDK functions.

Setup Required to Use the JavaScript SDK

Let's first explore the very basic setup required to use Yammer JavaScript SDK so it can integrate with external applications. The Yammer SDK for JavaScript doesn't have to be downloaded or installed. Instead you simply need to include a short piece of regular JavaScript code located on Yammer server (`https://c64.assets-yammer.com/assets/platform_js_sdk.js`) in your HTML. That will load the SDK on to your web pages or application interface.

The Yammer SDK reference is available at:

```
https://c64.assets-yammer.com/assets/platform_js_sdk.js
```

■ **Note** At the time of writing this book, c64 is the version released by Yammer. You should refer to the Yammer developer documentation for the latest SDK versions.

The following snippet of code shows the basic version of the JavaScript SDK. You should insert it in the `<head>` tag on each page you want to load it.

```
<script type="text/javascript" data-app-id="YOUR-APP-CLIENT-ID"
src="https://c64.assets-yammer.com/assets/platform_js_sdk.js"></script>
```

This script will load and initialize the SDK. You must replace the value in `data-app-id` with the ID of your own Yammer App. You can find this ID using the client `https://www.yammer.com/client_applications`, as explained in Chapter 3.

Another important configuration is the JavaScript origins section of your Yammer app's configuration. An *origin* is the URL of your web application, SharePoint site, or SharePoint-hosted app.

You need to enter all the URLs of your line-of business-applications. In our case study, this would be the SPDSUniversity SharePoint-hosted app. It's URL could be `https://spdsuniversity.sharepoint.com/sites/Dev` or `https://spdsuniversity-1a08e7eeb36b03.sharepoint.com/sites/Dev`.

That's all that is required from a setup point of view. In the next section, we will take a closer look at JavaScript SDK's authentication functions. You will learn about other JavaScript SDK's functions that allow you to call Yammer REST APIs from your line-of-business applications.

Authentication Using JavaScript SDK

The Yammer's JavaScript SDK provides a secure way to authenticate Yammer users in external applications. Yammer's JavaScript SDKs can be leveraged in a variety of applications, including HTML sites, web applications, Windows 8 apps, and SharePoint-hosted app on the Microsoft platform. In Chapter 4, you built a SPDSUniversity SharePoint-hosted app for SharePoint Online using the JavaScript SDK to authenticate the Yammer users. In this section, we will extend the functionality of that app to post and retrieve data from Yammer by using the JavaScript SDK.

First, let's explore the different authentication functions provided by the Yammer JavaScript SDK.

Authentication Functions

The Yammer JavaScript SDK includes core authentication functions to authenticate users and retrieve user data from Yammer into your line-of-business applications. The core authentication functions are the heart of the Yammer JavaScript SDK and easily can be invoked from client-side HTML code. Table 7-1 lists all the available authentication functions in the Yammer JavaScript SDK.

Table 7-1. *Yammer JavaScript SDK's Authentication Functions*

Function	Table Head
`yam.platform.loginButton`	Provides a "Log In with Yammer" button using simple HTML markup.
`yam.platform.GetLoginStatus`	Returns the Yammer user's login status and, if user is already logged in, it returns the access token.
`Yam.platform.logout`	This function is used to log out the logged in user.
`yam.platform.login`	Invokes the Yammer Login window in a popup. Ensure that you call this function inside a function(response) within `getLoginStatus`.

In the following section, you will learn more about each of the authentication functions listed in Table 7-1.

Function: loginButton

The simplest way to implement OAuth 2.0 authentication flow is to use the "*Sign In with Yammer*" button. You pass a selector parameter in the login function and second parameter is a callback function to handle the response. The HTML element such as `<span id="yammer-login"></span>` gets converted into a standard "Sign In with Yammer" button, as shown in Figure 7-1.

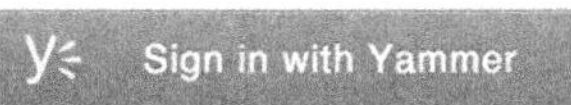

Figure 7-1. *Sign In with Yammer button*

Let's look at the syntax and parameters of the loginButton function.

Here is the syntax of the loginButton function:

```
yam.platform.loginButton(''#yammer-login'', [callback])
```

The loginButton function uses two parameters, listed in Table 7-2.

***Table 7-2.** loginButton Function Parameters*

Name	Type	Required
#selector	HTML element name as string	Yes
[callback]	Function	Yes

The complete implementation of the loginButton function is provided in the following code snippet:

```
<span id="yammer-login"></span>
<script>
yam.connect.loginButton('#yammer-login',
              function (resp) {
                  if (resp.authResponse) {
                      displayAuthResult(resp);
                  }
              });
</script>
```

When this button is clicked by user, it initiates the OAuth authentication workflow on Yammer. When the user approves or denies the Yammer app, the callback function will execute. To determine whether the user has logged in and has approved your Yammer app, you can check the resp.authResponse property value.

If the user isn't logged into your application or isn't logged into Yammer, you can use the Login window to prompt them to do both. If the user isn't logged into Yammer, he will first be prompted to log in. If he is accessing Yammer for the first time, he will be asked to grant permission to the Yammer app to access his data, as shown in Figure 7-2.

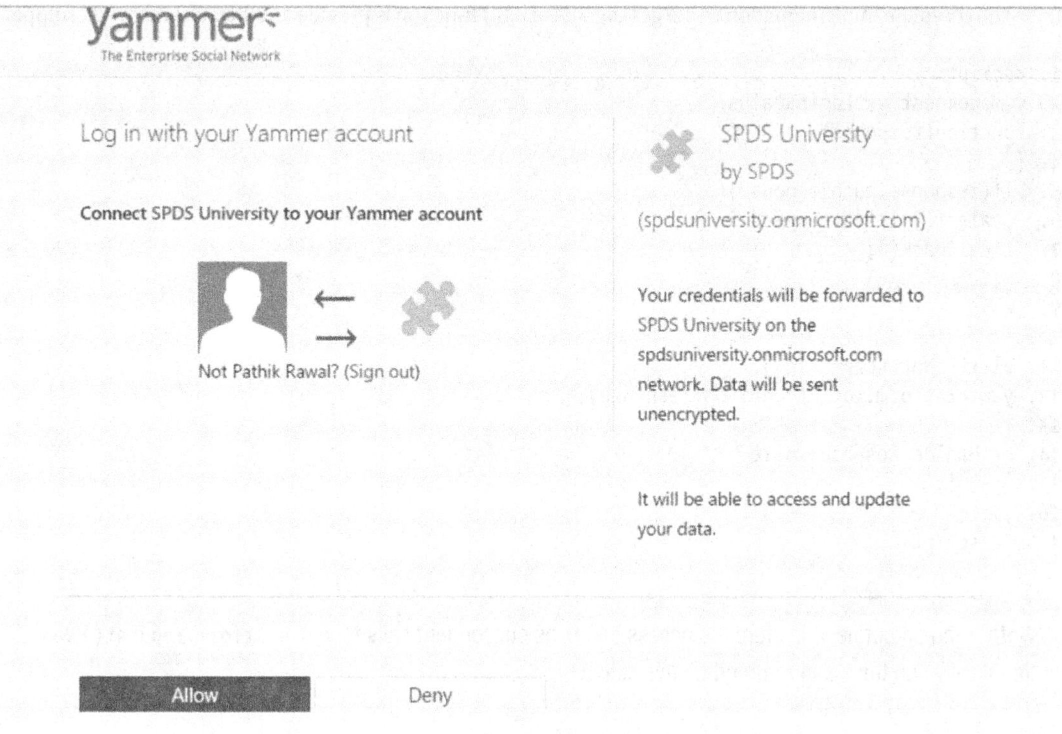

Figure 7-2. *Validation by Yammer to allow an external application to use the user's data*

Function: getLoginStatus

The JavaScript SDK function `getLoginStatus` can be called to determine whether the user is already logged into Yammer. The `GetLoginStatus` function takes two parameters—a callback function and Boolean parameter (true or false) to `forceRefresh`. When `getLoginStatus` is called for the first time, it calls the Yammer API. After a successful call, the callback function will be triggered. The server response is passed to the callback function.

Here is the syntax of the `getLoginStatus` function:

```
yam.platform.getLoginStatus(callback, [forceRefresh])
```

The `getLoginStatus` function uses two parameters, listed in Table 7-3.

Table 7-3. *getLoginStatus Function Parameters*

Name	Type	Required	Description
`[callback]`	Function	Yes	The callback function
`[forceRefresh]`	Boolean	No	If passed as false, then the cached response is returned; otherwise, the function is called again instead of the cached response

The complete implementation of the `getLoginStatus()` function is provided in the following code snippet

```
1. <script>
2. yam.connect.getLoginStatus(
3. function(response)
4. {
5.  if(response.authResponse){
6.    alert("Already Logged in");
7.    callback();
8.  }
9.  else
10. {
11. alert("Not Logged in");
12. yam.platform.login(function(response)
13. {
14. // Hanlde Resposne here
15.       };
16. });
17.  </script>
```

■ **Note** You do not need to store the access token, as subsequent calls to `yam.platform.request()` will automatically use the token returned by this call.

Let's explore this code snippet line by line:

- Line 2: The method `yam.connect.getLoginStatus()` gets the login status of the user.
- Line 3: This line has the callback function that gets called in response to the `getLoginStatus()` method.
- Line 5: The `if` block checks the Boolean field `response.authResponse` to determine if it is true or not.
- Lines 6 and 7: If `response.authResponse` is true then the `if` block is called and it calls the alert message to display the "Logged in" string. The developer can then write the code to call the REST APIs from line 5 on behalf of the logged in user. For demonstration purposed, a `callback()` function is called that can make further calls to the other Yammer APIs.
- Line 9: If `respone.authResponse=false` then the `else` block is called.
- Line 12: Within the `else` block, the line `yam.platform.login()` opens a window for the user to log in to Yammer.

Function: login

The `yam.platform.login()` function is an alternative way to trigger the Yammer login pop-up. This is different from the "Sign In with Yammer" button, which we explained earlier.

Here's the syntax of the `login` function:

```
yam.platform.login([opts], [callback])
```

The login function uses two parameters, listed in Table 7-4.

Table 7-4. *The login Function's Parameters*

Function	Description
[opts]	Object
[callback]	Function

Yam.platform.login() can be used with a GetLoginStatus() method, as shown in the following example:

```
yam.getLoginStatus(
  function(response) {
    if (response.authResponse) {
      console.log("logged in");
      console.dir(response); //print user information to the console
    }
    else {
      yam.platform.login(function (response) { //prompt user to login and authorize your app,
      as necessary
        if (response.authResponse) {
          console.dir(response); //print user information to the console
        }
      });
    }
  }
);
```

You should call the yam.platform.login() method inside a function(response) within getLoginStatus(), as shown in this example. The yam.platform.login() function prompts the user to log in using the Yammer Login screen and then the authorization screen appears so you can authorize your app. Once users take action, the pop-up is closed and the callback function is triggered.

Function: logout

The logout() function enables users to log out from Yammer directly from their business applications. You can check the login status of the user before calling this function, which will ensure that all components required for logout function are loaded.

The syntax of the logout function is as follows:

```
yam.platform.logout([callback])
```

The logout function uses one parameter, explained in Table 7-5.

Table 7-5. *The logout Function Parameters*

Name	Type	Required	Description
[callback]	Function	Yes	The callback function

Implementation of the logout function is very simple, as illustrated in the following code snippet:

```
yam.platform.logout(function (response) {
          // write your code here
})
```

So, now you have learned the various authentication functions provided by the Yammer JavaScript SDK to implement the authentication using OAuth 2.0 flow in your line-of-business applications. Next, you will learn about calling Yammer REST APIs using JavaScript SDKs.

Using the JavaScript SDK to Call Other REST APIs

Once you implement the authentication using OAuth 2.0 flow, you need to call the Yammer REST APIs to write or read data from Yammer in your business applications. Let's explore the functions provided by the JavaScript SDK to make REST APIs calls.

Additional Functions

The Yammer JavaScript SDK includes functions that allow developers to retrieve data from Yammer into their line-of-business applications. Table 7-6 lists the function in Yammer JavaScript SDK.

Table 7-6. *Yammer JavaScript SDK's Additional Function*

Function	Table Head
yam.platform.request	This function can be used to call all other Yammer REST APIs.

In the following section, you will learn about the yam.platform.request function in more detail.

Function: request

The Yammer JavaScript SDK also provides a function that can be used to call other REST APIs. This function can be used to read or write data to Yammer. For example, to post a message to a Yammer group or to post a private message on behalf of a user, you use the JavaScript SDK's yam.platform.request() method to call all the REST APIs.

Here's the syntax of the yam.platform.request function:

```
yam.platform.request(options)
```

The yam.platform.request() takes one parameter—Option—which contains four sub-parameters, as listed in Table 7-7.

Table 7-7. *yam.platform.request Function Parameters*

Name	Type	Required	Description
URL	String	Yes	REST API endpoint, for example, messages.json or activity.json
Method	String	Yes	POST or GET
Callback	Function	Yes	Success callback function
Callback	Function	Yes	Failure callback function

The yam.platform.request() makes Yammer API calls with a bearer token for the current users. The bearer token is set using the yam.platform.setAuthToken() method.

The complete implementation of the yam.platform.request function is provided in the following code snippet:

```
yam. platform.request({
                url: "messages.json",
                method: "GET",
                success: function (msg) {
console.dir ("Get was Successful!: " + msg);
},
                        error: function (msg)
{
 console.dir(msg);
}
})
```

You can make calls to the REST API without the hostname, as shown in the previous example. The previous example uses url:message.json instead of a complete hostname like https://api.yammer.com/api/v1/ messages.json. When calling REST APIs through the JavaScript SDK, you will need to use the api.yammer.com as documented on https://developer.yammer.com/yammer-sdks/.

In Exercise 7-1, you will learn to integrate SharePoint-hosted apps with Yammer using JavaScript SDK. Exercise 7-1 is an extension of Exercise 4-2. In Exercise 4-2, you learned how to implement OAuth 2.0 authentication, which uses JavaScript SDK's authentication function discussed in this chapter. So before you start Exercise 7-1, go back and work through Exercise 4-2 if you have not already done so.

Implementing Yammer Integration in a SharePoint-Hosted App Using JavaScript SDK

In Exercise 7-1, you will implement Yammer integration in a SharePoint-hosted app using JavaScript SDK. You need Visual Studio 2012 Professional or higher and Office Developer Tools for Visual Studio 2012. These can be downloaded from http://msdn.microsoft.com/en-us/office/apps/fp123627.

EXERCISE 7-1: MESSAGES MANAGEMENT: POST A MESSAGE TO A YAMMER GROUP

In this exercise, we will extend the functionality of the SharePoint-hosted app we built in Exercise 4-2 by adding more social features to it in order to post messages and so on.

1. Open the Visual Studio Solution SPDSUniversity SharePoint hosted-app for SharePoint Online that we developed in Exercise 4-2.

2. Add the following code to the `ContentPlaceHolderId="PlaceHolderMain"` for an input text box (to type the message to be posted) and button (to call the `post` message function) markup in `CustomActionTarget.aspx`.

```
<div style="position: absolute; top: 510px; left: 20px; width:
300px; height:80px; background-color: azure; border:dotted;
border-width:medium">
        <br />
          <input type="text" id="txtmessage" value="hi"
          style="width:250px; height:20px;"  />
        <br />
          <input type="button" onclick="postAMessage()"
          value="Post Message to Yammer" />
</div>
```

3. Add a function called `postAMessage()` to the section `ContentPlaceHolderId="PlaceHolderAdditionalPageHead"` in the `CustomActionTarget.aspx` file.

```
function postAMessage() {
          var ItemURL = "https://SPDSpetro.sharepoint.com/";
          var group_id = 4966305;
          var message = document.getElementById('txtmessage').value
          postMessagetoYammer(ItemURL, message, group_id);
}
```

   This function calls the `PostMessagetoYammer` function, defined in the `YammerCore.js`, by passing the `ItemURL`, the `message`, and the `group_id`.

   The `group_id` is hard-coded in this example; however, you can use the message retrieval REST API to get the `group_Id` to post a message to group.

4. Add a new JavaScript file by right-clicking on the project and choosing Add ➤ New Item ➤ Web ➤ JavaScript File, as illustrated in Figure 7-3. Enter `YammerCore.js` into the Name box.

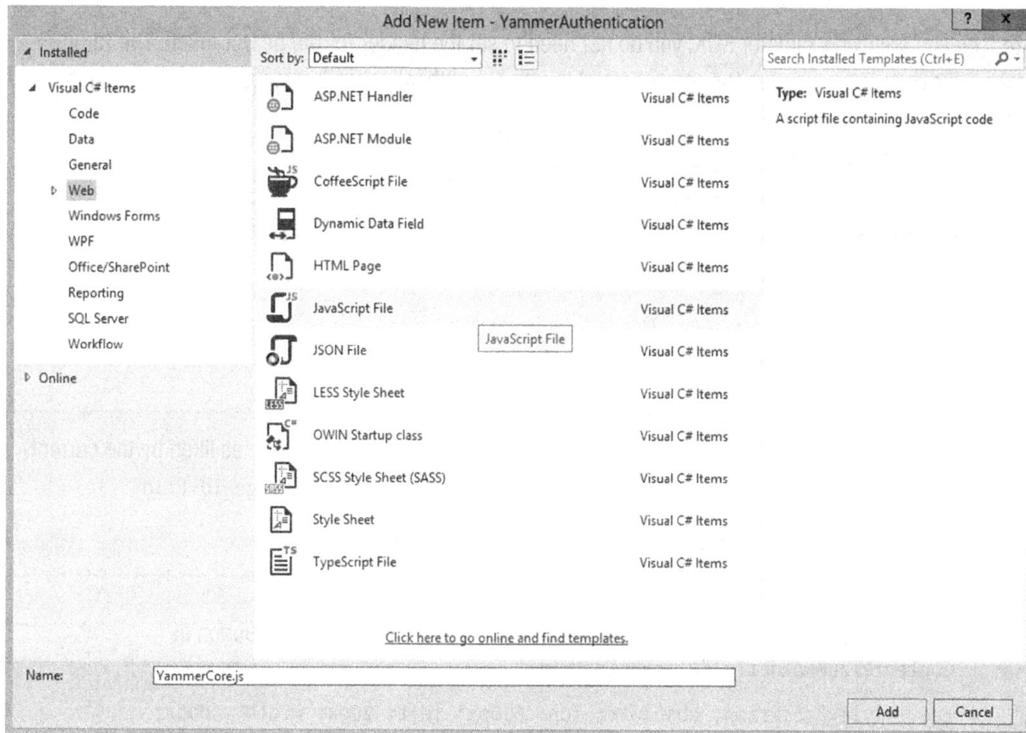

Figure 7-3. *Add a new JavaScript file and name it YammerCore.js*

5. Open `YammerCore.js` and add the following code:

```
function postMessagetoYammer(ItemURL, message, group_id) {
    var testMessage = { "body": "Hello Test, have you seen this" + ItemURL };
    yam.platform.request({
        url: "https://api.yammer.com/api/v1/messages.json",
        method: "POST",
       data: {
           "body": testMessage,
           "group_id": group_id
        } ,
        success: function (msg) {
            console.log("Message Posted Successfully");
        },
        error: function (msg) {
            console.log("Message Posting Error: " + msg.statusText);

        }
    });
}
```

■ **Note** As you are using Yammer SDK, you do not need to set the header for the bearer token. The Yammer SDK does it for your and generates the request header with the authentication bearer retrieved by using the OAuth flow.

6. Add the JavaScript reference to `YammerCore.js` in the section called `ContentPlaceHolderId="PlaceHolderAdditionalPageHead"` in the `CustomActionTarget.aspx` file.

```
<script src="../Scripts/yammercore.js"></script>
```

Messages Management: Like a Message

■ **Note** Yammer JavaScript SDK provides the following REST API to mark a message as liked by the current user. `https://www.yammer.com/api/v1/messages/liked_by/current.json?message_id=[:id]`

Where the `ID` represents the target message ID and `request` requires a `POST` method.

1. In `CustomActionTarget.aspx`, add a button's markup "Like a Message" button in `ContentPlaceHolderId="PlaceHolderMain"`.

```
<div style="position: absolute; top: 610px; left: 20px; width: 300px;
height:100px; background-color: azure; border:dotted; border-width:medium">
        Like A Message
        <br />
        Message Id <input type="text" id="txtmessageid" value="507867284"
        style="width: 250px; height: 20px;" />
        <br />

        <input type="button" onclick="likeMessage()" value="Like a
        Message on Yammer" />
        <br />
</div>
```

2. Add a function called `likeMessage()` to the `script` tag, which will be triggered on the "Like a Message on Yammer" button. This function then calls another function called `likeaMessage()`, which is defined in the `YammerCore.js` file.

```
function likeMessage() {
          var messageid = document.getElementById('txtmessageid').value;
          likeaMessage(messageid);
}
```

■ **Note** The `likemessage` function gets the message ID from the textbox and calls `likeaMessage`, defined in `YammerCore.js`, by passing the message ID.

3. Open `YammerCore.js` and add the following code to define a new function called `likeaMessage(messageid)`.

```
function likeaMessage(messageid) {

    var endpoint = "https://www.yammer.com/api/v1/messages/liked_by/
    current.json?message_id=[:id]".replace('[:id]', messageid)
     yam.platform.request({
        url: endpoint,
        data:'',
        method: "POST",
        success: function (msg) {
            console.log("Message liked Successfully");
        },
        error: function (msg) {
            console.log("Message Posting Error: " + msg.statusText);

        }
    });
}
```

This code snippet first forms the endpoint for invoking the "like a message" API. The endpoint is `https://www.yammer.com/api/v1/messages/liked_by/current.json?message_id=[:id]`, first replace the `[:id]` with the message ID of the message you would like to mark as liked. In this example, `message_id` is passed from `customActionTarget.aspx` using an input text box. The next code is the standard `yam.platform.request` call done by passing the URL (the endpoint we form in the first line of the function, data as empty string, `method:POST`, and callback functions to handle the success and failure scenarios.

Messages Management: Unlike a Liked Message

The Yammer JavaScript SDK provides following REST API, which is the same one we saw in the previous section, "Like a Message".

```
https://www.yammer.com/api/v1/messages/liked_by/current.json?message_id=[:id]
```

Where the `ID` represents the target message ID and `request` requires a `DELETE` method.

1. Add the following code to add a button to the `CustomActionTarget.aspx` file.

```
<div style="position: absolute; top: 810px; left: 20px; width: 300px;
height:80px; background-color: azure; border:dotted; border-width:medium">
        <input type="button" onclick="UnlikeMessage()" value="Unlike a Message
        on Yammer" />
        <br />
</div>
```

2. Add a function called `likeMessage()` to the `script` tag, which will be triggered on the "Like a Message on Yammer" button. This function then calls another function, called `likeaMessage()`, which is defined in the `YammerCore.js` file.

```
function UnlikeMessage() {
            var messageid = document.getElementById('txtmessageid').value;
            UnlikeaMessage(messageid);
}
```

3. Add the following code to define a function called `UnlikeaMessage` in the `YammerCore.js` file.

```
function UnlikeaMessage(messageid) {
    var endpoint = "https://www.yammer.com/api/v1/messages/liked_by/
    current.json?message_id=[:id]".replace('[:id]', messageid)
     yam.platform.request({
        url: endpoint,
        data:'',
        method: "DELETE",
        success: function (msg) {
            console.log("Message was unliked Successfully");
        },
        error: function (msg) {
            console.log("Message Posting Error: " + msg.statusText);

        }
    });
}
```

This code snippet first forms the endpoint for invoking the "unlike a message" API. The endpoint is `https://www.yammer.com/api/v1/messages/liked_by/current.json?message_id=[:id]`, so we need to replace the `[:id]` with the message ID of the message you would like to mark as unliked. In this example, the `message_id` is passed from `customActionTarget.aspx` using an input textbox. The next code is the standard `yam.platform.request` call created by passing the URL (the endpoint we form in the first line of the function, data as empty string, `method :DELETE` and call back functions to handle the success and failure scenarios.

Run the SharePoint-Hosted App

You have added all the necessary code for the SharePoint-hosted app, so you can now run the application and see the integration of the app with Yammer using JavaScript SDK in action.

1. In Solution Explorer, open the shortcut menu for the app in the SharePoint project, and then choose Deploy, as illustrated in Figure 7-4.

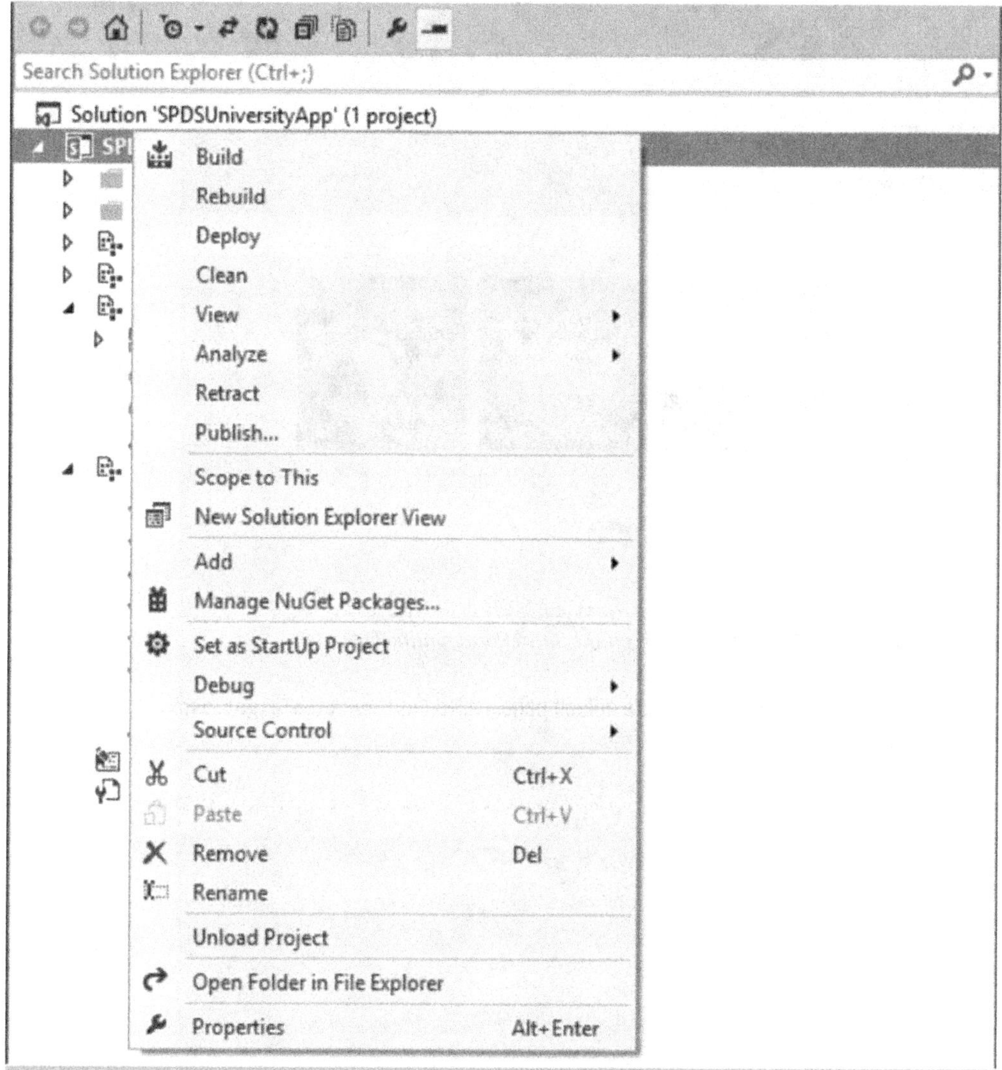

Figure 7-4. *Deploy the SharePoint-hosted app using Visual Studio*

2. Once the app is deployed, navigate to `https:// spdsuniversity.sharepoint.com/sites/dev/_layouts/15/start.aspx#/SitePages/DevHome.aspx` using your browser, as illustrated in Figure 7-5. Click on SPDSUniversityApp, as highlighted.

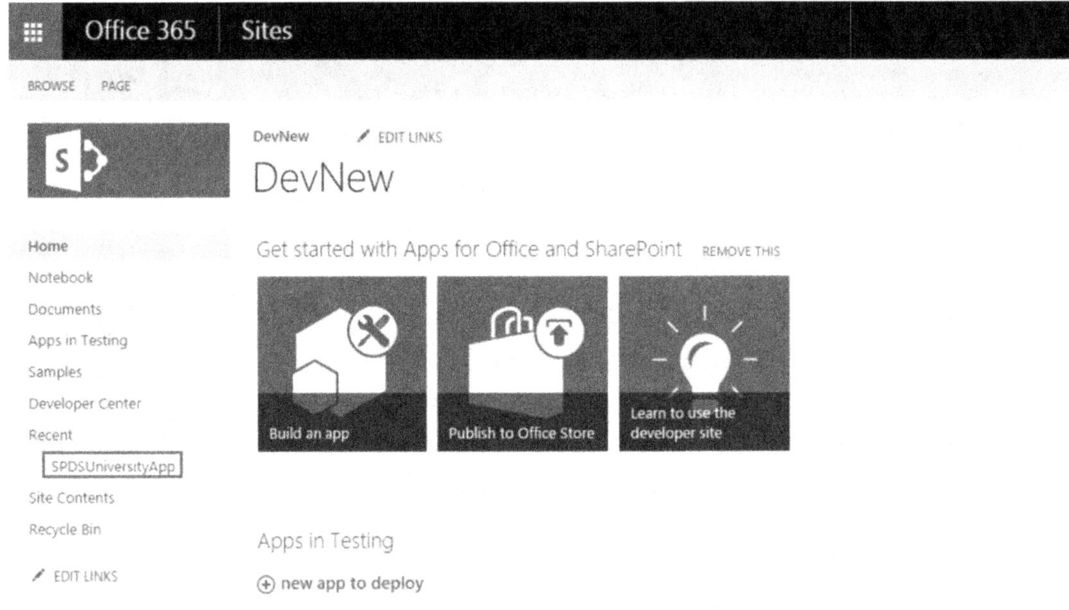

***Figure 7-5.** Deployed SharePoint-hosted app on the SharePoint Online Dev site*

3. You will be presented with the app's default page, called `CustomActionTarget.aspx`, as illustrated in Figure 7-6.

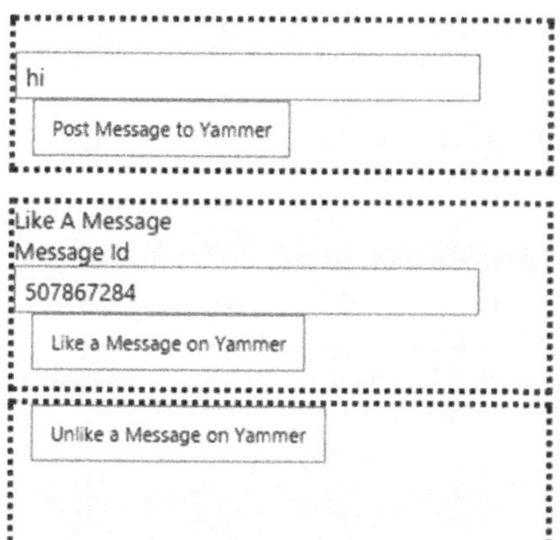

Figure 7-6. *SharePoint-hosted app's default page, CustomActionTarget.aspx*

4. Enter the URL of the SharePoint-hosted app, as shown in Figure 7-7. This should be the URL of the SharePoint web where your SharePoint-hosted app is deployed.

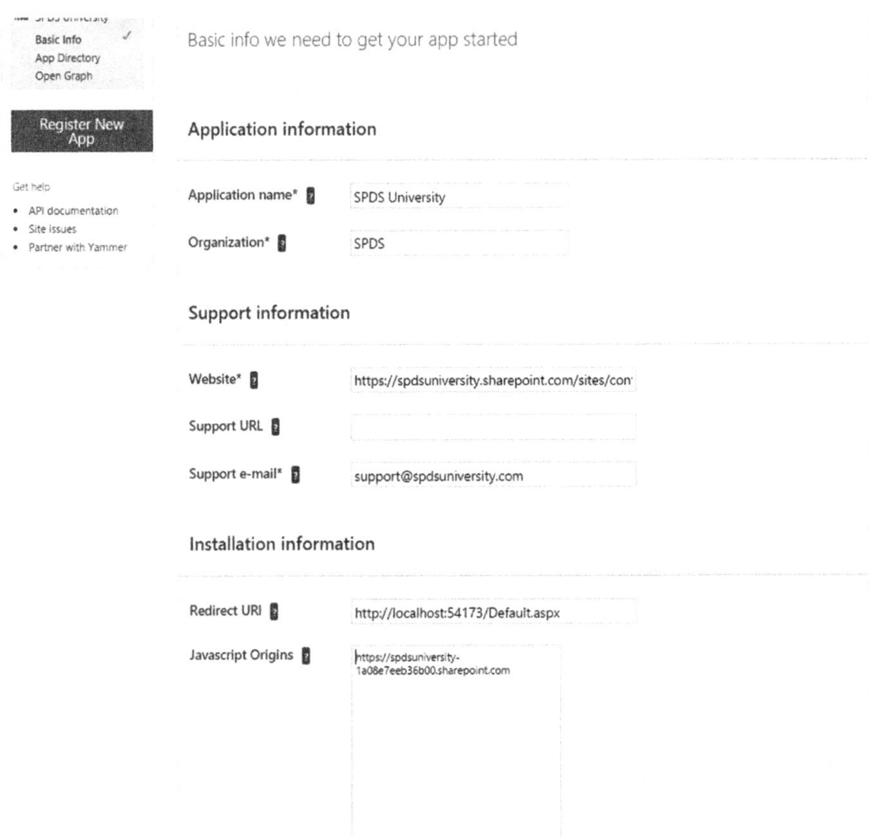

Figure 7-7. *Yammer app's JavaScript Origins section*

5. The first thing you need to do is log in using the "Log In with Yammer" button. Once you click on that button, you will be presented with Yammer's Login window, as shown in Figure 7-8. Enter your Yammer credentials and click on the Login button.

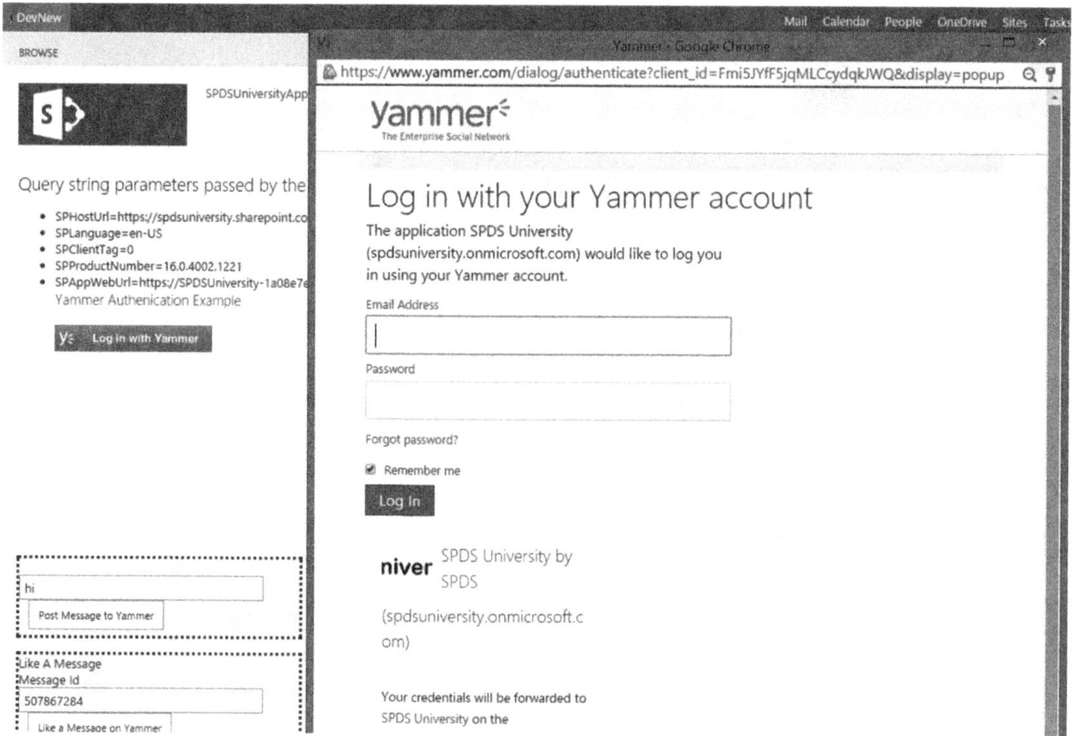

Figure 7-8. *Yammer's login window, which is initiated by clicking on the "Log In with Yammer" button*

6. After a successful login, you will be taken back to the `CustomActionTarget.aspx` page, where the `displayAuthResult()` function will display the access token for the logged-in user, which we already saw in Chapter 4. As illustrated in Figure 7-9, the page also has three `div` sections that display buttons and textboxes for posting a message, liking a message, and unliking a message.

BROWSE

Query string parameters passed by the custom action:

- SPHostUrl=https://spdsuniversity.sharepoint.com/sites/DevNew
- SPLanguage=en-US
- SPClientTag=0
- SPProductNumber=16.0.4002.1221
- SPAppWebUrl=https://SPDSUniversity-1a08e7eeb36b03.sharepoint.com/sites/DevNew/SPDSUniversityApp

Yammer Authenication Example

Welcome to Yammer!, The user ID is: 1541609272

User is now signed in to the app using Yammer

Log out from your Yammer account

Authentication Logs

```
=========
Access Token:
=========
user_id: 1541609272
network_id: 2022718
network_permalink: spdsuniversity.onmicrosoft.com
network_name: spdsuniversity.onmicrosoft.com
```

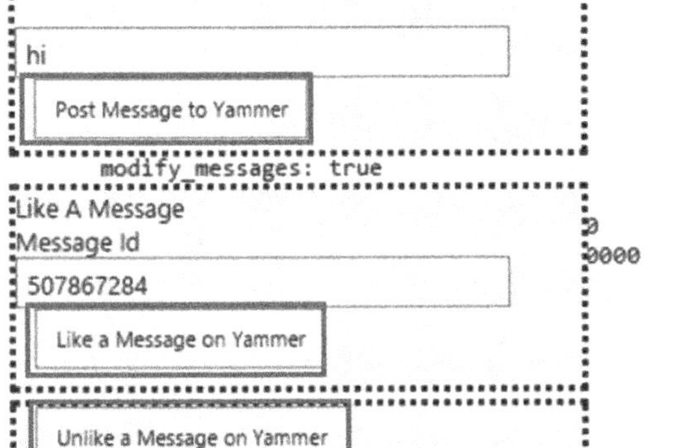

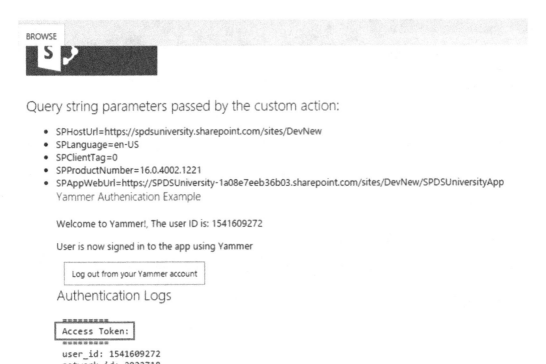

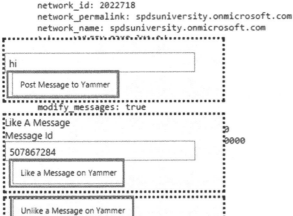

Figure 7-9. After successful login, the page displays the markup to test other features of the JavaScript SDK

So, in this exercise, we extended the SPDS University SharePoint-hosted app to integrate Yammer functionalities by using the Yammer JavaScript SDK.

In a similar manner, you can use the Yammer JavaScript SDK in your business application to provide authentication using Yammer and then read and write data to Yammer.

Summary

By now you are familiar with the Yammer SDKs released by Yammer. First, you learned about the Yammer JavaScript SDK, the authentication functions, and the other functions available in the SDK. You also learned to integrate a JavaScript-enabled application with Yammer. In the next chapter, you will learn how to integrate a Windows phone app with Yammer using the Windows Phone SDK.

CHAPTER 8

Building Social Apps Using Yammer Windows Phone 8 SDK

Pathik Rawal

In last chapter you learned about Yammer JavaScript SDK. The JavaScript SDK helps you integrate HTML-based line-of-business applications with Yammer. In this chapter, you will learn about the Yammer Windows Phone SDK, released by Yammer. The Windows Phone SDK allows you to integrate Windows phone apps with Yammer. You can leverage the Windows Phone SDK to allow users to log in to your Windows Phone SDK using Yammer. You can implement the "Sign In with Yammer" button using the Windows Phone SDK to speed up the registration process and build a functional login system in minutes.

Introduction to Windows Phone 8 SDK

Yammer Windows Phone SDK is an open source program that enables developers to build Windows mobile apps on the Yammer platform or integrate Yammer functionality into their existing Windows phone apps. Like Yammer's other SDKs for enterprise applications, the Windows Phone SDK helps organizations build more mobile capabilities and develop integrations with Yammer.

The Yammer Windows Phone SDK is a class library project that's best suitable for Microsoft Windows Phone 8 apps.

The Windows Phone SDK enables:

- Developers to authenticate users with OAuth 2.0 in a Windows phone app
- Developers to call into Yammer's API to integrate Windows phone app with Yammer
- Developers to call into Yammer's Open Graph and leverage social graph

The Windows Phone SDK is available at `https://github.com/yammer/windows-phone-oauth-sdk-demo`. This SDK consists of two projects:

- `Yammer.OAuthSDK`: A class library that contains helper classes for Windows phone app. The library provides methods for login, authorization processes, and other APIs calls.
- `OAuthWPDemo`: A sample project that demonstrates how to use the SDK to build the Windows Phone API for the Yammer network.

Note This chapter does not explain how to develop Windows Phone 8 mobile apps. Refer to MSDN or other Apress books to explore Windows Phone 8 app development.

P. Rawal and P. Rohilla, *Developing on Yammer*, DOI 10.1007/978-1-4842-0943-1_8

In the next section, you will learn about the basic setup required in order to leverage the Windows Phone SDK.

Setup Required to Use Windows Phone App 8 SDK

Before you learn about the different methods and functions, it's important to understand the basic setup required to integrate the Windows Phone SDK.

Step 1: Register Your Yammer App and Set the Redirect URI

Register a new Yammer app as explained in Chapter 3 and configure the redirect URI to a custom one. The redirect URI has be unique to your WP8 app. For example, `SPDSWP8App://Yammer`. Make sure the scheme name (in this case `SPDSWP8App`) is unique to your company and Windows phone 8 app.

Step 2: Create an Instance of the Yammer.OAuthSDK.Model.OAuthClientInfo Class

The Yammer App registered in your Yammer network is identified by a unique ClientID, a client secret key, and a redirect URI, as shown in Figure 8-1.

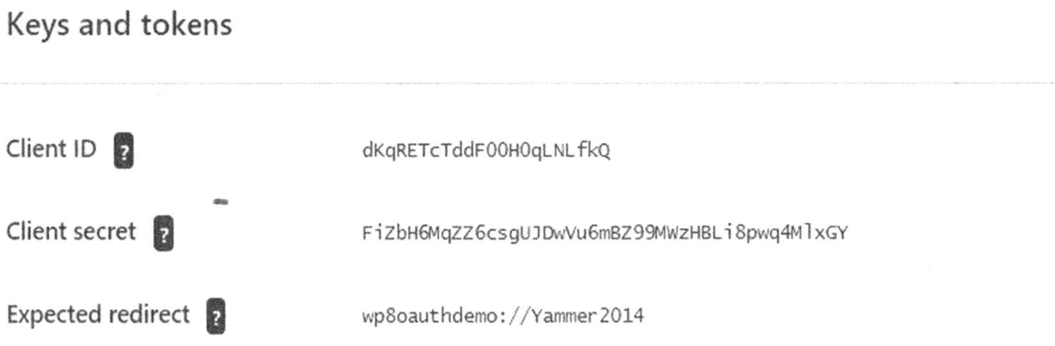

Keys and tokens

Client ID	dKqRETcTddF00H0qLNLfkQ
Client secret	FiZbH6MqZZ6csgUJDwVu6mBZ99MWzHBLi8pwq4MlxGY
Expected redirect	wp8oauthdemo://Yammer2014

Figure 8-1. *Registered Yammer app's keys and tokens*

The first step in setting up your Windows phone app is to create an instance of the class called `Yammer.OAuthSDK.Model.OAuthClientInfo`. This class defines the properties that store the Yammer App configuration values. The best place to do this is in the `resource` dictionary in your Yammer `App.xaml` file.

Adding Code to App.xaml

Define an object of class model `OAuthClientInfo` in the `App.xaml` file with the `ClientID`, `ClientSecret`, and `RedirectURI` values matching the Yammer app configuration values.

```
<model:OAuthClientInfo xmlns:model="clr-namespace:Yammer.OAuthSDK.Model;assembly=
Yammer.OAuthSDK" x:Key="MyOAuthClientInfo"
            ClientId="ZaV9YiPAdnqa273m3HTH5w"
            ClientSecret="BzLv9AsfUrVaCY7XTvgFBxjGizsxGK7BPcs5YftkVtE"
            RedirectUri="SPDSWP8App://Yammer" />
```

Adding Code to App.xaml.cs

You can now define a property in `App.xaml.cs`. A property declared in `App.xaml.cs` will be available application-wide. Add the following code in `App.xaml.cs` for the getter property.

```
public OAuthClientInfo MyOAuthClientInfo
{
    get
    {
        return Resources["MyOAuthClientInfo"] as OAuthClientInfo;
    }
}
```

Step 3: Configure a URI Association

This step is important from the user experience perspective, as during the login process in your Windows phone app, the user will be redirected to an IE browser Windows app. The developer needs to do URI association so that the after a successful login, users are redirected to the Windows phone app from the IE browser.

Configure Project Manifest "WMAppManifest.xml"

The configuration of URI association is done in the `WMAppManifest.xml` file, which is part of your Windows phone project.

The next step is to add an `Extensions` element in the app manifest file. Add the following code (below the tokens element) to `WMAppManifest.xml`. The `Extensions` element uses the `Protocol` element to specify the URI association (using a scheme name). Your `Extensions` element should look like this:

```
<Extensions>
  <Protocol Name="SPDSWP8App" NavUriFragment="encodedLaunchUri=%s" TaskID="_default" />
</Extensions>
```

Updating App.xaml.cs

Now you need to override the default URI-mapper class with the app's redirect URI in the `InitializePhoneApplication()` method in **App.xaml.cs**:

```
// Override the default URI-mapper class with our OAuth URI handler.
RootFrame.UriMapper = new OAuthResponseUriMapper(MyOAuthClientInfo.RedirectUri);
```

That is all the basic setup required to use the Windows Phone SDK in your Windows phone app. Exercise 8-1 demonstrates the step-by-step process to leverage the Windows Phone SDK, including the basic setup required in order to leverage the capabilities of Yammer's Windows Phone SDK.

Understanding Windows Phone SDK

Before we jump into the implementation of Yammer SDK for Windows Phone, let's explore the Windows Phone SDK's project structure and the functions provided by the SDK project. Later in this section, you will see the actual implementation of each function provided by the SDK.

Project "Yammer.OAuthSDK" Structure

`Yammer.OAuthSDK` is the C# class library project that contains all essential classes methods to integrate Yammer functionality into the Windows Phone App. This is a mandatory project you have to add to your Windows Phone App Visual Studio Solution to create an app for integration with Yammer. We will also explain how to implement this app in your project using an example later in this chapter.

Look at the class structure of the `Yammer.OAuthSDK` project, as shown in Figure 8-2.

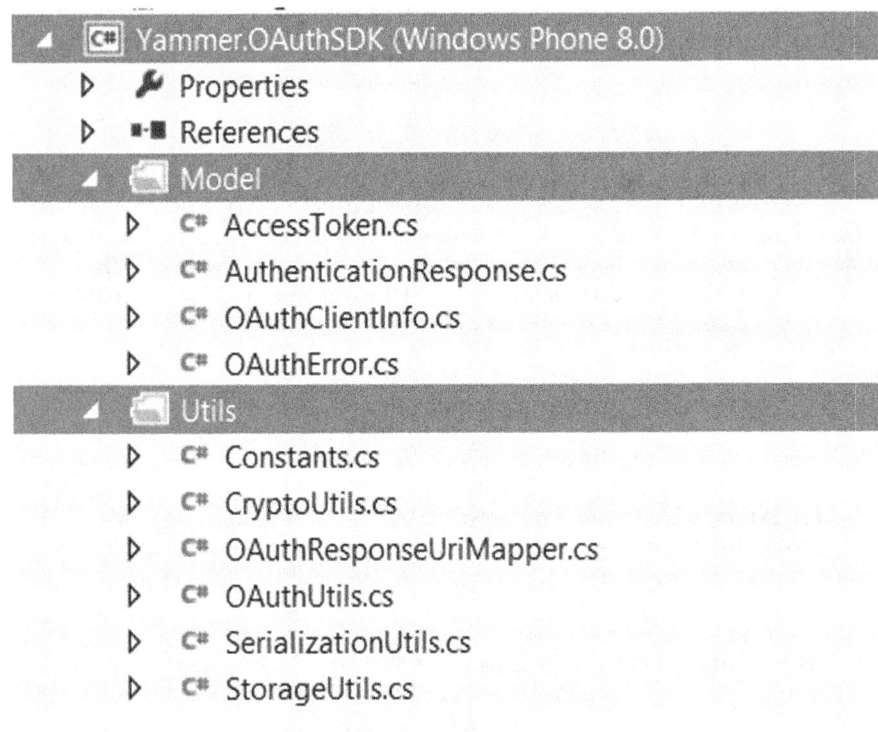

Figure 8-2. *Class structure of the Windows Phone SDK*

As you can see, this SDK project contains a folder named `Model` in the `Yammer.OAuthSDK` project. This folder contains all the model classes required for OAuth authentication for the Windows phone app.

All the classes under the `Model` folder are defined in the `Yammer.OAuthSDK.Model` namespace. The purpose of each class is listed in Table 8-1.

***Table 8-1.** List of Classes Available in the Yammer.OAuthSDK.Model Namespace*

Class Name	Purpose	Methods
AccessToken	The object that contains the actual access token.	Token
AuthenticationResponse	The root object that desterilizes from a Yammer OAuth API call response.	AccessToken OAuthError
OAuthClientInfo	Constants used to identify your app on the Yammer platform.	ClientId ClientSecret RedirectUri
OAuthError	Object used to deserialize an error response from a Yammer API call.	Type Message Code Stat HttpStatusCode HttpStatusDescription

There is another folder named Util in the Yammer.OAuthSDK project, also shown in Figure 8-1, that contains utility classes. All these classes are defined in the Yammer.OAuthSDK.Utils namespace. Table 8-2 provides details of these classes.

***Table 8-2.** List of Classes Available in the Yammer.OAuthSDK.Utils Namespace*

Class Name	Purpose	Available Methods
Constants	This class defines all constants for constants that point to the Yammer API endpoints and constants that are used as the URL parameters for the API calls and responses.	Private variable: ApiEndpoints OAuthParameters
CryptoUtils	Utils class to handle cryptographic and encoding related operations.	Private variable: redirectUri Method: GenerateUrlFriendlyNonce() EncryptAndStoreMapUri() DecryptStored() UrlTokenEncode() UrlTokenDecode()
OAuthResponseUriMapper	Converts a uniform resource identifier (URI) into a new URI to be redirected and based on the OAuth parameters received.	Private variable: redirectUri Method: OAuthResponseUriMapper() MapUri()

(*continued*)

Table 8-2. (*continued*)

Class Name	Purpose	Available Methods
OAuthUtils	Utils class to handle Yammer OAuth API operations.	Private variable: const string tokenFilePath const string nonceFilePath string AccessToken Method: LaunchSignIn() HandleApprove() GetJsonFromApi() DeleteStoredToken() HandleExceptions()
SerializationUtils	Utils class to handle serialization operations.	Private variable: Method: DeserializeJson()
StorageUtils	Utils class to handle storage-related operations.	Method: DeleteFromIsolatedStorage() WriteToIsolatedStorage() WriteToIsolatedStorage() ReadStringFromIsolatedStorage() ReadBytesFromIsolatedStorage()

The Yammer.OAuth.Model and Yammer.OAuthSDK.Utils namespaces both contain important and mandatory classes to support Yammer integration with the Windows phone app.

In the next section, we will deep dive into some important functions mentioned in these classes.

Important Methods of Yammer.OAuthSDK

Before developing a Windows phone app, let's look at the Windows Phone App SDK methods that are available in the Yammer.OAuthSDK.Utils namespace. Table 8-3 lists three important methods provided by the SDK.

Table 8-3. *Important Windows Phone 8 SDK Functions*

Method	Purpose
LaunchSignIn	Initiates the user login.
HandleApprove	Handles the OAuth approved response asynchronously by storing the information received from Yammer, like Code and State.
GetJsonFromApi	Calls the Yammer REST APIs asynchronously.

In the following section, you will dive deeply into each of these methods listed in Table 8-3. You will learn the actual implementation of each method with the syntax and parameter of each method.

LaunchSignIn Method

The LaunchSignIn method initiates the user login. Developers can invoke this method from a Windows phone app by using a "Login with Yammer" button. When called, this methods invokes the Internet Explorer browser on the Windows phone. The IE browser navigates to the Yammer login URL (https://www.yammer.com/dialog/oauth?client_id={0}&redirect_uri={1}&state={2}), which allows Yammer to authenticate the user as well as authorize the Yammer app.

The syntax of LaunchSignIn is as follows:

```
OAuthUtils.LaunchSignIn(clientId, redirectUri);
```

The LaunchSignIn method accepts two parameters, as listed in Table 8-4.

Table 8-4. *LaunchSignIn Method Parameters*

Name	Type	Required	Description
clientId	String	Yes	The client ID of your Yammer App.
redirectUri	String	Yes	The URL of your application where Yammer will redirect to after the authentication flow is complete.

The following code snippet provides the actual implementation of LaunchSignIn() method:

```
public static void LaunchSignIn(string clientId, string redirectUri)
{
    var ieTask = new WebBrowserTask();
    // need to generate and store this nonce to identify the request is ours when it
    comes back
    string nonce = CryptoUtils.GenerateUrlFriendlyNonce();
    StorageUtils.WriteToIsolatedStorage(nonce, nonceFilePath);
    string url = string.Format(Constants.ApiEndpoints.OAuthUserAuthentication, clientId,
    redirectUri, nonce);
    ieTask.Uri = new Uri(url, UriKind.Absolute);
    ieTask.Show();
}
```

HandleApprove Method

This is another very important method for Windows Phone SDK. HandleApprove is invoked after the user is redirected back to the Windows phone app. This method handles the OAuth-approved response asynchronously by storing the information received from Yammer, like Code and State.

The syntax of HandleApprove is as follows:

```
OAuthUtils.HandleApprove(clientId, clientSecret, Code, State,[ onSuccess],[onFailure])
```

The HandleApprove method accepts four parameters, as listed in Table 8-5.

***Table 8-5.** HandleApprove Function Parameters*

Name	Type	Required	Description
clientId	String	Yes	The client ID of your Yammer app.
client Secret	String	Yes	The clientSecret key of your Yammer app.
Code	String	Yes	The code value obtained back from Yammer on the RedirectUri callback.
State	String	Yes	The optional state value used to mitigate CSRF attacks.

The following code snippet provides the actual implementation of the HandleApprove() method:

```
public static void HandleApprove(string clientId,
    string clientSecret,
    string code,
    string state,
    Action onSuccess,
    Action onCSRF = null,
    Action<AuthenticationResponse> onErrorResponse = null,
    Action<Exception> onException = null)
{
    // we get the stored nonce from the Isolated Storage to verify it against the one we get
    back from Yammer
    string nonce = StorageUtils.ReadStringFromIsolatedStorage(nonceFilePath);
    if (state != nonce)
    {
        // might be a CSRF attack, so we discard the request
        if (onCSRF != null)
        {
            onCSRF();
        }
        return;
    }
    string url = string.Format(Constants.ApiEndpoints.OAuthAppAuthentication, clientId,
    clientSecret, code);
    var appAuthUri = new Uri(url, UriKind.Absolute);

    var webclient = new WebClient();

    OpenReadCompletedEventHandler handler = null;
    handler = (s, e) =>
    {
        webclient.OpenReadCompleted -= handler;
        if (e.Error == null)
        {
            // the token should have been sent back in json format, we use serialization to
            extract it
            AuthenticationResponse oauthResponse =
            SerializationUtils.DeserializeJson<AuthenticationResponse>(e.Result);
```

```
            AccessToken = oauthResponse.AccessToken.Token;
            onSuccess();
        }
        else
        {
            HandleExceptions(e.Error, onErrorResponse, onException);
        }
    };

    webclient.OpenReadCompleted += handler;
    // make the actual call to the Yammer OAuth App Authentication endpoint to get our
    token back
    webclient.OpenReadAsync(appAuthUri);
}
```

GetJsonFromApi Method

The GetJsonFromApi method calls the Yammer REST APIs asynchronously. Developers can use this method to call any REST APIs that do not require any additional parameters.

The syntax of GetJsonFromApi is as follows:

```
public static void GetJsonFromApi(Uri endpoint,  Action<string> onSuccess,
Action<AuthenticationResponse> onErrorResponse = null, Action<Exception> onException = null)
```

The GetJsonFromApi method accepts four parameters, as listed in Table 8-6.

Table 8-6. *GetJsonFromApi Function Parameters*

Name	Type	Required	Description
endpoint	String	Yes	An API URI endpoint that doesn't require any extra parameters.
onSuccess	String	Yes	Action to be executed if call is successful.
onErrorResponse	String	Yes	Action to be executed if you get an error response from Yammer.
onException	String	Yes	Action to be executed if there is an unexpected exception.

The following code snippet provides the actual implementation of the GetJsonFromApi() method:

```
public static void GetJsonFromApi(Uri endpoint,
    Action<string> onSuccess,
    Action<AuthenticationResponse> onErrorResponse = null,
    Action<Exception> onException = null)
{
    if (endpoint == null || onSuccess == null)
    {
        throw new ArgumentNullException();
    }
```

```
    var webclient = new WebClient();
    // We shouldn't use the url query paramters to send the token, we should use the header
    to send it more securely instead
    webclient.Headers[HttpRequestHeader.Authorization] = "Bearer " + AccessToken;

    DownloadStringCompletedEventHandler handler = null;
    handler = (s, e) =>
    {
        webclient.DownloadStringCompleted -= handler;
        if (e.Error == null)
        {
            var result = e.Result;
            // We just pass the raw text data response to the callback
            onSuccess(result);
        }
        else
        {
            HandleExceptions(e.Error, onErrorResponse, onException);
        }
    };

    webclient.DownloadStringCompleted += handler;
    webclient.DownloadStringAsync(endpoint);
}
```

Now that we have explained all the important requirements and structure of the Windows Phone SDK for Yammer integration, let's create a Windows phone app using this SDK.

Building a Windows Phone 8 App Using Yammer Windows Phone SDK

This section provides a step-by-step guide on creating a new Windows phone app. You will use the Yammer Windows Phone App SDK in your project and call Yammer REST APIs for groups, message, users, and so on. Finally, you'll use Visual Studio's emulator to test your app.

EXERCISE 8-1: BUILDING A WINDOWS 8 PHONE APP

Create New Project

1. If you already installed Visual Studio and the Windows Phone SDK tools, launch Microsoft Visual Studio.
2. The first screen presented to you is the Visual Studio start page, shown in Figure 8-3.

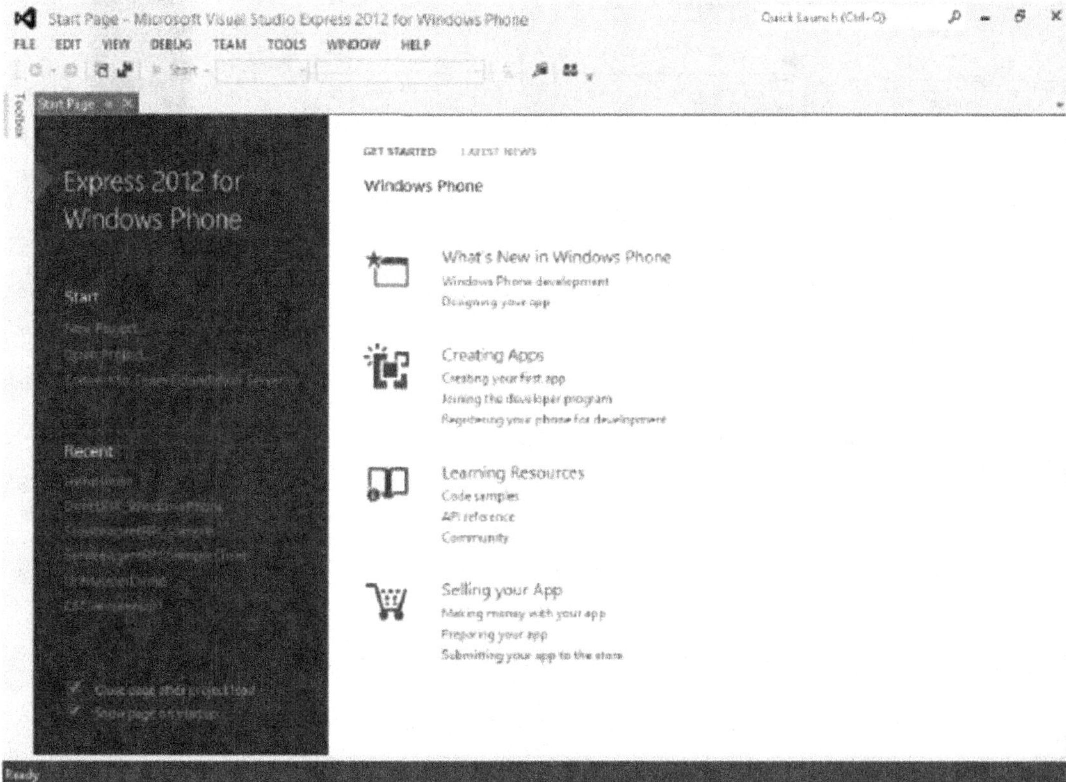

Figure 8-3. The Visual Studio start page provides a quick way to get started

3. On the left side of the start page, on the navigation pane, choose New Project. Alternatively, you can choose the File ➤ New Project ➤ Windows Phone App menu command.
4. This brings up the New Project window, where you can choose the type of project for the Windows phone app. Figure 8-4 demonstrates creating a simple Windows phone app from a Windows phone app template.

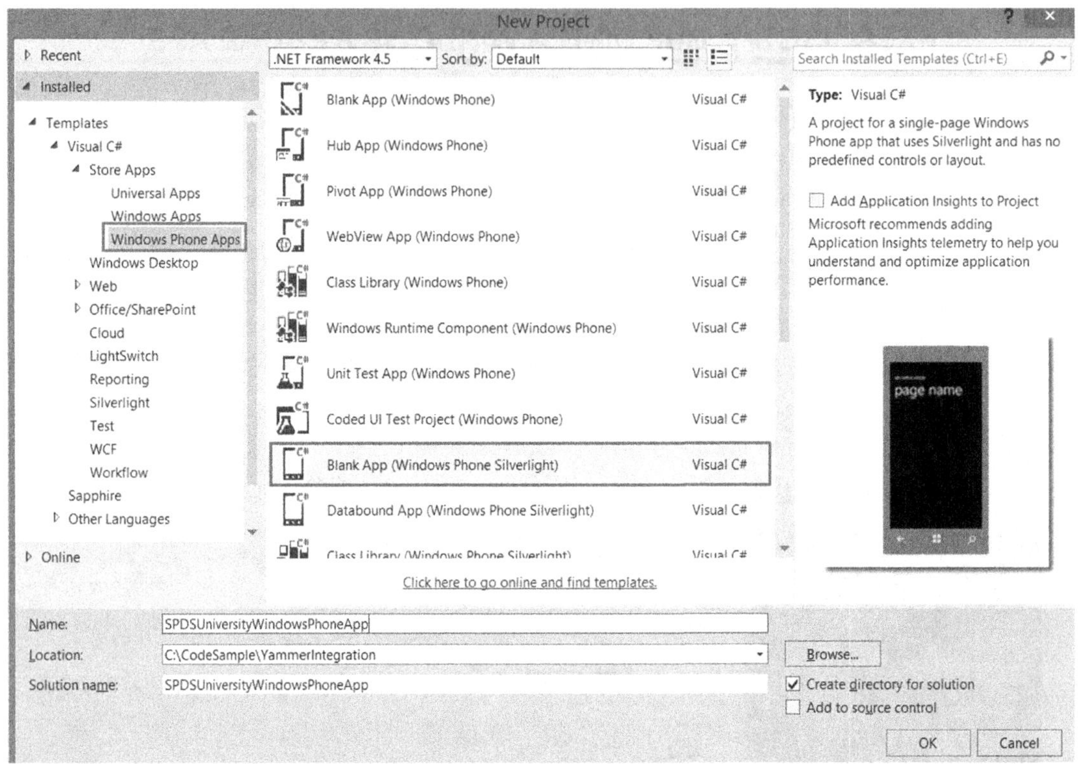

Figure 8-4. *Visual Studio provides a number of templates to choose from; to get started, select the Windows phone app*

5. Next you will be presented with a window to select the Windows app platform to target for this application. Choose Windows Phone 8.0.

New Windows Phone App Using Silverlight

Select the minimum Windows Phone version you want this app to target.

Target Windows Phone OS Version:

Windows Phone 8.0

Windows Phone 8.0

Windows Phone 8.1

OK Cancel

Figure 8-5. *Select the Windows phone version*

6. After the wizard finishes, you should have a structure in Solution Explorer that resembles Figure 8-6. The solution includes one Windows phone app project, which contains the app structure with an `App.xml` file.

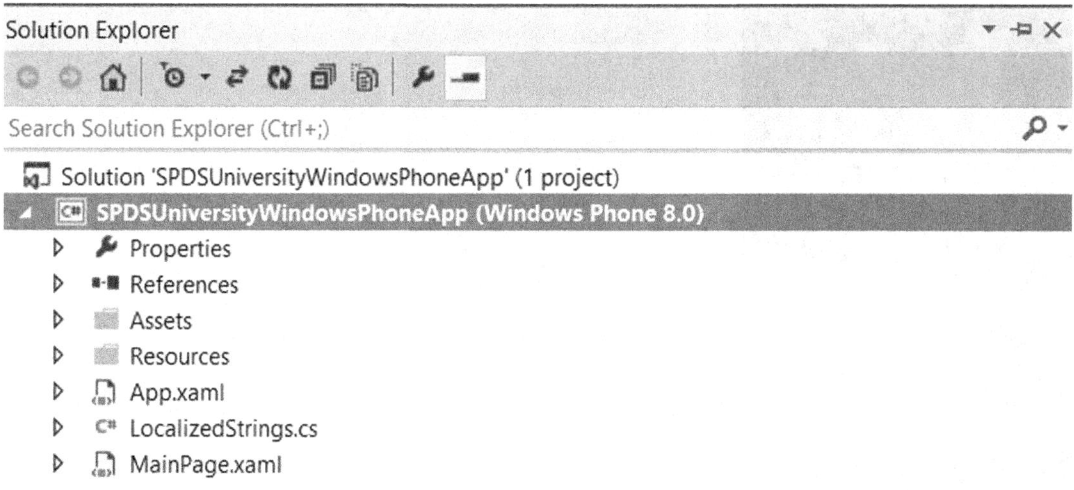

Figure 8-6. *Windows phone app project strucutre*

Add Yammer.OAuthSDK to the Solution

7. Download the Windows Phone SDK for Yammer from GitHub.

8. To add the `Yammer.OAuthSDK` project to your newly created solution, in the Visual Studio Solution Explorer, right-click on the solution name and then choose Add ➤ Existing Project, as demonstrated in Figure 8-7.

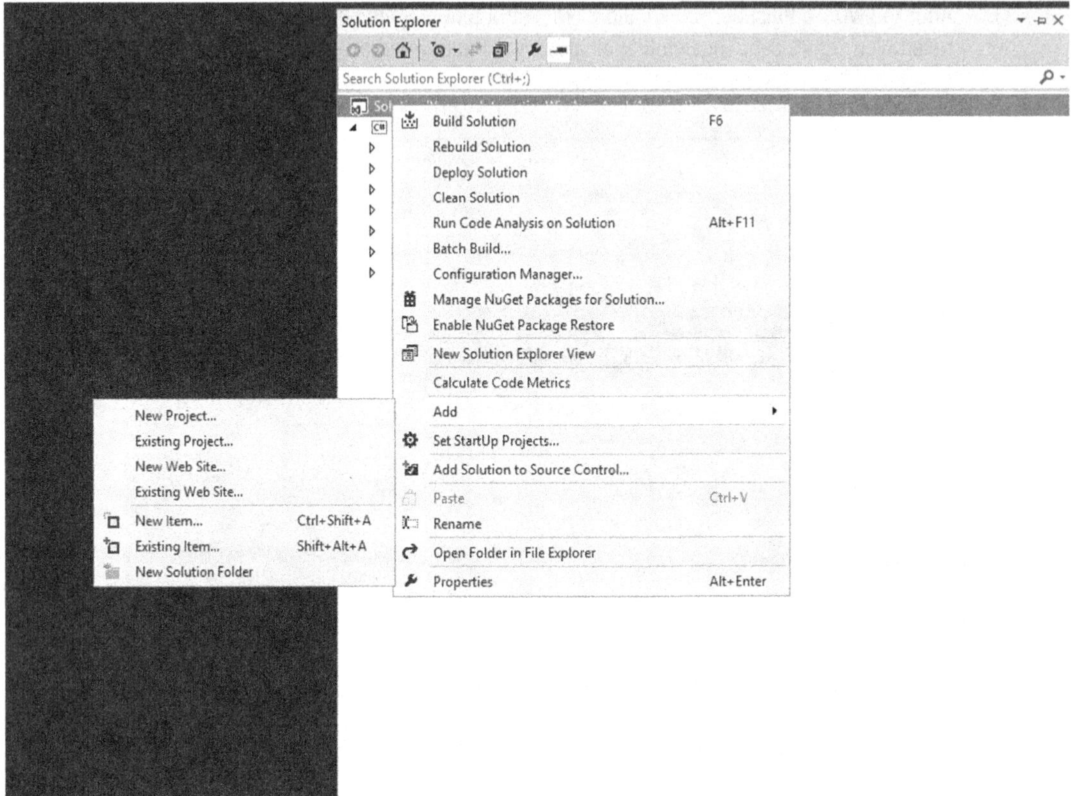

Figure 8-7. *To add an existing project to solution in Visual Studio*

9. Navigate to the folder where `Yammer.OAuth.SDK.csproj` is located (Figure 8-8).

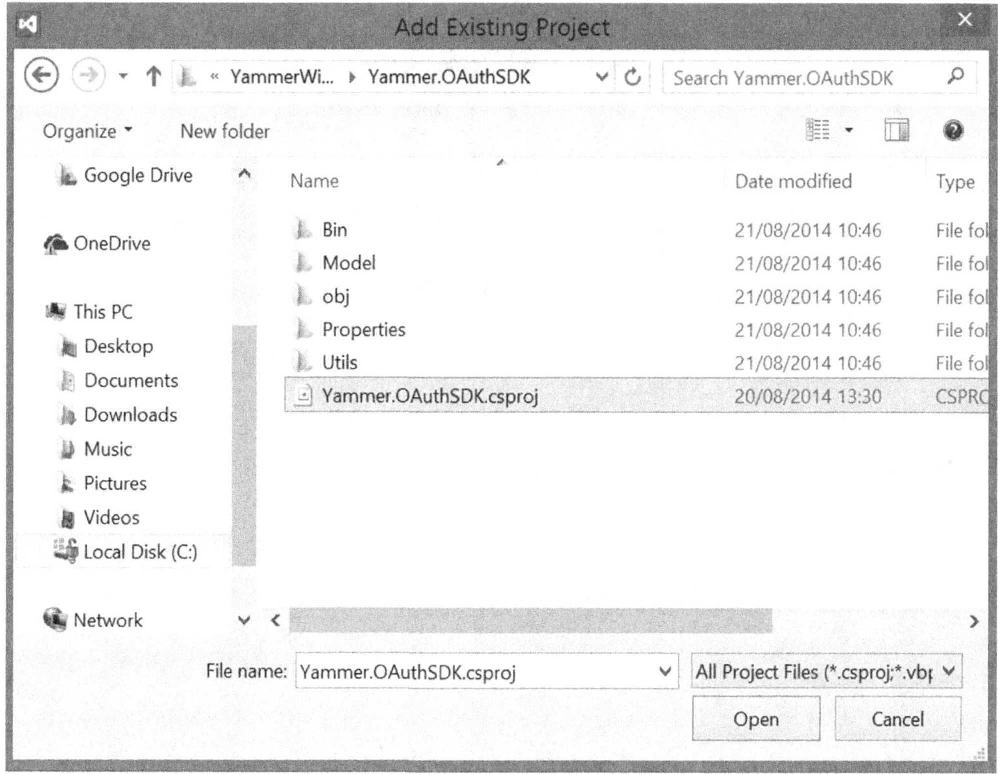

Figure 8-8. *Browse to the `Yammer.OAuthSDK` project file on your development machine*

10. Click open.

Referencing the Yammer.OAuthSDK to Windows Phone App Project

11. Once the Yammer Windows Phone SDK is added to your solution, you have to reference it in the Windows phone app project. In the Solution Explorer, expand the Windows phone app project, right-click on Reference and select Add Reference.

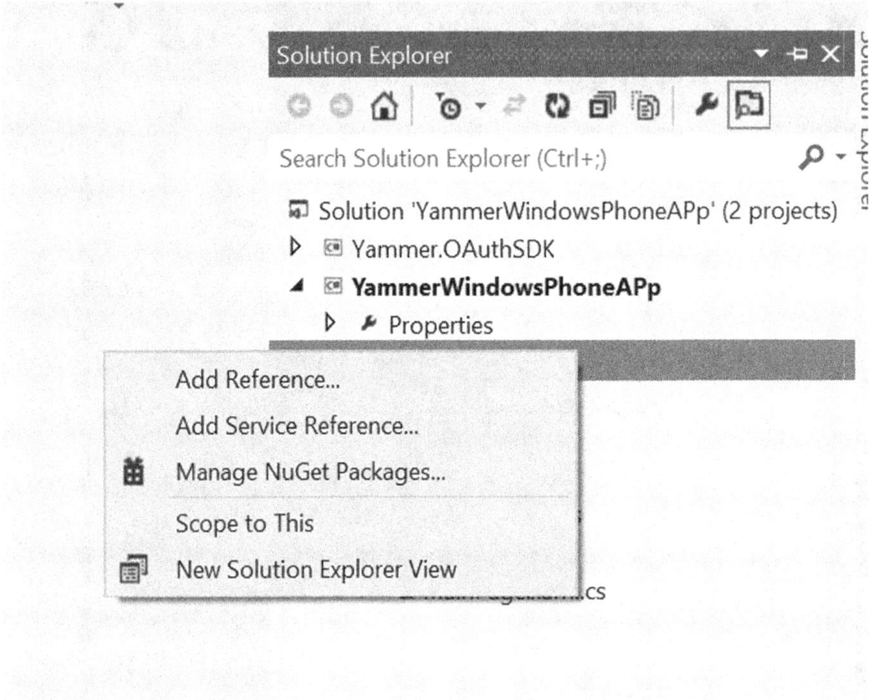

Figure 8-9. *To add the reference to the* `Yammer.OAuthSDK` *project that was added to the solution in the previous steps*

12. You'll will be presented with a dialog box, as demonstrated in Figure 8-10.

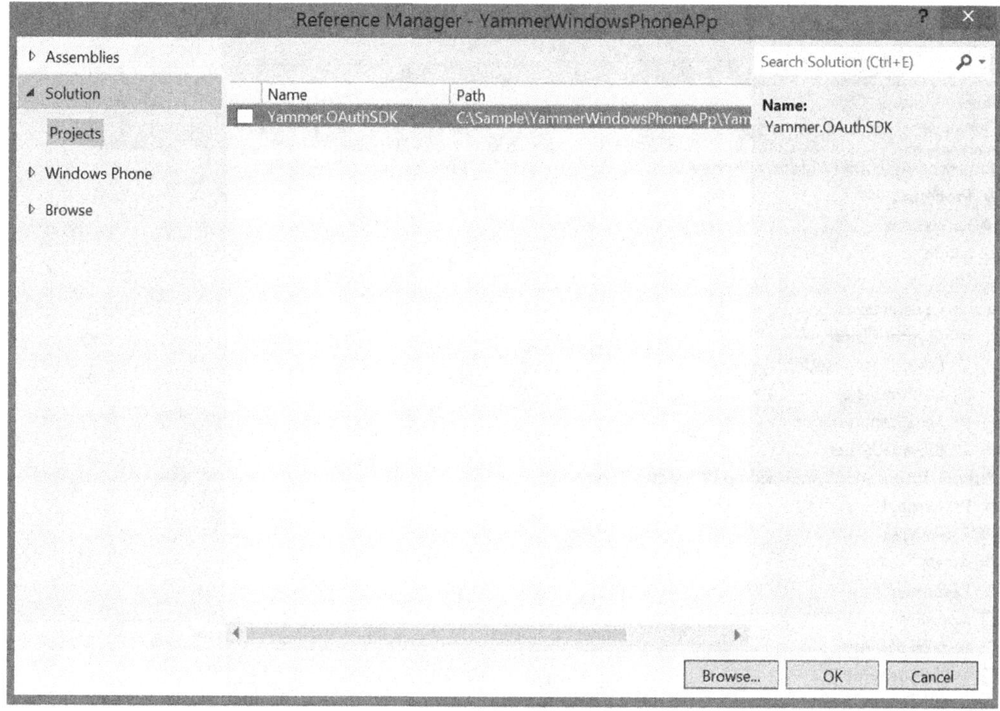

Figure 8-10. *Select the project from the list to be added as a reference*

13. From the right side of this dialog box, choose Solution ➤ Project ➤ Yammer.OAuthSDK and click OK.

Understanding the Visual Studio Solution Structure

14. Your solution should have two projects, as illustrated in Figure 8-11.

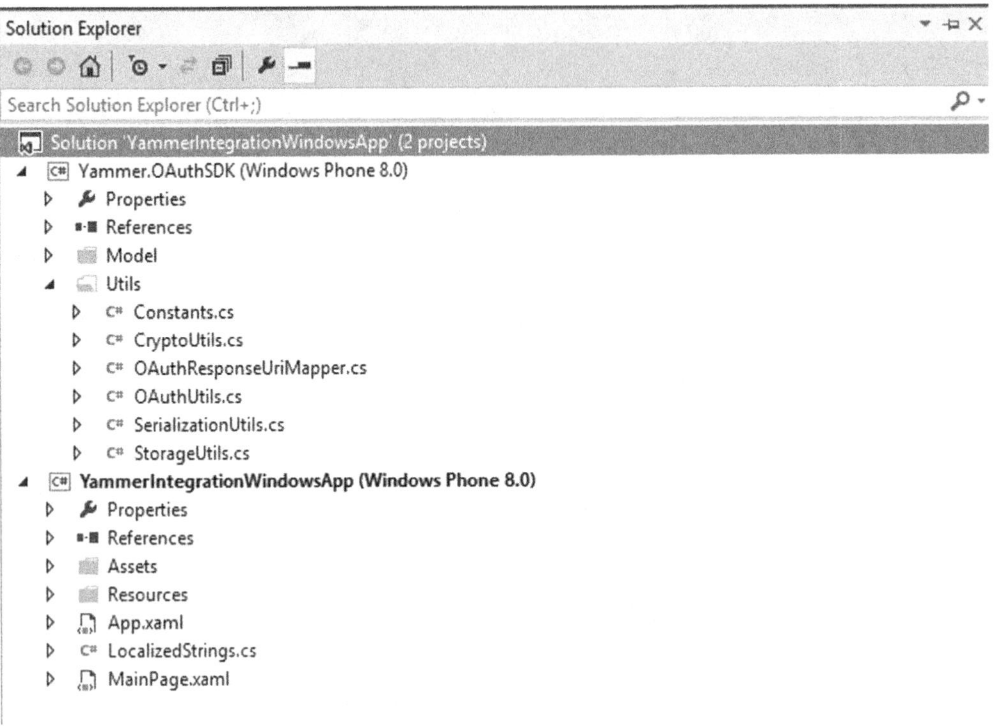

Figure 8-11. *Windows phone solution structure*

Table 8-7 lists the Windows Phone SDK's Visual Studio projects available in SDK.

Table 8-7. *Windows Phone SDK Projects*

Name	Description
`Yammer.OAuthSDK`	This is class library project that contains helper functions that allow you to integrate OAuth login and functions to make APIs calls.
`YammerIntegrationWindowsApp`	A sample Windows Phone 8 application that demonstrates how to set up and use these helper classes in an app.

Add an Extension: WMAppManifest.xml

We will start by adding an extension to the `WMAppManifest.xml` file. Since you'll be using Visual Studio Emulator to build and test this Windows phone app, the `redirect_uri` parameter must be set so that the IE browser on your Windows phone redirects the users to the Windows phone app after successful authentication and app authorization. To set up the `redirect_uri`, you need to set up the extension in the `WMAppManifest.xml` file.

The configuration of URI association is done in the `WMAppManifest.xml` file, which is part of your Windows phone project.

1. Add the following code snippet to `WMAppManifest.xml`, just below the `</Token>` tag:

```
<Extensions>
<Protocol Name="SPDSWP8App" NavUriFragment="encodedLaunchUri=%s"
TaskID="_default" />
</Extensions>
```

■ **Note** The `Protocol Name="SPDSWP8App"` should match the `App.xaml RedirectURI` of the Yammer app redirect URI configuration.

---

2. The next project file to modify is `App.xaml`. You'll use this file to configure the Yammer app configuration values like `ClientID`, `ClientSecret` key, and `RedirectURI`. These parameters are required in order to call the Yammer REST API from your Windows phone app. The best place to configure those parameters is in the `App.xaml` file within `<Application. Resources>`.
3. Open the `App.xaml` file by double-clicking on the filename in Visual Studio Solution Explorer.
4. Add the following code to the Application Resources section (tag name `<Application.Resources>`), directly below the `<local:LocalizedStrings>` tag.

```
<model:OAuthClientInfo xmlns:model="clr-namespace:Yammer.OAuthSDK.
Model;assembly=Yammer.OAuthSDK" x:Key="MyOAuthClientInfo"
            ClientId="Fmi5JYfF5jqMLCcydqkJWQ"
            ClientSecret="GBE5vp3mOUZuRVKqFPsXOA6eOLro95DOFVP5PPgSIIO"
            RedirectUri="SPDSWP8App://WPSample" />
```

The `redirectURI` in this configuration should match your `redirect_URI` in the Yammer's app configuration, as illustrated in Figure 8-12.

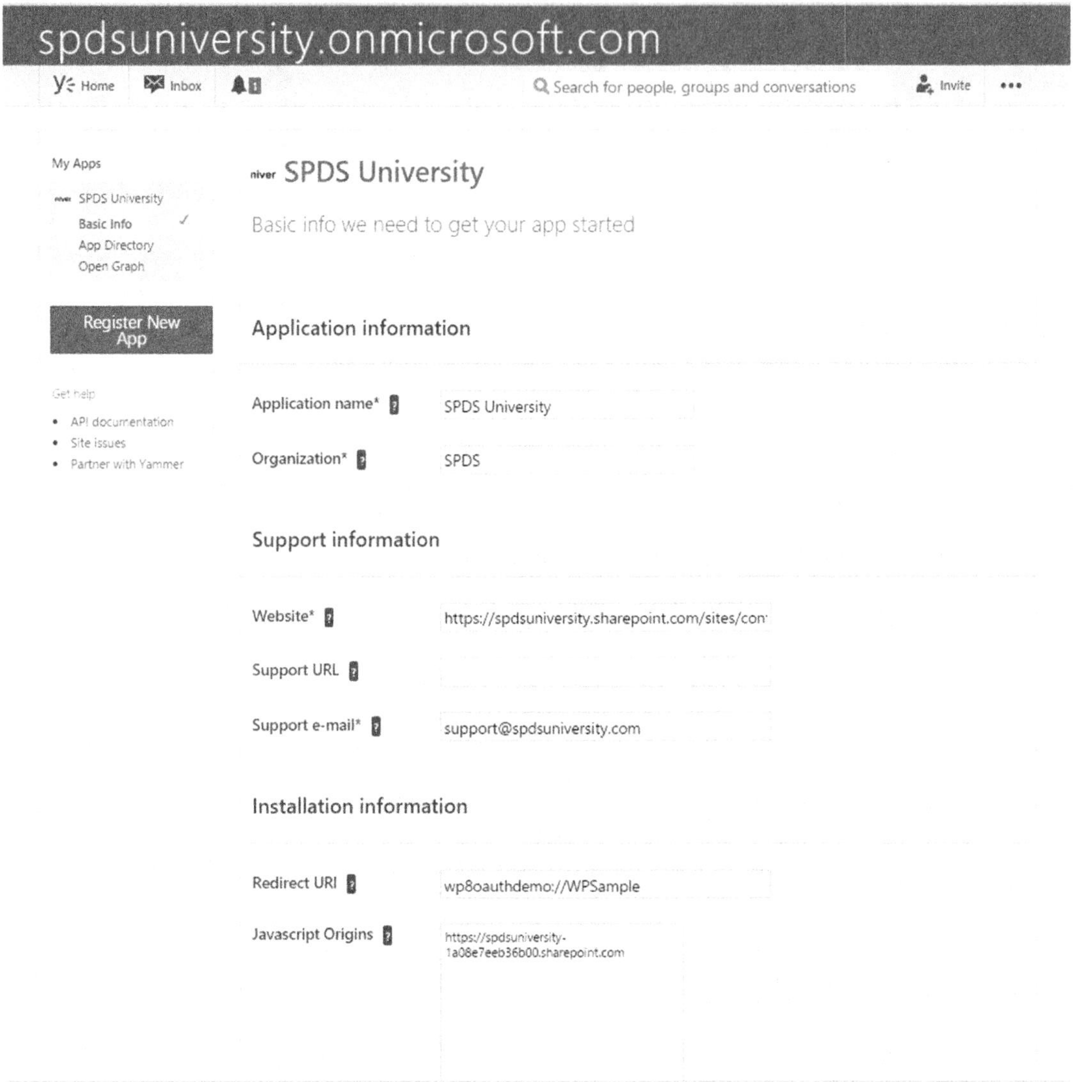

Figure 8-12. Ensure that your Yammer app's redirect URI matches OAuthClientInfo's redirect URI

■ **Note** The `clr-namespace` refers to the `Yammer.OAuthSDK.Model` class in the SDK library project you added in previous steps.

---

5. Open the `App.xaml.cs` file by double-clicking on the filename in the Solution Explorer. Add the following two lines of code to the `using` section on the top of the code-behind:

```
using Yammer.OAuthSDK.Model;
using Yammer.OAuthSDK.Utils;
```

6. Add the following code to declare an object of class `OAuthClientInfo` model class in the `App.xaml.cs` file. This object will be used to refer to the values for `ClientID`, ClientSecret key, and `RedirectURI`.

```
public OAuthClientInfo MyOAuthClientInfo
{
    get
    {
        return Resources["MyOAuthClientInfo"] as OAuthClientInfo;
    }
}
```

7. Now you'll modify the `InitializePhoneApplication` method within the `App.xaml.cs` file to override the default `URI-Mapper` class of the `RootFrame` with the `OAuth` URI handler, which will be used to redirect the user to the Windows phone app from the IE browser after the successful authentication and authorizations. Add the following code to the method:

```
// Override the default URI-mapper class with our OAuth URI handler.
            RootFrame.UriMapper = new OAuthResponseUriMapper(MyOAuthClientIn
            fo.RedirectUri);
```

■ **Note** `MainPage.xaml` is the default page with some UI element. It is actually a startup UI for the Silverlight application in the Windows phone app. Here, you can use the Silverlight controls for developing user interface with different layouts.

---

8. Open `MainPage.xaml` by double-clicking on the filename in the Solution Explorer. `MainPage.xaml` has the following markup code for the Windows phone page's title and app name. In the `StackPanel` named `x: Name="TitlePanel`, change it to the text block of your choice for the Yammer app name and main page title.

```
<!--TitlePanel contains the name of the application and page title-->
        <StackPanel x:Name="TitlePanel" Grid.Row="0" Margin="12,17,0,28">
            <TextBlock Text="SPDS University Windows Phone App"
            Style="{StaticResource PhoneTextNormalStyle}" Margin="12,0"/>
            <TextBlock Text="SPDS University" Margin="9,-7,0,0"
            Style="{StaticResource PhoneTextTitle1Style}"/>
        </StackPanel>
```

9. Add the following code in `<Grid x:Name="ContentPanel"`. This code contains the button markup code:

```
<!--ContentPanel - place additional content here-->
    <Grid x:Name="ContentPanel" Grid.Row="1" Margin="0,0,0,0">
        <Grid.ColumnDefinitions>
            <ColumnDefinition />
            <ColumnDefinition />
        </Grid.ColumnDefinitions>
        <Grid.RowDefinitions>
            <RowDefinition />
            <RowDefinition />
            <RowDefinition />
            <RowDefinition />
            <RowDefinition />
            <RowDefinition />
            <RowDefinition />
            <RowDefinition />
        </Grid.RowDefinitions>
        <Button Name="btnSignInWithYammer" HorizontalAlignment="Center"
        VerticalAlignment="Top" Click="btnSignInWithYammer_Click">
            <Image Source="Assets\yammer-signin.gif" Width="179" Height="28"
            Stretch="Fill" />
        </Button>
    </Grid>
```

■ **Note** Yammer-signin.gif: Use the image of your choice stored in the `Asset` folder of your Windows app solution. You can also download an image from `https://www.filepicker.io/api/file/KYDbdovdQAG9ABZoLLiT`.

---

10. Add the text block control markup to `<Grid x:Name="ContentPanel">` to store the token status. In the code-behind, we will use this text block to store the `status=Yes` if the Yammer app has already received the access token and `Status=no` if the access token for the current user has not been received. You can place this outside of the content panel grid:

```
<TextBlock x:Name="txbIsTokenPresent" Text="Is Token Present: No."
TextAlignment="Center" />
```

After you have defined all the markup in the `MainPage.xaml` page, you add the code to the code-behind class of `MainPage.xaml`.

11. Open `MainPage.xaml.cs` to add some code-behind to refer to the class library from a `Yammer.OAuthSDL` project like the `Yammer.OAUthSDK.Model` and `Yammer.OAUthSDK.Utils` classes.

```
using Yammer.OAuthSDK.Model;
using Yammer.OAuthSDK.Utils;
```

12. Declare three variables on top of the page class:

```
string clientId = default(string);
string clientSecret = default(string);
string redirectUri = default(string);
```

13. Next you need to read the Yammer app configuration values defined in `App.xaml` in the previous steps. To do that, add the following code to `MainPage.xaml`'s constructor (add the following code to the `InitializeComponent();`) to populate the `ClientID`, `ClientSecret`, and `RedirectUri` variables.

```
// we extract these values from the App's Resource Dictionary config
         clientId = ((App)App.Current).MyOAuthClientInfo.ClientId;
         clientSecret = ((App)App.Current).MyOAuthClientInfo.ClientSecret;
         redirectUri = ((App)App.Current).MyOAuthClientInfo.RedirectUri;
```

14. We added the login button markup in the `MainPage.xaml`, so now it is time to add an event handler code for the login button.

```
private void btnSignInWithYammer_Click(object sender, RoutedEventArgs e)
 {
     OAuthUtils.LaunchSignIn(clientId, redirectUri);

 }
```

- The `LaunchSignIn` method launches Internet Explorer using a `WebBrowserTask` to redirect the user to the proper user authentication endpoint (see `https://www.yammer.com/dialog/oauth?client_id={0}&redirect_uri={1}` which is defined in the `constants` class of the Yammer SDK.
- The `LaunchSignIn` method also stores the access token in an isolated space which will be used to make further calls.
- Generate and store this nonce to identify the request is yours when it comes back.

15. Add the `UpdateTokenMessage` method to the `MainPage.xaml.cs` file.

```
private void UpdateTokenMessage(bool isTokenPresent)
{
    Dispatcher.BeginInvoke(() => txbIsTokenPresent.Text = isTokenPresent ?
    txbIsTokenPresent.Text.Replace("No.", "Yes.") : txbIsTokenPresent.Text.
    Replace("Yes.", "No."));
}
```

The final method you'll add to the `MainPage.xaml.cs` file handles the redirect call. This is required as the IE browser window will redirect users to the Windows app after a successful user authentication. This method

Once the login is successful, the IE browser redirects users to `REDIRECT_URI`, which is configured in the Windows Phone App and `App.xaml.cs`'s `<Extension>` tag.

The Windows Phone App provides an `OnNavigatedTo()` event, which is used to handle the request.

16. Add the following code to implement the `OnNavigatedTo` method in `MainPage.xaml.cs`.

```
protected override void OnNavigatedTo(NavigationEventArgs e)
{
    base.OnNavigatedTo(e);

    // Check the arguments from the query string passed to the page.
    IDictionary<string, string> uriParams = NavigationContext.QueryString;

    // "Approve"
    if (uriParams.ContainsKey(Constants.OAuthParameters.Code) && uriParams.
    ContainsKey(Constants.OAuthParameters.State) && e.NavigationMode !=
    NavigationMode.Back)
    {
        OAuthUtils.HandleApprove(
            clientId,
            clientSecret,
            uriParams[Constants.OAuthParameters.Code],
            uriParams[Constants.OAuthParameters.State],
            onSuccess: () =>
            {
               UpdateTokenMessage(true);
            }, onCSRF: () =>
            {
                MessageBox.Show("Unknown 'state' parameter. Discarding
                the authentication attempt.", "Invalid redirect.",
                MessageBoxButton.OK);
            }, onErrorResponse: errorResponse =>
            {
                Dispatcher.BeginInvoke(() => MessageBox.Show(errorResponse.
                OAuthError.ToString(), "Invalid operation", MessageBoxButton.OK));
            }, onException: ex =>
            {
                Dispatcher.BeginInvoke(() => MessageBox.Show(ex.ToString(),
                "Unexpected exception!", MessageBoxButton.OK));
            }
        );
    }
    // "Deny"
    else if (uriParams.ContainsKey(Constants.OAuthParameters.Error) &&
    e.NavigationMode != NavigationMode.Back)
    {
        string error, errorDescription;
        error = uriParams[Constants.OAuthParameters.Error];
        uriParams.TryGetValue(Constants.OAuthParameters.ErrorDescription, out
        errorDescription);
```

```
            string msg = string.Format("error: {0}\nerror_description:{1}", error,
            errorDescription);
            MessageBox.Show(msg, "Error response is received.", MessageBoxButton.OK);

            OAuthUtils.DeleteStoredToken();

            UpdateTokenMessage(false);
        }

                    // if token already exist
        if (!string.IsNullOrEmpty(OAuthUtils.AccessToken))
        {
           // UpdateTokenMessage(true);
        }
    }
```

Code flow:

- First check the arguments from the query string passed to the page and store them in the dictionary object called `uriParams`.
- Check if the `uriParams` contains the code and state in the query string and the `NavigationMode != NavigationMode.Back`.
- If it contains code and state, then the user has approved (authorized) the app to use the user's data.
- Make a call to Yammer SDK's `HandleApprove` method to retrieve the access token.
- Finally, call the `UpdateTokenMessage` method to update the UI status flag of the token existence in isolated storage.

Run the Application

1. Build the solution and run the Windows phone app using the emulator, as shown in Figure 8-13.

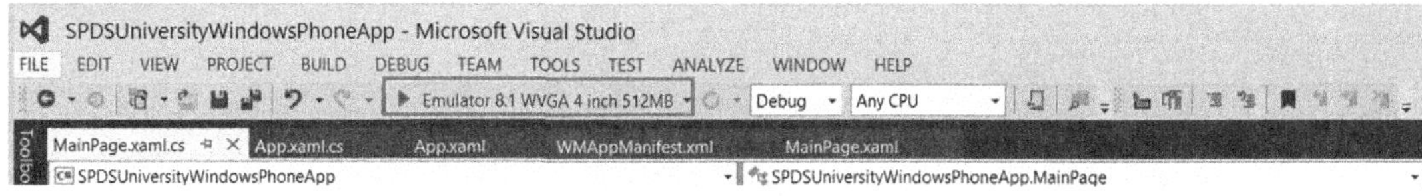

***Figure 8-13.** Run the Windows Phone App using the emulator*

2. In Run mode, the home page will look like Figure 8-14.

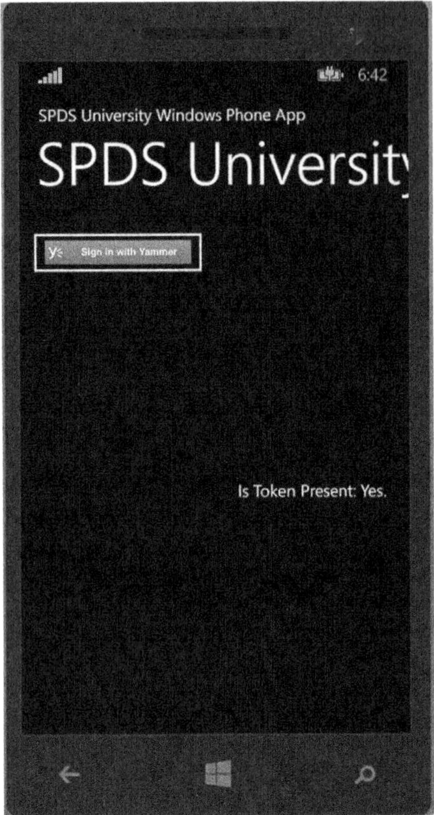

Figure 8-14. *Windows phone landing page*

When the Login with Yammer button is clicked, the Windows app will redirect you to the IE browser, as illustrated in Figure 8-15.

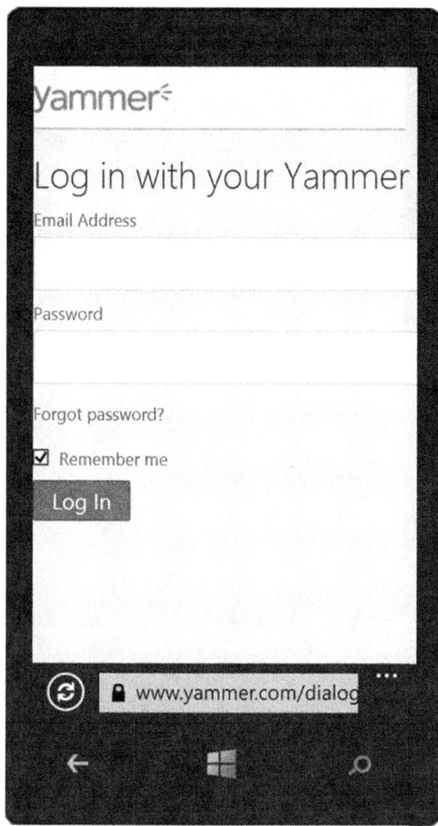

Figure 8-15. *The Yammer Login screen presented to the user in Internet Explorer*

3. Enter the login details and click on Log In.
4. The next screen presented is the app authorization screen. It allows users to allow or deny the Yammer app to access and update the user's data.

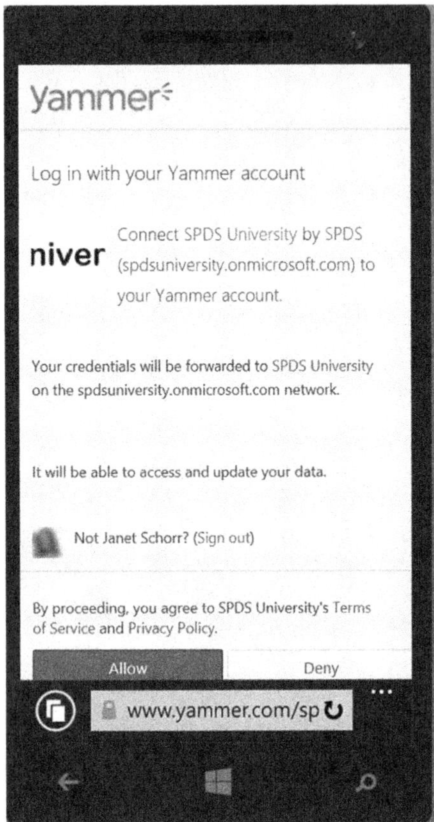

***Figure 8-16.** The OAuth process prompts the user to authorize the Yammer App*

5. After a successful log in to Yammer, IE will redirect you to the Windows phone home page again (as per the settings in the Yammer app ➤ Redirect_URI and the extension in `App.xaml.cs`).

Messages Management: Post a Message to Yammer's Group

Yammer Windows phone enables developers to post a message to Yammer on behalf of users from their Windows phone apps.

1. Modify `Constants.cs` (Project `Yammer.OAuthSDK`) by declaring a constant variable for the message endpoints in the public static class `ApiEndpoints`.

```
public const string Message = @"https://www.yammer.com/api/v1/messages.json";
```

2. Modify `OAuthUtils.cs` (Project `Yammer.OAuthSDK`). Add the following code to implement of the post message in the Windows phone SDK project's `OAuthUtils.cs` file.

```
public static void PostMessage(Uri endpoint, string method, string data,
    Action<string> onSuccess,
    Action<AuthenticationResponse> onErrorResponse = null,
    Action<Exception> onException = null)
{
    if (endpoint == null || onSuccess == null)
    {
        throw new ArgumentNullException();
    }

    var webclient = new WebClient();
    // We shouldn't use the url query paramters to send the token, we should
    use the header to send it more securely instead
    webclient.Headers[HttpRequestHeader.Authorization] = "Bearer " +
    AccessToken;
    // webclient.Headers["Content-Type"] = "application/json";

    UploadStringCompletedEventHandler handler = null;
    handler = (s, e) =>
    {
        webclient.UploadStringCompleted -= handler;
        if (e.Error == null)
        {
            var result = e.Result;
            // We just pass the raw text data response to the callback
            onSuccess(result);
        }
        else
        {
            HandleExceptions(e.Error, onErrorResponse, onException);
        }
    };

    webclient.UploadStringCompleted += handler;
    webclient.UploadStringAsync(endpoint, method, data);
}
```

3. Add the following code to MainPage.xaml for a button just below the "Log In to Yammer" button using the following code:

```
<Button Name="btnPostMsg" Grid.Row="1" HorizontalAlignment="Center"
Background="Black" VerticalAlignment="Top" Click="btnPostMsgYammer_Click">
                Post a Message
</Button>
```

4. Add a text block to store the response.

```
<TextBlock x:Name="txtResponses" Text="" TextAlignment="Center"
Grid.Column="1" Grid.Row="12" />
```

5. Add the following code to `MainPage.xaml.cs` for the button's click event handler.

```
private void btnPostMsgYammer_Click(object sender, RoutedEventArgs e)
{
    // Call this API to test if the auth token works
    var messageApiEndpoint = new Uri(Constants.ApiEndpoints.Message,
    UriKind.Absolute);
    String data = "body=We are in process of launching more technical
    trainings this year. Check our training portal home page for more details ";

    OAuthUtils.PostMessage(messageApiEndpoint, "POST", data, onSuccess:
    response =>
    {
        // we just dump the unformated json string response into a textbox
        Dispatcher.BeginInvoke(() => txtResponses.Text = "Message Posted");
    },
      onErrorResponse: errorResponse =>
      {
          Dispatcher.BeginInvoke(() =>
          {
              MessageBox.Show(errorResponse.OAuthError.ToString(), "Invalid
              operation", MessageBoxButton.OK);
              txtResponses.Text = string.Empty;
          });
      },
         onException: ex =>
         {
             Dispatcher.BeginInvoke(() =>
             {
                 MessageBox.Show(ex.ToString(), "Unexpected exception!",
                 MessageBoxButton.OK);
                 txtResponses.Text = string.Empty;
             });
         }
 );
    Dispatcher.BeginInvoke(() => txtResponses.Text = "Posting...");

}
```

In this method, YOU define a string variable called "`data`" which will hold the actual message to post. To post this message on a particular group, use the `group_id`. If `group_id` is omitted then the message will be posted to "`ALL Company`", which is your default group to post a message.

Once the message is constructed, call the `OAuthUtils.PostMessage` method by passing arguments. In addition, you can modify the data string variable to do the following.

Table 8-8. *Variable Available for Data String*

Variable	Example
Reply_to_Id	String data = "replied_to_id=432948966" + "&body=" + "Great!!";
Add Topics	String data = "group_id=4659506&body=A message with Topic" + "&topic1=" + "YammerBook!!";
Private Message	String data = "direct_to_id=1522209393&body=A message"; Where direct_to_id is the user ID
Share a Post	String data = "shared_message_id=433483891" + "&body=" + "Sharing an useful blog!!";

Messages Management: Like a Message

You can use the Yammer Windows Phone SDK to mark a message as Liked by the current user. Yammer provides `current.json` to support this activity. You'll need the `message_id` in order to mark a message as Liked. In the following example, the post message, which was used while posting a message, is used with method type set to `"POST"`. To like a message, the data parameter that was used as the message string to post is not required; therefore, it is passed as an empty string. The full URL of the `current.json` endpoint is:

```
https://www.yammer.com/api/v1/messages/liked_by/current.json?message_id=[:id]
```

where the `ID` represents the target message ID and method is the `POST` for marking a message as liked.

1. Declare a constant variable for the `current.json` endpoints in `Constants.cs` (Project `Yammer.OAuthSDK`).

```
public const string current = @"https://www.yammer.com/api/v1/messages/
liked_by/current.json";
```

2. Add a button's markup for the "Like a Message" button using the following code in `MainPage.xaml`:

```
<Button Name="btnlikemsg" Grid.Row="2" HorizontalAlignment="Center"
Background="Black" VerticalAlignment="Top" Click="btnLiketMsgYammer_Click">
                Like a Message
</Button>
```

3. Add the following code for the event handler for the button's click event to `MainPage.xaml.cs`:

```
private void btnLiketMsgYammer_Click(object sender, RoutedEventArgs e)
{
    // Call this API to test if the auth token works
    var messageApiEndpoint = new Uri(Constants.ApiEndpoints.current +
    "?message_id=508413888", UriKind.Absolute);
    String data = "";
```

```
        OAuthUtils.PostMessage(messageApiEndpoint, "POST", data,
        onSuccess: response =>
        {
            // we just dump the unformated json string response into a textbox
            Dispatcher.BeginInvoke(() => txtResponses.Text = "Message Liked");
        },
          onErrorResponse: errorResponse =>
          {
              Dispatcher.BeginInvoke(() =>
              {
                  MessageBox.Show(errorResponse.OAuthError.ToString(),
                  "Invalid operation", MessageBoxButton.OK);
                  txtResponses.Text = string.Empty;
              });
          },
             onException: ex =>
             {
                 Dispatcher.BeginInvoke(() =>
                 {
                     MessageBox.Show(ex.ToString(), "Unexpected exception!",
                     MessageBoxButton.OK);
                     txtResponses.Text = string.Empty;
                 });
             }
    );
        Dispatcher.BeginInvoke(() => txtResponses.Text = "Liking...");

}
```

Messages Management: Unlike a Liked Message

You can use the message endpoint method to unlike a message that was marked as Liked by the current users. You'll need `message_id` to unlike a message. The "mutator" method to unlike a message is `DELETE`.

1. We will add a `PostMessage` function with six parameters in the SDK. We need this method to pass the method parameter `DELETE`. Add the following code in the `OAuthUtils.cs` file:

```
public static void PostMessage(Uri endpoint, string method, string data,
    Action<string> onSuccess,
    Action<AuthenticationResponse> onErrorResponse = null,
    Action<Exception> onException = null)
{
    if (endpoint == null || onSuccess == null)
    {
        throw new ArgumentNullException();
    }
```

```
        var webclient = new WebClient();
        // We shouldn't use the url query paramters to send the token, we should
        use the header to send it more securely instead
        webclient.Headers[HttpRequestHeader.Authorization] = "Bearer " +
        AccessToken;
        // webclient.Headers["Content-Type"] = "application/json";

        UploadStringCompletedEventHandler handler = null;
        handler = (s, e) =>
        {
            webclient.UploadStringCompleted -= handler;
            if (e.Error == null)
            {
                var result = e.Result;
                // We just pass the raw text data response to the callback
                onSuccess(result);
            }
            else
            {
                HandleExceptions(e.Error, onErrorResponse, onException);
            }
        };

        webclient.UploadStringCompleted += handler;
        webclient.UploadStringAsync(endpoint, method, data);
    }
```

2. Add a button's markup for the "Unlike a Message" button using the following code in `MainPage.xaml`:

```
<Button Name="btnunlikemsg" HorizontalAlignment="Center" Background="Black"
VerticalAlignment="Top" Click="btnUnLikeMsgYammer_Click">
                        Unlike a Message
</Button>
```

3. Add an event handler for the unlike button to `MainPage.xaml.cs`:

```
/// <summary>
        /// UnLike a Message Button event handler to Like a message specified
        by message_Id
        /// </summary>
        /// <param name="sender"></param>
        /// <param name="e"></param>
        private void btnUnLikeMsgYammer_Click(object sender, RoutedEventArgs e)
        {
            // Call this API to test if the auth token works
            var messageApiEndpoint = new Uri(Constants.ApiEndpoints.current +
            "?message_id=508402750", UriKind.Absolute);
            String data = "";
```

```
            OAuthUtils.PostMessage(messageApiEndpoint, "DELETE", data,
            onSuccess: response =>
            {
                // we just dump the unformated json string response into a
                textbox
                Dispatcher.BeginInvoke(() => txtResponses.Text = "Message
                Unliked");
            },
              onErrorResponse: errorResponse =>
              {
                  Dispatcher.BeginInvoke(() =>
                  {
                      MessageBox.Show(errorResponse.OAuthError.ToString(),
                      "Invalid operation", MessageBoxButton.OK);
                      txtResponses.Text = string.Empty;
                  });
              },
                 onException: ex =>
                 {
                     Dispatcher.BeginInvoke(() =>
                     {
                         MessageBox.Show(ex.ToString(), "Unexpected
                         exception!", MessageBoxButton.OK);
                         txtResponses.Text = string.Empty;
                     });
                 }
         );
            Dispatcher.BeginInvoke(() => txtResponses.Text = "Unliking..");

         }
```

The previous event handler calls the same method that was called to like a message and post a message. The only difference is that the method type is `DELETE` instead of `POST`.

Messages Management: Retrieve All Messages

The Yammer REST API `https://www.yammer.com/api/v1/messages.json` enables developers to retrieve all messages for the current user. The Windows Phone SDK provides a method called `GetJsonFromApi` from the `OAuthUtil` class to retrieve all messages from Yammer and serialize the JSON to a .NET object. The following code snippet explains step-by-step how to call the SDK's method. It uses a separate phone application page that contains a list view object to display returned records.

4. Add a page to the Windows phone project. In Visual Studio's Solution Explorer, right-click on the Windows Phone Project and choose Add ➤ New Item.

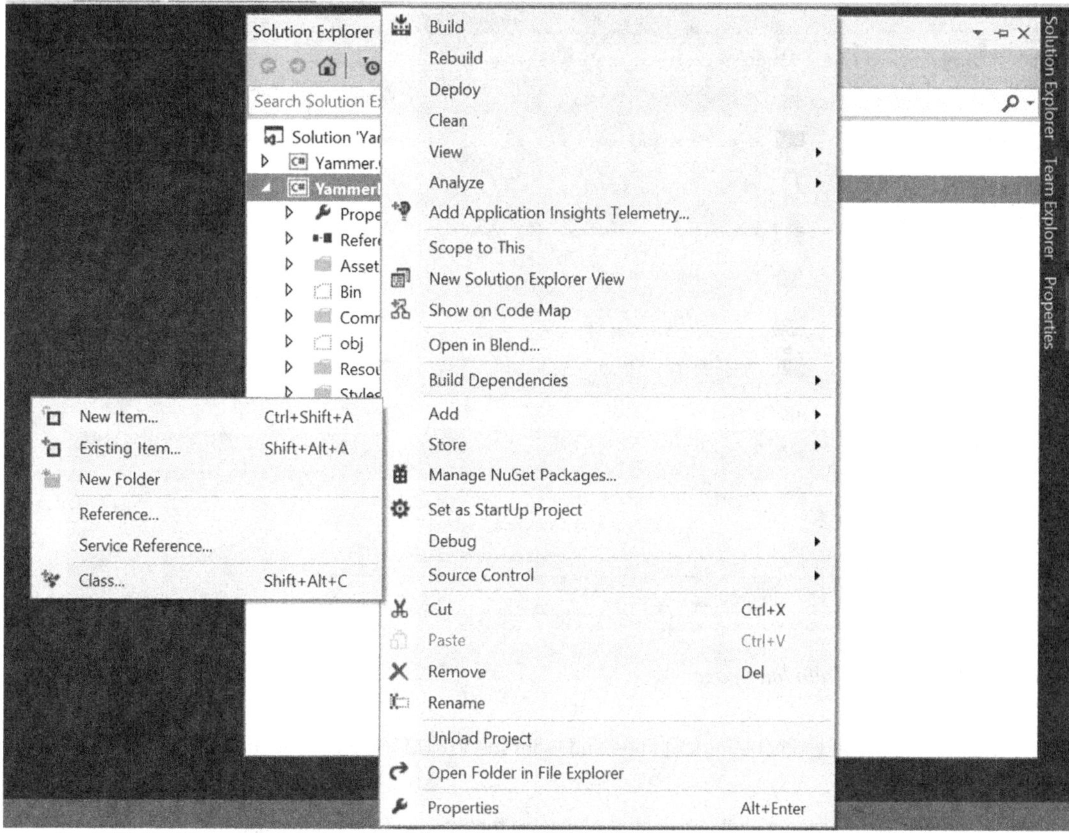

Figure 8-17. *Add a new page using Add New Item*

5. You'll be presented with the Add New Item screen, as shown in Figure 8-18.

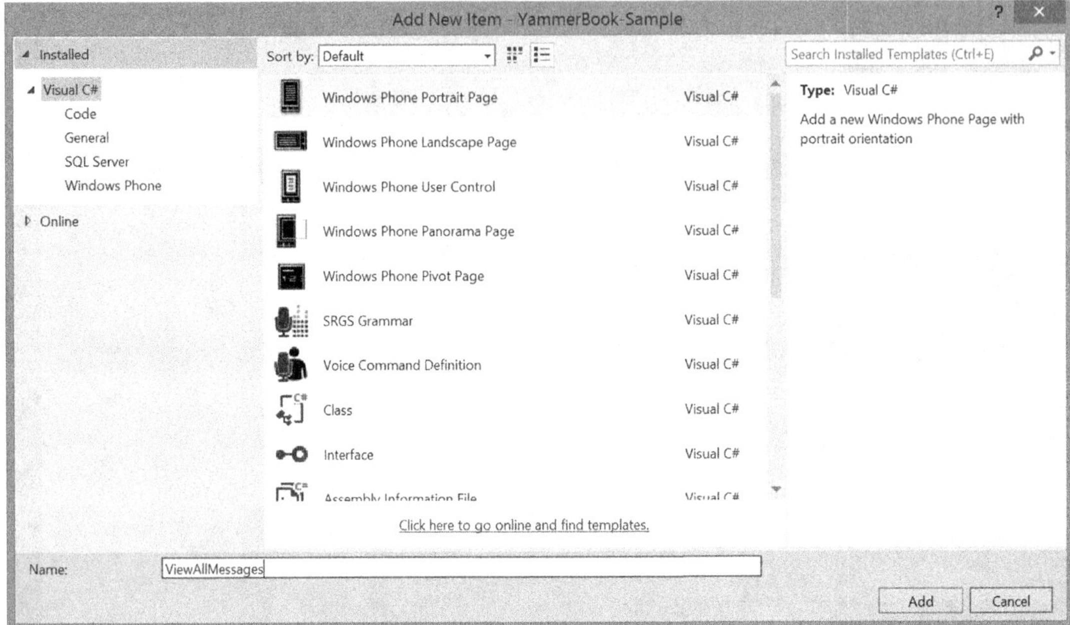

Figure 8-18. *Add a new windows page*

6. Select Windows Phone Portrait Page and enter the `ViewAllMessages` name. Click Add.

7. Since we're using a ListView control to display the retrieved messages, use the `App.xaml` file to define the styles. The styles are very basic with the intension of demonstrating the Yammer REST APIs' capabilities. Add the following code to the `App.xaml` file within the `<Application.Resources>` tags.

```
<Style x:Key="MessagesList" TargetType="ListBox">
            <Setter Property="Margin" Value="5"/>
            <Setter Property="Grid.Row" Value="1"/>
            <Setter Property="Background" Value="White"/>
        </Style>
        <Style x:Key="SimpleBlock" TargetType="TextBlock">
            <Setter Property="HorizontalAlignment" Value="Center"/>
            <Setter Property="FontSize" Value="18"/>
            <Setter Property="FontWeight" Value="Bold"/>
            <Setter Property="Foreground" Value="YellowGreen"/>
            <Setter Property="TextAlignment" Value="Left"/>
            <Setter Property="VerticalAlignment" Value="Center"/>

        </Style>
        <Style x:Key="TitleBlock" TargetType="TextBlock">
            <Setter Property="FontSize" Value="18"/>
            <Setter Property="FontWeight" Value="Bold"/>
            <Setter Property="Foreground" Value="WhiteSmoke"/>
```

```
        <Setter Property="TextAlignment" Value="Left"/>
        <Setter Property="VerticalAlignment" Value="Center"/>
    </Style>
```

This example uses the Yammer REST APIs that return the JSON object. In order to convert JSON to a .NET object, define a class and all the serializable properties for the object.

8. Add a new folder called `Common`, which will contain all common classes.

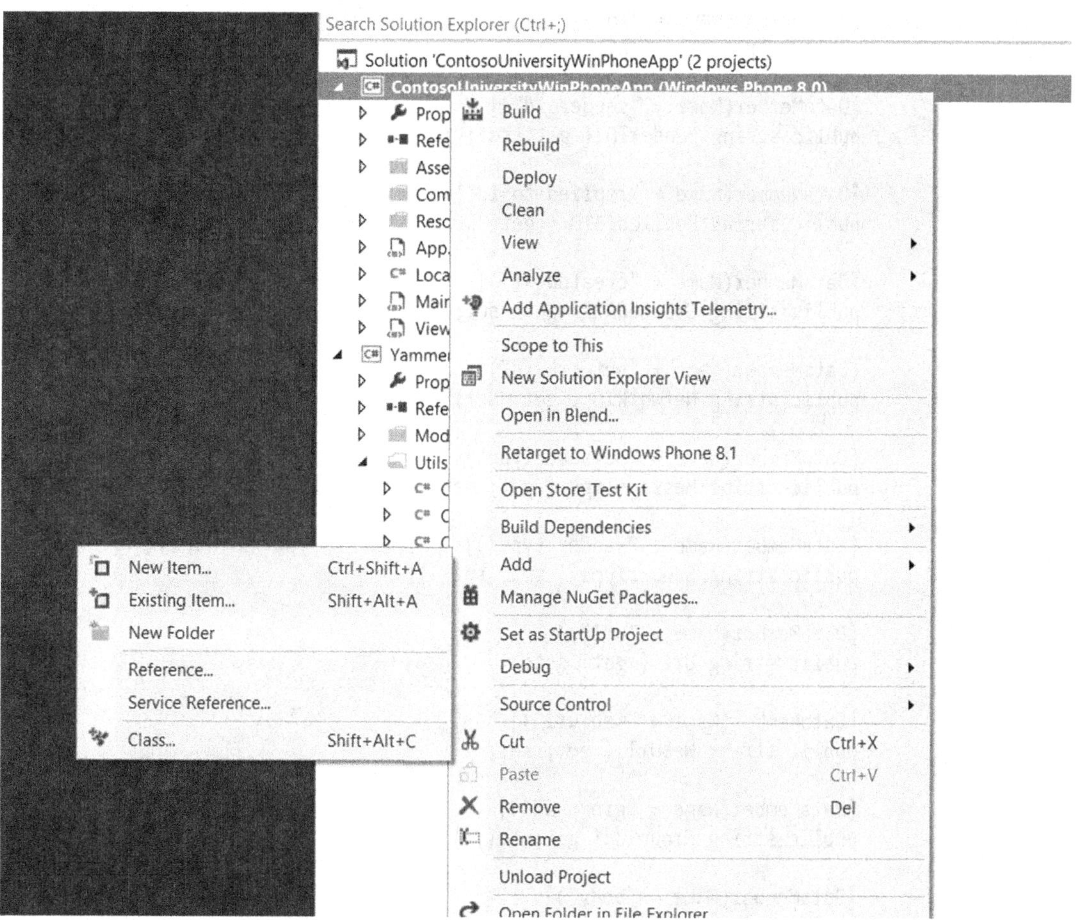

Figure 8-19. *Add a folder to the project*

9. Define a class for the message object and name it `YammerMessage`.

```
using System;
using System.Collections.Generic;
using System.Linq;
using System.Text;
using System.Threading.Tasks;
using System.Runtime.Serialization;
```

```
using System.Runtime.Serialization.Json;
using Yammer.OAuthSDK.Utils;
using SPDSUniversityWinPhoneApp.Common;

namespace SPDSUniversityWinPhoneApp.Common
{
    [DataContract]
    public class YammerMessage
    {
        [DataMember(Name = "id")]
        public string ID { get; set; }

        [DataMember(Name = "sender_id")]
        public string SenderID { get; set; }

        [DataMember(Name = "replied_to_id")]
        public string RepliedToID { get; set; }

        [DataMember(Name = "created_at")]
        public string CreatedAt { get; set; }

        [DataMember(Name = "network_id")]
        public string NetworkID { get; set; }

        [DataMember(Name = "message_type")]
        public string MessageType { get; set; }

        [DataMember(Name = "sender_type")]
        public string SenderType { get; set; }

        [DataMember(Name = "url")]
        public string Url { get; set; }

        [DataMember(Name = "web_url")]
        public string WebUrl { get; set; }

        [DataMember(Name = "group_id")]
        public string GroupId { get; set; }

        [DataMember(Name = "body")]
        public YammerMessageContent MessageContent { get; set; }

        [DataMember(Name = "rich")]
        public YammerMessageContent MessageContent1 { get; set; }

        [DataMember(Name = "thread_id")]
        public string ThreadID { get; set; }

        [DataMember(Name = "client_type")]
        public string ClientType { get; set; }
```

```
        [DataMember(Name = "client_url")]
        public string ClientUrl { get; set; }

        [DataMember(Name = "system_message")]
        public bool SystemMessage { get; set; }

        [DataMember(Name = "direct_message")]
        public bool DirectMessage { get; set; }

        [DataMember(Name = "chat_client_sequence")]
        public string ChatClientSequence { get; set; }

        [DataMember(Name = "content_excerpt")]
        public string ContentExcerpt { get; set; }

        [DataMember(Name = "language")]
        public string Language { get; set; }

        [DataMember(Name = "notified_user_ids")]
        public string notified_user_ids { get; set; }

        [DataMember(Name = "privacy")]
        public string privacy { get; set; }

        [DataMember(Name = "group_created_id")]
        public string group_created_id { get; set; }

        public YammerMessage()
        {

            this.MessageContent = new YammerMessageContent();
        }
    }

}
```

10. Define the `YammerMessageContent` class using the following code:

```
using System;
using System.Collections.Generic;
using System.Linq;
using System.Text;
using System.Threading.Tasks;
using System.Runtime.Serialization;
using System.Runtime.Serialization.Json;
using Yammer.OAuthSDK.Utils;
using SPDSUniversityWinPhoneApp.Common;
```

```
namespace SPDSUniversityWinPhoneApp.Common
{
    [DataContract]
    public class YammerMessageContent
    {
        [DataMember(Name = "parsed")]
        public string ParsedText { get; set; }

        [DataMember(Name = "plain")]
        public string PlainText { get; set; }

        [DataMember(Name = "rich")]
        public string RichText { get; set; }

    }

}
```

11. Define a class for the messages collection object using the following code:

```
using System;
using System.Collections.Generic;
using System.Linq;
using System.Text;
using System.Threading.Tasks;
using System.Runtime.Serialization;
using System.Runtime.Serialization.Json;
using Yammer.OAuthSDK.Utils;
using SPDSUniversityWinPhoneApp.Common;

[DataContract]
public class YammerMessages
{
    [DataMember(Name = "messages")]
    public List<YammerMessage> Messages { get; set; }

    public YammerMessages()
    {
        this.Messages = new List<YammerMessage>();
    }
}
```

12. Add the following code to the newly added class file. First add references to the class libraries:

```
using System.Runtime.Serialization;
using System.Runtime.Serialization.Json;
using Yammer.OAuthSDK.Utils;
```

13. Use the `ViewAllMessages.xaml` file to define the user interface to display messages retrieved from Yammer. To do this, use the following code snippet and add it to the `<Grid x:Name="ContentPanel">` grid control:

```
<ListBox x:Name="ListBoxAllMessage" ItemsSource="{Binding}" >
                <ListBox.ItemTemplate>
                    <DataTemplate>

                        <StackPanel Orientation="Vertical">
                            <Line Stroke="White" X1="0" Y1="25" X2="800"
                            Y2="25" />
                            <TextBlock Text="{Binding ID}"
                            Style="{StaticResource SimpleBlock}" />
                            <TextBlock Text="{Binding MessageContent.
                            PlainText}" Margin="5" Style="{StaticResource
                            TitleBlock}" />
                            <Line Stroke="White" X1="0" Y1="25" X2="800"
                            Y2="25" />

                        </StackPanel>

                    </DataTemplate>
                </ListBox.ItemTemplate>

            </ListBox>

            <TextBlock x:Name="txtResponses" Text="" TextAlignment="Center" />
```

The previous code uses a ListBox control with an item template. The item template defines a `StackPanel` to display a line, a text block for the message ID, a text block for the `MessageContent.PlainText`, and another line as a row separator. Define the appropriate binding as per the `YammerMessage` class definition.

The code-behind file of `ViewAllMessage.xaml` implements the server-side code that calls the Yammer REST API using the SDK's helper functions.

```
private void Loaddata()
{
    // Call this API to test if the auth token works
    var messageApiEndpoint = new Uri(Constants.ApiEndpoints.Message, UriKind.
    Absolute);

    OAuthUtils.GetJsonFromApi(messageApiEndpoint, onSuccess: response =>
    {
        byte[] byteArray = System.Text.UTF8Encoding.UTF8.GetBytes(response);
        MemoryStream res = new MemoryStream(byteArray);

        YammerMessages msgs =
        SerializationUtils.DeserializeJson<YammerMessages>(res);

        ListBoxAllMessage.DataContext = msgs.Messages;
```

```
            ListBoxAllMessage.ItemsSource = msgs.Messages;

            // we just dump the unformated json string response into a textbox
            Dispatcher.BeginInvoke(() => txtResponses.Text = "Messages Retrieved");
        },
          onErrorResponse: errorResponse =>
          {
              Dispatcher.BeginInvoke(() =>
              {
                  MessageBox.Show(errorResponse.OAuthError.ToString(), "Invalid
                  operation", MessageBoxButton.OK);
                  txtResponses.Text = string.Empty;
              });
          },
            onException: ex =>
            {
                Dispatcher.BeginInvoke(() =>
                {
                    MessageBox.Show(ex.ToString(), "Unexpected exception!",
                    MessageBoxButton.OK);
                    txtResponses.Text = string.Empty;
                });
            }
    );
        Dispatcher.BeginInvoke(() => txtResponses.Text = "Retrieving ...");
    }

    }
```

The `Loaddata` method calls the Windows Phone SDK's `GetJsonFromApi` method, which returns the JSON stream, which is then deserialized into a .NET object. Finally, the collection object called `msgs` of the `YammerMessages` class is assigned to `ListBox` as an `ItemsSource` property.

14. Use the following code snippet to reference the namespaces that the `ViewAllMessages.xaml` page will be using frequently.

```
using Yammer.OAuthSDK.Utils;
using Yammer.OAuthSDK.Model;
using Yammer.OAuthSDK.Utils;
using System.IO;
using System.Text;
```

15. Modify the page's `Constructor` method to call the `Loaddata()` method.

```
public ViewAllMessages ()
        {
            InitializeComponent();
            Loaddata();
        }
```

16. Now add a button control to the main windows phone page to allow users to navigate to the View All Messages page. Add the following code for a button control:

```
<Button Name="ViewallMessage" Grid.Row="4"  HorizontalAlignment="Center"
VerticalAlignment="Top" Click="ViewallMessage_Click">
             View All Messages
</Button>
```

17. `MainPage.xaml.cs`: Add an event handler for the ViewAllMessage button.

```
private void ViewallMessage_Click(object sender, RoutedEventArgs e)
{
    NavigationService.Navigate(new Uri("/ViewAllMessages.xaml",
    UriKind.Relative));
}
```

User Management: Retrieve all Users

In the previous section, you implemented code to retrieve all messages for the current user. Yammer is a social site and the most important actor on any social site are the users. We'll see how to retrieve Yammer's users using the REST APIs.

18. Add a `ViewAllUsers` phone page. We'll add another page to the existing project to display the users' properties on a grid view control. To add a page to your solution, in Visual Studio's Solution Explorer, right-click on the Windows Phone Project and then choose Add ➤ New Item (Figure 8-20).

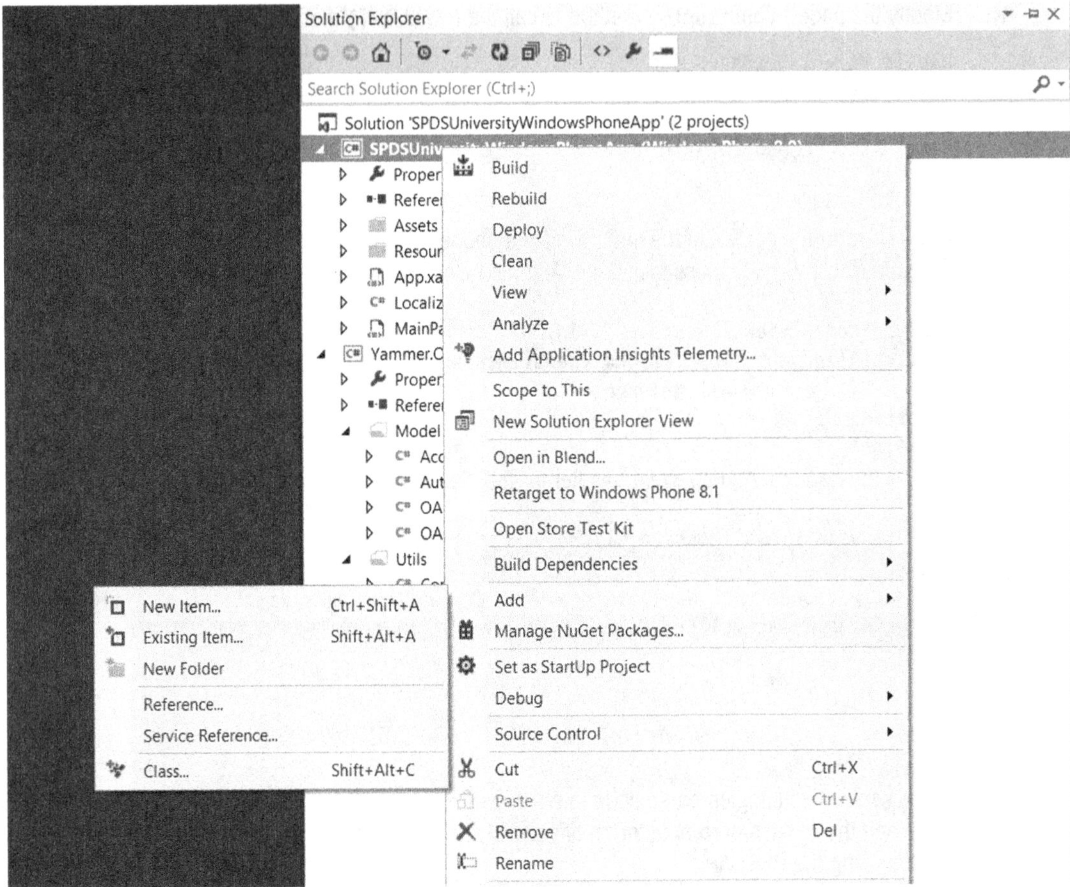

Figure 8-20. Adding a page using Visual Studio Solution Explorer

19. You'll be presented with the Add New Item screen. Select Windows Phone Portrait Page and enter the name `ViewAllMessages`. Click Add.

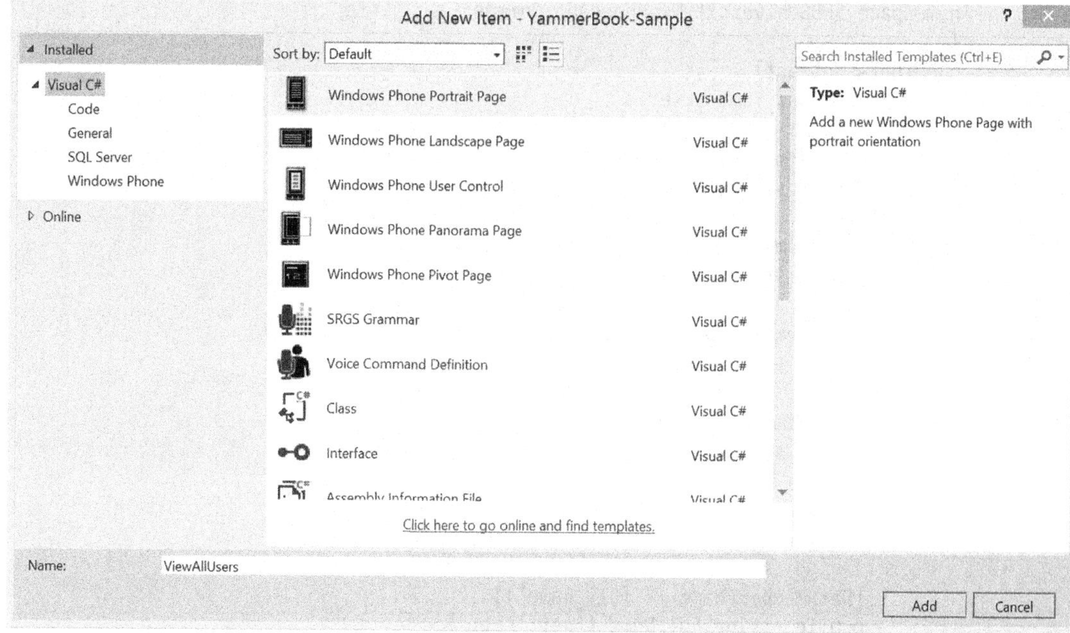

Figure 8-21. *Adding new items using the Add New Item screen*

20. Add an endpoint in the `Constants` class. Define a constant property in `Yammer.OAUthSDK`'s `Constants` class.

```
public const string allUsersUrl = "https://www.yammer.com/api/v1/users.json";
```

21. Add a new class for the Yammer users' data contract. The user object is very big in nature and it holds many properties that are stored in Yammer, like user's first name, last name, full name, department, title, and so on. Along with those properties, Yammer also stores the user's social graph like group members, followers, following, and so on. If you cannot use the class from this book directly, do not worry as the sample code is available for download.

```
using System;
using System.Collections.Generic;
using System.Linq;
using System.Text;
using System.Threading.Tasks;
using System.Runtime.Serialization;
using System.Runtime.Serialization.Json;
using System.IO;
using System.Diagnostics;
```

```
namespace SPDSUniversityWinPhoneApp.Common
{
    [DataContract]
    public class YammerUser
    {
        [DataMember(Name = "id")]
        public string UserID { get; set; }

        [DataMember(Name = "network_id")]
        public string NetworkID { get; set; }

        [DataMember(Name = "state")]
        public string AccountStatus { get; set; }

        [DataMember(Name = "job_title")]
        public string JobTitle { get; set; }

        [DataMember(Name = "expertise")]
        public string Expertise { get; set; }

        [DataMember(Name = "full_name")]
        public string FullName { get; set; }

        [DataMember(Name = "first_name")]
        public string FirstName { get; set; }

        [DataMember(Name = "last_name")]
        public string LastName { get; set; }

        [DataMember(Name = "url")]
        public string ApiUrl { get; set; }

        [DataMember(Name = "web_url")]
        public string WebUrl { get; set; }

        [DataMember(Name = "mugshot_url")]
        public string PhotoUrl { get; set; }

        [DataMember(Name = "mugshot_url_template")]
        public string PhotoTemplateUrl { get; set; }

        [DataMember(Name = "department")]
        public string Department { get; set; }

        [DataMember(Name = "contact")]
        public YammerContactInfo ContactInfo { get; set; }

        [DataMember(Name = "web_preferences")]
        public YammerSettingsAndFeedsAndGroups SettingsAndFeedsAndGroups
        { get; set; }
```

```
    [DataMember(Name = "previous_companies")]
    public List<YammerEmployer> PreviousEmployers { get; set; }

    [DataMember(Name = "schools")]
    public List<YammerSchool> Schools { get; set; }

    [DataMember(Name = "stats")]
    public YammerUserStats UserStats { get; set; }

    public YammerUser()
    {
        this.ContactInfo = new YammerContactInfo();
        this.SettingsAndFeedsAndGroups = new
        YammerSettingsAndFeedsAndGroups();
        this.PreviousEmployers = new List<YammerEmployer>();
        this.Schools = new List<YammerSchool>();
        this.UserStats = new YammerUserStats();
    }
}

[DataContract]
public class YammerUserStats
{
    [DataMember(Name = "followers")]
    public int Followers { get; set; }

    [DataMember(Name = "following")]
    public int Following { get; set; }

    [DataMember(Name = "updates")]
    public int Updates { get; set; }
}

[DataContract]
public class YammerSchool
{
    [DataMember(Name = "degree")]
    public string Degree { get; set; }

    [DataMember(Name = "description")]
    public string Description { get; set; }

    [DataMember(Name = "end_year")]
    public string EndYear { get; set; }

    [DataMember(Name = "start_year")]
    public string StartYear { get; set; }

    [DataMember(Name = "school")]
    public string School { get; set; }
}
```

```
[DataContract]
public class YammerEmployer
{
    [DataMember(Name = "description")]
    public string Description { get; set; }

    [DataMember(Name = "employer")]
    public string Employer { get; set; }

    [DataMember(Name = "end_year")]
    public string EndYear { get; set; }

    [DataMember(Name = "position")]
    public string Position { get; set; }

    [DataMember(Name = "start_year")]
    public string StartYear { get; set; }
}

[DataContract]
public class YammerSettingsAndFeedsAndGroups
{
    [DataMember(Name = "network_settings")]
    public YammerNetworkSettings NetworkSettings { get; set; }

    [DataMember(Name = "home_tabs")]
    public List<YammerGroupsAndFeeds> GroupsAndFeeds { get; set; }

    public YammerSettingsAndFeedsAndGroups()
    {
        this.NetworkSettings = new YammerNetworkSettings();
        this.GroupsAndFeeds = new List<YammerGroupsAndFeeds>();
    }
}

[DataContract]
public class YammerGroupsAndFeeds
{
    [DataMember(Name = "name")]
    public string Name { get; set; }

    [DataMember(Name = "select_name")]
    public string SelectName { get; set; }

    [DataMember(Name = "type")]
    public string Type { get; set; }

    [DataMember(Name = "feed_description")]
    public string Description { get; set; }
```

```
    [DataMember(Name = "ordering_index")]
    public int OrderingIndex { get; set; }

    [DataMember(Name = "url")]
    public string Url { get; set; }

    [DataMember(Name = "group_id")]
    public string GroupID { get; set; }

    [DataMember(Name = "private")]
    public bool IsPrivate { get; set; }
}

[DataContract]
public class YammerNetworkSettings
{
    [DataMember(Name = "message_prompt")]
    public string MessagePrompt { get; set; }

    [DataMember(Name = "allow_attachments")]
    public bool AllowAttachments { get; set; }

    [DataMember(Name = "show_communities_directory")]
    public bool ShowCommunitiesDirectory { get; set; }

    [DataMember(Name = "enable_groups")]
    public bool EnableGroups { get; set; }

    [DataMember(Name = "allow_yammer_apps")]
    public bool AllowYammerApps { get; set; }

    [DataMember(Name = "admin_can_delete_messages")]
    public bool AdminCanDeleteMessages { get; set; }

    [DataMember(Name = "allow_inline_document_view")]
    public bool AllowInlineDocumentView { get; set; }

    [DataMember(Name = "allow_inline_video")]
    public bool AllowInlineVideo { get; set; }

    [DataMember(Name = "enable_private_messages")]
    public bool EnablePrivateMessages { get; set; }

    [DataMember(Name = "allow_external_sharing")]
    public bool AllowExternalSharing { get; set; }

    [DataMember(Name = "enable_chat")]
    public bool EnableChat { get; set; }
}
```

```
[DataContract]
public class YammerContactInfo
{
    [DataMember(Name = "has_fake_email")]
    public bool HasFakeEmail { get; set; }

    [DataMember(Name = "email_addresses")]
    public List<YammerEmailAddresses> EmailAddresses { get; set; }

    [DataMember(Name = "phone_numbers")]
    public List<YammerPhoneNumbers> PhoneNumbers { get; set; }

    [DataMember(Name = "im")]
    public YammerIM IM { get; set; }

    public YammerContactInfo()
    {
        this.EmailAddresses = new List<YammerEmailAddresses>();
        this.PhoneNumbers = new List<YammerPhoneNumbers>();
        this.IM = new YammerIM();
    }
}

[DataContract]
public class YammerEmailAddresses
{
    [DataMember(Name = "address")]
    public string Address { get; set; }

    [DataMember(Name = "type")]
    public string Type { get; set; }

    public YammerEmailAddresses() { }

    public YammerEmailAddresses(string address, string type)
    {
        this.Address = address;
        this.Type = type;
    }
}

[DataContract]
public class YammerPhoneNumbers
{
    [DataMember(Name = "number")]
    public string PhoneNumber { get; set; }

    [DataMember(Name = "type")]
    public string Type { get; set; }
}
```

```
    [DataContract]
    public class YammerIM
    {
        [DataMember(Name = "provider")]
        public string Provider { get; set; }

        [DataMember(Name = "username")]
        public string UserName { get; set; }
    }

}
```

22. `MainPage.xaml`: Add the following code for a button control to the main Windows phone page to allow users to navigate to the View All Users page.

```
<Button Name="btnUsers" Grid.Row="5" HorizontalAlignment="Center"
VerticalAlignment="Top" Click="btnAllUserYammer_Click">
Get all Users
</Button>
```

23. `MainPage.xaml.cs`: Add the following code and the event handler for the "Get All User" button:

```
private void btnAllUserYammer_Click(object sender, RoutedEventArgs e)
{
    NavigationService.Navigate(new Uri("/ViewAllUsers.xaml",
    UriKind.Relative));
}
```

24. `ViewAllUsers.xaml`: Add the following code for the ListBox markup code:

In the <Grid x:Name="ContentPanel"> section, define the user interface to display messages retrieved from Yammer. To do this, use the following code snippet. Use the style properties you defined in previous sections of this chapter to "Retrieve All Messages".

```
<ListBox x:Name="ListBoxAllUsers" ItemsSource="{Binding}" >
                <ListBox.ItemTemplate>
                    <DataTemplate>

                        <StackPanel Orientation="Vertical">
                            <Line Stroke="White" X1="0" Y1="25" X2="800" Y2="25" />
                            <TextBlock Text="{Binding ID}" Style="{StaticResource
                            SimpleBlock}" />
                            <TextBlock Text="{Binding FullName}" Margin="5"
                            Style="{StaticResource TitleBlock}" />
                            <Line Stroke="White" X1="0" Y1="25" X2="800" Y2="25" />

                        </StackPanel>
```

```
                </DataTemplate>
            </ListBox.ItemTemplate>

        </ListBox>

        <TextBlock x:Name="txtResponses" Text="" TextAlignment="Center" />
```

The previous code snippet uses a ListBox control with an `Item` template. The `Item` template defines a `StackPanel` to display a line, a text block for the message ID, a text block for `MessageContent.PlainText`, and another line as a row separator. Define the appropriate binding as per the `YammerUsers` class definition.

25. `ViewAllUsers.xaml.cs`: Add the following code for the `LoadData` method.

The code-behind file of `ViewAllUsers.xaml.cs implements` the server-side code that calls the Yammer REST API using the SDK's helper functions.

```
private void Loaddata()
{
    // Call this API to test if the auth token works
    var messageApiEndpoint = new Uri(Constants.ApiEndpoints.allUsersUrl,
                             UriKind.Absolute);

    OAuthUtils.GetJsonFromApi(messageApiEndpoint, onSuccess: response =>
    {
        byte[] byteArray = System.Text.UTF8Encoding.UTF8.GetBytes(response);
        MemoryStream res = new MemoryStream(byteArray);

        List<YammerUser> users = SerializationUtils.DeserializeJson
        <List<YammerUser>>(res);

        ListBoxAllUsers.DataContext = users;
        ListBoxAllUsers.ItemsSource = users;

        // we just dump the unformated json string response into a textbox
        Dispatcher.BeginInvoke(() => txtResponses.Text = "Messages Retrieved");
    },
      onErrorResponse: errorResponse =>
      {
          Dispatcher.BeginInvoke(() =>
          {
              MessageBox.Show(errorResponse.OAuthError.ToString(), "Invalid
              operation", MessageBoxButton.OK);
              txtResponses.Text = string.Empty;
          });
      },
```

```
            onException: ex =>
            {
                Dispatcher.BeginInvoke(() =>
                {
                    MessageBox.Show(ex.ToString(), "Unexpected exception!",
                    MessageBoxButton.OK);
                    txtResponses.Text = string.Empty;
                });
            }
    );
        Dispatcher.BeginInvoke(() => txtResponses.Text = "Retrieving ...");
}
```

The `Loaddata` method calls the Windows Phone SDK's `GetJsonFromApi` method, which returns the JSON stream, which is then deserialized into a .NET object. The collection object messages of the `YammerUsers` class is then assigned to ListBox as an `ItemsSource` property.

26. Accessing namespaces: Use the following code to reference the namespaces that the page will be using frequently.

```
using System.Runtime.Serialization;
using System.Runtime.Serialization.Json;
using SPDSUniversityWinPhoneApp.Common;
using Yammer.OAuthSDK.Utils;
using Yammer.OAuthSDK.Model;
using System.IO;
using System.Text;
```

27. Modify page constructor method: Modify the page's `Constructor` method to call the `LoadData()` method.

```
public ViewAllUsers ()
        {
            InitializeComponent();
            Loaddata();
        }
```

User Management: View Data About the Current User

The Yammer REST API provides an endpoint `https://www.yammer.com/api/v1/users/current.json` to retrieve the current user's information. It includes profile information like username, job title, department, and contact info (email address, phone number, IM, and so on). Once you have the right permissions or the user has authorized your Yammer app to use her data, you can retrieve any piece of information belonging to a user node.

1. Add a page to the Windows phone project: In the sample application we are building, we'll add a new Windows phone page to display the user's information. To do that, add a new Windows phone page to your Windows phone project as you did in previous examples.

2. Add an endpoint in the `Constants` class: Define a `Constant` property in the `Yammer.OAUthSDK`'s `Constants` class.

```
public const string CurrentUserUrl = "https://www.yammer.com/api/v1/users/
current.json";
```

3. `ViewUserInfo.xaml`: Define the user interface to display user information retrieved from Yammer. To do this, use the following code snippet:

```
<Grid x:Name="ContentPanel" Grid.Row="1" Margin="12,0,12,0">
            <StackPanel Grid.Row="0" Margin="12,17,0,28">
                <StackPanel Orientation="Horizontal">
                    <TextBlock Text="User Name:" Margin="9,0,2,5"
                    Style="{StaticResource InputLabel}" />
                    <TextBlock x:Name="tbUserName" Text="" Margin="9,-7,2,5"
                    Style="{StaticResource InputLabel}"/>
                </StackPanel>

                <StackPanel Orientation="Horizontal">
                    <TextBlock Text="job_title:" Margin="9,-7,0,5"
                    Style="{StaticResource InputLabel}" />
                    <TextBlock x:Name="tbjob_title" Text="" Margin="9,-7,0,5"
                    Style="{StaticResource InputLabel}"/>
                </StackPanel>

                <StackPanel Orientation="Horizontal">
                    <TextBlock Text="Followers:" Margin="9,-7,0,2"
                    Style="{StaticResource InputLabel}" />
                    <TextBlock x:Name="tbFollowers" Text="" Margin="9,-7,0,5"
                    Style="{StaticResource InputLabel}" />
                </StackPanel>

                <StackPanel Orientation="Horizontal">
                    <TextBlock Text="Location:" Margin="9,-7,0,5"
                    Style="{StaticResource InputLabel}" />
                    <TextBlock x:Name="tbLocation" Text="" Margin="9,-7,0,5"
                    Style="{StaticResource InputLabel}" />
                </StackPanel>

                <TextBlock x:Name="txtResponses" Text=""
                TextAlignment="Center" />
            </StackPanel>
</Grid>
```

4. `ViewUserInfo.xaml.cs`: `Loaddata` method.

In the code-behind of the `ViewUserInfo.xaml.cs` file, you can use the same code that was used to retrieve the user list. The only difference is to replace the `List<YammerUser>` collection object with the `YammerUser` object as the returned JSON object will hold only one user's information. I also added a separator function called `RenderUI` by passing the deserialize JSON `YammerUser` object.

```
private void Loaddata()
{
    // Call this API to test if the auth token works
    var messageApiEndpoint = new Uri(Constants.ApiEndpoints.CurrentUserUrl,
    UriKind.Absolute);

    OAuthUtils.GetJsonFromApi(messageApiEndpoint, onSuccess: response =>
    {
        string s = response;
        byte[] byteArray = System.Text.UTF8Encoding.UTF8.GetBytes(response);
        MemoryStream res = new MemoryStream(byteArray);

        YammerUser YammerUser = SerializationUtils.DeserializeJson
        <YammerUser>(res);

        RenderUI(YammerUser);

        // we just dump the unformated json string response into a textbox
        Dispatcher.BeginInvoke(() => txtResponses.Text = "User Info
        Retrieved");
    },
      onErrorResponse: errorResponse =>
      {
          Dispatcher.BeginInvoke(() =>
          {
              MessageBox.Show(errorResponse.OAuthError.ToString(),
              "Invalid operation", MessageBoxButton.OK);
              txtResponses.Text = string.Empty;
          });
      },
         onException: ex =>
         {
             Dispatcher.BeginInvoke(() =>
             {
                 MessageBox.Show(ex.ToString(), "Unexpected exception!",
                 MessageBoxButton.OK);
                 txtResponses.Text = string.Empty;
             });
         }
 );
   Dispatcher.BeginInvoke(() => txtResponses.Text = "Retrieving ...");
}
```

5. RenderUI method: This is a very simple method that assigns the YammerUser's properties to the UI object to display the user information.

```
private void  RenderUI(YammerUser yammeruser)
{
    tbUserName.Text = yammeruser.FullName;
    tbjob_title.Text = yammeruser.JobTitle;
    tbFollowers.Text = yammeruser.UserStats.Following.ToString();

}
```

That's it! You can view the current user's information. You can extend the code to display the other pieces of user information like user stats (followers, following, and so on), group membership details, and more.

6. Accessing namespaces: Use the following code snippet to access namespaces that the page will be using frequently.

```
using Yammer.OAuthSDK.Model;
using Yammer.OAuthSDK.Utils;
using YammerBook_Sample.Common;
using System.IO;
using System.Text;

public ViewUserInfo ()
        {
            InitializeComponent();
            Loaddata();
        }
```

7. `MainPage.xaml`: Now you need to integrate the newly added page with `MainPage.xaml`. To do that, add another button control as you did in previous examples and write the code-behind `onClick` event handler to navigate to the newly added page. First, add the "View Current User Info" markup to `MainPage.xaml`:

```
<Button Name="btnViewUser" HorizontalAlignment="Center" Style="{StaticResource
TabItemFirst}" VerticalAlignment="Top" Click="btnViewUserYammer_Click">
       View Current User Info
</Button>
```

8. `MainPage.xaml.cs`: You'll need to implement a click event handler for the button you added to `MainPage.xaml`. To do this, open the `MainPage.xaml.cs` file and add the following code snippet.

```
private void btnViewUserYammer_Click(object sender, RoutedEventArgs e)
{
    NavigationService.Navigate(new Uri("/ViewUserInfo.xaml",
    UriKind.Relative));
}
```

User Management Search by Email Address

The Yammer REST API provides an endpoint called `https://www.yammer.com/api/v1/users/[:id].json` to retrieve the current users' information and it includes profile information like username, job title, department, and contact info (email addresses, phone number, IM, and so on). Once you have the right permission or the user has already authorized your Yammer app to use the user's data, you can retrieve any piece of information belonging to a user node. This is very similar to the REST API to view the current user; the only difference is that this API needs the user ID to retrieve the other user's data instead of the retrieving data for the logged-in user.

1. Add a page to Windows phone project.

In the sample application we are building, we'll add a new Windows phone page to display the user's information. For that, you need to add a new Windows phone page to your Windows phone project as you have done in previous examples. You can also use the same page used in the previous example, called `ViewUserInfo.xaml`, to display the other user data by using passing parameters between pages to decide on calling REST API for the current user or for other users. In this book, we are going to keep it simple and use another page to display other user information.

2. Add an endpoint in the Constants class. Define a constant property in `Yammer.OAUthSDK`'s `Constants` class.

```
public const string SearchUserByEmail= "https://www.yammer.com/api/v1/users/
by_email.json?email=";
```

3. Define the user interface to display user information retrieved from Yammer. For this, use the following code snippet.

```
<Grid x:Name="ContentPanel" Grid.Row="1" Margin="12,0,12,0">
            <StackPanel Grid.Row="0" Margin="12,17,0,28">
                <StackPanel Orientation="Horizontal">
                    <TextBlock Text="User Name:" Margin="9,0,2,5"
                    Style="{StaticResource InputLabel}" />
                    <TextBlock x:Name="tbUserName" Text="" Margin="9,-7,2,5"
                    Style="{StaticResource InputLabel}"/>
                </StackPanel>

                <StackPanel Orientation="Horizontal">
                    <TextBlock Text="job_title:" Margin="9,-7,0,5"
                    Style="{StaticResource InputLabel}" />
                    <TextBlock x:Name="tbjob_title" Text="" Margin="9,-7,0,5"
                    Style="{StaticResource InputLabel}"/>
                </StackPanel>

                <StackPanel Orientation="Horizontal">
                    <TextBlock Text="Followers:" Margin="9,-7,0,2"
                    Style="{StaticResource InputLabel}" />
                    <TextBlock x:Name="tbFollowers" Text="" Margin="9,-7,0,5"
                    Style="{StaticResource InputLabel}" />
                </StackPanel>

                <StackPanel Orientation="Horizontal">
                    <TextBlock Text="Location:" Margin="9,-7,0,5"
                    Style="{StaticResource InputLabel}" />
                    <TextBlock x:Name="tbLocation" Text="" Margin="9,-7,0,5"
                    Style="{StaticResource InputLabel}" />
                </StackPanel>

                <TextBlock x:Name="txtResponses" Text=""
                TextAlignment="Center" />
            </StackPanel>
</Grid>
```

4. `SearchUserInfo.xaml.cs`: `Loaddata` method.

In the code-behind of the `SearchUserInfo.xaml.cs` file, you can use the same code that was used to retrieve the user list. The only difference is to replace the `List<YammerUser>` collection object with the `YammerUser` object as the returned JSON object will hold only one user's information. I also added a separator function called `RenderUI` by passing the deserialize JSON `YammerUser` object.

```
private void Loaddata()
{
    // Call this API to test if the auth token works
    var emailaddress = "Rob.Bieber@Costco.com";
    var messageApiEndpoint = new Uri(Constants.ApiEndpoints.SearchUserByEmail +
emailaddress.ToString(), UriKind.Absolute);

    OAuthUtils.GetJsonFromApi(messageApiEndpoint, onSuccess: response =>
    {
        string s = response;
        byte[] byteArray = System.Text.UTF8Encoding.UTF8.GetBytes(response);
        MemoryStream res = new MemoryStream(byteArray);

        List<YammerUser> YammerUser = SerializationUtils.DeserializeJson
        <List<YammerUser>>(res);

        RenderUI(YammerUser[0]);

        // we just dump the unformated json string response into a textbox
        Dispatcher.BeginInvoke(() => txtResponses.Text = "User Info Retrieved");
    },
      onErrorResponse: errorResponse =>
      {
          Dispatcher.BeginInvoke(() =>
          {
              MessageBox.Show(errorResponse.OAuthError.ToString(), "Invalid
              operation", MessageBoxButton.OK);
              txtResponses.Text = string.Empty;
          });
      },
          onException: ex =>
          {
              Dispatcher.BeginInvoke(() =>
              {
                  MessageBox.Show(ex.ToString(), "Unexpected exception!",
                  MessageBoxButton.OK);
                  txtResponses.Text = string.Empty;
              });
          }
  );
     Dispatcher.BeginInvoke(() => txtResponses.Text = "Retrieving ...");
 }
```

5. RenderUI method: This is very simple method that assigns the YammerUser's properties to a UI object to display the user information.

```
private void  RenderUI(YammerUser yammeruser)
{
    tbUserName.Text = yammeruser.FullName;
    tbjob_title.Text = yammeruser.JobTitle;
    tbFollowers.Text = yammeruser.UserStats.Following.ToString();

}
```

That's it. You can view the current user's information. You can extend the code to display the other piece of user information like user stats (followers, following, and so on), group members, ship details, and so on.

6. Accessing namespaces: Use the following code snippet to namespaces that the page will be using frequently.

```
using Yammer.OAuthSDK.Model;
using Yammer.OAuthSDK.Utils;
using YammerBook_Sample.Common;
using System.IO;
using System.Text;
```

7. Modify the page constructor method. Modify the page's constructor method to call the LoadData() method

```
public SearchUserInfo ()
        {
            InitializeComponent();
            Loaddata();
        }
```

8. Now you need to integrate the newly added page with MainPage.xaml. To do that, you add another button control as you have done for previous examples and write the code-behind onClick event handler to navigate to the newly added page. First add the Search User Info markup to the MainPage.xaml file.

```
<Button Name="btnSearchUser" HorizontalAlignment="Center"
Style="{StaticResource TabItemFirst}" VerticalAlignment="Top"
Click="btnSearchUserYammer_Click">
Search User Info
</Button>
```

9. You need to implement a click event handler for the button you added to MainPage.xaml. To do this, open the MainPage.xaml.cs file and add the following code snippet:

```
private void btnSearchUserYammer_Click(object sender, RoutedEventArgs e)
{
    NavigationService.Navigate(new Uri("/SearchUserInfo.xaml", UriKind.Relative));
}
```

User Management" Retrieve All Users from a Group

The Yammer REST API provides an endpoint called `https://www.yammer.com/api/v1/users/in_group/[:id].json` to retrieve all users who are members of a Yammer group in your Yammer network.

10. Add a page to the Windows phone project.

In the sample application we are building, we'll add a new Windows phone page to display users who are member of a Yammer group. To do that, add a new Windows phone page to your Windows Phone project as you did in previous examples. You can also use the same page used in the `ViewAllUsers.xaml` example to display the user's list by using passing parameters between pages to decide on calling REST API for the current user or for other users. In this book, we going to keep it simple and use another page to display other user information.

11. Add an endpoint to the `Constants` class. Define a constant property to the `Yammer.OAUthSDK`'s `Constants` class.

```
public const string ViewUserinGroup = "https://www.yammer.com/api/v1/users/
in_group/";
```

12. Define the user interface to display the users list retrieved from Yammer. To do this, use the following code snippet:

```
<!--ContentPanel - place additional content here-->
        <Grid x:Name="ContentPanel" Grid.Row="1" Margin="12,0,12,0">
            <ListBox x:Name="ListBoxAllUsers" ItemsSource="{Binding}" >
                <ListBox.ItemTemplate>
                    <DataTemplate>

                        <StackPanel Orientation="Vertical">
                            <Line Stroke="White" X1="0" Y1="25" X2="800"
                            Y2="25" />
                            <TextBlock Text="{Binding Department}"
                            Style="{StaticResource SimpleBlock}" />
                            <TextBlock Text="{Binding FullName}" Margin="5"
                            Style="{StaticResource TitleBlock}" />
                            <Line Stroke="White" X1="0" Y1="25" X2="800"
                            Y2="25" />

                        </StackPanel>

                    </DataTemplate>
                </ListBox.ItemTemplate>

            </ListBox>

            <TextBlock x:Name="txtResponses" Text="" TextAlignment="Center" />
        </Grid>
```

13. `ViewAllUserinaGroup.xaml.cs`: `LoadData` method.

In the code-behind of the `ViewAllUserinaGroup.xaml.cs` file, you can use the same code that was used to retrieve the user list. The only difference is the REST API endpoint.

```
private void Loaddata()
{
    // Call this API to test if the auth token works
    var GroupId = 4659506;
    var messageApiEndpoint = new Uri(Constants.ApiEndpoints.ViewUserinGroup +
    GroupId + ".json", UriKind.Absolute);

    OAuthUtils.GetJsonFromApi(messageApiEndpoint, onSuccess: response =>
    {
        byte[] byteArray = System.Text.UTF8Encoding.UTF8.GetBytes(response);
        MemoryStream res = new MemoryStream(byteArray);

        List<YammerUser> users = SerializationUtils.DeserializeJson
        <List<YammerUser>>(res);

        ListBoxAllUsers.DataContext = users;
        ListBoxAllUsers.ItemsSource = users;

        // we just dump the unformated json string response into a textbox
        Dispatcher.BeginInvoke(() => txtResponses.Text = "Users Retrieved");
    },
      onErrorResponse: errorResponse =>
      {
          Dispatcher.BeginInvoke(() =>
          {
              MessageBox.Show(errorResponse.OAuthError.ToString(),
              "Invalid operation", MessageBoxButton.OK);
              txtResponses.Text = string.Empty;
          });
      },
         onException: ex =>
         {
             Dispatcher.BeginInvoke(() =>
             {
                 MessageBox.Show(ex.ToString(), "Unexpected exception!",
                 MessageBoxButton.OK);
                 txtResponses.Text = string.Empty;
             });
         }
);
    Dispatcher.BeginInvoke(() => txtResponses.Text = "Retrieving ...");
}
```

14. Accessing namespaces. Add the following code snippet to namespaces that the page will be using frequently:

```
using Yammer.OAuthSDK.Model;
using Yammer.OAuthSDK.Utils;
using YammerBook_Sample.Common;
using System.IO;
using System.Text;
```

15. Modify the page constructor method. Modify the page's constructor method to call the `Loaddata()` method.

```
public ViewAllUserinaGroup()
        {
            InitializeComponent();
            Loaddata();
        }
```

16. Now you need to integrate the newly added page with `MainPage.xaml`. To do that, you add another button control as you did in previous examples and write the code-behind `onClick` event handler to navigate to the newly added page. First add the "View Users in a Group Info" markup in the `MainPage.xaml`:

```
<Button Name="btnViewUserinGroup" HorizontalAlignment="Center"
Style="{StaticResource TabItemFirst}" VerticalAlignment="Top"
Click="btnViewUserinGroup_Click">
 View Users in a Group
</Button>
```

17. You need to implement a click event handler for the button you added to the `MainPage.xaml` file. To do this, open the `MainPage.xaml.cs` file and add the following code snippet:

Code Snippet: Use the MainPage.xaml.cs to handle the click event, OnClick users will be redirected to "ViewAllUsersinaGroup.xaml" page

```
private void btnViewUserinGroup_Click(object sender, RoutedEventArgs e)
{
   NavigationService.Navigate(new Uri("/ViewAllUsersinaGroup.xaml",
UriKind.Relative));
}
```

Run the Windows Phone App

18. Build the solution and run the Windows phone app using the emulator (Figure 8-22).

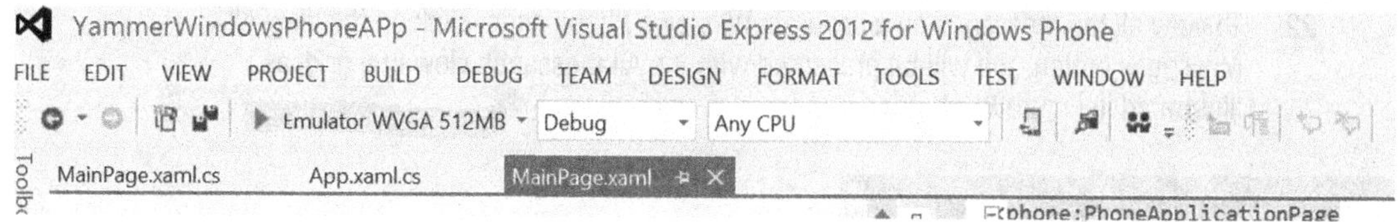

Figure 8-22. *Run the Windows phone app using the emulator*

19. In Run mode, the home page will look like Figure 8-23.

Figure 8-23. *Run the Windows phone app using the emulator*

20. Now click on the "Sign In with Yammer" button, which will initiate the OAuth authentication flow that you've seen in previous steps. After successfully logging in, you will be redirected to this home page.
21. To post a message on Yammer, click on "Post a Message". Likewise you will be able to like a message and unlike a message using those buttons. Note that we have hard-coded the `message_id` in the previous scenarios; however, you can use the "View All message" button to retrieve the messages and then use like or unlike.

22. To view all the messages on a separate Windows Phone page, click on the View All Messages button. You will be presented with the All messages view in a grid, as illustrated in Figure 8-24.

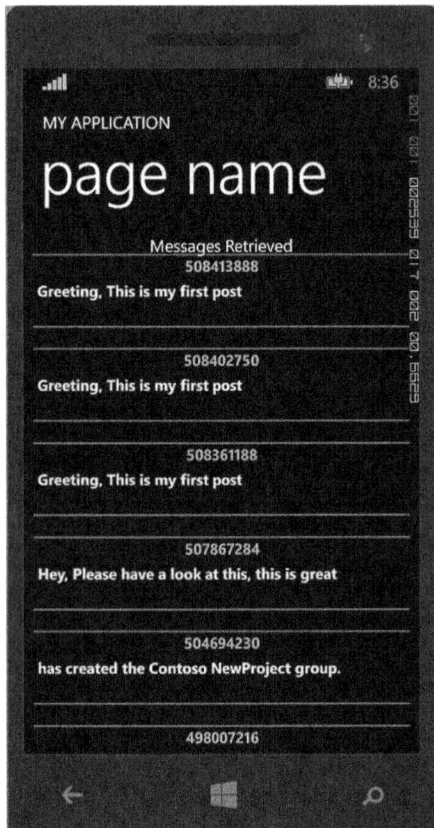

Figure 8-24. *View All Message page displays the message's ID and body*

In this exercise, you have learned how to integrate the Windows phone app with Yammer using the Yammer Windows Phone SDK.

Summary

By now you are familiar with the Yammer SDKs released by Yammer. In this chapter, you explored how to implement the "Sign In with Yammer" button using Yammer's SDKs for Windows Phone App and then learned how to implement Yammer features into the Windows Phone by using the Windows Phone SDK.

We hope this book has helped you understand the value of Yammer and develop integrations with Yammer using existing integration features. As the Yammer team keeps adding new features, we recommend that you follow `https://developer.yammer.com` to get the latest updates on new features that you can use to develop integration with Yammer.

Index

P. Rawal and P. Rohilla, *Developing on Yammer*, DOI 10.1007/978-1-4842-0943-1

T, U, V

W, X

Y, Z

Printed in the United States
By Bookmasters